HISTORY AS LITERATURE IN BYZANTIUM

Society for the Promotion of Byzantine Studies

Publications
15

HISTORY AS LITERATURE IN BYZANTIUM

Papers from the Fortieth Spring Symposium of Byzantine Studies, University of Birmingham, April 2007

edited by
Ruth Macrides

ASHGATE

Published by
Ashgate Publishing Limited
Wey Court East
Union Road
Farnham
Surrey, GU9 7PT
England

Ashgate Publishing Company
Suite 420
101 Cherry Street
Burlington
VT 05401-4405
USA

www.ashgate.com

British Library Cataloguing in Publication Data
Spring Symposium of Byzantine Studies (40th : 2007: University of Birmingham)
   History as Literature in Byzantium: Papers from the Fortieth Spring Symposium of
   Byzantine Studies, University of Birmingham, March 2007. – (Publications of the
   Society for the Promotion of Byzantine Studies)
   1. Historiography – Byzantine Empire – Congresses.
   I. Title II. Series III. Macrides, R. J.
   907.2′049502–dc22

Library of Congress Cataloging-in-Publication Data
Spring Symposium of Byzantine Studies (40th : 2007: University of Birmingham)
   History as Literature in Byzantium :Papers from the Fortieth Spring Symposium of
   Byzantine Studies, University of Birmingham, March 2007 / [edited by] Ruth Macrides.
     p.   cm. -- (Publications of the Society for the Promotion of Byzantine Studies)
   Includes bibliographical references and indexes.
   1. Byzantine Empire – Historiography – Congresses. 2. Historiography – Byzantine
   Empire – Congresses. 3. Byzantine Empire – History – Sources – Congresses.
   4. Byzantine literature – History and criticism – Congresses. I. Macrides, R. J.
   II. Title.
   DF505.S67 2007
   949.5′02072–dc22   2010021507

ISBN   9781409412069 (hbk)

SOCIETY FOR THE PROMOTION OF BYZANTINE STUDIES – PUBLICATION **15**

Mixed Sources
Product group from well-managed
forests and other controlled sources
www.fsc.org Cert no. SA-COC-1565
© 1996 Forest Stewardship Council
FSC

Printed and bound in Great Britain by
MPG Books Group, UK

Contents

From *History as Literature in Byzantium*, ed. Ruth Macrides. Copyright © 2010 by the Society for the Promotion of Byzantine Studies. Published by Ashgate Publishing Ltd, Wey Court East, Union Road, Farnham, Surrey, GU9 7PT, Great Britain.

Foreword

The contributions to this book derive from papers presented to the Fortieth Spring Symposium of Byzantine Studies on 'Byzantine History as Literature', held in Birmingham, 13–16 April 2007. Participants from three continents converged on the original home of symposia where, for once, truly spring-like weather conditions held, so that the daffodils blossomed in record time. The symposium coincided with the annual Classical Association meeting, as it had done 28 years earlier when Margaret Mullett and Roger Scott organized the Thirteenth Spring Symposium, from which *Byzantium and the Classical Tradition* emerged. That was still a time when every symposium met in Birmingham but not every symposium resulted in an edited book. To commemorate that earlier convergence of classicists and Byzantinists, Margaret Mullett addressed the 2007 joint meeting with 'History and truth, lies and fiction: Byzantium and the classical tradition, twenty-five years on'.

The symposium theme was divided into four sessions, each named after a prominent man or woman who has made pronouncements on literature and/or historical writing: David Lodge, Anna Komnene, Henry Ford and Steven Runciman. Fourteen speakers examined classicizing histories and chronicles from the sixth to the fourteenth centuries, asking questions about audience and aesthetics, narrative and narrator, stories and their reinterpretations and reconfigurations. Eighteen communications were given on topics related to the symposium theme. Some of these speakers were also Birmingham student assistants who took care of all manner of needs, with smooth efficiency.

The symposium certainly could not have taken place without the kind and generous support of a host of institutions and individuals. It is a pleasure to acknowledge their sponsorship here and thank the AHRC (doctoral training funds), Ashgate Publishing and Variorum, the British Academy, the J. F. Costopoulos Foundation, the Cyprus Ministry of Education and Culture, Nicholas and Matrona Egon, the Greek Ministry of Culture, the Hellenic Foundation, the Hellenic Society, the A. G. Leventis Foundation, Oxford University Press, the St Hilary Trust.

Warm thanks are due to John Smedley and Kirsten Weissenberg of Ashgate Publishing, for their exemplary support throughout the editorial process, and Rowena Loverance, series editor and head of the Publications Committee of the SPBS.

Ruth Macrides
Birmingham, September 2009

Editor's Preface

The words 'history' and 'literature' have been appearing in close association with each other with greater frequency in Byzantine studies over the last decade.[1] Although it has been the case that Byzantinists have always treated 'the literature of the empire as a body of historical source material', they have not always treated their historical source material as literature.[2] In 1990 Margaret Mullett wrote that it was rare for 'literature' to be given a section of its own at symposia and congresses, although she thought that historiography was an exception – 'it should now be the best understood area of Byzantine literature'.[3] The emphasis here is on 'should'.

'Still' is another word that must be emphasized. The literary analysis of historical works, chronographies and historiographies, is still in its early days for Byzantine studies. The literary dimension of historical writing is still considered the domain of others. The historian's work, it is thought, lies elsewhere, in the accumulation and corroboration of information about the past. Even though 'historiography was cut away from the branches of literature'[4] relatively recently, in the late eighteenth and nineteenth centuries, and made a discipline only then, we like to impute to medieval authors and medieval historiography characteristics of our own times – history as a discrete discipline of learning, and the historian's goal as that of uncovering, recording and explaining the past. Likewise we understand 'literature' to be separate and separable from history. Literature does not make for good history; it lacks 'the seriousness of

[1]   See the papers of the Third International Literary Colloquium at Nicosia in 2004: *L'écriture de la mémoire. La littérarité de l'historiographie*, eds. P. Odorico, P. A. Agapitos and M. Hinterberger (Paris, 2006); the Fourteenth Conference of the Australian Association for Byzantine Studies, Melbourne, 2004: *Byzantine Narrative: Papers in Honour of Roger Scott*, eds. J. Burke, U. Betka and R. Scott (Melbourne, 2006).

[2]   M. Mullett, 'Dancing with deconstructionists in the gardens of the muses: new literary history vs ?', *BMGS* 14 (1990), 258–75, here at 268.

[3]   Mullett, 'Dancing', 261–2, 263.

[4]   C.F. Robinson, *Islamic Historiography* (Cambridge, 2004), 84.

truthful historiography'.[5] We expect Byzantine authors of historical texts to be like us: serious, hardworking scholars.[6] But we have double standards. When, at times, they are like us, we refuse to admit it. Ingela Nilsson has pointed to techniques in our historical writing that we consider flaws in theirs: repetition of material taken from other sources is plagiarism in them or at the very least a lack of originality; in modern historical writing 'the sheer habit of repetition makes certain things come "true", so that the historian no longer has to prove them'. When our Byzantine authors deploy rhetorical methods, when they praise or blame or write to display their strengths as writers, we criticize their 'bias'. Yet modern historians also introduce their preferences and approaches in their works but do not recognize these as bias.[7]

Binary classifications abound; although they have outlived their usefulness, they are still with us: history vs. literature, truth vs. fiction, classicizing histories vs. popularizing chronicles, high-level Greek vs. the vernacular. It is still not uncommon to see Hans Georg Beck's 'Mönkschronik' article of 1965 cited approvingly but, in the very next sentence, overlooked without even a blush.[8] The features of Byzantine historical writing that are well known from the classical tradition in history writing, the very elements that gave Byzantine historical writing a high reputation as the most impressive literary achievement of Byzantine culture, are also held to be responsible for the 'distorting mirror' effect: they prevent their authors from portraying their own world and hinder modern historians in their efforts to reconstruct that world.[9] At best these are 'embellishments' that need to be stripped from the text so the core can be revealed, the core that alone is of value and interest. Literary critics have shown, on the contrary, that these 'embellishments' are 'facts' about the text, as useful

---

[5]   For the characterization of this attitude see I. Nilsson, 'Discovering literariness in the past: literature vs. history in the *Synopsis Chronike* of Konstantinos Manasses', in Odorico, *et al.*, eds, *L'écriture de la mémoire*, 15–31, here at 16–17.

[6]   W. Treadgold's response to J. Ljubarskij in the SO debate: '*Quellenforschung*', 5–73, here at 58.

[7]   I. Nilsson, 'To narrate the events of the past: on Byzantine historians, and historians on Byzantium', in Burke, *et al.*, eds, *Byzantine Narrative*, 47–58, here at 51–2.

[8]   See the discussion by Ljubarskij, *et al.*, '*Quellenforschung*', 11–12, and Treadgold's response, 59. Another dramatic example of this behaviour is H. Hunger's 'Trivialliteratur' section in *Die profane hochsprachliche Literatur der Byzantiner*, 2 vols (Munich, 1978), I, 253.

[9]   The Inaugural Lecture by C. Mango, 'Byzantine literature as a distorting mirror' (Oxford, 1975), repr. in Mango, *Byzantium and its Image* (London, 1984), which immortalized the phrase for Byzantinists, has proved a great stimulus to scholarship.

to our understanding and knowledge of the past as the other facts we are more keen to collect.[10] Yet, as a whole, historians of Byzantium are still not won over. Although we have perhaps stopped despising many, if not most, of the elements of Byzantine historical texts that have traditionally been considered intrusive and unhelpful – classicizing language, figures of speech, topoi, mimesis – we have not yet been persuaded of the need to undertake literary analyses of the works that are the backbone and substance of our own narratives. Texts are still edited and translated with no discussion given to their method of composition. Meanwhile, although chronicles are not impaired by all of the features of classicizing histories, they are not deemed worthy of literary analysis, since they are considered to lack literary pretension.

History *is* literature. The papers published here demonstrate what we can learn about Byzantium through literary readings of many of the main Byzantine historical texts of the sixth- to the fourteenth century and by an examination of the illustrated narratives of the twelfth- and fourteenth century. The work presented in this volume is fundamental to the further study of the main narratives of Byzantine history. For some, history studied as literature can be an end in itself. For others, it will be a means of determining how our knowledge of the past changes when the historical sources are read as literature.

---

[10]   R. M. Stein, 'Literary criticism and the evidence for history', in N. Partner, ed., *Writing Medieval History* (London, 2005), 67–87, here at 76: 'Sentence structure is as meaningful in its way as information about who won the battle'.

List of Contributors

Dmitry Afinogenov is a professor at Moscow University, where he teaches Byzantine Greek and the history of Byzantine literature while he also does research for the Russian Academy of Sciences. His main fields of interest are Byzantine historiography and hagiography, especially of the Iconoclast period, the interrelation of various texts from the so-called Dark Ages and the survival of lost Byzantine sources in Church Slavonic translations. He has also written several papers on Byzantine literary theory. A number of his publications deal with the restoration of image worship in 843 and its protagonists.

Athanasios Angelou is at present Dean of the Arts Faculty at the University of Ioannina, where he teaches Byzantine literature. Previously he taught at Royal Holloway and Kings College London. He has published the following texts: *Refutation of Proclus' Elements of Theology* by Nicholas of Methone (Athens/Leiden, 1984), and *Dialogue with the Empress-Mother on Marriage* by Manuel Palaiologos (Vienna, 1991). His other publications include articles on Byzantine intellectual history, focused on the views of Scholarios on Hellenic identity and the Fall of Constantinople. He has been Artistic Director of a series of cultural events centred on Byzantium, among which were a concert including Syrian chant with Guy Protheroe in St Paul's Cathedral, London (1998); *Versioni del Sacro* in San Marco, Venice (2001); *Voix de Byzance* in Brussels (2003); and a performance of music and readings at the Megaron, Athens (2006).

Elena N. Boeck is Associate Professor of Art History at DePaul University. Her current book project investigates the rise of illustrated histories in the Mediterranean world from the twelfth through the fourteenth centuries and explores the ideological motivations for visualizing history in Sicily, Bulgaria and Rus.

George T. Calofonos is a Byzantine historian, educated at the Centre for Byzantine, Ottoman and Modern Greek, Birmingham, specializing in the study of Late Antique and Byzantine dreaming. He has published on a variety of related subjects including dream theory, *oneirokritika*, incubation, dreams in historiography and hagiography, magic. A research associate of the Institute of Byzantine Research of the National Hellenic Research Foundation, Athens, he has contributed to the programme 'Dreaming in Byzantium: a database of dream-reports in Byzantine literature' and is co-editing, with Christine Angelidi, the forthcoming proceedings of the conference 'Dreams and Visions in Late Antiquity and Byzantium'. He is currently working on his book *Dream Divination in Byzantium: A Pagan Art in Christian Context*.

Brian Croke is Executive Director of the Catholic Education Commission, Sydney, as well as Adjunct Professor of History at Macquarie University and an Honorary Associate of the University of Sydney. He is the author of several articles and books on early Byzantine history and historiography, including *History and Historians in Late Antiquity* with A.M. Emmett (1983), *Studies in John Malalas* with E. Jeffreys and R. Scott (1990), *Christian Chronicles and Byzantine History* (1992), *The Chronicle of Marcellinus: Translation and Commentary* (1995), and *Count Marcellinus* (2001).

John Davis is a translation adviser at National Bank of Greece, Athens, while he also teaches a translation seminar at Athens University. He gained his PhD in Byzantine Philology from the University of Ioannina. He has published translations of contemporary Greek poetry as well as of an ekphrasis *On Spring* by Emperor Manuel Palaiologos. He hopes before long to complete for publication his critical edition of the fourteenth-century metaphrase of Niketas Choniates' *History*.

Stephanos Efthymiadis is Associate Professor at the Open University of Cyprus. He has published numerous studies on Byzantine hagiography, historiography and prosopography. He is the co-editor of *Niketas Choniates: a Historian and a Writer* (Pomme d'Or, Geneva, 2009), and is currently preparing a collective handbook on Byzantine hagiography.

Martin Hinterberger is Associate Professor of Byzantine Philology at the University of Cyprus. His research focuses on emotions in Byzantine literature, the language of Byzantine literature, as well as on autobiography and hagiography. He is currently working on a book about *Phthonos* in Byzantine literature.

Michael Jeffreys was trained as a classicist at Cambridge but wrote a London University PhD on the borders of Byzantium and Modern Greek. Most of his career was spent teaching Modern Greek to the children and grandchildren of Greek migrants in Sydney, Australia, where he became the Sir Nicholas Laurantus Professor at Sydney University. On returning to Britain with the new millennium he has turned to Byzantium, becoming the research manager for the continuing Prosopography of the Byzantine

World project, published as a huge online database. Most of his articles concern the period from the eleventh to the sixteenth centuries, but he has published a translation of the chronicle of John Malalas and a scattering of contributions to the literary and political history of Greece in the nineteenth and twentieth centuries.

Anthony Kaldellis is Professor of Greek and Latin at the Ohio State University. His studies on the reception of classical culture in Byzantium recently culminated in two monographs, *Hellenism in Byzantium* (2007) and *The Christian Parthenon* (2009). He has also translated many Byzantine authors into English, among them Hesychios, Genesios, Psellos and Prokopios (forthcoming).

Ruth Macrides is Senior Lecturer in Byzantine Studies at the Centre for Byzantine, Ottoman and Modern Greek Studies, University of Birmingham. She has edited and translated Byzantine legal texts, collected in *Kinship and Justice in Byzantium, 11th–15th centuries* (1999), and has published a translation and study of George Akropolites' *History* (2007). Among her articles are studies of Byzantine historical writing. At present she is working on late Byzantine ceremonial and preparing a study of Pseudo-Kodinos' work on court hierarchy and ceremony.

Paolo Odorico is Professor at the École des Hautes Études en Sciences Sociales, Paris. He is engaged in research on the history and the social context of Byzantine literature. His publications, which include editions of texts and their interpretation, range from early Byzantium to the Ottoman period. Among his publications are *Il prato e l'ape* (Vienna, 1986), *Digenis Akritas* (Florence, 1995), *Conseils et Mémoires de Synadinos* (Paris, 1996), *Le codex B de Saint-Jean-Prodrome de Serres* (Paris, 1998), *L'Akrite* (Toulouse, 2002), *Nicandre de Corcyre, Le voyage d'Occident* (Toulouse, 2003), and *Thessalonique, chroniques d'une ville prise* (Toulouse, 2005).

Stratis Papaioannou is William A. Dyer, Jr. Assistant Professor in the Humanities and Dumbarton Oaks Assistant Professor of Byzantine Studies at Brown University. He works on Byzantine literary aesthetics, epistolography, and concepts of self and desire. He is preparing a book-length study on medieval Greek self-representations, with an emphasis on Michael Psellos, while also working on an edition and translation of Psellos' letters.

Roger Scott retired from the University of Melbourne at the end of 2003 as Reader in Classics and is currently Principal Fellow in the School of Historical Studies. He is a former president of the Australian Association for Byzantine Studies. His main work has been on Byzantine chronicles, notably a translation and study of Malalas with an Australian group and a translation and commentary on Theophanes with Cyril Mango.

Teresa Shawcross is Assistant Professor at Amherst and Mt Holyoke College. Her recent research has been concerned with the eastern Mediterranean world of the late medieval period, with publications focusing on aspects of the social and cultural history of the Crusader States and the Byzantine Empire. Her book *The Chronicle of Morea: Historiography in Crusader Greece* was published in 2009.

Nicolette S. Trahoulia received her PhD in Art History from Harvard University. She is currently Professor of Art History at the American College of Greece. A major focus of her work has been to examine the role of art in expressing imperial ideology in the middle to late Byzantine period. She has done extensive research on the various manifestations of Alexander the Great in Byzantine times. Her present research examines the relationship of the visual arts to the literary genre of romance from the tenth to the twelfth centuries.

Konstantinos Zafeiris has taught in the Department of Mediaeval History at the University of St Andrews and as a temporary lecturer in the Institute of Byzantine Studies at Queen's University Belfast. He received his PhD from the University of St Andrews, for a dissertation entitled 'The *Synopsis Chronike* and its place in the Byzantine chronicle tradition: its sources (Creation–1081 CE)', and he is currently working on expanding his research on the text, and on Byzantine chronicle writing.

List of Abbreviations

AASS	Acta Sanctorum
AnBoll	*Analecta Bollandiana*
BMGS	*Byzantine and Modern Greek Studies*
BF	*Byzantinische Forschungen*
BNJ	*Byzantinisch-neugriechische Jahrbücher*
BSl	*Byzantinoslavica*
Byz	*Byzantion*
BZ	*Byzantinische Zeitschrift*
Cah Arch	*Cahiers Archéologiques*
DOP	*Dumbarton Oaks Papers*
EEBS	*Ἐπετηρὶς Ἑταιρείας Βυζαντινῶν Σπουδῶν*
GRBS	*Greek, Roman and Byzantine Studies*
Hell	*Ἑλληνικά*
JÖB	*Jahrbuch der Österreichischen Byzantinistik*
MGH, AA	Monumenta Germaniae Historica Auctores Antiquissimi
NE	*Νέος Ἑλληνομνήμων*
OCP	*Orientalia Christiana Periodica*
ODB	*The Oxford Dictionary of Byzantium*
PG	*Patrologia Graeca*
PLP	*Prosopographisches Lexikon der Palaiologenzeit*
REB	*Revue des Études Byzantines*
TM	*Travaux et Mémoires*
VV	*Vizantiiskii Vremennik*
ZRVI	*Zbornik Radova Vizantološkog Instituta*

Frequently cited publications:

Agathias, *History*: *Agathiae Myrinaei Historiarum Libri Quinque*, ed. R. Keydell (Berlin, 1967)

Akropolites, *History*: *Georgii Acropolitae Opera*, ed. A. Heisenberg, corr. P. Wirth (Leipzig, 1903; repr. Stuttgart, 1978)

Anna Komnene, *Alexiad*: D.R. Reinsch and A. Kambylis, *Annae Comnenae Alexias* (Berlin, 2001)

Attaleiates, *Historia*: I. Pérez Martín, *Miguel Attaliates Historia*, Nueva Roma 15 (Madrid, 2002)

Beck, '"Mönchschronik"': H.-G. Beck, 'Zur byzantinischen "Mönchschronik"', in A. Bauer, L. Boehm and M. Mueller, eds., *Speculum Historiale. Geschichte im Spiegel von Geschichtsschreibung und Geschichtsdeutung* (Freiburg and Munich, 1965), 188–97

Burke, *et al.*, eds., *Byzantine Narrative*: J. Burke, U. Betka, P. Buckley, K. Hay, R. Scott and A. Stephenson, eds., *Byzantine Narrative: Papers in Honour of Roger Scott* (Melbourne, 2006)

Choniates, *Historia*: *Nicetae Choniatae Historia*, ed. J.-L. van Dieten (Berlin and New York, 1975)

Constantine VII Porphyrogennetos, *De administrando imperio*: Constantine Porphyrogenitus, *De administrando imperio*, ed. G. Moravscik, trans. R.J.H. Jenkins (Washington, DC, 1967; repr. 1993)

Constantinides, *et al.*, eds., ΦΙΛΕΛΛΗΝ: C.N. Constantinides, N.M. Panagiotakes, E. Jeffreys and A. D. Angelou, eds., ΦΙΛΕΛΛΗΝ. *Studies in Honour of Robert Browning* (Venice, 1996)

Eastmond and James, eds., *Icon and Word*: A. Eastmond and L. James, eds., *Icon and Word: The Power of Images in Byzantium. Studies Presented to Robin Cormack* (Burlington, VT, 2003)

Evagrius, *Ecclesiastical History*: *The Ecclesiastical History of Evagrius with the Scholia*, ed. J. Bidez and L. Parmentier (London, 1898; repr. Amsterdam, 1964)

George the Monk: *Georgii monachi chronicon*, ed. C. de Boor, corr. P. Wirth (Leipzig, 1904; repr. Stuttgart, 1978)

Glykas: *Michael Glykas, Annales*, ed. I. Bekker (Bonn, 1836)

Gregoras: Nikephoros Gregoras, *Historia*, ed. L. Schopen, 3 vols. (Bonn, 1829–55)

Grigoriadis, '*Prooimion*': I. Grigoriadis, 'A study of the *prooimion* of Zonaras' chronicle in relation to other 12th-century historical *prooimia*', *BZ* 91 (1998), 327–44

Hunger, *Literatur*: H. Hunger, *Die hochsprachliche profane Literatur der Byzantiner*, 2 vols., Handbuch der Altertumswissenschaft, 12, 1–2 (Munich, 1978)

Jeffreys, ed., *Rhetoric*: E.M. Jeffreys, ed., *Rhetoric in Byzantium* (Aldershot, 2003)

Jeffreys, *et al.*, eds., *Studies in John Malalas*: *Studies in John Malalas*, ed. E. Jeffreys, B. Croke and R. Scott, Byzantina Australiensia, 6 (Sydney, 1990)

Kaldellis, *Procopius of Caesarea*: A. Kaldellis, *Procopius of Caesarea: Tyranny, History and Philosophy at the end of Antiquity* (Philadelphia, 2004)

Karpozilos, Βυζαντινοὶ Ἱστορικοί: A. Karpozilos, Βυζαντινοὶ Ἱστορικοὶ καὶ Χρονογράφοι, 2 vols. (Athens, 1997–2002)

Kazhdan, *A History of Byzantine Literature*: A. Kazhdan (in collaboration with L.F. Sherry and C. Angelidi), *A History of Byzantine Literature (650–850)*, The National Hellenic Research Foundation, Institute for Byzantine Research, Research Series 2 (Athens, 1999); A. Kazhdan, *A History of Byzantine Literature (850–1000)*, ed. C. Angelidi, The National Hellenic Research Foundation, Institute for Byzantine Research, Research Series 4 (Athens, 2006)

Kedrenos: *Georgii Cedreni Compendium Historiarum*, ed. I. Bekker, 2 vols. (Bonn, 1838, 1839)

Kinnamos, *Epitome*: *Ioannis Kinnamos, Epitome*, ed. A. Meineke (Bonn, 1836)

Lambros, 'Τραπεζουντιακὸν ὡροσκόπιον': S. Lambros, 'Τραπεζουντιακὸν ὡροσκόπιον τοῦ ἔτους 1336', *NE* 13 (1916), 33–50

Leo the Deacon: *Leonis diaconis Caloensis Historiae libri decem*, ed. C.B. Hase (Bonn, 1828)

Ljubarskij, *et al.*, 'Quellenforschung': J. Ljubarskij, *et al.*, 'Quellensforschung and/or Literary Criticism: Narrative Structures in Byzantine Historical Writings', *Symbolae Osloenses* 73 (1998), 5–73

Macrides, 'The Historian in the History': R. Macrides, 'The Historian in the History', in C. N. Constantinides, *et al.*, *ΦΙΛΕΛΛΗΝ*, 205–24

Magdalino, ed., *New Constantines*: P. Magdalino, ed., *New Constantines: The Rhythm of Imperial Renewal in Byzantium, 4th–13th Centuries* (Aldershot, 1994)

Maguire, ed., *Byzantine Court Culture*: H. Maguire, ed., *Byzantine Court Culture from 829 to 1204* (Washington, DC, 1997)

Malalas, *Chronographia*: *Ioannis Malalae Chronographia*, ed. I. Thurn (Berlin and New York, 2000); trans. E. Jeffreys, M. Jeffreys, R. Scott, *et al.*, Byzantina Australiensia, 4 (Melbourne, 1986)

Manasses: *Constantini Manassis Breviarum Chronicum*, ed. O. Lampsidis, 2 vols. (Athens, 1996)

Mango and Scott, eds., *The Chronicle of Theophanes Confessor*: C. Mango and R. Scott, eds., with the assistance of G. Greatrex, *The Chronicle of Theophanes Confessor: Byzantine and Near Eastern History, AD 284–813* (Oxford, 1997)

Mansi: J.D. Mansi, *Sacrorum conciliorum nova, et amplissima collectio* (Florence, 1759–98)

Mullett and Scott, eds., *The Classical Tradition*: M. Mullett and R. Scott, eds., *Byzantium and the Classical Tradition* (Birmingham, 1982)

Nikephoros, *Short History*: Nikephoros, Patriarch of Constantinople, *Short History*, ed. and trans. C. Mango, Dumbarton Oaks Texts 10 (Washington, DC, 1990)

Odorico, *et al.*, eds., *L'écriture de la mémoire*: P. Odorico, P. A. Agapitos, M. Hinterberger, eds., *L'écriture de la mémoire: La littérarité de l'historiographie*.

Actes du IIIe colloque international philologique, Nicosie 6–8 mai 2004, Dossiers byzantins 5 (Paris, 2006)

Patria: Th. Preger, *Scriptores originum Constantinopolitanarum* (Leipzig, 1901–1907; repr. 1989)

Photios, *Bibliotheke*: R. Henry, *Photius Bibliothèque*, 9 vols. (Paris, 1959–77)

PLRE: *The Prosopography of the Later Roman Empire*, eds. A.H. Jones, J.R. Martindale, and J. Morris, 3 vols. (Cambridge, 1971–92)

Procopius: *Procopii Caesariensis opera omnia*, ed. J. Haury, 4 vols. (Leipzig, 1905, 1906, 1913; repr. 1962–64)

Psellos, *Chronographia*: *Michele Psello, Imperatori di Bisanzio*, ed. S. Impellizeri, 2 vols. (Milan, 1984)

Psellos, *Or. for.*: *Orationes forenses et acta*, ed. G.T. Dennis (Stuttgart and Leipzig, 1994)

Psellos, *Or. paneg.*: *Michaelis Pselli Orationes panegyricae*, ed. G.T. Dennis (Stuttgart and Leipzig, 1994)

Psellos, *Phil. min.* I: *Michael Psellus Philosophica Minora*, ed. J.M. Duffy, I (Stuttgart and Leipzig, 1992)

Psellos, *Poem.*: *Michaelis Pselli Poemata*, ed. L.G. Westerink (Stuttgart and Leipzig, 1992)

Psellos, *Theologica* I: *Michael Psellus, Theologica*, ed. P. Gautier, I (Leipzig, 1989)

Pseudo-Symeon: F. Halkin, 'Le règne de Constantin d'après la chronique inédite du Pseudo-Symeon', *Byz* 29–30 (1960), 7–27

Sathas, ed., *Mesaionike Bibliotheke*: K.N. Sathas, ed., *Mesaionike Bibliotheke*, 7 vols. (Venice, 1872–94; repr. Athens, 1972)

Sode and Takács, eds., *Novum Millennium*: C. Sode and S. Takács, eds., *Novum Millennium: Studies on Byzantine History and Culture Dedicated to Paul Speck* (Aldershot, 2001)

Skylitzes, *Synopsis Historion*: *Ioannis Scylitzae Synopsis historiarum*, ed. I. Thurn (Berlin and New York, 1973)

Symeon the Logothete: *Symeonis Magistri et Logothetae Chronicon*, ed. S. Wahlgren (Berlin and New York, 2006)

SynChron/Skoutariotes: K.N. Sathas, ed., *Mesaionike Bibliotheke*, VI (Venice, 1894; Athens, 1972)

Talbot–Sullivan: A.-M. Talbot and D. Sullivan, *The History of Leo the Deacon: Byzantine Military Expansion in the Tenth Century*, Dumbarton Oaks Studies 41 (Washington, DC, 2005)

Theophanes, *Chronographia*: *Theophanis chronographia*, ed. C. de Boor, 2 vols. (Leipzig, 1883,1885)

Theophanes Continuatus, *Chronographia*: *Theophanes Continuatus, Ioannes Cameniata, Symeon Magister, Georgius Monachus*, ed. I. Bekker (Bonn, 1838)

Theophylact Simokatta, *History*/*EH*: *Theophylacti Simocattae, Historiae*, ed. C. de Boor (Leipzig, 1887), repr. P. Wirth (Stuttgart, 1972)

Tzetzes, *Chiliades/Historiae*: *Ioannis Tzetzae Historiae*, ed. P.A.M. Leone (Naples, 1968)

Xanthopoulos, Nikephoros Kallistos: *Ecclesiasticae Historiae*, *PG* 145–7, 3 vols. (Paris, 1857–66)

Zonaras, *Epitome*: *Ioannis Zonarae epitome historiarum*, ed. I. Dindorf I (Leipzig, 1868), II, III, ed. T. Büttner-Wobst (Bonn, 1897)

Note: Abbreviations of ancient works not listed above are given according to the Liddell & Scott dictionary.

List of Illustrations

Note on Spelling of Names

The proper names of persons who lived in the period up to and including the reign of Heraclius are given in Latinized form; thereafter in close transliteration from the Greek: for example, the emperor Theodosius, the Patriarch Macedonius, but Photios.

SECTION I
Aesthetics

1. The aesthetics of history: from Theophanes to Eustathios

Stratis Papaioannou[*]

In societies that possess a historiographical tradition, historiography is only a small part of a much larger framework. This is the cultural mechanism of the making of 'history', the various ways in which a society produces its own past, its collective memory. The main thrust of this production is usually of an ideological nature: it empowers communities, groups and individuals, and is manifested in institutional structures, performed ritual, and other forms of representation.[1] In Byzantium, the state, church, monasteries and schools – to name the most significant Byzantine social formations – brought forth various historical pasts with their concomitant ideological baggage. That production was accompanied by rituals and representations that made the past present in Byzantine everyday life and served to form communal and personal identities. Indeed, it would not be an exaggeration to claim that, from imperial and monastic ceremony to church homiletics, from iconography to school rhetoric, narratives of a historical past were one of the main products of Byzantine culture.[2]

---

[*] I am grateful to Michael Ennis and Paul Robertson for their help in finishing the manuscript for publication. An earlier, shorter, version of this paper appears in P. Rousseau and J. Raithel, eds., *A Companion to Late Antiquity* (Chichester and Malden, MA, 2009), 17–28.

[1] A provisional definition of 'ideology' is employed here; ideology is understood as the production of social meaning (in our case, the 'past'), which offers the basic script for the formation of identities. Cf. various essays collected in S. Žiček, *Mapping Ideology* (London, 1994); see further P. Bourdieu, *The Logic of Practice*, trans. R. Nice (Stanford, CA, 1990), esp. 73, on the notion of the 'enactment of the past', as well as F. Jameson, *The Political Unconscious: Narrative as a Symbolic Act* (Ithaca, NY, 1981), on narrative and the formation of communal or personal identities. Historiography, we should note, reached a wider (yet still not a *major*) audience only very recently; cf. P. Gay, *The Naked Heart* (The Bourgeois Experience: Victoria to Freud 4; New York, 1995), 185–221.

[2] For aspects of this making of the Byzantine past see, e.g., P. Magdalino, 'The distance of the past in early medieval Byzantium (7th–10th centuries)', *Ideologie e*

It is in this wider framework of a culture's 'creation' of its past that we are to locate the narratives of Byzantine historiography. Undeniably, these narratives and their particular version of the past were the product of a specific historical moment: an author or authors that pursued personal aspirations and addressed the needs of an immediate, intended, and often limited audience.[3] Simultaneously, however, these narratives adopted the wider Byzantine tropes of the making of the past, thus becoming embedded in larger ideological projects to one degree or another. At closer inspection, these narratives, though arguably a minor part of the Byzantine construction of the past, reveal wider ideological preoccupations that Byzantine historians rehearse and, occasionally, also expose and challenge.

What will be discussed in this paper pertains to only a small set of such ideological concerns and their rehearsal or critical negotiation by Byzantine historians. I shall focus, that is, on historiographical 'aesthetics', those principles that regulate the how of historiography, namely the form, style and representational potential of historical writing. Which were some of the most prominent aesthetic principles put forth by Byzantine historians, will be my main question. As will become clear, the normative meaning of 'aesthetics' should be juxtaposed with the literal meaning of the 'aesthetic', that which is immediately available and, more importantly, appealing to the senses, the *aestheseis*. This juxtaposition is necessary, because normative aesthetics can in fact be either pro- or anti-aesthetic in force; aesthetic norms may, that is, support or – which is more often the case in Byzantium – oppose appreciation of material form and style. This crucial interplay between the awareness of aesthetic rules and the investment in aesthetic appearance will be a governing theme of what follows. The importance of aesthetics in Byzantine historiography, especially its literary aesthetics, has been the focus of several recent volumes; this essay asks whether we can detect a consciousness of this importance in Byzantine writing itself.[4]

---

pratiche del reimpiego nell'alto medioevo [= *Settimane di studio del Centro Italiano di studi sull'alto medioevo*, 46 (1999)], 115-46; R. Macrides and P. Magdalino, 'The Fourth Kingdom and the rhetoric of Hellenism', in Magdalino, ed., *The Perception of the Past in Twelfth-Century Europe* (London, 1992), 117–56; and Magdalino, ed., *New Constantines*.

3   Here the questions of the circulation and formation of manuscripts that contain historiographical works, as well as of the intended and actual audience of Byzantine historiography, or of the type of reading that Byzantine historiographers envisioned for their texts, are crucial ones; for some bibliography see the essays of Brian Croke and John Davis in this volume.

4   The bibliography on the texts discussed below is extensive; for a recent overview of Byzantine historiography see Karpozilos, Βυζαντινοί Ἱστορικοί, vols. 1–2, to be read with Kazhdan, *A History of Byzantine Literature (650–850)* and Kazhdan, *A History of Byzantine Literature (850–1000)*, as well as A. Markopoulos, 'Byzantine history writing at the end of the First Millennium', in P. Magdalino,

The power of precise signs

Let me begin with a tale recorded most likely before Theophanes the Confessor completed his universal chronicle in the 810s. The tale relates, in the shortest of narratives, a significant aspect of Byzantine aesthetics. The story is recounted in the *Parastaseis Syntomoi Chronikai*, the notorious collection of descriptions of Constantinopolitan monuments written in the eighth- or early ninth century.[5] Two friends – one of whom is the narrator – visit an abandoned part of the City in order to, as the narrator claims, 'narrate-and-explain (*historesai*) the statues (*eikonas*)' that exist there.[6] Coming upon and standing before a statue (*stele*) of an imposing late antique figure, they stop and marvel at it (*thaumazein*). Suddenly, the statue falls and kills the narrator's friend. Utterly shocked, the narrator first tries to hide the body, but then reports the event to the authorities. People gather amazed at the miraculous event (again, *thaumazein*). A 'philosopher' divines that, according to writings of the past (here attributed to a 'Demosthenes'!), the statue's fall was the work of divine

---

ed., *Byzantium in the Year 1000*, The Medieval Mediterranean: Peoples, Economies and Cultures, 400–1500 45 (Leiden, 2003), 183–97. Recent works that deal with Byzantine historiography and its complicity with literature: Ljubarskij, *et al.*, '*Quellenforschung*', 5–73; U. Criscuolo and R. Maisano, eds., *Categorie linguistiche e concettuali della storiografia bizantina: atti della quinta Giornata di studi bizantini, Napoli, 23–24 aprile 1998* (Naples, 2000); A. Markopoulos, *History and Literature of Byzantium in the 9th–10th Centuries* (Aldershot, 2004); Odorico, *et al.*, *L'écriture de la mémoire*; Burke, *et al.*, *Byzantine Narrative*; and L. B. Mortensen and P. A. Agapitos, eds., *Medieval Narratives between History and Fiction: From the Centre to the Periphery of Europe, 1100–1400* (Notre Dame, IN, forthcoming), see especially the article by P.A. Agapitos, 'In Rhomaian, Frankish and Persian lands: fiction and fictionality in Byzantium'. I would like to thank Panagiotis Agapitos for allowing me to read a copy of this article before its publication. On the aesthetics of history in general see further R. Barthes, 'The discourse of history', *Comparative Criticism* 3 (1981), 7–20; H. White, *The Content of the Form: Narrative Discourse and Historical Representation* (Baltimore, MD, 1987); and, especially, G. M. Spiegel, *The Past as Text: The Theory and Practice of Medieval Historiography* (Baltimore, MD, 1997).

[5] See *Parastaseis* §§ 27–8. For the *Parastaseis* see A. Cameron and J. Herrin, *Constantinople in the Early Eighth Century: The Parastaseis Syntomoi Chronikai*, Columbia Studies in the Classical Tradition 10 (Leiden, 1984) as well as L. James, '"Pray Not to Fall into Temptation and Be on Your Guard": pagan statues in Christian Constantinople', *Gesta* 35 (1996), 12–20.

[6] *Historein* in this first meaning – what I translate as 'narrate-and-explain' – indicates an *act of knowledge* that affirms both a knowing subject and a system of knowledge; cf. S. Goldhill, 'The naive and knowing eye: ecphrasis and the culture of viewing in the Hellenistic world', in S. Goldhill and R. Osborne, eds., *Art and Text in Ancient Greek Culture*, Cambridge Studies in New Art History and Criticism (Cambridge and New York, 1994), 213–39.

providence. In response, the emperor orders that the statue be buried, 'for it was impossible for it to be destroyed'. The narrator concludes with an all-too-familiar exhortation to his Byzantine reader: 'Studying these things in truth (*aletheia*), pray not to fall into temptation, and beware when you behold the old statues, especially the pagan ones'.

As the story suggests, what collapses upon the head of the unfortunate Byzantine viewer is not simply a statue; it is also, one might say, a system of knowledge. A method of viewing, a mode of representation, and, for our purposes here, a type of history making seem to be at stake.[7] By the end of the story, aesthetic marvel has been replaced by miraculous wonder. An awesome materiality (the statue [*stele*] is *pacheia*, heavy and thick) has been hidden. This materiality has been buried under a prescriptive discourse of moral imperative and clarity. The narrator tells us that he has studied 'with precision' (*akribeia*) and he is 'making visible' (*phaneroun*) that which he is narrating. 'Explanatory narrative' (*historia*) is progressively replaced by 'truth' (*aletheia*). This truth is meant to be transparent: this is a 'precise' truth that is based upon past textual authorities, that is to be interpreted by an authority in the present, and that, perhaps most significantly, is enforced by imperial power.

The movement from the old to the new, as thematized in this short tale, implies the completion of a cultural change. It is as if the dangerously aesthetic – focused on appearance, matter and sensation – ancient past is now safely buried.[8] A new aesthetics of history making with its emphasis on morality and its link to tradition and imperial authority seems to replace what is presented as an earlier material aesthetics. The new aesthetics, we should note, was an inherited one. The story alludes to some seminal aesthetic imperatives such as clarity, transparency, and moral correctness, imperatives promoted by Christian late antique discourse. At the heart of much Christian aesthetics, which Byzantium inherited, was the depreciation of exterior appearance and the suppression of individual subjective authorship for the sake of objective authority – in short, the valuing of objective truth over and against subjective aesthetic form.[9]

---

[7]   For the wider context of this 'collapse' see A. Cameron, *Changing Cultures in Early Byzantium* (Aldershot, 1996).

[8]   For statues as aesthetic objects see S. Papaioannou, 'Animate statues: aesthetics and movement', in C. Barber and D. Jenkins, eds., *Reading Michael Psellos* (Leiden, 2006), 95–116.

[9]   For a preliminary discussion of this aesthetics see S. Papaioannou, 'Der Glasort des Textes: Selbstheit und Ontotypologie im byzantinischen Briefschreiben (10. und 11. Jh.)', in W. Hörandner, J. Koder and M. Stassinopoulou, eds., *Wiener Byzantinistik und Neogräzistik: Beiträge zum Symposion Vierzig Jahre Institut für Byzantinistik und Neogräzistik der Universität Wien im Gedenken an Herbert Hunger* (Wien, 4.–7. Dezember 2002) (Byzantina et Neograeca Vindobonensia 24; Vienna,

Such notions were substantiated by Byzantium's 'fathers' in a voluminous discursive production that formed the logic of great parts of Byzantine speech and ideology. (Think, for instance, of Gregory of Nazianzus and his immanent presence in writers as diverse as George the Monk and Michael Psellos, and in imperial, ecclesiastic and monastic contexts alike.) : Furthermore, Christian aesthetics introduced a significant change in the history of writing and discursive representations of the past. By the fifth century, narratives of a fictional past – most notably the Greco-Roman novel – gradually disappear from the literary production and are replaced by hagiographical tales that never acknowledge their possible fictionality. That is, the conscious production of fiction with any historiographical pretences dies out.[10] In cultural terms, such a disappearance is an inseparable feature of the gradual decline and end of the production of new, freestanding sculpture (the last recorded new statue was made during late antiquity in the seventh century).[11] This suppression of fiction and concurrent 'burying' of statues in Byzantium – fiction and statues both being inescapably aesthetic artistic signs – are related symptoms of a significant theoretical stance inherited from Early Byzantium.

Byzantine chroniclers knew these imperatives well. When they come to narrate their historical past, they define clearly, especially in their *prooimia*, the aesthetic presuppositions that govern their writing of history.[12] Theophanes the Confessor is perhaps the first of these writers to dwell on the topic in the *prooimion* to his *Chronographia*.[13] Like the narrator of the

---

2004), 324–36, and *idem*, 'Gregory and the constraint of sameness', in J. Børtnes and T. Hägg, eds., *Gregory of Nazianzus: Images and Reflections* (Copenhagen, 2006), 59–81. The terms 'objective' and 'subjective' are used with some caution here; they refer to the preference for divine absolute truth over and against human self-reflexive knowledge.

[10] For a discussion see G.W. Bowersock, *Fiction as History: Nero to Julian* (Berkeley, CA, 1994).

[11] See C. Mango, 'Antique statuary and the Byzantine beholder', *DOP* 17 (1963), 53–76, and *idem*, 'Epigrammes honorifiques, statues et portraits à Byzance', in B. Kremmydas, C. Maltezou and N. M. Panagiotakis, eds., Ἀφιέρωμα στὸν Νίκο Σβορῶνο, I (Rethymno, 1986), 23–35.

[12] Byzantine *prooimia* have been extensively catalogued and studied in the still-valuable study of H. Lieberich, *Studien zu den Proömien in der griechischen und byzantinischen Geschichtschreibung* (Munich, 1899–1900) to be read with R. Maisano, 'Il problema della forma letteraria nei proemi storiografici bizantini', *BZ* 78 (1985), 329–43, Grigoriadis, '*Prooimion*', 327–44, and L. R. Cresci, 'Ποικιλία nei proemi storiografici bizantini', *Byz* 74 (2004), 330–47.

[13] On Theophanes see Mango and Scott, eds., *The Chronicle of Theophanes Confessor*. On the immediate context of the revival of the interest in the past in the early ninth century see I. Ševčenko, 'The search for the past in Byzantium

Parastaseis, Theophanes too speaks of the precision (*akribeia*) with which he composed his work. Precision here means absence of subjective mediation. Theophanes claims that all events are presented in their correct order (*taxis*) without any interpretative rearrangement by the historian himself who can only display his ignorance (*a-mathia*). Similarly, some decades later, George the Monk declares that his narrative presents 'the entire truth' (*aletheia*) without any embellishment, but with 'most transparent clarity' (*sapheneia enargestate*). His discourse is 'plentiful of content' and void of 'fashioned words and artistic constructions'. It is written without hiding falsehood behind a 'most forceful method of construction'. His is a discourse that will narrate a past in which pagan idols, fictions and myths are overthrown: a discourse that will teach salvation; a discourse of direct 'vision' (*theoria*) that does not alter or deceive 'sense-perception' (*aisthesis*).[14]

Similar statements abound in other sources.[15] The metahistorical principles promoted by these statements define a historiography that provides continuity with the past. Historiographical memory functions as a means both for making the past present and for demanding that what is moral and good from the past be repeated. Therefore, the past and the present are to become one, continuous, through history.[16] This is, for example, the point made in the *prooimion* of the tenth-century *Life of the Emperor Basil* (known as *Vita Basilii*). Basil I is presented here as both a perfect representative of the Roman imperial past of Byzantium and an example that must be imitated by later emperors. This double quality of Basil is brought into the narrative by speaking of him as a 'statue'.[17] This statue is *not*, like ancient sculpture can be – as some Byzantines see it – an

---

around the year 800', *DOP* 46 (1992), 279–93. The citations that follow come from Theophanes, *Chronographia,* 3–4.

[14]   George the Monk, 1–5. The text is to be dated perhaps in *ca.* 843–45; see D. Afinogenov, 'The date of Georgios Monachos reconsidered', *BZ* 92 (1999), 437–47. On the late antique sources of George's wording in the *prooimion* see Karpozilos, Βυζαντινοί Ἱστορικοί, I, 233–42.

[15]   The *prooimia* of the historical works of writers as diverse as John Skylitzes, Leo the Deacon and Niketas Choniates with their emphasis on truth, discursive clarity, and the moral response expected from the reader testify to the ubiquity of this aesthetics. John Skylitzes, specifically, while accusing other historians for failure in *akribeia*, praises George Synkellos and Theophanes for employing a simple discourse that 'almost *touches the essence* of the events' (*Prooimion* to his *Synopsis Historion,* 3–4). Finally, *akribeia* and *aletheia* are recurrent criteria in Photios' judgments of style (see, e.g., *Bibliotheke* 60.19b: 58.24–5).

[16]   For this concept of memory see, e.g., G. M. Spiegel, 'Genealogy: form and function in medieval historical narrative', *History and Theory* 22 (1983), 43–53, with K. L. Klein, 'On the emergence of memory in historical discourse', *Representations* 69 (2000), 127–50.

[17]   Theophanes Continuatus, *Chronographia* (= *Vita Basilii*), ch. 1: 211.

object of aesthetic admiration. Rather, his statue is a new kind of object that displays continuity with the Roman tradition and requires moral repetition in the Byzantine present. Basil's statue, as the author tells us, stands in for all of Roman history; as such, namely as an 'archetype', this statue incites moral action, what the author calls imitation, *mimesis*.[18] Notably, the Greek word used in the *Life* for 'statue' is *andrias* – rather than the more general terms *stele* or *eikon*, the aesthetically charged *agalma*, or the pagan term *eidolon*. This usage is not coincidental. *Andrias* alludes to the manliness that defines much of the morality that these Byzantine narratives propagate. The morality that oversees the making of the past in Byzantium is always also *andro*-centric; and this is something to keep in mind.[19]

The emphasis on continuity defines the historical narratives so much so that they come full circle and ultimately focus on the sensational mediation of the past, which their authors repeatedly criticize. For instance, Theophanes' chronicle is full of visible signs, *semeia*, that make the presence of both God and the past directly accessible to the reader. The reader can see, hear, and perceive with his senses past events. The history of Byzantium's past is presented as a competition of signs – that is, the emergence of new Christian signs and the destruction of pagan ones. For example, we read of Constantine's mother, Helen, who discovers the Holy Cross under a pagan temple and statue (*agalma*) of Aphrodite in Jerusalem, while later, in Constantinople, Constantine erects his own statue (*andrias*) as part of the construction of his new city. Julian, soon after Constantine's death, installs an effigy (*xoanon*) of himself in direct contest with a statue (*andrias*) of Christ. Julian also attempts to converse with an image (*eidolon*) of Apollo, who is silenced, however, by the holy relics of a Christian martyr. And so on.[20] These narratives, as is the case with much Byzantine writing,

---

[18] This *prooimion* echoes the preface of Diodorus of Sicily's *Bibliotheca Historica*. Like Diodorus, the Byzantine author speaks of the immortal 'mouth of history', yet he has left out Diodorus' explicit – and characteristically Greco-Roman – affirmation of the 'power of discourse' (1.2.3–6). On the rehabilitation of the statue metaphor here see P. A. Agapitos, 'Ἡ εἰκόνα τοῦ αὐτοκράτορα Βασιλείου Αʹ στὴ φιλομακεδονικὴ γραμματεία 867–959', *Hell* 40 (1989), 285–322, at 311.

[19] Constantine VII Porphyrogennetos repeats this emphasis on instituting the emperor as a manly statue (*andrias*) in his preface to the *De administrando imperio*, *Proem* 37. Similarly, Lucian – to cite here an earlier example – in his description of proper history-writing compares history with the manly beauty of an 'athlete': *How to Write History*, 9.

[20] Theophanes, 25–26, 28, 49–50. The same competition between ancient/pagan and triumphant Roman/Christian signs is the force behind a work that in its outlook (namely its linguistic idiom and poetic aspiration) appears to be entirely different from Theophanes' work; I am referring to Constantine of Rhodes and his *Ekphraseis* of Constantinopolitan statues, ed. Legrand (1896), a text dedicated to Constantine VII.

are structured around 'perceptual grids', often showing little interest in comprehending the content of historical events.[21] More or, perhaps, *rather* than an understanding of the past, the reader must gain a direct sensation of it.

The aesthetics of presenting history in truth and inciting morality are thus paradoxically manifested through materially aesthetic narratives. At the level of theory, Byzantine historiographical aesthetics propagates an *anti*-aesthetic stance (a fear against any sense-oriented embellishment or artificiality). At the level of narrative, history-writing indulges in the aesthetic power of representation and the 'thick' texture of historical events.[22] The result is incongruous. While Byzantine historians – and Byzantine narrators in general – adopt a pose of self-obliteration, a kind of *Selbstauslöschung* that a modern historicist like Leopold von Ranke would envy, they, in effect, impose upon the historical past the most subjective, and often most fictional, of narratives.[23] Truth reigns in metahistorical declarations; yet, as any reader of Byzantine narrative knows, truth can be dispensable in historiographical practice.

This approach is evidently self-contradictory, but only from our perspective. For Byzantine historiographers the self-professed reign of truth and the simultaneous silencing of its fictionality was the basis for the authority claims that these writers raised to their Byzantine readers.[24] For the norms that govern their narratives, are the very same norms with which Byzantine institutions, through ritual and representation, brought forth hegemonic versions of the past. Whether in ceremony or public rhetoric, coinage or religious iconography, truth was professed in Byzantium, but only with the mechanisms – the staging, the artistry, indeed the fiction – of the production of that truth hidden.[25] Two examples may suffice. One is the staging of the Roman *imperium* as scripted in the *Book of Ceremonies*. The other is the creation of the Christian past through ritual by the triumphant

---

[21]   On this see Spiegel, 'Genealogy', 46. We should not forget that, in a Byzantine context, the word *historia* has built into its semantic field the emphasis on sense-perception, as *historia* could simply mean 'picture,' 'image'; cf. H. Maguire, *Art and Eloquence in Byzantium* (Princeton, NJ, 1981), 9.

[22]   In this paradox of theoretical proclamations of *truth* and, simultaneously, narrative pursuits of *fiction*, Byzantine historiography is not alone; a quick glance at most Byzantine hagiography would give the same impression.

[23]   On modern historicism see Gay, *The Naked Heart*, 198–210 and 414–18.

[24]   Cf. T. Whitmarsh, *Ancient Greek Literature* (Cambridge and Malden, MA, 2004), 116–120 on the Thucydidian deployment of similar techniques.

[25]   These are, it seems, always the workings of *power*; cf. M. Foucault, *History of Sexuality* I (New York, 1978), 86: power's 'success is proportional to its ability to hide its own mechanisms'.

translations of relics.[26] Through somewhat institutionalized practices, the Byzantines would often rather marvel and repeat than remember and understand. In a context where authority was constructed by such means, Byzantine historians were somewhat conditioned to follow certain dominant ideological premises. But this is only half of the story.

The appeal of sculpted objects

After at least the mid-eleventh century, a different stance in the historiographical aesthetics becomes evident. Valuation of the aesthetic form of history is both voiced through statements and explored in narrative attempts. An eloquent example of the former is Michael Attaleiates' dual introduction to his *Historia* (1070s?), and of the latter aspects of John Zonaras' narrative practice in his *Epitome Historion* (second half of the twelfth century). The *prooimion* proper of Attaleiates' *Historia* would perfectly satisfy the expectations of a Byzantine reader.[27] Attaleiates parades terms like 'clear teaching', 'concise and simple diction', 'pattern for imitation' and 'immortal memory' in order to describe his understanding of what history-writing is about, the stylistic form he has adopted, and his intended effect upon his audience. Historiographical continuity with the past is proclaimed through what purports to be a non-aesthetic narrative; Attaleiates will not adopt, as he tells us, any 'double-speak' or 'fiction', *diploe* or *mythos*.

Attaleiates has, however, prefaced his history also with a brief speech (perhaps intended for performance) in which he offers his work to the 'Emperor [Nikephoros] Botaneiates' (*Historia* 2–4). Here, his historiographical practice is presented with terms that evoke appeal to the senses.Attaleiates will not simply narrate manly 'deeds' and explain 'causes' of events; he will also 'extend his narrative or, rather, season it, as if with some delicacies, with signs [*semeiois*] that occurred unexpectedly … also weaving into the fabric certain scientific expositions on natural phenomena [*physikas technologias*] and the appearances of animals'. 'Simply put,' Attaleiates tells us, 'I have completed a *variegated* book [*poikilen biblon*],

---

[26]   Cf. A. M. Cameron, 'The construction of court ritual: the Byzantine *Book of Ceremonies*', in D. Cannadine and S. Price, eds., *Rituals of Royalty: Power and Ceremonial in Traditional Societies* (Cambridge and New York, 1987), 106–36, with B. Flusin, 'Construire une nouvelle Jérusalem: Constantinople et les reliques', in M. Amir Moezzi and J. Scheid, eds., *L'Orient dans l'histoire religieuse de l'Europe: L'invention des origines* (Brepols, 2000), 51–70, and H. A. Klein, 'Sacred relics and imperial ceremonies at the Great Palace of Constantinople', in F. A. Bauer, ed., *Visualisierungen von Herrschaft* (Istanbul, 2006), 79–99.

[27]   Attaleiates, *Historia*, 5–6.

like a garden nourishing many a flower'. The fact that Attaleiates introduces aesthetic variety as a seminal historiographical principle challenges his own disavowal of artistry and fiction as outlined in the *prooimion* proper.[28] Attaleiates flirts with the notion that historiography may be something more than mere transparent presentation of the past.

Many decades later, John Zonaras questions the dominant tropes of Byzantine historiography, both in his metahistorical statements and, occasionally, in the formation of his narrative.[29] Let me look here at a single example of the latter.[30] Like Theophanes the Confessor, Zonaras mentions the statue erected by Constantine while founding his new City.[31] In Zonaras, however, Constantine's statue is not inscribed, as in Theophanes, within a narrative context of cultural competition between the defeated pagan and victorious Christian signs. While Zonaras does indeed note the Christianization of the statue (Constantine, we are told, had nails from Christ's Holy Cross hammered to the head of the statue), the twelfth-century historian exhibits this most notable sign of imperial power as an aesthetic product of the Greco-Roman past. The statue, Zonaras reports, was originally a depiction of Apollo, brought to Constantinople from Ilion, the ancestral city of ancient Rome. Most importantly, it is a statue that 'displayed the *precision* [*akribeia*] of an *ancient* hand that could fashion objects that are almost breathing'. *Akribeia* is here restored to its original Hellenistic meaning, for it refers to a principle of artistry, verisimilitude and life-likeness.[32] As opposed to Theophanes who speaks of Constantine's statue as an *andrias*, Zonaras' statue of Constantine is an *agalma* – a term that Theophanes reserves for, e.g., the pagan statue of Aphrodite.[33] For

---

[28]   On Attaleiates' two prefaces see further the notes in I. Pérez Martín, *Miguel Attaliates Historia*, Nueva Roma 15 (Madrid, 2002), 231–5; see also Cresci, Ποικιλία'.

[29]   On Zonaras' *Epitome* see further I. Grigoriadis, *Linguistic and Literary Studies in the Epitome Historion of John Zonaras* (Thessalonike, 1998).

[30]   Regarding the former, it may suffice to note here that, in his *prooimion*, Zonaras surprisingly declares that his historiography will *not* be characterized by precision (*akribeia*); rather, his text will be varied, while its author (whom Zonaras calls 'its father') will assume the voices and styles of others; *Epitome*, I, 1–6. See further Grigoriadis, 'Prooimion'.

[31]   Zonaras, *Epitome*, III, 17–18.

[32]   In Greco-Roman aesthetic theory, precise transparency is appreciated not merely for the representation of truth, but also for the enlivening artistry involved in producing a transparent representation; cf. A. D. Walker, 'Enargeia and the spectator in Greek historiography', *Transactions of the American Philological Association* 123 (1993), 353–77.

[33]   Theophanes, 28 (on Constantine's *andrias*) with 26 (on Aphrodite's *agalma*); the term *agalma* is used only two more times in Theophanes' *Chronographia* (50 and 176), in reference again to *pagan* statues.

Zonaras, the statue is a manifestation of imperial ideology but also an object of aesthetic delight.[34]

At this juncture, it is Michael Psellos who emerges as the strongest and, I believe, most influential voice.[35] Leaving aside for now the discursive strands that support this influential voice, let me turn briefly to Psellos' *Chronographia* in order to treat both its implicit practice and stated theory.

We do not possess Psellos' *prooimion* to his *Chronographia*. But if we bring to mind Psellos' intense authorial self-referentiality attested in all of his texts (most famously in this one), it is likely that Psellos did write an introductory preface.[36] I would suggest that this preface was left out from the surviving manuscript (the famous twelfth-century *Parisinus Graecus* 1712, which preserves the *Chronographia*). This omission might have satisfied what seems to be the intention behind the making of this twelfth-century history book: the intention is one of creating a continuous chronicle-like universal narrative that leads from the so-called Pseudo-Symeon's chronicle to Leo the Deacon to Psellos, namely from the creation of the world to the late eleventh century. In order to make Psellos' history cohere nicely with such linear historiography, the beginning of Psellos' text, I believe, needed to be excised.[37]

---

[34] It is no coincidence that this statue also falls, killing several Constantinopolitan pedestrians. This collapse, however, which happens during Zonaras' lifetime, is not a sign of a mysterious presence, as in the *Parastaseis*, but functions rather as a metaphor for Zonaras' critique of contemporary imperial power; on this aspect of Zonaras' work see P. Magdalino, 'Aspects of twelfth-century Byzantine *Kaiserkritik*', *Speculum* 58/2 (1983), 326–46 (repr. in Magdalino, *Tradition and transformation in medieval Byzantium* [Aldershot, 1991], study VIII).

[35] This influence is felt in Zonaras and perhaps Attaleiates too; for Psellos and Zonaras see Grigoriadis, *Linguistic and Literary Studies*, while for Attaleiates and Psellos see D. Krallis, 'Attaleiates as a reader of Psellos', in Barber and Jenkins, eds., *Reading Michael Psellos*, 167–91.

[36] Cf. Psellos, *Letter* 28, ed. E. Kurtz and F. Drexl, *Michael Psellus. Scripta minora magnam partem adhuc inedita II, Epistulae* (Milan, 1941), pp. 38–9, with Lucian, *How to Write History*, 53–4, on the importance of the right *prooimion*.

[37] On the *Parisinus* see N. Panagiotakes, Λέων Διάκονος, *EEBS* 34 (1965), 1–138, at 42–84, with A. Markopoulos, Ἡ Χρονογραφία τοῦ Ψευδοσυμεών καὶ οἱ πηγές της (Ioannina, 1978), 30–38, and K. Snipes, 'Notes on Parisinus Graecus 1712', *JÖB* 41 (1991), 141–61; see also *idem*, 'The Chronographia of Michael Psellos and the textual tradition and transmission of the Byzantine historians of the eleventh and twelfth centuries', *ZRVI* 27/28 (1989), 43–62. I owe to Professor Diether Reinsch the information (communicated in conversation) that the *Parisinus* is to be dated in the late twelfth century. Now, given Psellos' admiration for the rhetorical aesthetics of Dionysius of Halicarnassus (see, for example, G. Aujac, 'Michel Psellos et Denys d'Halicarnasse: Le traité sur la composition des éléments du langage', *REB* 33 [1975], 257–75), should we speculate that Psellos – if he ever indeed wrote a

Be that as it may, Psellos repeatedly returns to defining his historiographical aesthetics within the *Chronographia*. Here, I shall look at only one of the many metahistorical statements Psellos offers in his lengthy narrative about Constantine IX Monomachos. The statement appears after a report regarding the death of Maria Skleraina, Monomachos' mistress, approximately a third of the way into the sixth book of the *Chronographia*.

> To include within the texture [*hyphen*] of this history everything that the emperor did upon the occasion of her death – the laments he wept, the deeds he performed, his passionate mourning, overcome as he was like a child by this suffering [*pathos*] – to include all this would be redundant. Discoursing in petty and, as it were, fine details about each thing done or said is not the work of historians, but the work of those engaged in blame … or those mounting praises … Now, if I myself have occasionally used such features from which I am urging historians to refrain, this should not cause wonder. For the discourse of history [*logos historias*] is not thus defined [*oristai*] so as to be polished, sculpted all around entirely [*apexesthai*]. It must also contain some excursions and digressions, whenever this is fitting. The historian must quickly round up what has intervened, and, while using the rest in supplementary fashion [*en parergois*], conclude everything towards his main subject.[38]

It is not uncommon for a Byzantine narrator to find pleasure in his digressions – what would Byzantine historiography be, after all, without them? Nor is it entirely uncommon for a Byzantine writer to assert the value of such digressions.[39] Not as common, however, for Byzantine and, even, Roman Greek aesthetics is, I believe, the implicit metaphor that Psellos evokes in reference to the 'discourse of history', the aesthetic principles with which Psellos has invested this metaphor, and the narrative strategies that this metaphor is aiming to justify and explain.

---

prooimion – imitated Dionysius' preface to his *Roman Antiquities*? That preface suggests, among other things, that the historian is to create with his writing a 'memorial' of his own soul; this would be an idea that Psellos might have liked. Indeed, Dionysius' preface was a rather forgotten source of prooimiastic wisdom for Byzantine historiographers who preferred the more moralistic Diodorus of Sicily; on this preference for Diodorus see Lieberich, *Studien zu den Proömien*.

[38]   *Chronographia* 6.70.

[39]   Cf. Theophanes Continuatus (= *Vita Basilii*), ch. 56: 294.3–7, or Photios, *Bibliotheke*, 83.65a:191.14–17 on Dionysius of Halicarnassus and his historiographical deviations. Attaleiates (*Historia*, 177.17–18) is careful to ask for the reader to excuse him when altering his style towards the 'pleasure of tragedy' by inserting a digressive *ethopoiia*.

The implicit metaphor is none other than the parallelism of discourse with the material surface of statues.[40] A sculpted object, as opposed to a painted image or a transparent sign, is how Psellos imagines history-writing. The metaphor immediately suggests sense-oriented aesthetics; indeed, a few lines later Psellos tellingly refers to his narrative on Monomachos as a 'woven and textured body', a *hyphainomenon soma* (6.74) – a metaphor that in his writing carries associations of texture, bodiliness, fabrication, embellishment or fiction, as well as of a characteristically feminine activity.[41] More specifically, the artistic sculpting that Psellos evokes is a controversial one. Unlike classical or post-classical ideals of sculpture, the Psellian 'statue' of history does not have its surfaces carved, polished and perfected.[42] Rather than clarity, visible unity, and perfection, Psellos invests his metaphor with the valuation of a rather anomalous statue that, defined by the subjective will of its creator, crosses boundaries.[43] Psellos has deviated from the norms prescribed for others – this is the point of this metahistorical statement.

The comparison of history with an anomalous sculpted object is placed within, and aims to justify, the equally anomalous narrative strategy employed in Psellos' lengthy presentation of Monomachos' rule. In this sixth book of the *Chronographia*, Psellos folds multiple digressions.[44] The following are, in my opinion, two of the most significant. The first is Psellos' notorious autobiographic intrusion in Chapters 36 through 46; the second

[40]   *Apoxeein* is the verb that Psellos typically uses in order to describe the sculpting of real or metaphorical statues; see, e.g., *Chronographia* 3.14, *Orat. for.* 2.236–7, and *Theologica* I, 113.15–18.

[41]   On the connotations of weaving in Psellos see, e.g., *Theologica* I 30.44 (on weaving and style), *Orat. for.*, 1.795–7 (fictional as well as *heretical* weaving of dogmas), *Chronographia* 6.159 (on Zoe abandoning the typical female task of weaving), and, especially, *Letter* 24 (on Psellos' *artistic* weaving of discourse): P. Gautier, 'Quelques lettres de Psellos inédites ou déjà éditées', *REB* 44 (1986), 111–97, here 174–5; cf. Lucian, *How to Write History*, 48 (on the 'weaving' of the body of history).

[42]   The classic statement on the perfectly carved out and polished statue is to be found in Plotinus, *Enneads* 1.6.9 (notably Plotinus uses the verb 'apoxeein'). Psellos was familiar with the Plotinian notion; see, e.g., *Theologica* I, 67.21–2. See further Lucian, *How to Write History*, 23 and 48 on history-writing as the making of a well-ordered (and manly) body, and 50–51 on the *sculpting* task of the historian ('xeein' is again one of the verbs employed).

[43]   Cf. how in an essay on philosophy *Phil. min.* I 2.76–84, Psellos describes rhetoric as 'law in itself [*auto-nomothesia*]' which 'fashions [*apoxeei*]' other types of discursive practice. See also how the verb 'apoxeein' is ascribed by Psellos to the *creative* power of nature; see *Chronographia* 6.126 (on nature and its making of the body of Monomachos).

[44]   This part of the *Chronographia* dates to the early 1060s.

is the equally notorious presentation of the imperial trio of Monomachos, Zoe and Maria Skleraina in Chapters 50 through 69, with an emphasis on Psellos' expressedly sympathetic view of Maria, Constantine's mistress.[45] Both digressions – the one with the author's self-promotion, the other with its emphasis on erotics – would cause the dismay of Roman or Byzantine Greek normative literary aesthetics.[46] Both would be considered a supplementary work, a *parergon*, which Psellos, despite his many excuses, has turned into his main *ergon*.

What unites the two digressions is the undercurrent that marks both narratives: the promotion of an aestheticization of discourse. Both Psellos and Maria Skleraina are praised for their discursive 'charms'. Psellos' 'pleasures' (*hedone*) and Maria's ability in 'narrative' (*diegeisthai*) are the cause for a *passion of desire* that has captivated Monomachos who desires both Maria (sexually) and Psellos (intellectually).[47] When Psellos and Maria, the two main subjects, actually meet on the stage of Psellos' narrative (6.60–61), words like *historia* and *akribeia* are removed from their Byzantine moral or ontological connotations and are restored to precisely the aesthetic meaning that the unfortunate viewers in the *Parastaseis* were forced to abandon.[48] Maria, we read (6.61), asks Psellos about the meaning of pagan 'myths', often contributing thoughts of her own that she derives from 'those who have studied these matters with precision [*ton*

---

[45]   Maria is one of the few characters that receive a consistently unambiguous praise in the *Chronographia*. For Psellos' well-known *intrusion* in his historiographical narrative see J. N. Ljubarskij, 'Man in Byzantine historiography from John Malalas to Michael Psellos', *DOP* 46 (1992), 177–86, with *idem*, 'New trends in the study of Byzantine historiography', *DOP* 47 (1993), 131–8, and, especially, Macrides, 'The Historian in the History', 205–24.

[46]   Lucian, for instance, remarks how digressions 'feminize' the manly, Herculean body of history (*How to Write History*, 10), while in an epigram attributed to either Photios or Leo the Philosopher readers are advised not to look at the 'supplementary' erotic sight (*parergos thea*) afforded by the reading of Achilles Tatius' love-story (*Anthologia Graeca* 9.203). Similarly, John Skylitzes in his *Prooimion* (cf. above note 15) blames others, including Psellos, for writing history 'as a supplementary work [*parergos*]' or for 'putting forward a subject-matter *pertaining to themselves* [*oikeian hypothesin*]'; he then describes his own historiographical method as 'having *polished* [*apo-xesantes*] everything found to be close to what is fictional [*mythodous*]'.

[47]   See *Chronographia* 6.45–6 on Psellos, with 6.50–51 and 60 on Maria. Cf. also Psellos' funerary poem in honour of Maria, *Poem*. 17; there (esp. lines 14–117) Maria is described as a 'living statue' and is praised by Psellos for her bodily appearance and discursive charms that render her an object of desire (*pothos*) that turns her viewers into stone!

[48]   Indeed, what Psellos restores here is Greco-Roman (as opposed to late antique) aesthetics; cf. above note 32.

akribounton]'. She, 'with linguistic precision [*akribos*]', inquires about the 'narrative [*historia*]' that underlies a Homeric line uttered, most likely by Psellos himself, during a ceremonial procession. The Homeric line identifies Maria with that primary object of desire, Helen.[49] Here, at the heart of Psellos' narrative about Monomachos, Maria's and Psellos' 'tongues', their discursive *akribeia* and openness to fictional *historia*, are instituted as those aesthetic objects that potentially define the fabric of history-writing and the desires of history-reading.[50] With Psellos' *Chronographia*, the aesthetics of a fictional vs. moral and gynocentric vs. androcentric narrative become an acknowledged ingredient of history-writing.[51]

Psellos' indulgence in the aesthetics of history promotes a new type of narrative that foregrounds rather than effaces rhetoric as well as gynocentric writing.[52] This is the kind of history explored by Anna Komnene's *Alexiad* (written in the 1140s?). Margaret Mullett has poignantly shown the 'novelisation', that is the fluidity of rhetorical genres and the flirtation with 'possible worlds', that constitutes Anna's narrative.[53] For this essay, let me draw attention to the several 'statues' (*agalmata*) that inhabit Anna's history. The statue metaphor is used in key moments in order to describe,

---

[49]   Kaldellis has suggested, rightly I believe, that it is Psellos himself who utters the allusive praise of Maria; see A. Kaldellis, *The Argument of Psellos' Chronographia* (Leiden, 1999), 140.

[50]   Cf. 6.60 with 6.46 and 161 on Maria and Psellos respectively. Next to the 'tongues' of Psellos and Maria, we should add the 'statues' (*agalmata*; notably, Psellos does not use the term *andrias*) of Constantine Monomachos (6.125), of, especially, Zoe who is also praised for her discursive virtues (5.22 and 4.16), and, ultimately, the 'statue' of discourse itself as discussed above.

[51]   Anthony Kaldellis (*The Argument of Psellos' Chronographia*, esp. 132–66) makes a further case for the *political* – and not simply historiographical – significance of Psellos' rehabilitation of both rhetoric and the 'body'. Much of his argument is conducive to Psellos' aestheticization of history-writing that is proposed here. Nevertheless, the details of that political significance remain to be discussed especially in reference to one of the suggestions of Kaldellis' *Argument* for which I remain sceptical, namely that Psellos is promoting a purely Platonic as well as agnostic (often Machiavellian) political agenda.

[52]   By '*gyno*-centric' I refer here to two things: (a) the promotion of female characters (and especially their speech) at the foreground of historical narrative, and (b) what would have been regarded in Byzantium as 'effeminate' aesthetics, namely an aesthetics that is focused on sensuality as well as the expression and incitement of emotions.

[53]   M. Mullett, 'Novelisation in Byzantium: narrative after the revival of fiction', in Burke, *et. al., Byzantine Narrative*, 1–28. On Anna see further T. Gouma-Peterson, ed., *Anna Komnene and Her Times* (New York and London, 2000).

among others, Anna's parents.[54] In two of these instances, metaphorical 'statues' interrupt Anna's main narrative, and cause moments of what one could call metanarrative crisis.[55] By indulging in the aesthetic and emotional appeal of exterior beauty witnessed in these statues, Anna, like Psellos, reflects on the value of such temporary and notably gynocentric digressions. Such digressions, Anna suggests, deviate from the normative and generic Byzantine aesthetics of a *historia* that is focused on truth rather than appearance and defies the effeminate expression of, and being affected by, emotions.[56]

Indeed, Anna begins and concludes her *Alexiad* by challenging Byzantine normative historiographical principles, what she calls the '*ethos* of *historia*' (Proem. 1.3).[57] While in the *prooimion* she is anxious to avoid giving voice to *pathos*, Anna finally can do nothing but submit to her emotions, introducing a further subversive usage of the statue metaphor. At the very end of the *Alexiad*, while speaking of her incomparable grief due to the loss of her parents and husband, she expresses the wish : to have been turned into 'a stone .... becoming insensitive (*pros petran ... an-aisthetos echousa*)'. As Anna remarks, she wishes to become desensitized as the mythological Niobe who was turned into a body of rock, thereby protected from *pathos* and grief.[58] Here, the aesthetic dimension of history is drawn to its limits. Anna's wish for petrification manifests her acknowledged inability to transcend the senses in a kind of ontological permanence promised in, say, Theophanes' *Chronographia* and the *Life of the Emperor Basil*. Anna cannot and will not raise a historiographical statue of virtue and manly stability; instead, she will remain human, affected by emotions.[59] Anna's unrealizable wish to become stone marks her unwillingness to write *his*-tory.[60]

---

[54]   *Alexiad* 1.12, 3.2–4, and 12.3, where the word *agalma* is used and aesthetics is evoked. Anna also refers to *andrias* with the connotation of masculinity in 12.4 (on the statue of Constantine), 13.2 (on soldiers), 13.12 (Bohemond on himself), and, most importantly, 14.4.7 (on Alexios as a steadfast and immovable *andrias*).

[55]   See especially 1.12.3 and 3.2.4.

[56]   See also 4.8.1.

[57]   Following Polybius, *Historiae* I.14, a *prooimion* also excerpted in Constantine VII Porphyrogennetos, *De sententiis* 108, ed. U. P. Boissevain, *Excerpta historica iussu imp. Constantini Porphyrogeniti confecta, vol. 4: excerpta de sententiis* (Berlin, 1906).

[58]   *Alexiad* 15.11.23–4.

[59]   Cf. this passage (15.11.23–4) with her earlier promotion of a statuesque Alexios (14.4.7 and note 54 above).

[60]   On ancient *his-tory* see P. Cartledge, 'The silent women of Thucydides: 2.45.2 re-viewed', in R. M. Rosen and J. Farell, eds., *Nomodeiktes: Greek Studies in Honor of Martin Oswald* (Ann Arbor, MI, 1993), 125–32. It should be noted that there are two significant allusions within Anna's reference to Niobe: the first is its mention by Achilles to Priam near the *end* of Homer's *Iliad* as an example of mourning and the

After Anna's *Alexiad*, one might turn to Constantine Manasses' universal chronicle, the *Synopsis Chronike*, dedicated to the *sebastokratorissa* Eirene, wife of Andronikos Komnenos. This writing of history is blatantly indulgent in Psellian aesthetic pleasures, free from Anna's anxieties.[61] (This is, after all, the time when the conscious production of fiction and interest in sculpture are revived in premodern Greek culture, after a silence of several centuries.) In Manasses' text, normatively Byzantine narrative signs have receded (the word *semeion* is virtually absent). They are replaced by the distinctive ingredients of premodern fiction: heroic acts, statuesque bodies, powerful men who express their suffering and emotions, beautiful and attractive women, women actively involved in the making of history, dialogues, dreams, love-stories, poisonous apples, terrible eunuchs.[62] The chronicle is written with the stylistic devices distinctive of contemporary fiction (it should be remembered that Manasses is the author of one of four fictional romances produced in the twelfth century). His text is written in verse, like the majority of the novels of this period. It contains elaborate Homeric-like metaphors, several short digressive narratives, encomia, rhetorical addresses, and evocations of the audience (a marker of public performance). With several maxims of timeless morality that usually conclude the narration of an event (*gnomai*), Manasses enters the fabric

---

second is Psellos' use of Niobe in *Letter* 118, ed. Sathas, *Mesaionike Bibliotheke*, V, 365. Indeed, of the several references to Niobe in premodern Greek literature, Psellos is both – as far as I can tell – the first of the medieval period and the first ever who adopts the feminine pathos of Niobe *autobiographically* and speaks of it in the first person singular; Anna consciously, I believe, revives Psellos' autobiographic voice.

[61]   Diether Reinsch has recently dated the *Synopsis Chronike* in the years 1150 to 1153; 'Die Palamedes-Episode in der Synopsis Chronike des Konstantinos Manasses und ihre Inspirationsquelle', in M. Hinterberger and E. Schiffer, eds., *Byzantinische Sprachkunst: Studien zur byzantinischen Literatur gewidmet Wolfram Hörandner zum 65. Geburtstag*, Byzantinisches Archiv 20 (Berlin, 2007), 266–76, see esp. 268–9. On the literarization of historiography in Manasses see I. Nilsson, 'Discovering literariness in the past: literature vs. history in the *Synopsis Chronike* of Konstantinos Manasses', and D. R. Reinsch, 'Historia ancilla litterarum? Zum literarischen Geschmack in der Komnenenzeit: Das Beispiel der Σύνοψις Χρονική des Konstantinos Manasses', in Odorico, *et al.*, *L'écriture de la mémoire*, 15 31 and 81–94 respectively, with Agapitos, 'In Rhomaian, Frankish and Persian Lands'. For a comparable trend in the Medieval West see G. M. Spiegel, *Romancing the Past: The Rise of Vernacular Prose Historiography in Thirteenth Century France*, The New Historicism 23 (Berkeley, CA, 1993).

[62]   See, e.g., *Synopsis Chronike* 725f. (dreams), 816–39 and 1381f. (*eros*), 2597–9, 2622–34 and 3447–53 (women), 2662–99 (poisonous apple), 2757–8 (terrible eunuch), 3133–4, 3326–32, 3392, 3570–77 (male *pathos* and its expression), 3214–20, 3496f., 3665–6 (heroic? acts), 3338–54 (dialogue), 6578 (statuesque appearance).

of his history, expresses his opinion, and allows his audience to distance themselves from the past by looking at their own present condition.[63] With such themes and rhetorical techniques, the historian exposes the rhetorical character of his historical work. Manasses turns the past into a stage for rhetoric.

It is time to arrive at Eustathios of Thessalonike, writing towards the end of the twelfth century. A reader of Eustathios' conclusion to his *On the Capture of Thessalonike* is led to believe that not much has changed between Theophanes' precise truth along with the victorious signs that mediate it and Eustathios' tale of Byzantine defeat, pain and suffering.[64] Addressing his fellow 'citizens and fellow martyr/athletes' as well as 'the young', Eustathios claims that he has narrated, in a manner of precision (*akriboun*), what has befallen their city and that he has raised as a pillar (*ana-steloun*) an 'image [*eikona*] of teaching'. Disrespecting the 'painted image (*diazographesin*)', Eustathios continues, would equal disrespect towards 'truth (*aletheian*)' itself, with the inevitable effect of future repetition of suffering.[65] Thus despite the fact that this tale is one of loss rather than victory, the ontological continuity of narrative with truth and the moral response that this continuity demands seem to define the traditional horizon of Eustathios' metahistory.[66]

Yet, at the beginning of his narrative, Eustathios provides us also with the clearest affirmation of the Byzantine consciousness of the aesthetic form of the making of history. In his *prooimion* (*Protheoria*, 3–4), Eustathios makes a distinction between the narration of past events and the narration of contemporary ones. The historian of the past, according to Eustathios, often theologizes, expands his discourse, and unsparingly applies cosmetics to his expression for the sake of beauty. He becomes infatuated with descriptions and presents much for the sake of pleasure. He might even, Eustathios claims, 'behave like a dancer', and place in the foreground 'strange stories', while he artistically contrives discourses for 'showing off'. Eustathios, being a historian of the present, as he continues to argue, will do something different. For him, the history of the present is to be a mixture of styles, ranging from simplicity to elaborate rhetoric. That the historian of the past is charged with profuse rhetoricality may

---

[63]   See, e.g., verses 3246–61 with the author's explicitly digressive intrusion into his text concluded with a *gnome*. On this function of *gnomai* see H. Morales, *Vision and Narrative in Achilles Tatius' Leucippe and Clitophon* (Cambridge, 2004), 106–30.

[64]   *On the Capture of Thessalonike* 158, ed. S. Kyriakidis, *Eustazio di Tessalonica. La espugnazione di Tessalonica* (Palermo, 1961); the text dates to 1185–86.

[65]   *Ibid.*, 158. John Kinnamos, writing after 1176, similarly speaks of historiography as the creation of 'immortal pillars': *Epitome* 3–4.

[66]   The single 'statue' mentioned in Eustathios' narrative is a metaphorical *andrias* of immorality (44).

be a rhetorical gesture by Eustathios himself. It is founded, nevertheless, upon the same acknowledgement that Psellos, Anna, Manasses, and other Byzantine historians articulated or implemented (though, we should admit, in no consistent, comprehensive or unidirectional fashion): history-writing cannot but be affected by rhetoric's ornate and varied forms, its *aesthetics*.

SECTION II
Audience

2. Uncovering Byzantium's historiographical audience

Brian Croke

One of Byzantium's better-known manuscript images is that of an author – Niketas Choniates according to the inscription – writing his lively history of the events leading to the sack of Constantinople by the Latins in 1204 and its uncertain aftermath. Modelled on the standard Byzantine representation of an evangelist or scribe, Choniates is depicted in an idealized setting, possibly at Nicaea where he ended up after 1207 with the remnant of the Byzantine imperial court. He is holding a stiff sheet on which he is writing. On the lectern in front of him lies another sheet, presumably a previous version of his history now being revised or a rough copy.[1] This image of Choniates immediately evokes some key questions: What did he think he was doing as he put pen to paper? Who did he think he was writing for? How did he expect, or know, that his new words would be communicated to his audience? Did he produce his history in instalments over several months or years? How did his projected audience influence the shape and style of his work, how he wrote and what he wrote about? How large was his audience and what criteria influenced their response to his work? How can modern historians and readers know what audience he had in mind, anyway?

Once we embark on answering these questions for Choniates we can discover that even the author's own education and occupation, his culture and literary style, tell us something about the nature of his audience. He was one of the best-educated men of his day who spent long winter evenings reading the ancient Greek historians,[2] and he enjoyed the highest imperial positions, at one stage *logothetes ton sekreton*. He wrote in a style befitting his elevated culture and literary capacity, a style that resonated with his bureaucratic and imperial contemporaries at the courts of the

---

[1] Vindob. gr. 53 with I. Spatharakis, *The Portrait in Byzantine Illuminated Manuscripts* (Leiden, 1976), 153–5, 157–8.

[2] Oration 12, ed. J.-L. van Dieten, *Nicetae Choniatae Orationes et Epistulae* (London and New York, 1972), 117.

Angeloi before 1204 and Theodore I Laskaris at Nicaea who had clear expectations of what such a work should provide.[3] If he dedicated his history to any individual that fact is no longer known, but in writing his preface his potential audience was at the front of his mind. Part of this audience is future generations, although some are waiting for it more immediately, 'gaping in eager expectation',[4] so he confidently insists. He does not identify these eager ones. 'I humbly request the forbearance of those into whose hands [my history] may fall', he goes on to explain, in case his audience should be critical of his style. In speaking here of 'willing listeners' (τοῖς φιλακροάμοσι)[5] he would appear to envisage his history being read aloud to his audience. Then he strikingly suggests that he aspires to reach the ears of blacksmiths 'covered with soot', soldiers and women.[6] However unrealistic Choniates' ambition was, throughout the history his narrative consciously engages the audience and lets us speculate about whom he is addressing. For example, in concluding a discussion of the emperor Manuel's setback in 1158/59, with the escape from custody of his cousin and rival Andronikos and the revolt of Styppeiotes, he advises that 'I insert these events into my history to show my readers (τοῖς ἀναγινώσκουσιν) how unreasonable a thing wickedness is and how difficult it is to guard against it'.[7] To complicate matters further, it is clear from the variegated manuscript tradition that Choniates produced different versions of the history himself, both before and after his ignominious flight from Constantinople as it was being burnt and ransacked in 1204, with a final revision in 1215/17.[8]

Each extant manuscript of Choniates' history, the earliest dating from 1286,[9] represents a conscious and identifiable expansion of his audience and sometimes provides a glimpse of audience reaction as individual readers comment and annotate. 'You're lying', one wrote in the margin of an early manuscript.[10] Another burst out: 'You declare in your [preface] that

---

[3]   J. Harris, 'Distortion, divine providence and genre in Nicetas Choniates's account of the collapse of Byzantium 1180–1204', 19–31. On Choniates' History: Hunger, *Literatur*, I, 429–41.

[4]   Choniates, *Historia*, 3.40–41.

[5]   Choniates, *Historia*, 2.27.

[6]   Choniates, *Historia*, 3.52–7.

[7]   Choniates, *Historia*, 111.26–7.

[8]   A. J. Simpson, 'Before and after 1204: the versions of Niketas Choniates' *Historia*', *DOP* 61 (2006), 189–221.

[9]   Oxford, Bodleian MS Roe 22, fols. 423r–447r, with A. Turyn, *Dated Greek Manuscripts of the Thirteenth and Fourteenth Centuries in the Libraries of Italy* (Urbana, IL, 1973), 47–8, and Simpson, 'Before and after 1204', 205–12.

[10]   Par. gr. 1778, in J.-L. van Dieten, ed., *Nicetae Choniatae Historia* (Berlin and New York, 1975), xx1.

a learned style is the lucid style, and then you compose in an oracular and high-flown manner'.[11] Sometimes we know exactly who copied and owned a manuscript of the history, such as the influential teacher and bibliophile John Chortasmenos who made his copy of Choniates at Constantinople in 1391.[12] In addition, effort was later put into creating an entirely new version of Choniates' history, a so-called *metaphrasis*, in which the author's high style was simplified.[13] This version has been taken to signify a whole new audience for the history, but this need not be so.[14]

If we want to uncover the Byzantine historiographical audience, these are the questions we need to ask of all historiographical texts. Yet because the evidence is so scanty and elusive they are difficult to answer in detail and it would appear that no comprehensive attempt has ever been made to address them. More complicated still is evaluating how the Byzantine audience for history changed between the fourth and fifteenth centuries. The likely places to look for hints of the Byzantine historiographical audience and how it changed are therefore the dedications and commissions of historiographical works, occasions of public recitation or presentation of the works, citations of such works by later authors, different versions of a work, individual manuscripts of a work, and traces of how the author's narrative consciously engages the audience.

Focusing on the historian's audience highlights the essential literary dimension of Byzantine historiographical texts. A history's or chronicle's style and character are invariably shaped and judged by literary tradition and audience expectation. In recent years increasing attention has been paid to the Byzantine author and the construction of the narrative, but the nature and role of the audience, at least for history writing, deserve closer scrutiny.[15] This paper is designed to do no more than open up

---

[11] Scholion quoted in Grigoriadis, '*Prooimion*', 339.

[12] Van Dieten, ed., *Nicetae Choniatae Historia*, xxv.

[13] J.-L. van Dieten, 'Bemerkungen zur Sprache der sog. vulgärgriechischen Niketasparaphrase', *BF* 6 (1979), 37–77.

[14] G. Cavallo, *Lire à Byzance* (Paris, 2006), 92; E. Trapp, 'Learned and vernacular literature in Byzantium: dichotomy or symbiosis?', *DOP* 47 (1993), 116; I. Ševčenko, 'Some additional remarks to the report on levels of style', *JÖB* 32 (1982), 228 (a reminder of the complexity of such metaphraseis and their use by the best-educated scholars). See also the contribution of John Davis in this volume.

[15] The various contributions led and concluded by Ljubarskij, '*Quellenforschung*', 5–93, and the papers in Odorico, *et al.*, eds., *L'écriture de la mémoire* and in Burke, *et al.*, eds., *Byzantine Narrative*. On the audience itself, not much has changed since A. Kazhdan and G. Constable, *People and Power in Byzantium* (Washington, DC, 1982), 102: 'The problem of the audience for Byzantine literary works has hardly been touched. The question itself seems vague and undefined and must be asked in another way if it is to be clarified'.

the question of Byzantium's historiographical audience on the widest possible front, propose occasional conclusions and suggest further lines of investigation. Even though it is recognized that historiography represents one of Byzantium's greatest literary achievements, it was always a marginal activity for a small and relatively narrow audience.

c. 350 to c. 640

Byzantine historiography originated in a relatively secure and stable world of well-resourced cities with strong civic institutions including well-educated teachers and good collections of books. At Constantinople in particular there was an imperial library from c. 350.[16] The capacity to write historical works, have them copied and appreciated, arose from a traditional rhetorical education during which students read Thucydides and other historians. They then deployed them in their own compositions, the *progymnasmata*, which practised a particular literary model such as 'narrative' (διήγημα).[17] Although they were educated in diverse places, almost all historians from Eunapius in the fourth century to Theophylact in the seventh- wrote their histories in Constantinople and found their initial audience there. The major audience for any new work of history was the local cultural and political elite, in effect the civic and ecclesiastical aristocracy.[18] A more precise understanding of this audience awaits further research. Meanwhile, research on the audience for Greek and Roman historical works is only now emerging and will surely cast new light on the Byzantine audience too.[19] As in Roman times, an early Byzantine

---

[16]   A. Kazhdan, *La produzione intelletuale in Bisanzio* (Naples, 1983), 145–6.

[17]   B. Gibson, 'Learning Greek history in the ancient classroom: the evidence of the treatises on progymnasmata', *Classical Philology* 99 (2004), 103–29; T. Morgan, *Literate Education in the Greek and Roman Worlds* (Cambridge, 1998), 220–21; Hunger, *Literatur*, I, 92–120. In the case of Libanius in the fourth century we see clearly the importance of Thucydides in the rhetor's classroom: Libanius, *Or* 1.148–50 (the loss and rediscovery of his favourite working copy of Thucydides); focus on prose writers: *Ep.* 379.5, 9; 894.23; *Or.* 35.12, with R. Cribiore, *Gymnastics of the Mind* (Princeton, NJ, 2001), 144.

[18]   H. Hunger, 'The importance of rhetoric in Byzantium', in Mullett and Scott, eds., *Byzantium and the Classical Tradition*, 44–5.

[19]   A beginning was made by A. Momigliano, 'The historians of the ancient world and their audiences: some suggestions', *Annali della Scuola Normale Superiore di Pisa* 3/8 (1978), 59–75, repr. in *Sesto Contributo alla storia degli studi classici e del mondo antico* (Rome, 1980), 361–76. More recently I. O. Martin, 'Lectores y publico de la historiografia griega', *Estudios Clásicos* 44 (2002), 125–47, esp. 133–47 (on Byzantine historians); R. Nicolai, 'The place of history in the ancient world', in J. Marincola, ed., *A Companion to Greek and Roman Historiography* (Oxford, 2007), 13–

historian's new work would first be shared with his closest friends and associates who had a chance to comment, cavil or compliment.[20] In some cases we know who sought the author's efforts in the first place. Eunapius, for instance, wrote with certain individuals in mind beginning with the emperor Julian's physician, Oribasius, who had urged him to write his history and provided helpful notes and reports. Then there were what Eunapius calls the 'most cultivated men of our age' (οἱ τοῦ καθ'ἡμᾶς βίου μακρῷ προεῖχον κατὰ παιδείαν), who also encouraged his work.[21] They were the educated civic gentry of Sardis and nearby cities. Eutychianus, a relative of Paul the Silentiary, commissioned the history of Agathias[22] in the 570s, and its initial circulation or reading would have been within Agathias' close circle.

Generations of Byzantine historians were influenced by Lucian of Samosata's advice in the second century on how to write history.[23] Lucian presumes the historian first reached his audience by way of a public reading.[24] We know that historians from the time of Herodotus, in both Greek and Latin, had their historical works declaimed publicly, sometimes winning prizes for their efforts,[25] although the early Byzantine evidence for this practice is slender. In the early seventh century Theophylact Simokatta's history was presented orally, perhaps to the learned circle around the Patriarch Sergius[26] or to an even larger audience in an auditorium (*akroaterion*) that was moved to tears by Theophylact's account of the death of the Emperor Maurice and his family.[27] One can

---

26, esp. 23–5; and J. Marincola, 'Ancient audiences and expectations', in A. Feldherr, ed., *The Cambridge Companion to Roman Historians* (Cambridge, 2009), 11–23.

[20]   R. J. Starr, 'The circulation of literary texts in the Roman world', *Classical Quarterly* 37 (1987), 213–23; J. W. Iddeng, '*Publica aut peri!* The releasing and distribution of Roman books', *Symbolae Osloenses* 81 (2006), 58–84.

[21]   Eunapius, fr. 1, fr. 15: R. C. Blockley, ed. and trans., *The Fragmentary Classicising Historians of the Later Roman Empire* (Liverpool, 1983), 10–11, 20–21.

[22]   Agathias, *prooimion*, 11:5.17–22.

[23]   R. Maisano, 'Il problema della forma letteraria nei proemi storiografici bizantini', *BZ* 78 (1985), 330.

[24]   Lucian, *How to Write History*, 23, 28 (a 20-hour recitation!), 29, 39. Lucian recounts the importance of keeping one's ears open at readings of historians: *How to Write History*, 7.

[25]   A. Chaniotis, *Historie und Historiker in den griechischen Inschriften*, Epigraphische Beiträge zur griechischen Historiographie (Wiesbaden and Stuttgart, 1988), 290–324.

[26]   A. M. Taragna, 'L'écriture de l'histoire chez Théophylacte Symocatta', in Odorico, *et al.*, eds., *L'écriture de la mémoire*, 67–84, and J. Frendo, 'History and panegyric in the Age of Heraclius', *DOP* 42 (1988), 147.

[27]   Theophylact Simocatta, *History*, 8.12.3–4: 309, cf. Taragna, 'L'écriture de l'histoire chez Théophylacte Symocatta', 75.

easily envisage other striking set pieces being performed to an interested audience at Constantinople: Priscus' account of his journey to the court of the Hun King Attila in 449,[28] Procopius' account of the sieges of Naples and Rome in 536/37,[29] or the lawyer Agathias' account of the trial of Gubazes in 556.[30]

The early Byzantine historians generally wrote in imitation of the ideals their teachers had promoted. A critical component of that literary process was the emphasis on rhetorical elements involving careful construction of speeches and other set pieces (expository, argumentative, encomiastic and invective) that signalled the historian's distinctive skills to a like-minded audience.[31] That explains why speeches (and letters designed to be read aloud) form such a major part of most historical works. In Procopius' history, for instance, there are 100 speeches and 44 letters, while Theophylact included 18 speeches and 7 letters. It also explains why contemporary historians intended histories of their own times to be read aloud. At Constantinople, students, historians and audience alike would have noted the statue of Thucydides, the model historian, in the baths of Zeuxippos near the imperial palace that depicted him declaiming a speech from his history.[32] No less important, however, was the reading audience for the historian, and for both listeners and readers it is important to note the precise literary strategies the historian used to engage them.

For the sake of their audience, the Byzantine historians regularly display a clear sense that the story needs to follow a defined shape usually labelled its 'logos'. Reminding the audience periodically of exactly how the 'logos' is unfolding, is an integral part of any historiographical narrative.[33] It also implies certain literary expectations on the part of the audience to which the author must consciously respond. Procopius demonstrates his authorial control and his sensitivity to the expectations of his audience when he says, for instance, that 'since the narration of the history (ὁ τῆς ἱστορίας λόγος) has brought me to this point I must explain … (4.12)', while Agathias suggests that 'at this point I should like to add for the convenience of the reader the following clarification …' (2.27.9), Menander advises how he kept his narrative from getting too long,[34] and Theophylact

---

[28]   Priscus, fr. 11.2: Blockley, ed. and trans., *The Fragmentary Classicising Historians*, 246–79.

[29]   Procopius, *Wars* 5.10.36–6.2.38.

[30]   *Historiai*, 4.1–11.

[31]   Cf. M. Fox, 'Dionysius, Lucian and the prejudice against rhetoric in history', *Journal of Roman Studies* 91 (2001), 76–93.

[32]   *Anth. Pal.* 2.372–6.

[33]   M. Hinterberger, in Ljubarskij, '*Quellenforschung*', 35.

[34]   Menander, fr. 6.2–3: R. C. Blockley, *The History of Menander the Guardsman* (Liverpool, 1985), 88–9.

pulls himself up thus: 'Therefore I must return to the continuity of the narrative, wheeling round the history that is perhaps running a little off course' (3.18.4, cf. 8.11.12). All these historians link their narrative with references to other parts of their text, referencing backwards and forwards. This narrative self-awareness is designed to help an audience keep track of the story and can be found in all Byzantine historians right down to the fifteenth century. It demonstrates the shared understanding by writer and audience about how a work of history should flow and what constitutes not only its content but also its stylistic boundaries of detail and relevance.[35] In writing Byzantine historical texts there were definite rules of the game and they were policed by author and audience alike.

Such criteria also apply to the emerging new models for writing history, namely church history and chronography. In literary terms all the church historians from the fourth- to the seventh century exhibit the same sense as other historians of what is appropriate to the narrative, of guarding against excesses of opinion, digression or documentation, and of alerting the reader to the unfolding story. The author himself is very much part of the history and there is a consistent awareness of the writer's audience and its expectations. Theodoret, for example, reminds his audience in the 440s that he is deliberately refraining from overwhelming them with detail (*Historia Ecclesiastica* 2.25, 5.21), while Socrates' narrative of the church from Constantine to Theodosius II denotes a highly literate audience because he encourages them to seek out and read works such as the treatises of Didymus the Blind (*HE* 4.25) and the sermons of John Chrysostom (6.4). He also includes a list of attendees at the Council of Nicaea in 325 because it would be appreciated by 'lovers of learning' (φιλομαθεία: 1.13), and Evagrius reticently included particulars of fifth-century buildings in Antioch but argued that such matters would be 'not without their attraction to lovers of learning' (φιλομαθέσιν: *HE* 1.18). So there is a clear understanding that the prime audience for an ecclesiastical historian was the cultured and highly literate aristocracy of Constantinople, Antioch and elsewhere; in other words, much the same audience as for Eunapius and Procopius.

An audience sometimes heard a work written in instalments and revised in response to its reaction. Agathias, for instance, introduces his third book with an apology to his audience for not proceeding fast enough because his day job as a lawyer was keeping him too busy. Moreover, some of his audience had been critical of his previous books so he dismisses them with the comment that he was only writing to please himself 'just as people with no ear for music enjoy their own singing' (3.2–7). Eunapius went further and produced a whole new version of his history in response

---

[35]   I. Nilsson and R. Scott, 'Towards a New History of Byzantine literature', *Classica et Mediaevalia* 58 (2007), 323.

to criticism that it was too anti-Christian in tone and content.[36] We may not be wrong to assume public readings of the church historians too, with each new instalment taking account of audience reaction. Socrates tells us he had to revise the first book when additional material was pointed out to him (1.1) and the prefatory explanation of style before Book 6 implies that some readers had passed critical comment, just as Book 5 is introduced by an explanation of the relevance of secular events in a church history (5.1). Readers or listeners of earlier books had evidently been critical of such material.

Greek and Roman historians and philosophers recited their works to small scholarly circles in a *theatron*, but they also performed in an auditorium for larger and less-educated groups who were no less used to formal rhetoric and found their works enjoyable.[37] Lucian envisaged the historian's audience as including a mixed or culturally wider range of people, the 'hoi polloi', and he encouraged historians to ensure their style was accessible to these listeners as well.[38] Indeed, Eunapius was aware that his history soon became known and appreciated by the 'hoi polloi', who were always clamouring for more detail, however inaccurate, and many lesser historians would oblige them.[39] All they were interested in was the particulars of the story. This audience would have included the large number of local and imperial officials and functionaries, as well as the military hierarchy, the generals and leading military officers around the court. They normally had a level of literacy that certainly enabled them to read the histories of Priscus and Procopius if so inclined. The imperial soldier and official Marcellinus, for example, writing in Latin for the Emperor Justinian, appears to have focused his account on a local audience of Illyrian soldiers and courtiers.[40] The Spanish general Theodosius became emperor in 379 and then spent most of his reign at Constantinople, where he was especially fond of history books,[41] while another general turned emperor, Maurice, spent his evenings in the palace reading histories and he offered financial incentives to potential historians such as Menander.[42]

---

[36]   Photios, *Bibliotheke*, cod. 77 (Eunapius), I, 159.26–36.

[37]   J. Maxwell, *Christianization and Communication in Late Antiquity: John Chrysostom and his Congregation in Antioch* (Cambridge, 2006), 19.

[38]   Lucian, *How to Write History*, 44.

[39]   Eunapius, fr. 66: Blockley, *The Fragmentary Classicising Historians*, 100–101, τοὺς πολλούς.

[40]   B. Croke, *Count Marcellinus and his Chronicle* (Oxford, 2001), 94–101; W. Treadgold, *The Early Byzantine Historians* (London, 2007), 234–5.

[41]   *Epitome de Caesaribus* 48.11, ed. M. Festy, *Pseudo-Aurélius Victor, Abrégé des Césars*, Collection des Universités de France (Paris, 1999).

[42]   Menander, fr. 1: Blockley, *The History of Menander the Guardsman*, 40–41.

Theophylact notes too that the general Philippicus in the 580s was a keen consumer of military history (1.14.1).

This wider audience existed for the church historian too. Socrates seeks to justify his straightforward style by explaining that he was aiming at a much wider readership than just his rhetorically educated peers (*HE* 6, praef. 3–5). He argues that if he were to employ a highly wrought literary style his work would be inaccessible to the 'general public and the uneducated' (τοὺς πολλοὺς καὶ ἰδιώτας). For Socrates their main interest is simply to know about events, not to marvel at the fancy phraseology in which they are couched. So his style is pitched in such a way as to appeal simultaneously to the educated (εὐπαιδεύτοις) and the uneducated (ἰδιώτας). As for the other new early Byzantine historiographical model, the chronicle, its audience was meant to find it useful for the practical purpose of seeing the order of events in God's time and of understanding how the present related to the past.[43] Most of the early Byzantine chronicles are no longer extant, but the earliest one to survive and prosper was that of John Malalas, who was an imperial government bureaucrat in Antioch in the 530s writing for a local audience.[44] It used to be thought that works such as the chronicle of Malalas and the *Chronicon Paschale* involved a distinctly different and culturally inferior audience compared to that for Procopius, namely the uneducated masses and undereducated monks.[45] Now the picture is more subtle and complex.[46]

From the fourth- to the seventh century there was a core audience for works of history, comprising the cultural elite and a wider group of less educated but still relatively literate civil and military officials and others. However, there was no tightly prescribed nexus between the social and intellectual composition of this audience and the particular mode

[43] C. Mango, 'The tradition of Byzantine chronography', *Harvard Ukrainian Studies* 22/3 (1988–89), 360–72.

[44] B. Croke, 'Malalas, the man and his work', in Jeffreys, *et al.*, eds., *Studies in John Malalas*, 1–25, further elaborated in Treadgold, *The Early Byzantine Historians*, 235–9.

[45] The classic statement is in K. Krumbacher, *Geschichte der byzantinischen Literatur*, 2nd edn. (Munich, 1897), reflected in N. Wilson, 'Books and readers in Byzantium', in *Byzantine Books and Bookmen* (Washington, DC, 1975), 14, but effectively challenged by Beck, '"Mönchschronik"', 188–97. As observed by Ljubarskij, '*Quellenforschung*', 11, and 'New trends in the study of Byzantine historiography', *DOP* 47 (1993), 133, Beck's corrective is usually disregarded, with a good example being S. Runciman, 'Historiography', in A. R. Littlewood, ed., *Originality in Byzantine Literature, Art and Music* (Oxford, 1995), 60–61. In theory, Hunger, *Literatur*, I, 253–4 is tentative, but in practice he reinforces the Krumbacher paradigm (257–78).

[46] R. Scott, 'Malalas and his contemporaries', in Jeffreys, *et al.*, eds., *Studies in John Malalas*, 67–85.

of presenting the past (history, church history, chronicle). We should therefore be cautious about erecting sharp boundaries of genre between these different literary modes. By around 640 this historiographical culture, based on each new generation immersing itself in Thucydides and Herodotus, and mastering their language, had come to a shuddering halt. No one continued Theophylact, nor was there a church historian to continue Evagrius, nor a chronicler to extend the story of the *Chronicon Paschale*. The combination of periodic plague along with the Persian invasion, followed by the Arab expansion that engulfed the eastern Roman world so quickly in the seventh century, totally disrupted the connected Byzantine urban economy and bureaucracy. All the activities dependent on it, education and literary production foremost among them, contracted along with the potential audience for historiographical texts.[47] It was the best part of another two centuries before the three Byzantine historiographical modes and their audiences emerged again into a changed cultural and religious landscape.

c. 640 to c. 1050

If 640 marks a decisive ending to the historiographical culture of Late Antiquity, then 800 arguably marks an equally decisive resurrection of history-writing and the audience for it.[48] In the intervening period education had shrunk severely, but it had not disappeared. There were individuals still able to impart a traditional literary education at Constantinople, while in Syria and Palestine a solid education was still available for someone like John of Damascus.[49] Even in a remote Armenian town in the first half of the seventh century, the mathematician Ananias of Shirak could find a teacher who among his collection of books had some historians, even if it was just Thucydides and Herodotus, and also chronicles, presumably Eusebius and one or more of his continuators, perhaps even Malalas.[50] Yet there was very

---

[47]   Treadgold, *The Early Byzantine Historians*, 393–9.

[48]   I. Ševčenko, 'The search for the past in Byzantium around the year 800', *DOP* 46 (1992), 279–93.

[49]   Documents in the Genizah archive also suggest that Greek was being taught in the eighth century well beyond the borders of the Byzantine world, as noted by C. Holmes, 'Written culture in Byzantium and beyond: contexts, contents and interpretations', in Holmes and J. Waring, eds., *Literacy, Education and Manuscript Transmission in Byzantium and beyond* (Leiden, 2002), 23 (hereafter, Holmes and Waring, eds., *Literacy*).

[50]   Ananias of Shirak, *Autobiography* (trans. F. C. Conybeare, 'Ananias of Shirak (A.D. 600–650 ca.)', *BZ* 6 [1897], 572–84), cf. P. Lemerle, *Byzantine Humanism*, trans. H. Lindsay and A. Moffatt (Canberra, 1986), 90–93.

little historiographical writing of any kind between the seventh and the ninth centuries and hardly any copying of manuscripts. Literary capability had been severely curtailed.[51]

By 800, interest in the past and writing about it was re-emerging in the expanding monasteries that were becoming a focus for educating monks and others who learnt to read by mastering the Psalter rather than Homer and Thucydides. The coenobitic reforms of Theodore the Studite, who had enjoyed a traditional rhetorical education at Constantinople in the 770s, gave impetus to reading and being read to together in community, as well as to copying and lending of manuscripts by monasteries. Generally, monastic education was limited and reading was confined to biblical, liturgical and hagiographical books, so the audience for old and new historical works was slender.[52] The numerous foundation documents for Byzantine monasteries (*typika*) occasionally specify the library's contents and what they lent to each other.[53] Together the *typika* underscore the marginality of secular literature, not least historical texts, for a monastic audience. So too the manuscripts copied by monks in their scriptoria were almost entirely scriptural, liturgical or spiritual. It has been calculated that 89 per cent of all extant manuscripts from the ninth to the eleventh centuries are religious in content, while the remaining 11 per cent include only a tiny number of historical texts.[54] The exception that proves the rule is the monk Ephraem, who copied Polybius in 947, but he came late to monastic life as a highly educated man.[55]

Taking the well-known example of Patmos, we find that in its later catalogue dated to 1200 there were no historians but there was a 'chronographer' in an 'old book' – that is, probably a sixth- or seventh century uncial manuscript without an ascribed author.[56] In the later eleventh century Michael Attaleiates' will established a new monastery, and the detailed provisions include a list of books. Among them was a copy of a 'chronikon' in Attaleiates' hand;[57] the other books donated to the library after the founder's death included one that commenced with

---

[51]   J. Haldon, *Byzantium in the Seventh Century* (Cambridge, 1990), 425–35.

[52]   G. Cavallo, 'ΠΟΛΙΣ ΓΡΑΜΜΑΤΩΝ – Livelli di istruzione e uso di libri negli ambienti monastici a Bisanzio', *TM* 14 (2002), 95–113.

[53]   J. Waring, 'Literacies of lists: reading Byzantine monastic inventories', in Holmes and Waring, eds., *Literacy*, 165–86.

[54]   Cavallo, *Lire à Byzance*, 3.

[55]   Cavallo, 'Livelli di istruzione', 111–12.

[56]   C. Astruc, 'L'inventaire (1200) du trésor de la bibliothèque de Patmos', *TM* 8 (1981), 28.

[57]   P. Lemerle, *Cinq études sur le XIe siècle* (Paris, 1981), 89, who takes it to be Attaleiates' own history, but it would be unusual to so describe it and its actual title appears to have been *historia*.

a 'chronikon'.[58] Then in 1132 the Norman monarch Roger II established a well-educated group of monks in a new monastery of the Holy Saviour in Messina. Its *typikon* tells us that there were 'scribes and calligraphers, and teachers of our sacred books who were sufficiently trained in profane literature'. Moreover the library included 'historical works', but we are left to guess which ones.[59] Around the same time, in his Cypriot monastery Neophytos the Recluse possessed two 'short chronicles'.[60]

All these instances of anonymous 'chronicles' or 'chronographers', from the sixth to the eleventh centuries, suggest a pattern. It would appear that what is being referred to here is the sort of chronological summary we find in the *'chronographikon syntomon'* of the Patriarch Nikephoros, which is a short and simple table of rulers to 821 preserved anonymously in most manuscripts,[61] like so many other similar fragmentary ninth- and tenth century chronicles.[62] Yet each manuscript had a conscious author and a projected audience. Moreover, it was a widespread audience since there are so many extant copies and versions. In reality these chronicles functioned as a sort of reference work required for each library to accompany its scripture and other sacred literature. It was the chronological key to sacred reading and the story of the Christian nation to date. That explains the predominance of such chronographies in monasteries, but they could also be owned by others such as the middle-ranking official Eustathios Boïlas in the eleventh century, whose library contained 'two chronographers'.[63]

Besides reading and listening, monks occasionally turned their hand to composing their own historical works for some particular audience, beginning with Synkellos and Theophanes.[64] While they both will have had access at different points to the imperial and patriarchal libraries, they may also have had some texts in their own monasteries at the time of writing and had to borrow others, including Malalas and Procopius, which

---

[58]   Diataxis, 1272, in P. Gautier, 'La Diataxis de Michel Attaliate', *REB* 39 (1981), 95.

[59]   J. Thomas and A. C. Hero, eds., *Byzantine Monastic Foundation Documents*, 5 vols. (Washington, DC, 2000), 2, 645 (26: Luke of Messina).

[60]   C. Galatariotou, *The Making of a Saint: The Life, Times and Sanctification of Neophytos the Recluse* (Cambridge, 1991), 23, 26–8. Neophytos may have borrowed these works rather than owned them himself.

[61]   C. Mango, *Nikephoros, Patriarch of Constantinople* (Washington, DC, 1990), 2–4.

[62]   For example, the *Ekloge Historion* in Par. gr. 854 from the time of Basil I and an extension of it to 1118 in Vindob. Theol. gr. 133 with Hunger, *Literatur*, 1, 332–3 and Karpozilos, Βυζαντινοί Ἱστορικοί, II, 531–76.

[63]   Lemerle, *Cinq études*, 25.

[64]   Assuming, for our purposes, two separate authors well known to each other. Details in Mango and Scott, eds., *The Chronicle of Theophanes Confessor*, xliii–lxiii.

Theophanes used. In his preface Theophanes explains how he laboriously composed his own work in about 816. He goes on to say explicitly that 'his readers (οἱ ἀναγινώσκοντες) may be able to know in which year of each emperor what event took place'. He consciously recognizes that his readers may find his work of value or not, and expresses reservations about the reader being overwhelmed by his detailing the evil actions of the Emperor Nikephoros in 810/811.[65] At no point does he suggest a work like his might be read out loud to an audience rather than studied personally, although he may have acquired his own knowledge of certain texts such as Procopius and Theophylact from attending public readings.[66]

Theophanes' audience grew, and a century later the chronicle was taken up by the Emperor Constantine VII, who utilized it in his treatise *De administrando imperio*.[67] It was continued in quite different ways by two readers, Genesios (dedicated to Constantine VII) and Theophanes Continuatus (also dedicated to the emperor but including his own contribution on Basil I), as well as by John Skylitzes. Meanwhile, later in the ninth century George the Monk followed Synkellos and Theophanes' example and produced a world chronicle to his own day. George's chronicle in effect combined more thoroughly and smoothly than Theophanes had done material previously contained separately in chronicles and ecclesiastical histories, so there were no more church histories until the lonely example of Nikephoros Kallistos Xanthopoulos in the fourteenth century.[68] George envisaged and achieved a broad audience for his work, which continued generation after generation. In particular, he considered that he was counteracting the 'high and pompous' style of previous historians by expressing the same events in a more open style.[69] This

---

[65]   Theophanes, AM 6303 (pp. 488, 492).

[66]   J. Ljubarskij, 'Concerning the literary technique of Theophanes the Confessor', *BSl* 56 (1995), 32. Theophanes does take advantage of traditional stories and refashion them to suit his own purpose and audience, as explained by R. Scott, '"The events of every year arranged without confusion": Justinian and others in the Chronicle of Theophanes Confessor', in Odorico, *et al.*, eds., *L'écriture de la mémoire*, 49–66. See also the contributions of Scott and Afinogenov in this volume.

[67]   Constantine Porphyrogenitus, *De administrando imperio*, ed. G. Moravcsik and trans. R. J. H. Jenkins, rev edn. (Washington, DC, 1967), 17 (80–83); 21 (84–93); 25 (102–7).

[68]   D. Afinogenov, 'Some observations on genres of Byzantine historiography', *Byz* 62 (1992), 31.

[69]   George the Monk, *Prooimion*: 1–5, with Maisano, 'Il problema della forma literaria nei proemi storiografici bizantini' (as in note 23), 329–43.

was a different approach, or at least a different language register, but not necessarily a different audience.[70]

As culture and education revived and expanded in the ninth century, new opportunities and interest emerged in reading earlier secular and ecclesiastical literature.[71] By itself the *Bibliotheca* of Photios represents a one-man historical audience, or possibly the core of a wider reading circle.[72] What is important about the *Bibliotheca* is its testimony to what manuscripts of historical works were at least available to an educated and literary-minded person at Constantinople in the ninth century, and without too much effort.[73] Moreover, Photios' evaluations of individual authors provide an insight into how an historiographical audience read and compared the books of historians. Most historians who had written in Greek from Herodotus onwards could be located by Photios and read critically. In the course of his evaluative summary of so many historians, Photios reveals that the overriding criteria were literary. He demonstrates that still in the ninth century there was a shared understanding of what constituted 'the law of history'.[74] By that he means the same concerns we see in historians and church historians from the fourth century; that is, attention to scale, relevance, style, and a suspicion of innovation. These are clearly the fundamental components of a successful historical narrative and what the audience, represented here by Photios, expected.

By the end of the ninth- and into the tenth century it seems that the audience for history-writing was growing once more as the Byzantine world recovered lost territory and acquired new wealth and confidence. Literacy was expanding. Historiography too was transformed.[75] The move from uncial to the bureaucratic minuscule script facilitated copying

---

70   Hunger, *Literatur*, I, 257–8 is generally disposed to consider Byzantine chronicles as being designed for 'the broad public of the average Byzantine' (cf. 263). He sees George's audience as essentially monastic (347) and his simpler language level as customized to the capability of this audience (350); modified by Afinogenov, 'Some observations on genres of Byzantine historiography', 13–33.

71   Kazhdan and Constable, *People and Power in Byzantium*, 130–35, 197.

72   Wilson, 'Books and readers', 14; L. Canfora, 'Il "Reading Circle" intorno a Fozio', *Byz* 68 (1998), 222–3; *idem*, 'Le "cercle des lecteurs" autour de Photius: une source contemporaine', *REB* 56 (1998), 269–73.

73   Explained in detail in B. Croke, 'Tradition and originality in Photius' historical reading', in Burke, *et al.*, eds., *Byzantine Narrative*, 59–70.

74   Photios, *Bibliotheke*, cod. 77 (Eunapius), 159.18–19: ὁ τῆς ἱστορίας ... νόμος.

75   A. Kazhdan and A. W. Epstein, *Change in Byzantine Culture in the Eleventh and Twelfth Centuries* (Berkeley, CA, and London, 1985), 204; R. Scott, 'The classical tradition in Byzantine historiography', in Mullett and Scott, eds., *Byzantium and the Classical Tradition*, 61–74.

of manuscripts for a new audience. The earliest extant manuscripts of both Thucydides (*Laur.* 69.2) and Herodotus (*Laur.* 70.3) date from the tenth century, as does that of Cassius Dio.[76] They have been identified as having been copied from the manuscripts in the imperial library used by Constantine Porphyrogennetos in his vast project of compiling categories of extracts from historians.[77] Each manuscript itself represents the conscious act of production for one or more readers, but most of the time we have no way of knowing who they were although literary men as different as Arethas of Caesarea and Leo the Mathematician evidently owned manuscripts of Thucydides,[78] while the imperial soldier and official Kekaumenos recommended reading historians and appears to have been familiar with Dio and Procopius.[79] He had completed at least the earlier stages of a traditional education.[80]

While Thucydides and later historians such as Procopius were now increasingly being read and copied, they had no imitators. There had not yet been any successor to the history of Theophylact in the early seventh century, unless we count Nikephoros whose *Breviarium* follows Theophylact in a key manuscript (*Vat. gr.* 977).[81] One way of making more digestible the considerable bulk of the ancient and early Byzantine historians still available was to extract and summarize them systematically. That was a key purpose of Constantine VII's project to compile extracts from the major historians under different categorical headings – on embassies, on conspiracies, on sayings. The volumes of extracts are large and unwieldy,

---

[76]   A. Diller, 'Notes on Greek codices of the tenth century', *Transactions and Proceedings of the American Philological Association* 78 (1947), 186.

[77]   J. Irigoin, 'Survie et renouveau de la littérature antique à Constantinople (IXe siècle)', *Cahiers de Civilisation Médiévale* 5 (1962), 301; *idem*, 'Centre de copie et bibliothèques', in *Byzantine Books and Bookmen* (Washington, D.C., 1975), §19; Martin, 'Lectores', 137.

[78]   Arethas: Lemerle, *Byzantine Humanism*, 270 and 301 (citing links to manuscripts of Xenophon, Diodorus and Cassius Dio); Leo: R. Browning, 'Byzantine Scholarship', *Past and Present* 28 (1964), 8 (repr. in *Studies on Byzantine History, Literature and Education* [London, 1977], study XIII).

[79]   C. Roueché, 'The literary background of Kekaumenos', in Holmes and Waring, eds., *Literacy*, 113; M. Mullett, 'Writing in early medieval Byzantium', in R. McKitterick, ed., *The Uses of Literacy in Early Mediaeval Europe* (Cambridge, 1990), 166; G. Cavallo, 'Alfabetismi e letture a Bisanzio', in B. Mondrain, ed., *Lire et écrire à Byzance* (Paris, 2006), 106–7; G. Buckler, 'Writings familiar to Cecaumenos', *Byz* 15 (1940–41), 133–43, but unnecessarily reluctant to concede that Kekaumenos knew Procopius (133–4).

[80]   Roueché, 'The literary background of Kekaumenos', in Holmes and Waring, eds., *Literacy*, 112, and *idem*, 'The rhetoric of Kekaumenos', in Jeffreys, ed., *Rhetoric in Byzantium*, 37.

[81]   Nikephoros, *Short History*, 19–23.

and would not be used other than by the same educated audience for the original histories. Interestingly, Constantine makes no literary or categorical distinction between Diodorus and Procopius on the one hand, and Malalas and George the Monk on the other. They are lumped together as 'chronicles' for a single audience.[82] Yet the project appears to have failed. Certainly it did not expand or diversify the Byzantine historiographical audience at all.

By the later tenth century an audience for more recent histories had reappeared, although most of the new histories are now lost except for Genesios, Kaminiates, Theophanes Continuatus (preferably, *Scriptores post Theophanem*), Symeon the Logothete, and Leo the Deacon. Genesios enjoyed a courtly audience, having been invited to write his history by Constantine VII because no one had recounted the empire's story from the time of Leo V (813–20): 'I have completed this book of history as you commanded, O emperor, after much study and great labours', so he notes.[83] It would have been a similar audience for the various *Scriptores post Theophanem*, where a consistent aristocratic and imperial bias has been detected. In a later section of the *Scriptores*, possibly the work of Theodore Daphnopates who was a leading official at the court of Romanos I and a prolific writer, an audience of listeners is implied.[84] Kaminiates, on the other hand, wrote his account of the Arab capture of Thessalonike in 904 very soon after but for a provincial audience. He explains that it was a letter from a certain Gregory, a member of a well-off clerical family, that prompted him to write as an exile in Tarsus where he found his immediate audience.[85] Occasionally during what is cast as an epistolary reply Kaminiates directly addresses Gregory and the account was probably written to be read out in Gregory's circle, just as Eustathios recited his account of a later capture of Thessalonike in 1185.

Genesios addresses his audience directly ('O listeners, ὦ ἀκροαταί),[86] in noting what the patriarch John the Grammarian says in declining to give

---

[82]   Cf. E. Patlagean, 'Discours écrit, discours parlé. Niveaux de culture à Byzance aux VIIe–XIe siècles', *Annales: Economies, Sociétés, Civilisations* 34 (1979), 268–9.

[83]   Genesios, *On the Reigns*, ed. A. Lesmueller-Werner and I. Thurn (Berlin and New York, 1978), praef., with Hunger, *Literatur*, I, 367–71, Karpozilos, Βυζαντινοί Ἰστορικοί, II, 475–91, and A. Kaldellis, *Genesios: On the Reigns of the Emperors* (Canberra, 1998), ix–xxviii (for a critical overview of author and context).

[84]   Theophanes Continuatus (*Vita Basilii*) ch. 56:294.4–5: τὰς τῶν ἐντυγχανόντων ἀκοάς.

[85]   Hunger, *Literatur*, I, 357–9; D. Frendo and A. Fotiou, *John Kaminiates. The Capture of Thessalonike* (Perth, 2000), xxvii–xl.

[86]   Genesios, *On the Reigns*, 4.3, translated by Kaldellis, *Genesios*, 74, as 'readers', relying on D.M. Schenkeveld, 'Prose usages of ἀκούειν "to read"', *Classical Quarterly*

up his position after the restoration of icons in 843, and in dealing with the deposition of Patriarch Ignatios. The patriarch was confined in the tomb of the seventh-century emperor Constantine IV Kopronymos, who had died of dysentery, so Genesios says bluntly: 'All of you know what his pain was like who have experienced dysentery and other afflictions brought on by cold'.[87] Indirect traces of the tenth- and eleventh-century audience can also be identified in the historians' narratives. The signalling to the audience of events yet to be told, or previously recounted, which had always been an integral part of any Byzantine historian's narrative strategy, emerges prominently in the history of Leo the Deacon.[88] It is also frequent in the various *Scriptores post Theophanem*,[89] but less so in Symeon the Logothete.[90] Likewise, the traditional sense of what the historian can and cannot do, and what content is 'noteworthy' or not, is embedded in the unwritten compact between author and audience. Leo the Deacon has a clear appreciation of the proper sequence of an historical narrative (καθ' εἱρμὸν τοῦ λόγου).[91] One of the *Scriptores post Theophanem* is likewise conscious of indicating to his audience the importance of treating particular events within the framework of the narrative,[92] and Kaminiates reminds his audience of this central task.[93]

From the ninth century Byzantine historiography saw a changing interest on the part of the writer and audience in the human and personal

---

42 (1992), 129–41. However, here as elsewhere in the Byzantine historians, the plain meaning of 'hear' makes perfect sense and should be preferred.

[87]   Genesios, *On the Reigns*, 4.18.

[88]   E.g. Leo the Deacon, 1.5:12.2; 2.1:17.2; 4.7:66.12–13; 5.1:75.1; 6.1:93.1–2; 9.12:157.23.

[89]   E.g. Theophanes Continuatus, 2.3:42.7–8; 2.6:45.8–9; 2.12:55.11; 3.1:84.16; 3.35:132.2; 4.22:174.1; 4.23:176.5; 5.35:264.9–11; 6.16:409.10–11; 6.1:436.18–19.

[90]   E.g. Symeon the Logothete, 136.83:339.639.

[91]   Leo the Deacon, 2.6:24.10–11; 2.10:31.14: πρὸς τὸν εἱρμὸν; 4.10:70.3–4; 4.11:72.18–19: τὸν λόγον τοῦ εἱρμοῦ; 5.4:81.10–11: τὸν λόγον ... τοῦ εἱρμοῦ; 5.9: 91.20–23: verbose writers unduly stretch out their narratives; 9.5:148.1; 10.10:176.12-13: κατὰ μέρος εἰς τοὺς ἑαυτῶν καιρούς.

[92]   Theophanes   Continuatus,   2.8:49.17–19;   3.41:139.15–17;   4.17:167.17; 4.27:185.15–16; 4.44:210.16–17; 5.47: 280.9–10; 5.51:288.11–12; 5.72:314.3–5; 5.73:316.13–14; 5.87:329.4–5; 6.42:428.3: ἄξιον δὲ διηγήσασθαι; Constantine Porphyrogennetos, 6.17:448.15–16, 6.18.449.4, 6.33.456.4, 6.48.463.8–9; Romanos, 6.2:470.19–20.

[93]   John Kaminiates, *De expugnatione Thessalonicae*, ed. G. Böhlig (Berlin and New York, 1973), 74; *The Capture of Thessaloniki*, trans. Frendo and Fotiou, 125: 'If I wished to furnish a detailed narrative of the hardships and overcrowding to which we were continually subjected during that voyage, most people would think that I was romancing and departing from that strict adherence to truth that I promised at the outset of my account would be the guiding principle of my writing'.

agent in history, and it is widely considered to be a distinguishing mark of historiography and the expectations of its audience.[94] By the mid-eleventh century it was clear that the relatively large audience enjoyed by Procopius and Agathias in their day had gone. Likewise the overlapping audiences for history, church history and chronicle had now dissolved into one as the boundaries of the different literary modes had loosened and converged, although some specialist chronicles were still compiled. Yet the educated historiographical audience still shared the culture and literary background of the author and had a set of expectations, reinforced by tradition, about length, balance, style and relevance within which the author consciously worked.

c. 1050 to c. 1300

The 'Golden Age' of Byzantine historiography and its audience was the eleventh, twelfth and thirteenth centuries, before and after 1204, which produced the works of Psellos, Eustathios, Attaleiates, Skylitzes, Bryennios, Anna Komnene, Manasses, Glykas, Zonaras, Kinnamos, Choniates, Akropolites, Pachymeres and others. Almost all these writers of histories were, as they always had been, highly educated literary figures and public officials who happened to produce an historical work among many others such as speeches and encomia, *ekphraseis*, philosophical and theological treatises, poetry and letters. They learnt their skills in the schools of the capital, now complemented by the higher institutions of philosophy and law in which some of them were directly involved. Moreover, their pattern of education in grammar and rhetoric was as heavily based on Homer and Thucydides as it had been in the fifth and sixth centuries, and each new generation of students devised and practised their *progymnasmata* and other exercises on historical topics.[95] The intellectual Michael Italikos

---

[94]   Scott, 'The classical tradition', 61–74; A. Kazhdan and S. Franklin, *Studies on Byzantine Literature of the Eleventh and Twelfth Centuries* (Cambridge, 1984), 192; J. Ljubarskij, 'Man in Byzantine historiography from John Malalas to Michael Psellus', *DOP* 46 (1992), 177–86; Macrides, 'The Historian in the History', 205–24; A. Markopoulos, 'Byzantine history writing at the end of the First Millennium', in P. Magdalino, ed., *Byzantium in the Year 1000* (Leiden, 2003), 186. However, when one considers the corresponding engagement of the early Byzantine historians such as Priscus and Agathias in their own histories, as well as the church historians such as Socrates, Sozomen and Evagrius, then the novelty of this feature in the ninth century may well be over-emphasized.

[95]   G. Cavallo, 'Le tracce per una storia della lettura a Bisanzio', *BZ* 95 (2002), 423–44, at 438.

in the 1150s was part of a circle that read Herodotus and Thucydides,[96] while his formidable scholarly contemporary John Tzetzes enjoyed a deep knowledge of Thucydides and other historiographical writers.[97] The learned bishop Theophylact of Ochrid recommended to his friend the bishop of Pelagonia the reading of ancient histories, presumably meaning at least Herodotus and Thucydides.[98] By now, too, manuscripts of the historians and chroniclers were being acquired by the Athonite monasteries.[99] What readers of Thucydides learnt, at least in the case of Psellos in the eleventh century, was 'innovation in diction, tightly packed meaning, ungraceful but intellectual quality, composition which is not revolutionary, variety in the formulation of his thoughts'. For Gregory of Corinth, it was Procopius who was the recommended rhetorical model because 'in his political and deliberative oratory [he] has a competitive and elaborate quality and is not simply a narrator'.[100] The wars of Athens and Sparta and of Justinian were clearly incidental.

Despite greater authorial intervention by Byzantine historians and chroniclers, they are not always forthcoming about their intended audience. It helps when a particular work is commissioned by or dedicated to someone. Attaleiates dedicated his history to Nikephoros Botaneiates,[101] perhaps responding to an imperial commission. Anna Komnene relates that the empress Eirene Doukaina commissioned the history of Nikephoros Bryennios and encouraged others to write up the deeds of her husband Alexios (*Alexiad* 15.11), while Manasses dedicated his chronicle to the *sebastokratorissa* Eirene (wife of Andronikos Komnenos) and he may well have recited it, wholly or partly, in her *theatron*.[102] Most commissions and

---

[96] Michael Italikos, *Lettres et Discours*, ed. P. Gautier (Paris, 1972), Ep. 18, with Cavallo, 'Tracce', 429.

[97] N. G. Wilson, *Scholars of Byzantium* (London, 1982), 191. In his *Chiliades* or *Historiae*, Tzetzes cites not only Herodotus, Thucydides and Xenophon, but also Ctesias, Ephorus, Theopompus, Dionysius, Diodorus, Dio Cassius, Malalas, Procopius and Theophylact Simokatta. On one occasion he refers to Diodorus and Ephorus and 'all the *chronographoi*' (*Hist.*, 12.253). Elsewhere he refers anonymously to '*chronikoi*' (1.321; 2.88; 3.57, 324, 349; 4.224; 12.253, 254). One early manuscript of Thucydides (Palatinus Heidelbergensis gr. 252) contains marginalia by Tzetzes.

[98] M. Mullett, *Theophylact of Ochrid* (Birmingham, 1997), 101.

[99] S. Rudberg, 'Les manuscrits à contenu profane du Mont-Athos', *Eranos* 54 (1956), 174–85.

[100] Psellos, 'Essay on learning literature', quoted in Wilson, *Scholars of Byzantium*, 173, cf. Cavallo, *Lire à Byzance*, 4–5; Gregory: quoted in Wilson, *Scholars*, 186.

[101] Attaleiates, *Historia*, 2–4.

[102] M. Mullett, 'Aristocracy and patronage in the literary circles of Comnenian Constantinople', in M. Angold, ed., *The Byzantine Aristocracy, IX–XIIth Centuries*, British Archaeological Reports, International Series, 221 (Oxford, 1984), 179, cf.

dedications were more local and personal. Michael Psellos ascribes the impetus for his *Chronographia* to 'senators and clerics' who were concerned at the loss of any record of important events[103] and directly addresses Constantine Leichoudes, 'O dearest of friends' (*Chron.*, 6.73). Zonaras says he was encouraged to write by friends when they saw that he now had time in his isolated monastic life.[104] A special category of historical commissions is formed by those particular manuscripts that are illustrated or prepared in a more deluxe form. Skylitzes and Manasses come immediately to mind, and each of these expensive productions would have had their own imperial or aristocratic patron.[105]

A more complex problem is determining exactly how a new historical work was communicated to its audience in the eleventh, twelfth and thirteenth centuries. The final third, at least, of Attaleiates' history had been proposed for oral presentation,[106] which may be so, and Eustathios took four hours to declaim his linguistically sophisticated account of the capture of Thessalonike in 1185, noting that the historian can choose his words 'to please the listener' (πρὸς χάριν ἀκοῆς) but be fearful of misleading the 'future listener' (ἀκουσόμενον).[107] The hint of oral delivery keeps obtruding in the historians' texts. Psellos (*Chron.*, 6.21) once says he has some brief preliminary comments 'for the friendly listener' (πρὸς τὴν φιλήκοον ἀκοήν), and Kinnamos notes that the Byzantine soldier Hikanatos 'achieved feats worthy of telling and hearing'.[108] As a listener, on the other hand, Psellos suggests that individuals could remember particularly striking incidents or anecdotes they once heard recounted but without being able any longer to recall the precise author. For instance, in his *Historia syntomos* he says he heard from some writer or other (τινος ... τῶν συγγραφέων ἤκουσα) about the death of Gallienus, and later how in the 960s the empress Theophano decided to support Tzimiskes against her husband Nikephoros Phokas (ἀκούω δέ τινος τῶν συγγραφέων).[109]

Cavallo, *Lire à Byzance*, 42–3. In one manuscript (Vind. Phil. gr. 149) he is depicted presenting his work to Eirene (details in Spatharakis, *The Portrait in Byzantine Illuminated Manuscripts*, 158).

[103]   Psellos, *Chronographia*, 6.22.

[104]   Zonaras, *Epitome*, I, 4.7–11.

[105]   See the article by Elena Boeck in this volume.

[106]   Martin, 'Lectores', 129. On one occasion (*Historia*, 201.24–5) Attaleiates worries that his audience (ἀκροατῶν) will think he is eulogizing rather than describing.

[107]   Eustathios, *The Capture of Thessaloniki*, trans. J.R. Melville Jones, Greek text ed. S. Kyriakidis (Canberra 1988), prooimion 2.17; 18.6.

[108]   Kinnamos, *Epitome*,155.13–14.

[109]   Psellos, *Historia syntomos*, 47 (ed. W. J. Aerts [Berlin and New York, 1990], 30.25–6) on Gallienus and 104 (98.69) on Theophano. In both cases Aerts

Choniates advises that he has decided to withdraw parts of his history because they would have been repetitive and 'would only satiate those who are fond of listening', and again 'the reports of the impious acts perpetrated in the Great Church are unwelcome to the ears'.[110] Then, finally, there is Glykas, who in the preface to his chronicle advises that it is not lengthy otherwise it would 'overload the ears of listeners'.[111]

In all these cases an oral audience is envisaged so it is no surprise to find a manuscript designed specifically for public reading. The famous Madrid manuscript of Skylitzes has clear and exaggerated punctuation marks that reflect Skylitzes' aural sense, and its neat semi-uncial script lent it to public reading in a way that the usual minuscule of that time did not.[112] If Skylitzes was considered apt for such a reading then Kedrenos who virtually copied him would perhaps qualify too.[113] At the same time, the historians' prefaces also envisage an audience of private readers. Skylitzes says that reading his history can only help the remembering of it and as he progresses he is prepared to reiterate something said earlier 'to make it clearer for the reader',[114] while Psellos offers some examples of plots against Constantine IX then leaves others to his readers[115] – that is, he assumes they would know. On another occasion he speculates that one day his history will be read by Constantine, son of Michael VII.[116]

The revival of rhetoric in the eleventh century created many new opportunities to hear polished performances by well-educated officials, and sometimes these were historical accounts. Students under the tutelage of the *maistores* at Constantinople numbered 200 to 300 at any one time and the immediate audience for a new history would have been in the tens, not hundreds.[117] These officials, teachers and students arguably constitute the

---

unnecessarily avoids translating ἀκούω in its plain sense as 'heard', preferring 'understood' and 'learn from' (99); cf. Psellos, *Chronographia*, 1.4 (Basil II): τῶν … περὶ ξυγγραφέων ἤκουσα (listening to more recent historians on Basil II).

[110] *Historia*, 125.42–5; 573.13–14.

[111] Glykas, 4.1–2: καὶ πάνυ καταβαρύνει τὰς ἀκοάς.

[112] J. Burke, 'The Madrid Skylitzes as an audio-visual experiment', in Burke, *et al.*, eds., *Byzantine Narrative*, 145–6.

[113] As proposed by R. Maisano, 'Note su Giorgio Cedreno e la tradizione storiografica bizantina', *Rivista Internazionale di Studi Bizantini e Slavi* 3 (1983), 237–54.

[114] Skylitzes, *prooimion* 4.51–4, 93.44–5.

[115] Psellos, *Chronographia*, 6.134: τοῖς ἀναγινώσκουσι.

[116] Psellos, *Chronographia*, 7.13 (Michael VII): ἀναγνωσεταί μου τὸ σύγγραμμα.

[117] Wilson, 'Books and readers', 1–15, with A. Markopoulos, 'De la structure de l'école byzantine. Le maître, les livres et le processus educatif', in Mondrain, *Lire et écrire*, 86–7.

total readership for any new historical work.[118] In fact, we can probably now say that as Choniates was writing his history he knew exactly who he was writing for, and may have personally known almost all of the individuals who would make up his immediate audience. Moreover, as the prosopographical tools become more available and familiar the historians' circle of listeners and readers may be able to be defined in more detail. Further, histories were made public in the same way as other works – that is, through circulation to patron and associates or even a special public reading in a local literary circle (*theatron*) where groups of friends and courtiers met regularly to hear new works being promulgated. This meant inevitably that the immediate audience for history was not necessarily different from the audience for letters, encomia and poetry.[119] According to Psellos, there were distinct cultural levels in eleventh-century Byzantium: the advanced students of the language (λόγιοι ἄνδρες περιττοί), the educated 'listeners' (ἐλλόγισμοι ἀκροαταί) and the less cultivated ones (ἰδιώτιδες ἀκοαί).[120] They reflect similar levels already noticed in the fifth century, but they are not necessarily mutually exclusive audiences for historical works. Indeed, Psellos himself seems to have produced his high-style *Chronographia* and his lower-style *Historia syntomos* for the same audience,[121] while the *sebastokratorissa* Eirene had requested, so Manasses tells us, 'a work that is simple and easy to understand'.[122] This is surely another signal of diverse historiographical forms or styles for the same educated audience, rather than a lower-level one.[123] In the mid-thirteenth century Akropolites sought to make his history 'intelligible to everyone'

---

[118]   Mullett, 'Aristocracy and patronage in the literary circles of Comnenian Constantinople', 174–80.

[119]   Mullett, *Theophylact of Ochrid*, 39–40.

[120]   Psellos, 'Encomium on Symeon Metaphrastes', elucidated in G. Cavallo, 'Lo scritto a Bisanzio, tra communicazione e ricezione', in *Communicare et significare nell'alto medievo. Settimane di Studio* (Spoleto, 2005), 1–4.

[121]   Assuming Psellan authorship of the *Historia syntomos*, cf. Macrides, 'The Historian in the History', 211, and C. Holmes, *Basil II and the Governance of Empire (976–1025)* (Oxford, 2005), 122–3, n. 3.

[122]   Constantine Manasses, *Synopsis Chronike*, ed. I. Bekker (Bonn, 1837), vv 7–9. The conscious linguistic discipline of Manasses' chronicle partly explains its popularity and its wide range of readers, cf. E. M. Jeffreys, 'The attitude of the Byzantine chroniclers towards ancient history', *Byz* 49 (1979), 236.

[123]   Cf. I. Nilsson, 'Discovering literariness in the past: literature *vs.* history in the *Synopsis Chronike* of Konstantinos Manasses', in Odorico, *et al.*, eds., *L'écriture de la mémoire*, 15–31, esp. 17, n. 9.

(τοῖς πασῖν εὔγνωστος) and Skoutariotes' chronicle was aimed at a well-educated audience.[124]

Historiography, like other rhetorical genres, was essentially interactive,[125] so Byzantine historical authors in this period are forever interjecting, pontificating, cautioning, speculating, directing and elucidating as they engage with their audience. These authorial interventions could profitably be collected, catalogued and analyzed under headings like these. For present purposes, it will suffice to focus on certain specific dimensions of this process of narrative engagement between author and audience. The audience is made most immediate when the historian addresses it directly, as do Psellos[126] and Anna Komnene (*Alexiad*, 11.3, 12.9). On many occasions Michael Glykas addresses his son (usually γινώσκε δὲ, ἀγαπητέ, ὅτι),[127] while Skoutariotes also addressed his readers directly.[128] Then there is the Byzantine historian's preoccupation with the narrative structure which scholars have occasionally dismissed as pedantic or too fussy.[129] However, it is a characteristic inherited from the classical tradition but deployed in a distinct way by each historian. Some are more closely occupied with guiding their audience than others, especially Skylitzes in the eleventh century and Kinnamos in the twelfth. Indeed, Kinnamos would appear never to leave the reader time to work things out for herself. He is regularly noting, 'now I am going to explain this', 'now I will show how that happened', or retrospectively – 'But let the narrative return to its previous subject'.[130] Psellos takes note of returning to his main narrative (*Chron.*, 5.10), while Anna is also conscious that, as she put it on one occasion (*Alexiad*, 1.16), 'these speculations have carried me off the main

---

[124]   K. Zafeiris, 'Narrating the past: elements of littérarité in the *Synopsis Chronike*', in Odorico, *et al.*, eds., *L'écriture de la mémoire*, 34.

[125]   M. Mullett, 'Rhetoric, theory and the imperative of performance: Byzantium and now', in Jeffreys, ed., *Rhetoric*, 153.

[126]   Psellos, *Chronographia*, 5.9 (Michael V): ὅπως ἂν μὴ θαυμάζητε; 6.37 (Constantine IX): καὶ μοι συμμαρτυρήσετε οἱ τήμερον τὸν λόγον ἀναγινώσκοντες. Cf. Macrides, 'The Historian in the History', 216–17.

[127]   E.g. Glykas, 312.3, 423.9, 429.11, 430.11, 431.6, 440.4, 443.19, 457.12, 464.5, 465.9, 471.3, 488.1, 492.9, 492.21, 495.14, 499.6, 502.9, 505.9, 506.16, 551.15, 576.14.

[128]   *SynChron*, 3.13 with Zafeiris, 'Narrating the past', 36, 45–6.

[129]   E.g. Hunger, *Literatur*, I, 370 on a 'certain pedantry' in Leo the Deacon's 'anxious effort' to keep his chronology intact.

[130]   Kinnamos, *Epitome*, 128.23. Some specific instances in Kinnamos are: 'It was this Frederick who ruled the Germans after Conrad for reasons which will be related in the subsequent narrative' (72.1–3); 'we shall make much account [of Roger II, Norman king] in the following books' (37.15–16); 'I shall at once show why the Hungarians clashed with the Romans' (104.23–4) and on Raymond of Antioch 'who had departed from mankind in a way which I will now relate' (122.2–3); and 'what the facts of Andronikos' flight were I shall now relate' (232.12).

road of my history. We must get my horse back on the right path again' (cf. 2.2; 2.6; 6.6, 11.6). Anna also speaks of it being incumbent on the historian to summarize deeds and decrees of an emperor with some care ('not crassly', 3.6) and has a clear notion of those events that form the proper subject of history (deploying the standard phrase of earlier historians (ὁ τῆς ἱστορίας λόγος, 3.8). Reflecting on her mother's interest in theology and philosophy Anna is prompted to say more but the 'law of history' (θεσμὸς ἱστορίας) prevents her.[131] Similarly, Choniates is preoccupied on occasion with the need to guide the reader through his unfolding story, 'to proceed with the sequence of my narrative', as he says, and 'let the narrative take us back once again to the turning point so that we may continue with our history'. He is concerned with what he calls the 'sequence of this history' and its 'original design'.[132] Akropolites employs the same narrative signposts for his audience and the same literary devices,[133] as does also Manasses.[134]

Another frequent literary device of Byzantine historians that reflects awareness of their audience is the decision to include or exclude some episode or fact on the grounds that it is, or is not, of interest to an audience. The traditional word is 'axion', and such phrases have a formulaic flavour about them. Kinnamos, for example, claimed it was 'worthwhile' to describe the manner of the emperor John Komnenos' demise in 1143, and later 'I come to a recollection of this woman's deed which is still worthy of admiration'.[135] Niketas Choniates is able to say, 'let the following events which are worthy of narration and remembrance be recorded in this history', and then, 'I have omitted those actions not worthy of the telling.' Later on, in relation to a prophecy, he confesses that 'I must not neglect to record another noteworthy event', and of the Emperor Andronikos 'for the sake of continuity it will be best not to omit anything noteworthy'.[136] We find this

---

[131]   *Alexiad*, 5.9. Cf. G. Buckler, *Anna Comnena. A Study* (Oxford, 1929), 24–5 on use of 'logos' in history.

[132]   *Historia*, 645.84–8; 580.85–6. See the article of Athanasios Angelou in this volume.

[133]   Akropolites, *History*, §15:27.15–16: awareness of length; §37:57.16–20: however winding, the narrative is following a clear course – *dromos*; §32:50.6–8: continuing narrative; §65:138.19–20: authorial control as the narrative moves in sequence – καθ'εἱρμὸν τὰ τῆς ἱστορίας. There are backwards and forwards references pointed out to the reader, as well as geographical transitions in the narrative: to east (§68:143.21–2), to west (§8:12.22–4), to Constantinople (§27:44.6–7; §37:57.16–18), to emperors (§15:26.10–11), to Bulgaria (§20:32.25); cf. R. Macrides, 'George Akropolites' Rhetoric', in Jeffreys, ed., *Rhetoric*, 201–11.

[134]   Manasses, *Synopsis Chronike*, 1472–5; 2230: τοῦ δρόμου καὶ τοῦ λόγου; 2553–4: τὸν λοιπὸν δρόμον τῆς ἱστορίας; 6722.

[135]   Kinnamos, *Epitome*, 24.9–10; 37.4–5; also 62.22.

[136]   *Historia*, 114.15; 125.42–5; 219.71–2; 225.60–226.63.

feature also in Attaleiates,[137] Anna Komnene,[138] Akropolites,[139] and even in the verse chronicle of Manasses.[140] Psellos provides an important witness to this central feature of the historian's engagement with his audience. In describing the death of Zoe in 1050 (*Chron.*, 6.70) he says that he will desist with the detailed reaction to her passing, but that it is a tension in history to include the right amount of detail. Following the precepts of Lucian of Samosata in his essay on how to write history, Psellos claims historical narrative (ὁ λόγος τῆς ἱστορίας) has no boundaries around these things, but the historian should always return quickly to his narrative flow. All historians are aware of the need to ensure the audience that their work is balanced and not unduly lengthy. Choniates speaks for them all in reducing his account of Alexios III – 'to make a long story short, lest I be guilty of saying too much and thus exposing my work to censure'.[141]

The sequence and shape of the narrative dictates an appropriate point at which particular events can be treated. Audiences would be well aware of this and happy to be reminded. Psellos tells us that he saw the empress Zoe towards the end of her eventful life and 'about her I will write at the appropriate point in my history' (*Chron.*, 2.5); similarly for John the Eunuch, 'whom I will discuss at the appropriate point in my history' (4.4, cf. 4.19). Kinnamos points out how the emperor Manuel's deeds are magnified by accounts at court and panegyrics, '[b]ut the history will describe this at the right moment, at present let us keep to what lies before us'.[142] Virtually the same phraseology is used by Choniates,[143] as well as earlier by Skylitzes[144] and Anna Komnene.[145]

All these different sorts of narrative signposts for the reader or listener are an integral part of the historian's self-awareness and overall literary strategy. They are found in almost all Byzantine historians and chroniclers, but their frequency means they are simply taken for granted by modern readers. Yet their function is important precisely because they are so frequent and because they indicate the author's preoccupation with ensuring the audience is following the shape of the story being narrated. This has been demonstrated recently for texts as different as those of

---

[137] *Historia*, 70.14, 229.4–12, 223.19, 303.4, 303.4.

[138] *Alexiad*, 1.13.

[139] *History*, §39:63.15–64.1.

[140] Manasses, 854, 4197.

[141] *Historia*, 483.45–6.

[142] *Epitome*, 192.22–193.1.0

[143] For example, in speaking of John Komnenos he advises that more will be said 'at the proper time': Choniates, *Historia*, 107.30–31; cf. 87.94–5; 171.41–2.

[144] Skylitzes, 11.68–9; 28.17–18; 118.50–52.

[145] E.g. *Alexiad*, 6.8, 10.8, 10.11, 13.6.

Skylitzes and Skoutariotes.[146] Perhaps it is a hallmark of the oral narrative that remains in the historian's text even if the main audience are readers, not listeners. This particular feature of Byzantine narrative would repay more extensive investigation. Likewise, the distorting effect of the shared contemporary perspective of author and audience, at least for Skylitzes, Choniates and Anna Komnene, is only now being properly understood.[147] Whether Choniates or any of the other 'Golden Age' historians ever succeeded in reaching the intended blacksmiths, soldiers and women cannot be known, but it definitely should not be ruled out.[148]

1300 to 1460

Byzantine society and culture may have contracted severely by the beginning of the fourteenth century, but it still clung to the cultural practices and apparatus that characterized its more glorious past. Certainly, a strong engagement with hearing, reading and writing about that past ensured the survival of the Byzantine historiographical audience. In fact, most of the extant manuscripts of Greek and Byzantine historians date from this period or have been preserved because they were owned and studied by Palaiologan scholars. Despite enduring lengthy periods of intense religious conflict and civil war, discovering and promoting the past glories of Hellenic and Roman culture and history was the preoccupation of a range of literary groups at Constantinople. Most notable were those around Nikephoros Gregoras (1290/91–1358/61) and Demetrios Kydones (1324–98), as well as the bookish emperors John VI Kantakouzenos (1295–1383) and Manuel II Palaiologos (1350–1425).[149] All of them were actively engaged in the political struggles of their day with one eye on the example of Thucydides. Demetrios Kydones, for instance, tells us he used to gather friends around to listen to readings about 'the wars of the Romans and

---

[146]   Skylitzes: C. Holmes, 'The rhetorical structures of Skylitzes' *Synopsis Historion*', in Jeffreys, ed., *Rhetoric*, 191; Skoutariotes/*SynChron*: Zafeiris, 'Narrating the past', 41.

[147]   Holmes, *Basil II*, 171–239 (on Skylitzes); P. Magdalino, 'The pen of the aunt: echoes of the mid-twelfth century in the *Alexiad*', in T. Gouma-Peterson, ed., *Anna Komnene and her Times* (New York and London, 2000), 15–43 (on Anna), and *idem*, 'Aspects of twelfth-century Byzantine *Kaiserkritik*', *Speculum* 58 (1983), 326–46 (on Choniates).

[148]   Cf. H. Hunger, 'Überlieferungsgeschichte der byzantinischen Literatur', in M. Meier *et al.*, ed., *Geschichte der Textüberlieferung der antiken und mittelalterlichen Literatur* (Zurich, 1964), 450.

[149]   Hunger, *Literatur*, I, 245; Cavallo, 'Tracce', 430–31; *idem*, *Lire à Byzance*, 72–4.

the histories of the Greeks told by Thucydides',[150] while Kantakouzenos produced 'one of the masterpieces of Byzantine literature'[151] by emulating the Athenian model in his own history that is so replete with speeches.[152]

The great polymath Maximus Planoudes (1260–1330) worked in the imperial palace as a scribe and taught at the Chora monastery at Constantinople. He read and annotated manuscripts of Zosimus (Vat. gr. 176) and Thucydides (Monac. gr. 430), while also using Xiphilinos' copy of Dio.[153] He will have particularly influenced Gregoras, who was also a prodigious scholar. Gregoras' activity was focused on his school and library at the Chora, and among the extant autograph manuscripts of Gregoras as annotator is found Herodotus (Angel. gr. 83) and Zosimus (Vat. gr. 176), as well as Polybius, Diodorus (Par. gr. 1665) and Arrian.[154] At the request of Manuel Kantakouzenos, son of John VI, he also transcribed Thucydides, whom he tellingly labelled a 'rhetor', not a historian.[155] In addition, Gregoras wrote a lengthy (37 books) and detailed history from 1204 to 1359. At one stage he was a protégé of Theodore Metochites (1270–1332), who was another of the great students of the Hellenic tradition and whose wealth had been instrumental in rebuilding the Chora and its library, where he spent his final years. Both Gregoras and Metochites were senior officials at the court of Andronikos II, and while Metochites evidently never wrote history himself he considered Thucydides the greatest of all authors.[156] Likewise, Gregoras' learned friend at Thessalonike Thomas Magistros (1275?–1347) regarded Thucydides as his favourite author.[157] Two of his pupils, Demetrios Triklinios (fl. 1300–1325) and Gregory Akindynos, included an interest in the historians in their repertoire. In fact, there are

---

[150]   R. J. Loenertz, *Démétrius Cydonès Corrrespondance*, Studi e Testi 186 (1956), *Ep.* 98:135.26–30.

[151]   W. Treadgold, *A History of the Byzantine State and Society* (Stanford, CA, 1997), 830.

[152]   A. Kazhdan, 'L'Histoire de Cantacuzène en tant qu'oeuvre littéraire', *Byz* 50 (1980), 279–335.

[153]   C. N. Constantinides, *Higher Education in Byzantium in the Thirteenth and Early Fourteenth Centuries, 1204–c.1310* (Nicosia, 1982), 76.

[154]   Details in D. Bianconi, 'La biblioteca di Cora tra Massimo Planude e Niceforo Gregora, una questione di mani', *Segno e testo* 3 (2005), 416–34, with manuscripts itemized at 412–18.

[155]   Wilson, *Scholars of Byzantium*, 260.

[156]   Details in I. Ševčenko, 'Theodore Metochites, Chora et les courants intellectuels de l'époque', in *Ideology, Letters and Culture in the Byzantine World* (London, 1982), study VIII, 28.

[157]   F. Tinnefeld, 'Intellectuals in late Byzantine Thessalonike', *DOP* 57 (2003), 158–9.

two extant manuscripts of Herodotus (Angel. gr. 83, Laur. 70.6 – copied in 1318) associated with Demetrios.[158]

Over the same decades there were several others around the imperial court who were no less engaged in reading, annotating and copying the works of earlier historians. Nikephoros Moschopoulos (d. 1322–32) owned a large library at Constantinople that included many historians, and in the following century another prolific scholar and writer with diverse literary interests, John Chortasmenos (1370–1437), who owned a Choniates manuscript. Moreover, the histories written at this time demonstrate the influence of the Byzantine tradition by employing the characteristic literary ways of acknowledging and interacting with the writer's audience. Gregoras, for instance, carefully guides the reader/listener with references forwards and backwards to earlier and later events,[159] as well as advising on the value of including or excluding certain content from his narrative (logos),[160] while Kantakouzenos' more intense and subjective account of a narrower period (1320–56) clearly signals for his audience the direction of the narrative.[161]

The Byzantine historiographical audience may have become narrowly restricted by the fourteenth century, but in the literary and court circles of Constantinople and Thessalonike it remained active and focused on preserving its distinguished tradition from the fifth- to the thirteenth century. Scholars still gathered in their *theatra* to listen to each other's new work or earlier works.[162] As Byzantium disappeared its historiographical audience was busy borrowing, studying and replicating manuscripts of historians, and utilizing their reading to describe and explain their own circumstances. The histories of Chalkokondyles and Kritovoulos written after the demise of Byzantine Constantinople in 1453 are in some ways the most Thucydidean of all. The survival of much of the Greek tradition of historiography that later so influenced the west is owed to the attentive and productive Byzantine historiographical audience of the thirteenth, fourteenth and fifteenth centuries, but they also had their favourites among later Byzantine historians.

---

[158]   Martin, 'Lectores', 144.

[159]   E.g. (Books 1 to 5 only): Gregoras, I, 35.14–15; 28.9–10; 62.3–4: 'My advancing narrative will show this'; 117.3; 144.7–10; 180.15; 209.15.

[160]   E.g. (Books 1 to 5 only): Gregoras, I, 80.13–14: 'after the history has reached this point it is not proper to be silent on the Scyths. We will discuss them as the narrative progresses'; 62.3: 'my history almost passed over ...'; 68.7–8; 123.1–3: need 'to repeat so as not to interrupt the flow of the narrative'; 148.19; 171.4–5.

[161]   References conveniently collected in Kazhdan, 'Cantacuzène', 323.

[162]   Constantinides, *Higher Education*, 150.

Conclusion

From the fourth century to the fifteenth, most Byzantine history writing emerged from, and primarily for, a small highly educated and self-contained cultural elite around the court and government at Constantinople, Nicaea and provincial centres. They accessed historiographical works by attending readings in a private salon (*theatron*) or public auditorium, or by borrowing copies from friends, patrons or libraries, civic and monastic. Historical writers worked within the literary tastes and expectations of their audience, which differed considerably from a modern one. It is therefore considered 'a sad commentary on the taste of the Byzantine public' that the *Chronographia* of Psellos has survived in but a solitary manuscript, whereas there are numerous extant manuscripts of what are deemed lesser works such as those of Kedrenos and Zonaras.[163] Certainly it is true that Psellos and Leo the Deacon would be lost to us were it not for Par. gr. 1712, while the *Scriptores post Theophanem* and Bryennios owe their present existence to a single manuscript. However, there are numerous Byzantine manuscripts of the whole of Herodotus and Thucydides, and much of Diodorus, Dionysius of Halicarnassus and Cassius Dio, Polybius and Arrian, while among Byzantine writers the best preserved are George the Monk (more than 30 manuscripts) and Manasses (more than 70).[164] The relative popularity of different historical works with a Byzantine audience highlights their enduring preference for the best-told stories of Byzantium's Greek, Roman and Christian heritage and a comprehensive compendium of the period between then and the living present.

---

[163] Quote from C. Mango, *Byzantium: The Empire of New Rome* (London, 1980), 246; cf. Patlagean, 'Discours', 274, lamenting that there is only one manuscript of the *Scriptores post Theophanem* but numerous ones of Symeon Metaphrastes' saints lives.

[164] Cf. Hunger, *Literatur*, I, 243.

3. Anna Komnene and Niketas Choniates 'translated': the fourteenth-century Byzantine metaphrases

John Davis

While Henry Ford's famous verbal drubbing of history just ninety years ago may not throw much light on the intellectual, social and political function of history, it surely says something about the spirit of the modern age.[1] Interestingly, at a concert by U2 in Sarajevo just over ten years ago – still within the geographical orbit of Byzantium – while the 'old' Yugoslavia was disintegrating, the lead singer of the band, Bono, recommended to the 50,000 people in the audience that they 'forget the past' and look only to the future. Henry Ford and Bono, it could be argued, were both condemning, perhaps legitimately, the use of history as a tool to perpetuate belligerence: history and tradition sustaining national or ethnic animosity, ensnaring mankind in fetters of hatred, social regression, cynical manipulation by ruling elites and, ultimately, moral bankruptcy. A serious indictment, indeed – though it is just one side of the coin.

Historians like to believe that a knowledge of history enables us to avoid the errors of the past. Terror, tyranny and incompetence in the sphere of public administration are aberrations that diverge from the norm of rational behaviour and – a historian might argue – betray lack of historical awareness. Modern-day economists often fall into the same trap, believing that human beings will always make rational choices when it comes to matters of economic self-interest. Be that as it may, and regardless of whether history is in fact just one damned thing after another, Niketas Choniates – one of the authors considered in this paper – stresses from the outset that history serves as a textbook on proper and improper conduct

---

[1] 'History is more or less bunk. It's tradition. We don't want tradition. We want to live in the present, and the only history that is worth a tinker's damn is the history that we make today' – interview with Charles N. Wheeler, *Chicago Tribune*, 25 May 1916. Ford, of course, has secured a place for himself in the history books not as a philosopher of history but as a motorcar manufacturer.

for the generations to come: he provides us, that is, with living paradigms of behaviour to be emulated or shunned. In his preface he also states, perhaps rather formulaically, that history is a βίβλος ζώντων, 'the book of the living'.[2] In a sense, this statement not only tells us that what we are about to read is going to be a lesson in human affairs – that is, *real* human affairs and conduct, setting up a mirror to society and how it has come to be the way it is – but also serves as a literary-critical signpost informing us that we are entering the medieval non-fiction department.

That said – and as others point out in this volume – it should be borne in mind that non-fiction, as in the case of great historical writing of any age, does not imply that the work will be lacking in the rhetorical paraphernalia that makes a work of writing distinctly (to our modern eyes, at any rate) literary. Monika Otter recently gave a nice summary of the situation:

> The mental habit of regarding historiography as a transparent medium with no literary substance of its own, a self-effacing text that simply shows things 'as they really were' ('wie es eigentlich gewesen'), derives from nineteenth-century historicism. To classical, medieval and early modern Europeans, history was not a separate academic discipline, but a subsection of rhetoric (as was poetry and what we would call fictional narrative).[3]

We can let this observation serve as a kind of yardstick by which to measure the metaphrases of the late Palaiologan period – that is, the 'declassicizing' reworkings of Anna Komnene's *Alexiad*, Niketas Choniates' *History*, and Nikephoros Blemmydes' rhetorical essay on royal conduct, the *Basilikos Andrias*, or *Imperial Statue*. Broadly speaking, these texts endeavour to recast in a simpler linguistic register the information given in their sources: inevitably, therefore, a considerable proportion, though not all, of the rhetorical wealth and subtlety of the originals is reduced or omitted.

The language, or register, of these metaphrases has been termed very studiedly by Eideneier (and subsequently adopted by Herbert Hunger[4]) as a 'Schrift-Koine'.[5] The metaphrases, in effect, are instances of what is known

---

[2]   Choniates, *Historia*, 2.20.

[3]   M. Otter, 'Functions of fiction in historical writing', 109, in N. Partner, ed., *Writing Medieval History* (London, 2005), 109–30.

[4]   See the relevant discussion in H. Hunger and I. Ševčenko, *Des Nikephoros Blemmydes Βασιλικὸς ἀνδριάς und dessen Metaphrase von Georgios Galesiotes und Georgios Oinaiotes*, Wiener Byzantinischer Studien XVIII (Vienna, 1986), 30.

[5]   H. Eideneier, review of H. Hunger, *Anonyme Metaphrase zu Anna Komnene. Alexias XI–XIII. Ein Beitrag zur Erschliessung der byzantinischen Umgangssprache*, Wiener Byzantinische Studien XV (Vienna, 1981), in *Südostforschungen* 41 (1982), 589–90.

as intralingual translation – that is, not of translation from one language into another, such as from Greek into English, but of one form or register of the language into another form or register of the same language.[6]

Both Anna Komnene's *Alexiad* and Niketas Choniates' *History* are notable for their intricate blend of historical and linguistic awareness. That is, on the one hand they follow the pattern of serious historical composition, including research, considered assessment of the data, and careful arrangement and exposition of the material; on the other, they drape their narratives in a rich mantle of rhetorical and literary artifice, which, as Athanasios Angelou discusses in this volume, involves not only the use of a vast armoury of rhetorical devices and techniques but also, in the hands of the best practitioners, a sophisticated alternation of detailed focus and grand vistas. These works therefore offer a complex historical account. They are subtle and complex monuments to the cultural spirit of the ancient Roman (i.e. Greek) intellectual tradition.

It will always remain intriguing and perhaps, for many modern spectators of the Byzantine world, baffling that one side-effect of upholding this intellectual tradition involved making it obscure to the majority of those that claimed to live and converse within the sphere of its influence. One need only recall the scribal note, referred to also by Brian Croke,[7] in the margin of one of the manuscripts (MS Vindobonensis Hist. gr. 53, f. 2v) containing Choniates' original:[8]

> I've no idea what you're going on about here, Choniates.
> You tell us that it's wise to express yourself clearly, and
> then proceed to write in riddles.

It is worth recalling that this reader of the text made this remark on just the second leaf, and it would seem unlikely, given the speed at which frustration had set in, that he reached folio 323 without skipping much of the material in between. One result of this curious linguistic tension was

---

[6] R. Jakobson, 'On linguistic aspects of translation', in R. A. Brower, ed., *On Translation* (Cambridge, MA, 1959), 232–9, repr. in R. Schulte and J. Biguenet, eds., *Theories of Translation: An Anthology of Essays from Dryden to Derrida* (Chicago, IL, 1992), 144–51, esp. 145, where he distinguishes three types of translation: 1) intralingual translation, or rewording (an interpretation of verbal signs by means of other signs in the same language), 2) interlingual translation or translation proper (an interpretation of verbal signs by means of some other language), and 3) intersemiotic translation or transmutation (an interpretation of verbal signs by means of signs of nonverbal sign systems).

[7] Above, 26–7.

[8] Choniates, *Historia*, xxxii, 'Οὐκ οἶδα τί φῇς ἐνθάδε Χωνιάτα, σοφὸν τὸ σαφὲς συγγράφων εἶναι λέγεις, εἶτα γριφώδη καὶ βαραθρώδη γράφεις'.

that at some stage an individual or group of individuals saw fit to translate the histories of Niketas Choniates and Anna Komnene into a simpler idiom that, besides any other purpose it might have served, could be intelligible to a wider readership.

There are, however, several fundamental questions regarding the circumstances under which these metaphrases were created that are well-nigh impossible to answer. One of the main reasons for this is that the manuscripts preserving the texts of the historical metaphrases are all mutilated. In the case of Anna Komnene's *Alexiad*, there is only one surviving manuscript of the metaphrase. And to make matters worse, this manuscript is a seventeenth-century copy of a Byzantine codex once in the Vatican but today lost.[9] And the surviving text contains just two-and-a-half chapters of Anna's original fifteen. As so often happens with such manuscripts, the folios at the beginning and end – in other words, the folios that normally contain a note by the author, the scribe or others involved in the production of the manuscript – are lost. The result is that the translation is anonymous, its date of production obscure, and the reasons for its existence a matter for debate and conjecture.

However, other evidence allows us to make some reasonable hypotheses. At a palaeography conference held in Wolfenbüttel in 1983, Giancarlo Prato presented a paper that, while dealing with another topic, has important implications regarding the date of the metaphrase of the *Alexiad*.[10] Prato demonstrated that the key manuscript – Parisinus Coislin 311 – containing the text of Anna's original *Alexiad* was not, as had previously been thought, a manuscript of the twelfth century, but in fact dates to around 1300 or shortly thereafter. He produced evidence indicating that MS Parisinus Coislin 311 belonged to a larger group of manuscripts that had been copied in a deliberately archaizing scribal hand.[11] This re-dating has important implications for the metaphrase of the *Alexiad*. The importance lies in the

---

[9]   H. Hunger, *Anonyme Metaphrase zu Anna Komnene. Alexias XI–XIII. Ein Beitrag zur Erschliessung der byzantinischen Umgangssprache*, Wiener Byzantinische Studien, Band XV (Vienna, 1981), 13–18.

[10]   G. Prato, 'I manoscritti greci dei secoli XIII e XIV: note paleografiche', in *Paleografia e codicologia Greca: Atti del II Colloquio internazionale (Berolino-Wolfenbüttel, 17–21 ottobre 1983)* (Alessandria, 1991), I, 131–49.

[11]   Prato, 'I manoscritti greci', 139–40. The other manuscripts of this group include Bucharest, Accademia Rumena 10 (parchment) containing works by Nikephoros Blemmydes; two manuscripts containing works by Plato, Vat. gr. 225 and 226, which had been dated to the twelfth century; and Vat. gr. 1302 with works by Theophrastos, Pseudo-Aristotle and Diogenes Laertius. On this fashion for archaizing scripts see also N. G. Wilson, *Scholars of Byzantium* (London and Baltimore, MD, 230: 'There is little doubt that .. [the] archaising script belongs to a fashion current in the reign of Andronicus II'.

fact that, according to the modern editor of the *Alexiad* metaphrase, Herbert Hunger, it was MS Parisinus Coislin 311 that in all likelihood provided the text from which the metaphrast worked.[12] In other words, given this evidence, we are compelled to assume that the metaphrase of the *Alexiad* was not made in the twelfth or thirteenth centuries,[13] but later, in the early years of the fourteenth century.

When we turn to the Choniates metaphrase we have firmer foundations on which to suggest possible answers to the questions posed above. About seventy years ago, Franz Dölger expressed the view that the metaphrase of Choniates' *History* must have been made by Choniates himself. This view itself had a venerable history, because Hieronymus Wolf, in 1557, in his preface to the *editio princeps*, had assumed the same, though it was based on his collation of just three manuscripts of the *History*, one of which was the metaphrase.[14] However, the latest editor of the *History*, J.-L. van Dieten, was categorical in his refutation of this view: there is every reason to believe that Choniates himself had nothing to do with the metaphrase of his historical work, the most important being the numerous misinterpretations of Choniates' text that occur in the metaphrase. If Choniates died in around 1217, we can safely assume that the metaphrase of his work was produced after that date.[15]

The total number of manuscripts containing the text of the metaphrase of Choniates' *History* is four. Again, none of them survives intact and we are deprived of scribal notes, prefaces or colophons that might otherwise have given us some information regarding the why and wherefore of its production. However, the two oldest surviving manuscripts of the metaphrase are, on palaeographical and codicological grounds, very close in date, and they bear a number of changes that suggest that one of them may have functioned as a kind of draft translation, which has been polished up somewhat in the other. They are the kind of changes, one can reasonably argue, that make sense only if the manuscripts were close in date to the initial production of the metaphrase. The watermarks on the paper of the oldest manuscript, Monacensis gr. 450, suggest a date somewhere between the late 1320s and the mid-1340s.[16] Thus, this happens to be close to the likely time of production of the metaphrase of Anna Komnene's *Alexiad*. One of the other three Choniates metaphrase manuscripts is

---

[12] Hunger, *Anonyme Metaphrase*, 18.

[13] Hunger, *Anonyme Metaphrase*, 15, suggests that the metaphrase may have been made as early as the period of Latin rule.

[14] For a discussion of this issue, see J.-L. van Dieten, 'Bemerkungen zur Sprache der sogenannten vulgärgriechischen Niketasparaphrasen', *BF* 6 (1979), 37–40.

[15] V. Katsaros, 'A contribution to the exact dating of the death of the Byzantine historian Nicetas Choniates', *JÖB* 32/3 (1982), 83–91.

[16] See Choniates, *Historia*, xxxiii–xxxiv.

part of a composite manuscript that also contains an autograph work by the late fourteenth-century emperor Manuel II Palaiologos, Parisinus gr. 3041.[17] It is tempting to think that the translated text, besides the original, may have been associated with imperial circles in some way. Indeed, the *Alexiad* manuscript discussed above was part of a large, elegantly written group of manuscripts that seem, according to Giancarlo Prato, to have been produced for a large, well-stocked library.[18] Such a library could well be associated with court circles, if not the imperial library itself, which would again suggest that the Choniates metaphrase also may have been associated with court circles.

By taking a closer look at the metaphrases, we may gain an idea of the ways in which they seem to work, what they strive to retain from the original, what they change, and what features they have in common.

This first passage is taken from the chapter in Choniates' *History* dealing with the reign of Isaac II Angelos (1185–95). It is contained in three of the metaphrase manuscripts, and has not been previously published.[19] The episode describes the passage of the army of Frederick Barbarossa through Byzantium on its way to the Holy Land in May 1190. His armies were subject to constant harassment from Turkish forces, encouraged by the Byzantines, who had every reason to be wary of the religious and military zeal of the crusaders. Here Choniates describes a German soldier who had been separated from his regiment and had to fend off the Turks on his own:

---

[17] See Choniates, *Historia*, xxxvi–xxxvii.

[18] Prato, 'I manoscritti greci', 139–40.

[19] Previously published fragments of the Choniates metaphrase can be found in Van Dieten, 'Bemerkungen', 41–61, with extensive discussion of the language and style; E. Miller, *Recueil des Historiens des Croisades, Historiens grecs*, I (Paris, 1875), 342–482 (this volume, whose apparatus criticus contains a large section of the metaphrase, can be downloaded as a pdf file from the website of the Bibliothèque nationale de France); J. C. Davis, 'A passage of the "Barbarograeca" metaphrase of Niketas Choniates' *Chronike Diegesis*: retranslated or revised?', *Symmeikta* 10 (1996), 127–42; and various much smaller fragments in the apparatus criticus of Bekker's edition of the *History* for the Bonn corpus. I hope one day to publish a critical edition of the entire Choniates metaphrase.

Choniates, *Historia*, 414.85–415.15

Κατὰ δὲ τὴν ἀνάβασιν ταύτην λέγεται
Ἀλαμανόν τινα, πελώριον τὸ σῶμα, τὴν
ἰσχὺν ἀπροσμάχητον, τῶν ὁμοφύλων
ἐπὶ πλεῖστον ἀπολειφθῆναι. καὶ τὸν μὲν
ἀνύειν ποσὶ τὴν ὁδὸν ἀνειμένοις ἐκ τοῦ
χαλινοῦ τὸν ἵππον ἐφέλκοντα τῇ ὁδοιπορίᾳ
καμόντα, τῶν δ' ἐξ Ἰσμαὴλ ἀθροισθῆναι
περὶ αὐτὸν ὑπὲρ τοὺς πεντήκοντα,
κρατίστους ἅμα πάντας καὶ τὰς οἰκείας
τάξεις ἀπολιπόντας. οἱ μὲν οὖν ὡς ἐς
κύκλωσιν αὐτὸν διειληφότες περιετόξευσαν,
ὁ δὲ τῷ εὐρεῖ σάκει σκεπόμενος καὶ τῇ τῶν
ὅπλων θαρρῶν στεγανότητι γεγηθὼς
ἐπορεύετο ἀτίνακτος κατὰ πρῶνα ἢ
πρόβολον τοῖς τῶν ἐναντίων βλήμασι
καὶ ὧν καὶ δεικνύμενος. ὡς δ' ἐκείνων εἰς
γενναῖόν τι δράσειν ὑπὲρ τοὺς ἄλλους
ἐπαγγελλόμενος ἀπέθετο μὲν τὸ τόξον
ὡς οὐκ ὀνήσιμον, τὴν δ' ἐπιμήκη μάχαιραν
ἐξερύσας καὶ τὸν ἵππον ἐς δρόμον ἀνεὶς
ἀγχωμάλως ἐπεβάλετο μάχεσθαι, αὐτὸς
μὲν ὅσα καὶ ἀκρώρειαν ὄρους ἢ ἀνδριάντα
χάλκεον ἔπαιε τὸν Ἀλαμανόν, ὁ δὲ τὸ
ξίφος σπασάμενος παχείᾳ καὶ ἡρωϊκῇ
χειρί, βριθὺ καὶ μέγα καὶ στιβαρόν,
πλήττει τὸν ἵππον ἐπιδοχμίως περὶ τοὺς
πόδας καὶ ἄμφω τοὺς ἔμπροσθεν ὡς οὐδ'
ἀγροῦ τις χόρτον ἀποδιεῖλεν. ὡς δ' ἐπὶ
γόνυ κλιθεὶς ὁ ἵππος ἔτι τὸν ἀναβάτην
ἐρειδόμενον εἶχε τῇ ἐφεστρίδι, ἐκτείνας
ὁ Ἀλαμανὸς τὸν βραχίονα κατὰ μέσης
τῆς τοῦ Πέρσου κόρσης τὴν σπάθην
κατήνεγκεν. ἡ δὲ τῇ οἰκείᾳ τε ἀντιτυπίᾳ
καὶ τῇ τοῦ φέροντος γενναιότητι οὕτως
ἀξιοθαύμαστον εἰργάσατο τὴν τομήν,
ὡς τὸν μὲν πληγέντα διαιρεθῆναι διχῆ,
κακῶς δὲ καὶ τὸν ἵππον ἐς νῶτον παθεῖν
διαπτάντος τὴν ἀστράβην τοῦ πλήγματος,
τοὺς δὲ λοιποὺς Πέρσας πρὸς τὴν τοιαύτην
θέαν καταπλαγέντας μηκέτι ἀποθαρρῆσαι
τὸν μεθ' ἑνὸς πόλεμον. καὶ οἱ μὲν οὕτως, ὁ
δὲ ὡς λέων τῇ οἰκείᾳ πεποιθὼς ῥώμῃ οὐκ
ἐπέτεινε τὴν πορείαν, ἀλλὰ βάδην ὁδεύων
περὶ ὀψίαν τοῖς ὁμογενέσι προσέμιξεν,
ἔνθα ηὐλίσαντο.

Metaphrase

Λέγεται δὲ κατὰ τὸν δρόμον ἐκεῖνον
Ἀλαμανόν τινα ἄνδρα ὑψηλὸν καὶ μέγαν
καὶ ἀνδρεῖον ἐναπομείναντα ἀπὸ τῆς
αὐτοῦ συντάξεως πεζὸν ἐρχόμενον, καὶ
τὸν ἵππον αὐτοῦ ἐκ τοῦ χαλινοῦ σύροντα,
ὡς ἀποσταθέντα ἰδόντες δὲ αὐτὸν Τοῦρκοι
πλείονες τῶν πεντήκοντα μεμονωμένον
ὄντα, περιεκύκλωσαν αὐτὸν καὶ ἐτόξευον.

ὁ δὲ θαρρῶν εἰς
τὰ ἑαυτοῦ ἅρματα, ἐδέχετο τὰς σαγίτας
ἐπὶ τοῦ σκουταρίου οὗ ἐν ταῖς χερσὶν
ἐκράτει, καὶ χαίρων ἐπορεύετο μὴ ἀλλάξας
ποσῶς τὸ βῆμα τῶν ποδῶν αὐτοῦ. εἰς δὲ ἐκ
τούτων ἀνδρεῖόν τι πράξαι μέλλων, ῥίψας
τὸ τόξον καὶ τὴν σπάθην αὐτοῦ γυμνώσας
καὶ εἰς χεῖρας λαβών, τόν τε ἵππον αὐτοῦ
ἐγκράξας, ὥρμησε κατὰ τοῦ Ἀλαμάνου,
καὶ ἔκρουε τοῦτον ἐπάνω τοῦ κασσειδίου,
καὶ ἐφαίνετο ὡς πέτραν κρούων· καὶ ὁ
Ἀλαμάνος τὴν ἰδίαν σπάθην ἀνὰ χεῖρας
λαβών, κρούει τοὺς ἐμπροσθίους πόδας
τοῦ ἵππου τοῦ Τούρκου καὶ οὕτως αὐτοὺς
ἔκοψεν ὥσπερ χόρτον·

καὶ ὁ ἵππος ἐπὶ γόνυ πεσών, ἔτι τὸν
Τοῦρκον ἔχων ἐπάνω τῆς σέλας, κρούει
πάλιν ὁ Ἀλαμάνος τὸν Τοῦρκον κατὰ
μέσης τῆς κεφαλῆς, καὶ τῇ ἀντιτυπίᾳ
τοῦ κρούσματος καὶ τῇ χειρὸς ἀνδρείᾳ
ἀξιοθαύμαστον εἰργάσατο τὴν πληγήν·
ἐχώρησε γὰρ τοῦτον εἰς μέρη δύο, καὶ
τὴν σέλαν αὐτοῦ, καὶ ἐτραυμάτισε καὶ
τὸ ἄλογο, καὶ ἔπεσε τὸ ἥμισυ μέρος τοῦ
σώματος ἀνὰ μέρος καὶ τὸ ἥμισυ ἀνὰ
μέρος. ἰδόντες δὲ οἱ ἕτεροι Τοῦρκοι τὸ
γεγονός, οὐκ ἐθάρρησαν πολεμῆσαι αὐτῷ·
ἀλλὰ ἀφέντες αὐτόν, ἔφυγον.
αὐτὸς δὲ ὡς λέων τῇ οἰκείᾳ δυνάμει
θαρρῶν, μετὰ ἀνέσεως ἐπορεύετο, καὶ
πρὸς ἑσπέραν εἰς τὸν στρατὸν ἔφθασε.

It is said that on that same road one of the Germans – a man of gigantic stature and a mighty warrior – straggling behind his troop, came walking along, leading his horse by its reins. And the Turks saw that he had fallen behind and was alone and, being over fifty in number, surrounded him and started shooting at him with their arrows. The German, however, was quite confident in his arms, and took the arrows on the shield he held in his hands, and happily st. ode along without so much as changing his pace. One of them [i.e. one of the Turks] decided to try to perform a feat of bravery and threw down his bow and drew out his sword. Spurring on his horse, he charged at the German, and smote him on his helmet, but it was as if he had struck a rock. The German, drawing his own sword, slashed at the front legs of the Turk's horse, and sliced through them as if mowing grass. And as the horse collapsed on its knees with the Turk still sitting in the saddle, the German struck again at the Turk: right through the middle of his head. And the force of the blow and the might of his arm worked truly remarkable damage: for it sliced him in two, together with his saddle, even hacking into the horse. And the one half of his body fell to one side, and the other half fell to the other. When the other Turks saw this, they dared not fight with him and let him go. He, like a lion confident in his own strength, just walked calmly on, reaching his regiment's camp in the evening.

This is one of those digressions of Choniates that are of little significance as far as the bigger historical picture and narrative is concerned but nevertheless provide an opportunity for particularly effective dramatic focus.[20] The language of the metaphrase is somewhat awkward when placed beside the original, though it nonetheless captures the fearsome – and fearless – demeanour of the German warrior. Notably, while Choniates piles up a list of adjectives in lines 22–3 (βριθὺ καὶ μέγα καὶ στιβαρόν), these are simply left out of the metaphrase. There is much one can talk about in any extract of the metaphrase; here we can note a number of changes that can be seen to recur throughout the entire metaphrase.

For instance, the metaphrast consistently renders Choniates' term 'Perses' with 'Tourkoi'. We see the passive infinitive construction (line 4: ἀπολειφθῆναι) rendered by an active form (here a participle: ἐναπομείναντα), a change that we see again further down (in lines 31–2, ὡς τὸν μὲν πληγέντα διαιρεθῆναι διχῆ, rendered ἐχώρησε γὰρ τοῦτον εἰς μέρη δύο). Groups of words, such as βάδην ὁδεύων in Choniates (line 39) are turned into simple verbs (here: ἐπορεύετο, line 34), and various lexical items that are clearly of a learned, literary origin, such as εὐρεῖ σάκει (line 11, from Homer) are rendered by the very 'modern' σκουτάριον (line 10), or τῇ οἰκείᾳ πεποιθὼς ῥώμῃ (line 38) with the metaphrast's τῇ οἰκείᾳ

δυνάμει θαρρῶν (lines 33–4), and so on. Within this one paragraph we see the metaphrast progress from the word ἵππος, as in Choniates of course, to ἄλογο, as in the vernacular. Notably, in line 15 of the metaphrase, we see the word ἵππος used with the particle τε: here the metaphrast sticks to classical usage, though admittedly easily intelligible classical usage, of two lexical items, but one could argue that from the moment he decides to use τε he is obliged to keep the noun to which it is attached – ἵππος – in its classical form. A more general point concerning this passage is that the metaphrase has, broadly speaking, sought to reproduce the whole of the original more or less in its entirety.

Another significant feature of the Choniates metaphrase is that Choniates' digressions from the main thread of the story, whose role is as much didactic as literary, are frequently omitted. The examples are numerous, but one particularly striking example is the long introduction to the chapter describing the events immediately after the fall of the City to the crusaders. In Choniates' original there is a long digression on Solon and the foolishness of the Athenians who failed to heed his words of warning prior to the tyrant Peisistratos seizing power in their city.[21] Choniates sought to make a parallel between the conduct of the citizens of Athens in antiquity and the citizens of Constantinople in his own day: 'If', he says, 'Solon, whose wisdom is famed throughout the world, succeeded with his words in provoking shame at the assembly of the Athenians, he did not manage to persuade them to resist Peisistratos' ambitions.' Choniates then goes on to make a bitter criticism of the general political situation in Byzantium immediately before the sack of the City. He says, 'Exactly the same would have happened in our land, even if someone had offered to help govern our affairs, whose rulers' – he adds caustically – 'were brought up in luxury and idleness.'[22]

Characteristically, the metaphrast omits this entire passage. It is a literary and moral digression that does not comprise an essential part of his narration of events. The metaphrast is interested first and foremost in rendering the basic narrative of the history rather than reproducing its literary finery.

When we look at the *Anonymous Metaphrase* of Anna Komnene's *Alexiad* we come across precisely the same phenomena. Compare, for instance, two sentences where Anna describes the naval encounter of Byzantine and Pisan ships near Rhodes in 1098/99.[23] Note how Anna's text is rich with seething, briny alliteration, particularly in the last parenthesis:

---

[21] Choniates, *Historia*, 583.4–585.49.

[22] Choniates, *Historia*, 584.21–6.

[23] Hunger, *Anonyme Metaphrase*, §69 (pp. 42–3).

Anna Komnene, *Alexiad* 11.10.4

ἐπεὶ δ' ἅμα καὶ συστροφὴ ἀνέμου τὴν θάλατταν ἀθρόον ἐπεισπεσοῦσα διετάραττε, τάς τε ναῦς συνέτριβε καὶ μονονοὺ βυθίζειν ἠπείλει (ἐρρόχθει γὰρ τὸ κῦμα, ἐτετρίγεσαν αἱ κεραῖαι τά θ' ἱστία διερρήγνυντο).

Anonymous metaphrase

ἐγερθεῖσα δὲ καὶ ἡ θάλασσα ἀνέμου συστροφῇ ἐκ τοῦ παραυτίκα τά τε καράβια συνέτριβε καὶ καταποντίζειν αὐτὰ ἐφοβέριζεν· ἀνέβαινον γὰρ τὰ κύματα ἕως ἄνωθεν τῶν κεραταρίων καὶ τὰ κατάρτια ἐτζακίζοντο.

The gale, suddenly blowing onto the sea, stirred it up, pounded on the ships and threatened to sink them (for the water roared, the yard-arms cracked, and the masts were split through).

A comparison of the two versions shows us that the metaphrast has transformed almost everything. Not only have specific words been rendered with words that are closer to contemporary usage (as in the case of κερατάρια, κατάρτια and the passive form of the verb τζακίζω), but the syntax of the text has been dismantled and then reassembled, such as in the case of θάλασσα, transformed now into the subject of the clause, while ἀνέμου συστροφῇ functions in the metaphrase as an instrumental dative (unusually, because the metaphrast often prefers to avoid the dative). Further, the metaphrast prefers to use the plural κύματα, to the generic κῦμα of Anna.

The entire *Anonymous Metaphrase* follows this general pattern. It is interesting to compare this sentence with a passage dealing with a similar subject in the Choniates metaphrase. The sentence here is taken from Book VI of the reign of Manuel Komnenos, where there is a short digression on a dream of Manuel's at the time of his campaign against the Turks in 1176–77. Manuel, it should be remembered, attached immense importance to dreams and astrology.

Choniates, *Historia*, 190.87–92

Βασιλεὺς μὲν γὰρ ἡνίκα ἦν κατὰ Περσῶν ἐκστρατεύειν προθέμενος, ἐδόκει καθ' ὕπνους ὁρᾶν ὡς εἰς στρατηγίδα νῆα ἐμβὰς αὐτός τε καὶ συχνοὶ τῶν ἐπιτηδείων τὴν Προποντίδα ἀνελέγετο, αἴφνης δὲ συμπεσεῖν τὰ ἐξ Εὐρώπης τε καὶ Ἀσίας ὄρη, ὡς ἀφανισθῆναι μὲν τῆς νηὸς θραυσθείσης τὸ ἐμπλέον ἅπαν, αὐτὸν δὲ μόλις ἐκδοθῆναι τῇ χέρσῳ ταῖς χερσὶ νηχόμενον.

Metaphrase

Ὁ γὰρ βασιλεὺς ὅτε κατὰ τῶν Τούρκων ἐκστρατεύειν ἔμελλεν, ἔδοξεν αὐτῷ καθ' ὕπνους ὅτι ἦν εἰς κάτεργον αὐτὸς καὶ ἕτεροι πολλοὶ τῶν ἀρχόντων μετ' αὐτοῦ, καὶ ἀνέβαινε κατὰ τὸ στενὸν τοῦ Ἱεροῦ, καὶ ἐξαίφνης τὰ ὄρη τῆς δύσεως καὶ τῆς ἀνατολῆς συμπεσεῖν καὶ συμμιγῆναι καὶ τὸ κάτεργον ὅλον τζακισθῆναι, τὸν δὲ βασιλέα πλέοντα μόλις τὴν στερεὰν ἐξελθεῖν.

At the time when the emperor was embarking on campaigning against the Turks, he dreamt that he boarded a flagship along with many of his close associates and sailed into the Propontis, but suddenly the mountains of Europe and Asia appeared to collapse and everything in the shattered vessel was lost, while he was barely able to swim to dry land.

Choniates' ἔνικα is rendered as ὅτε, the Persians are Turks, we have ἔδοξεν ὅτι rather than ἐδόκει plus infinitive, the ναῦς becomes κάτεργον (generally interchangeable with καράβιον throughout the Choniates metaphrase), the ἐπιτήδειοι are his fellow ἄρχοντες, the Propontis is the Stenon of the Hieron, Europe and Asia become simply the west and the east, ἀφανισθῆναι becomes τζακισθῆναι, and, finally, the emperor comes out (ἐξελθεῖν) onto the στερεάν, rather than χέρσῳ. Furthermore, while ἔδοξεν is initially followed by the ὅτι construction, it is later used with infinitives.

Correspondences of this kind between the two metaphrases are repeated and consistent. A close comparison of the entire text of both metaphrases reveals numerous and remarkable affinities. I list some of these:

First, the same frequent use of the phrase ἐκ τοῦ παραυτίκα, corresponding to prepositional phrases and adverbs of the type ἐκ τοῦ παρευθύ, εὐθύ, ἀθρόον, παραχρῆμα, and so on.

Second, a strong liking for the verb οἰκονομῶ to render a variety of words and phrases in the original texts meaning or implying 'prepare', 'make provision for', 'construct', 'manage'. Another such verb used in a very specific sense by both texts is the word καινοτομῶ, meaning, characteristically for this period, 'waste', 'squander' or 'destroy'.

Third, there is a long list of individual vernacular words and terms that are identical translations in both the Anna and Niketas metaphrases, such as ἄσπρο, βουνό, γυρεύω, ἐγκράζω, γλυτώνω, καβαλλαρικός, καβαλλάριος, καβαλλικεύω, καράβιν, κατούνα, κατουνοτόπια, κοντάρι, κουρσεύω, λόγγος, μάγουλον, μανάρα, πεζεύω, πόρτα, πετζί, πρόβοδος, ροῦχον, σακούλια, σέλα, σούδα, τέντα, τζάγρα, τζακίζω, φωνάζω, χαντάκι, plus many more. Indeed, when it comes to the vernacular words, calculations indicate that about 80 per cent of such words in the *Alexiad* metaphrase are found used in exactly the same way in the metaphrase of Choniates' *History*.[24]

Fourth, besides a host of grammatical and syntactical features that are encountered in both metaphrases, there is also precisely the same tendency to expand the meanings of specific words very frequently. For instance, in certain cases where the original text has just one word, the metaphrases consistently translate with two. Sometimes these pairs of words seem to be

---

[24]   For a list of such words in the *Alexiad* metaphrase see Hunger, *Anonyme Metaphrase*, 251–4.

inseparable. Two such examples are the rendering of δωρεαὶ in both Anna and Niketas by the phrase δωρεαὶ καὶ εὐεργεσίαι, and the rendering of πόλεις by πόλεις καὶ χῶραι or κάστρα καὶ χῶραι.

It would be tedious to extend the list any further, but the point I am making is, I think, clear: there are strong reasons – stylistic and linguistic, as well as the loose chronological coincidence I mentioned earlier – to suspect that the same individual, or group of individuals, was involved in the translation of both. If this is indeed the case, we need to date the *Alexiad* metaphrase to the same time as the Choniates metaphrase, i.e. somewhere in the 1330s or 1340s.

One further comment about the language of these two translations vis-à-vis the so-called 'high-style' originals of Anna Komnene and Niketas Choniates: verbs of motion in both Anna and Niketas are many and varied. For instance, the verbs Choniates uses in the opening sentences of the second book on the reign of Manuel Komnenos:

Choniates, *Historia*, 72.10–12	Metaphrase
ἐν ᾧ δὲ τὴν ἐπὶ τῶν Ἱεροσολύμων οὗτοι ἐβάδιζον, παρημειφότες μὲν τὰ Ῥωμαίων ὅρια, τῆς δ' ἄνω Φρυγίας ἁπτόμενοι Λυκαονίας τε καὶ Πισιδίας...	ἐξελθόντες ἀπὸ τῶν ὁρίων τῶν Ῥωμαίων, καὶ πρὸς τὰ Ἱεροσόλυμα πορευόμενοι καὶ διὰ τῆς ἄνω Φρυγίας διερχόμενοι, Λυκαονίας τὲ καὶ Πισιδίας...

The italicized participles of Choniates are reduced to derivatives of ἔρχομαι. This small but very pervasive feature leads me to another point that needs to be made with regard to the metaphrases as a whole. The overall quality that distinguishes them is this radical simplification of the original text. Scholars in the past have used a variety of terms to describe these translations. H.-G. Beck, for example, preferred to use the Greek word 'metaphrase' rather than the German 'Übersetzung' or the much-used 'paraphrase'.[25] Van Dieten always used the term 'paraphrase' when discussing the translation of the *Chronike Diegesis*.[26] Hunger's edition of the translation of Anna's *Alexiad* uses the term 'metaphrase' (indeed he states his reasons for preferring the term 'metaphrase' to 'paraphrase'),[27] as does also Hunger's and Ševčenko's edition of the translation of Nikephoros Blemmydes' *Imperial Statue*. More

---

[25]   H.-G. Beck: *Das byzantinische Jahrtausend* (Munich, 1978), 150; "Die griechische volkstümliche Literatur des 14. Jahrhunderts", *Actes du XIVe Congrès International des Études Byzantines* (Bucharest, 1974), 125–38, esp. 126–8; *Geschichte der byzantinischen Volksliteratur* (Munich, 1971), 6; 'Überlieferungsgeschichte der byzantinischen Literatur', in *Geschichte der Textüberlieferung der antiken und mittelalterlichen Literatur*, 1 (Zurich, 1961), 449–50.

[26]   J.-L. van Dieten: 'Bemerkungen'; 'Noch einmal über Niketas Choniates', *BZ* 57 (1964), 302–28; and in his edition of Choniates, *Historia*.

[27]   Hunger, *Anonyme Metaphrase*, 7 and n. 2.

recently, in his history of the Greek language, Geoffrey Horrocks uses the rather nice musical term 'transposition' to describe the process by which these late Palaiologan translations were recast,[28] while Robert Browning, in his article 'A fourteenth-century prose version of the *Odyssey*', stated that these works had undergone a process of 'declassicisation'.[29] The truth is, all of these attempts to describe these unusual translations are more or less accurate, the lowest common denominator being simplification.

One may ask, can these metaphrases be seen to fit into a more general literary–cultural pattern in (late) Byzantium? Broadly speaking, metaphrastic activity (i.e. the recasting of texts in another register, whether higher or lower) implies a complex substratum of sociolinguistic issues and involves conscious engagement with stylistic levels (as, for example, in the various statements on style in the imperial handbooks of Constantine VII Porphyrogennetos)[30] as well as, in other cases, the 'transposition' of already-existing texts into another stylistic level (as in Symeon Metaphrastes' project to rewrite the 148 vitae of the *Menologion* in the later tenth century).[31] Interestingly, in the fourteenth century we see again further translations of saints' lives into a higher register.[32] The fact of the matter is that with the appearance of the Palaiologan historical metaphrases we are faced for the first time with a sustained effort to translate substantial and highly prestigious prose texts 'down' a few notches on the stylistic scale. It could

[28] G. Horrocks, *Greek: A History of the Language and its Speakers* (London and New York, 1997), 166 and 196–200.

[29] R. Browning, 'A fourteenth-century prose version of the *Odyssey*', DOP 46 (1992), 27–36, esp. 29; and *idem*, 'The language of Byzantine literature', in S. Vryonis Jr., ed., *The 'Past' in Medieval and Modern Greek Culture* (Malibu, 1978), 103–33, esp. 125.

[30] See the discussions in Browning, 'The language of Byzantine literature', 118–19, 125, and Horrocks, *Greek*, 179–204. Generally, these provide extremely good broad orientation through the evolving stylistic and linguistic preferences of Byzantine writers. Besides these two works, of course, key studies on stylistic levels are those of I. Ševčenko, 'Levels of style in Byzantine prose', *JÖB* 31/1 (1981), 289–312, and E. Trapp, 'Learned and vernacular literature in Byzantium: dichotomy or symbiosis?', *DOP* 47 (1993), 69–76.

[31] C. Høgel's 'The redaction of Symeon Metaphrastes: literary aspects of the Metaphrastic martyria', in Høgel, ed., *Metaphrasis: Redactions and Audiences in Middle Byzantine Hagiography* (Oslo, 1996), 7–21, and *Symeon Metaphrastes: Rewriting and Canonization* (Copenhagen, 2002) comprise major reassessments of the tenth-century Metaphrastic project. Høgel's account extensively revises the earlier assessment of P. Lemerle, *Le premier humanisme byzantin* (Paris, 1971), 293–4.

[32] A.-M. Talbot, 'Old wine in new bottles: the rewriting of saints' Lives in the Palaeologan period', in S. Ćurčić and D. Mouriki, eds., *The Twilight of Byzantium: Aspects of Cultural and Religious History in the Late Byzantine Empire. Papers from the Colloquium held at Princeton University 8–9 May 1989* (Princeton, NJ, 1991), 15–26.

be argued, plausibly, that this was linked to a certain Byzantine cultural insecurity in the mid-fourteenth century, which reflected the political circumstances of the age, a by-product of which was the commissioning of these metaphrases. Translation proper (i.e. interlingual translation), especially from Latin into Greek, also experienced a flowering in the fourteenth century, notably with Maximos Planoudes at the dawn of the century,[33] and later with the extensive translation work of Demetrios Kydones.[34] However, apart from implying an opening-up of cultural pores, this is probably not directly associated with the intralingual metaphrastic activity of the mid-century.

Before reconsidering the possibility of a commissioned translation project, it is worth looking at the relation the historical metaphrases may have with another translation of the 1340s, the *Basilikos Andrias*, or *Imperial Statue*, by Nikephoros Blemmydes.[35] The linguistic level of the *Imperial Statue* is remarkably close to the two histories, although the subject matter and vocabulary are very different, which makes comparison more problematic. For example, verbs of motion are rarely encountered in the *Imperial Statue*, the presence of which provides a very useful comparative tool in the other metaphrases. However, besides the similar *extent* to which the original has been transformed, there are a number of other strong similarities: certain words do occur much as in the *Alexiad* and the Choniates metaphrases, for instance, the favourites οἰκονομῶ (to render διατίθεμαι, παρασκευάζω and πρυτανεύω), παραυτίκα (to render παραχρῆμα), and twin sets of words such as ἐζήτει καὶ παρεκάλει to render ἐξαιτοῦμαι, which display what Hunger called 'Abundanz' – the tendency to expand – in the metaphrase, as we saw earlier in the case of δωρεαὶ and πόλεις.

However, one very useful difference between the *Imperial Statue* and the metaphrases of the histories is that it is preserved in its entirety, and its title tells us the names of the authors of the metaphrase – George Oinaiotes[36]

---

[33]   See the recently published *editio princeps* of M. Papathomopoulos, I. Tsavari and G. Rigotti, eds., Αὐγουστίνου Περὶ Τριάδος βιβλία πεντεκαίδεκα, ἅπερ ἐκ τῆς Λατίνων διαλέκτου εἰς τὴν Ἑλλάδα μετήνεγκε Μάξιμος Πλανούδης. Εἰσαγωγή, Ἑλληνικὸ καὶ Λατινικὸ κείμενο, Γλωσσάριο, Academy of Athens – A. Manousis Library 3 (Athens, 1995), and M. Papathomopoulos, ed., *Anicii Manlii Severini Boethii De consolatione philosophiae. Traduction grecque de Maxime Planude*, Academy of Athens: Corpus philosophorum medii aevi. Philosophi byzantini 9 (Athens and Brussels, 1999).

[34]   See especially A. Glycofrydi-Leontsini, 'Demetrius Cydones as a translator of Latin texts', in C. Dendrinos, J. Harris, E. Harvalia-Crook and J. Herrin, eds., *Porphyrogenita, Essays on the History and Literature of Byzantium and the Latin East in Honour of Julian Chrysostomides* (Aldershot, 2003), 175–85.

[35]   See note 4 above.

[36]   *PLP* 3528. See also Hunger, *Anonyme Metaphrase*, 31–5.

and George Galesiotes[37] – about whom we do know some facts, the most notable being that George Galesiotes was in charge of the *sakellion* of the Church between about 1330 and 1346.[38] Significantly, these dates coincide with the dating we prefer for the historical metaphrases.

There are a number of reasons to suspect that perhaps all three of these translations belong to a common translation project of the mid-fourteenth century that was designed to provide a young prince (the obvious candidate being the young John V Palaiologos) with key textbooks on imperial conduct and imperial history of the crucial Comnenian century. Recall that one of the manuscripts of the Choniates metaphrase (contained in the composite MS Parisinus gr. 3041) may well have been part of the imperial library.[39] While this amounts to informed conjecture, it might explain one other aspect of the historical metaphrases. They seem to have been somewhat hurriedly produced, and imperfections remain, while they make no sustained effort to render effectively the more erudite literary aspects of the originals. If they are the product of some kind of literary salon such as those Ševčenko hints at in his study 'Society and intellectual life in the 14th century',[40] they are not exactly showpieces, although they do occasionally have their entertaining moments. As we have seen, they keep to the basic flow of the narrative, they are careful to include all the historical details, they preserve the drama, but they do not attempt to provide the reader with a full rendering of the literary frills and embellishments of the original, although they do occasionally don a kind of literary cloak of their own, usually of a somewhat biblical colour, which, given the period and society, hardly comes as a surprise: in other words, they serve the somewhat pedestrian, though by no means ignoble, task of conveying the historical substance of the originals. In the margins of the text contained

---

[37] *PLP* 21026.

[38] The full title of the work is Τοῦ σοφωτάτου κυροῦ Νικηφόρου τοῦ Βλεμμύδου λόγος περὶ βασιλείας μεταφρασθεὶς πρὸς τὸ σαφέστερον παρὰ τοῦ σακελλίου τῆς μεγάλης ἐκκλησίας διακόνου κυροῦ Γεωργίου Γαλησιώτου καὶ τοῦ Οἰναιώτου κυροῦ Γεωργίου τῶν λογιωτάτων ἀνδρῶν καὶ ῥητόρων.

[39] This manuscript, which, as noted, is a composite manuscript, is discussed in detail by G. T. Dennis, 'Four unknown letters of Manuel II Palaeologus', *Byz* 36 (1966), 35–40; *idem*, *The Letters of Manuel II Palaeologus*, CFHB 8 (Washington, DC, 1977), xxi–xxiv; A. Angelou, *Dialogue on Marriage with the Empress Mother* (Vienna, 1992), 8–9, and C. Dendrinos, *An annotated critical edition (editio princeps) of Emperor Manuel II Palaeologus' treatise* On the procession of the Holy Spirit, unpublished doctoral dissertation of the University of London (Royal Holloway College, 1996), esp. 430–47. The relationship in this manuscript between the Choniates metaphrase and the various texts of the emperor Manuel II is not clear.

[40] I. Ševčenko, *Society and Intellectual Life in Late Byzantium* (London, 1981), study I, 88.

in MS Parisinus gr. 3041 are some childish sketches, of boats and faces.[41] Could these be the idle scribbles of a bored young prince?

If, then, these translations *are* related to the mid-fourteenth century court, would it be legitimate to view them as serving a sordid role such as that despised by Henry Ford and Bono? Are they perhaps cheap versions of key texts designed for the hasty education of a member or members of the ruling elite, a crib for acquiring easy knowledge of the history of the state, and a grimy tool for holding on to power? The years between 1342 and 1347 were an all-time low for the Byzantine state, when the emperor John was still a boy and his foreign mother, Anne of Savoy, may also have been in need of a crash course in Byzantine politics.[42] These unstable years put a seal on the fragmentation and decline of what was left of Byzantium, and the metaphrases could be taken as a kind of linguistic reflection of this. Or are they, after all, the product of an earnest group of literary amateurs who were keen to open up otherwise inaccessible, learned texts, an example of what Hans-Georg Beck referred to as the 'desire of the Byzantines not to allow linguistic barriers to come between them and their own historical self-awareness'?[43] Ultimately, it is impossible to give a definitive answer. Whatever the case, and whatever the literary shortcomings of the metaphrases compared with their majestic originals, they undoubtedly suggest that those who read them were far from considering history to be 'bunk'.

---

[41]   MS Parisinus gr. 3041, fols. 253, 268 and 270ᵛ.

[42]   The civil wars of the 1340s are famously described by John VI Kantakouzenos (ed. L. Schopen, II [Bonn, 1831], 12.4–9) as the worst in the history of the Roman state: ἐπεὶ δὲ μετὰ τὴν Ἀνδρονίκου τοῦ νέου τελευτὴν ὁ χαλεπώτατος τῶν πώποτε μνημονευομένων τοῖς Ῥωμαίοις πρὸς ἀλλήλους πόλεμος ἀνερριπίσθη, ὃς ὀλίγου δεῖν πάντα ἀνατέτραφε καὶ διέφθαρκε, καὶ τὴν εὐδαίμονα καὶ μεγάλην τῶν Ῥωμαίων βασιλείαν ἀσθενεστάτην καὶ ὥσπερ εἴδωλον ἀπέδειξε τῆς προτέρας.

[43]   Beck, *Geschichte der byzantinischen Volksliteratur*, 6.

SECTION III
Narrator

4. Psellos and 'his emperors': fact, fiction and genre

Michael Jeffreys

The *Chronographia* of Michael Psellos is the most attractive literary work of the Byzantine eleventh century. One may hear even non-Byzantinists discuss the character of Constantine Monomachos or the efforts of Romanos Diogenes to resurrect the Byzantine army. They will have read a translation in a modern language, probably that in English in the Penguin Classics series.[1] By making the *Chronographia* so readable, Psellos has given its version of the history of the period a dominant position in all subsequent historiography. It influenced Skylitzes and Attaleiates, his contemporaries, in both positive and negative ways.[2] It has eclipsed, as we shall see, everything else that Psellos himself wrote. Since first publication in 1874, it has been edited several times and widely translated, dominating both primary and secondary bibliography for the mid-eleventh century. So powerful a text must be analyzed with special rigour, read against the grain, and deconstructed. I offer a contribution in this spirit.

By the second or third reading, for me at least, the *Chronographia* is just as attractive but less persuasive. Psellos speaks so much about himself that we begin to question the emerging authorial personality. There is a large bibliography on the subject,[3] much of it with a strong moral line (or at times with theoretically based determination not to show moral prejudice). Psellos' value as a historian is undermined, though he is allowed some marks for originality. He is accused of rampant self-centredness, morbid self-justification, and the constant manufacture of dramatic situations.

---

[1]   Trans. E. R. A. Sewter, *Fourteen Byzantine Rulers* (London, 1953; revised edn. Harmondsworth, 1966).

[2]   Psellos' connections with them are conveniently summarized by Hunger, *Literatur*, I, 372–93.

[3]   Examined by E. Pietsch, *Die Chronographia des Michael Psellos: Kaisergeschichte, Autobiographie und Apologie* (Wiesbaden, 2005), esp. 6–20 (henceforth Pietsch, *Chronographia*); see also V. Katsaros, 'Τὸ δραματικό στοιχεῖο στὰ ἱστορικὰ ἔργα τοῦ 11ου καὶ 12ου αἰώνα', in P. Odorico et al., eds., *L'écriture de la mémoire*, 281–316, esp. 294–302.

My own reaction at this level is to see him as the ultimate name-dropper, one who must constantly have said, 'As the emperor told me yesterday', or even more, 'As I told the emperor'. There is a good Greek word for this: *parresia*, access to the powerful and open and convincing address to them. The Psellos of the *Chronographia* is so obsessed with *parresia* that we mistrust him, as we mistrust such persons in our world. Is he concealing something? Or is our mistrust confusing cultural situations that should be kept distinct? This is not a trivial issue, because Psellos and his emperors interact on approximately a third of the pages of the *Chronographia*. What Psellos says and does in these passages is important, while what the emperors say and do includes some of the most memorable and influential scenes in the book.

Since the subject is well trodden and the methodology to be used elusive, a short article like this had better find a single useful issue on which to formulate a relevant question and answer it. I have chosen the following: in the passages of the *Chronographia* where Psellos describes himself in contact with emperors, is he trying to reflect what 'really happened', with whatever degree of distortion, or is he using some other strategy? If answers must be plotted on a continuum rather than in black or white, where on the continuum should we place them? Most possible approaches to the text must begin by testing it like this, and on the results subsequent lines of enquiry will depend.

To evaluate the *Chronographia* in these passages, we need comparative material, covering events from different points of view or different literary frameworks. Skylitzes and Attaleiates will help. But if we go beyond the genre of history to other surviving contemporary texts with historical content, we are again swamped by Psellos: there are several dozen speeches with historical references,[4] more than 500 letters,[5] often useful for our purpose, many poems,[6] and hundreds of small treatises,[7] a handful

---

[4] More than 50 are contained in Michael Psellus, *Oratoria minora*, ed. A. R. Littlewood (Leipzig, 1985) (henceforth *Or. min.*), and *Orationes panegyricae*, ed. G. T. Dennis (Stuttgart and Leipzig, 1994) (henceforth *Or. paneg.*). But there are a number more yet to receive an edition later than the middle of the twentieth century.

[5] E. Papaioannou, 'Das Briefcorpus des Michael Psellos. Vorarbeiten zu einer kritischen Neuedition, *JÖB* 48 (1998), 67–118 (henceforth Papaioannou, 'Das Briefcorpus').

[6] *Michaelis Pselli Poemata*, ed. L.G. Westerink (Stuttgart and Leipzig, 1992) (henceforth *Poem.*).

[7] See Michael Psellus: *Theologica* I, ed. P. Gautier (Leipzig, 1989); *Theologica* II, eds. L. G. Westerink and J. Duffy (Munich and Leipzig, 2002) (henceforth *Theologica* II); *Philosophica minora* I, ed. J. Duffy (Stuttgart and Leipzig, 1992); *Philosophica minora* II, ed. D. J. O'Meara (Leipzig, 1989) (four volumes containing a total of more than 250 texts, mostly brief).

with historical interest. Unlike the *Chronographia*, most of this other work is virtually unknown. I shall here examine speeches and letters, reading Psellos against Psellos, to see how far this other historical material supports or undermines the narrative of the *Chronographia*. The method, suggested long ago by the Greek critic Ioannis Sykoutris,[8] has been surprisingly neglected, but provides useful results. Conclusions will be both literary and historical.

The most significant texts, and the least known, are the letters. These are very numerous – they are awaiting a consolidated edition[9] – and they are often difficult to read and hard to put into context, while the epistolary genre is notoriously perilous for historical use. These are presumably the reasons why the letters are almost universally neglected in discussions of the *Chronographia*. But half of them are available in twentieth-century editions, the nineteenth-century edition of Sathas is not bad, and many of them seem to me to make intelligible statements on persons and situations recognizable from the *Chronographia*. A thorough reading of the letters has led directly to the writing of this paper.

To put in context the methodology of reading one narrative against another, it will be best to start with a very obvious clash between two of Psellos' works from other genres, neither letters nor the *Chronographia*. It concerns two speeches on the patriarch Michael Keroularios written in 1058 and 1060. The first is the prosecution speech against Keroularios when imprisoned by Isaac I.[10] He was to be tried in Thrace, as he was too popular in the capital, but he died on arrival there, so the speech was not delivered. Its framework is forensic, but its rhetoric of uncompromising vilification derives from the *psogos*.[11] Keroularios is accused of heresy, rebellion, murder, sacrilege and indifference. Heresy involved religious performances by John and Niketas, founders of Nea Moni (Chios), with a female associate, Dosithea. These tainted Keroularios, as he had invited them to the patriarchate. Dosithea, a possible feminist heroine, is attacked with full patristic misogyny. Keroularios is accused of double rebellion,

---

[8]   His proposal is analyzed and put into its intellectual context by E. de Vries-van der Velden: 'The letters of Michael Psellos, historical knowledge and the writing of history', in W. Hörandner and M. Grünbart, eds., *L'épistolographie et la poésie épigrammatique* (Paris, 2003), 121–35.

[9]   For details, see Papaioannou, 'Das Briefcorpus'.

[10]   Michael Psellus, *Orationes forenses et acta*, ed. G. T. Dennis (Stuttgart and Leipzig, 1994), 1–103 (henceforth *Or. for.*).

[11]   This seems a regular pattern, to judge from the only other preserved example of an eleventh- or twelfth-century forensic speech: see P. Magdalino, 'The *Bagoas* of Nikephoros Basilakes: a normal reaction?', in L. Mayali and M. M. Mart, eds., *Of Strangers and Foreigners (Late Antiquity–Middle Ages)* (Berkeley, CA, 1993), 47–63.

quick to drive out the fading Michael VI but slow to accept his successor
Isaac. A few deaths involved in stopping a full-scale assault on the capital
are ascribed personally to Keroularios as murders. Sacrilege was the
careless exposure of tombs in demolishing a church. Indifference was
ignorance of the bible and theology, and undertaking patriarchal duties
when visibly too bored or angry to approach God.

Within two years Psellos gave another long oration on Keroularios in
front of his tomb, before the next patriarch Constantine Leichoudes and
the new imperial pair, Constantine X and Eudokia, Keroularios' niece.[12]
This time the genre is encomium ending in hagiography. Keroularios'
theology has now become immaculate, and his handling of the transition
from Michael VI to Isaac is called masterful. In this version, as Keroularios
reaches Thrace for his trial (in fact his death), Psellos' undelivered *psogos*
turns into angelic choirs conducting the saintly patriarch to heaven. The
differences are great, but easily explicable. At one level, they are an extreme
form of the ambivalence towards Keroularios seen throughout Psellos'
work, especially his letters.[13] He was often positive, especially when the
patriarch sent him fish (S56–9), but negative when churchmen whom
Keroularios probably controlled persecuted him for unorthodox theology
(S139, M16). The charge is important if, as Anthony Kaldellis shows,
Psellos was a major source of theological instruction.[14] The two speeches
are rhetorical reactions to similar events under different patronage and
opposite political circumstances: the nervous hostility of Isaac demanded
condemnation and *psogos*; the wounded reverence of Constantine and
Eudokia needed encomium and hagiography. There are no untruths or
fictions, just different genres occasioned by different contexts.

Let us now turn our attention to the *Chronographia*, testing Psellos'
connections to the emperors he served, searching for more serious
discrepancies.[15] The chapter on Constantine IX Monomachos is by far the
longest and contains far more methodological discussion than any other,

---

   12   Sathas, ed., *Mesaionike Bibliotheke*, IV, 303–87.

   13   References to letters in this paper will come from four collections, each
referred to by collection abbreviation and letter number: Sathas, ed., *Mesaionike
Bibliotheke*, V (abbreviated S); E. Kurtz and F. Drexl, *Michaelis Pselli Scripta minora
magnam partem adhuc inedita* II (Milan, 1941) (K–D); P. Gautier, 'Quelques lettres de
Psellos inédites ou déjà éditées', *REB* 44 (1986) 111–97 (G); E. V. Maltese, 'Epistole
inedite di Michele Psello', *Studi Italiani di Filologia Greca* III 5 (1987) 82–98, 214–23,
and 6 (1988) 110–34 (M). There is also a single letter edited by Papaioannou, 'Das
Briefcorpus', 110–12 (Pap).

   14   A. Kaldellis, 'The date of Psellos' theological lectures and higher religious
education in Constantinople', *BSl* 63 (2005), 143–51.

   15   There is a highly intelligent analysis of Psellos' relationships with the
different emperors of the *Chronographia* by Jakov Ljubarskij, *Michail Psell. Ličnost'i*

leading me at least to give it a major role in the genesis of the whole.[16] We shall check this reign first. Then I shall examine Isaac I and Constantine X, where I think clear insights are available to guide discussion. Finally I shall tidy up the others: Theodora and Michael VI, followed by Eudokia, Romanos IV, Michael VII and even Nikephoros III, at the start of whose reign I date Psellos' death. The discussion will include scattered narratological comment on the *Chronographia*. Several proposals by Ljubarskij, especially in an issue of the periodical *Symbolae Osloenses*,[17] have now been seriously taken up by Efthymia Pietsch.[18] I will summarize here some of her conclusions with further hints as to how analysis might continue, especially via simple criteria of point of view and narrative focalization.

The *Chronographia* in its sole complete manuscript[19] comes after the text of Leo the Deacon, whose narrative it also continues chronologically. Psellos starts on **Basil II** as an omniscient narrator, with little concern to explain his sources. Later he introduces himself into the text as a witness to some of its most dramatic scenes, like the poison-ravaged corpse of **Romanos III** (4.4)[20] and the dying **Michael IV** in his Bulgar triumph (4.50). In the reign of **Michael V**, Psellos as narrator becomes more prominent. He was working in the palace when the people attacked, rode round the city watching the rioters (5.27), and later observed the emperor Michael at Stoudios after his abdication (5.39–43). He was bearing witness to extraordinary situations, but not yet integral to the action.

Constantine IX Monomachos

In this reign the narrative changes completely. It was Monomachos who gave Psellos his high position at court, and the *Chronographia* amply confirms a close relationship. We are at the emperor's elbow in every

---

tvorčestvo (Moscow, 1978), consulted in revised form in the Greek translation Ἡ προσωπικότητα καὶ τὸ ἔργο τοῦ Μιχαὴλ Ψελλοῦ (Athens, 2004), 305–23.

[16]   One might object that a major dimension of the book's structure suggests a diachronic plan, tracking the effectiveness of Byzantine rulers, declining from Basil II and returning to a high level with Isaac I. But even in this framework Psellos (and his readers) are far more seriously challenged by the decline and its results in the reign of Constantine IX than in any other.

[17]   Ljubarskij, *et al.*, 'Quellenforschung', 5–21.

[18]   E. Pietsch, *Die Chronographia des Michael Psellos* (as in note 3) (henceforth Pietsch, *Chronographia*).

[19]   Par. gr. 1712.

[20]   References to the *Chronographia* will be in this form, with the book number and the section number in Arabic numerals. The edition used is that of S. Impellizeri (*Michele Psello, Imperatori di Bisanzio*, 2 vols. [Milan, 1984]).

crisis of his reign. We witness relationships with his empress Zoe, two successive mistresses, and the marginal characters who enjoyed and abused his trust. Narratological mechanisms for this change are discussed at length by Pietsch.[21] I shall summarize her ideas with my own coloration. In one way Psellos, as an imperial secretary, simply had close access to Monomachos and chose to report it. But this is complicated by Psellos' long, traditional discussions over historical impartiality, intense yet largely bogus. He must have intended the impression of Monomachos given in the *Chronographia* to be extremely negative. But by pretending to be anxious neither to criticize his imperial benefactor nor favour him unduly, making comparisons that turn out to be invalid and using the *reductio ad absurdum* in a creative way, he could slip in negative points with added barbs of credibility, particularly when stories of the emperor's stupidity end up on the credit side as Psellos balances his character. Psellos' other works on Monomachos, when allowance is made for genre, do not differ from the *Chronographia*. The speeches[22] are well informed and adulatory, while the letters[23] show him losing patience with an irrational and unpredictable master, and deciding, for various reasons, to retreat to a monastery.

Isaac I Komnenos

Psellos' account in the *Chronographia* of his relationship to Isaac begins with an embassy on which he was sent by Michael VI after his defeat by Isaac in the civil war of 1057 (7.15–33). He was accompanied by Constantine Leichoudes and a certain Alopos. The next few days form a climax of the work. The focalization of narrative is on Psellos himself, making the reader share his terror, amazement and triumph, in a role more independent than any he assumed under Monomachos. Narrative of the embassy makes a vivid and memorable text, helping to raise tension by postponing details of the outcome, rejecting a more omniscient line.

The ambassadors are to offer the victorious Isaac the role of caesar as deputy and successor to Michael, with other guarantees (7.15–20). It is unlikely Isaac will accept. He welcomes them politely, but holds negotiations in the middle of his army to overawe them (7.22–31). Psellos was spokesman. We hear of his beating heart, the angry opposition of

---

[21]   Pietsch, *Chronographia*, 66–97.

[22]   *Or. paneg.*, 1–106 (seven speeches).

[23]   Letters referring to his departure for the monastery include S114 and S115, over problems of returning to court after his tonsure; S36, S37, K–D191 and G17, all to John Xiphilinos, the friend who had gone to Olympos before him; and S185, K–D170 and K–D267, to monks on Olympos who were advising him over his entry there.

surrounding troops, and the technical skill of his rhetoric. Isaac quietens the troops and, amazingly, agrees. The ambassadors report back to Michael VI before returning to Isaac (7.32–3). All is going well when the negotiations are interrupted by events elsewhere. Isaac's supporters in the capital enlist the aid of Keroularios, as discussed in the two speeches of Psellos with which we began. Michael is forced to abdicate, and Isaac occupies the city peacefully (7.34–8).

The narration continues with his triumphal entry. Psellos fears for his life, as representative of the loser, but Isaac compliments his conduct as ambassador. Before entering the capital, they have a philosophical debate (7.39–43), culminating in a request by Isaac for advice on rulership, which Psellos eagerly provides.[24] Isaac appoints him *proedros* and a major counsellor. As Isaac's rule continues, the *Chronographia* allows us to view his private as well as his public face (7.44–50). There is some support in other texts of Psellos for a close relationship to Isaac. In his hagiographic encomium of Keroularios, he expresses surprise that one so close to Isaac as he had no warning of the patriarch's arrest.[25] There is also a long letter (K–D156) of advice to Isaac on his Danube campaign, discussing the obduracy of the Pecheneg leader Selte, and warning of possible treachery from other Pechenegs.

The *Chronographia* expresses regret at the failure of Isaac's zealous attempts to reform Byzantine public finances, blaming him sorrowfully for trying too much too soon (7.51, 58–63). It mentions several groups who might have opposed him, but describes no actual opposition, apart from Keroularios. In fact Isaac's failure seems to result from an accident. In the *Chronographia*, after returning from the Danube, he overtaxes himself while hunting and catches a bad chill (7.73). In Skylitzes and Attaleiates, he is struck by lightning while hunting, Skylitzes mentioning a boar that ran into the sea.[26] Am I alone in suspecting this mixture of motives and unlikely accidents? I have no insights to suggest into this problem, but a general sense that something is being concealed.

The emperor was carried to the palace. The *Chronographia* shows Psellos visiting him the next day, finding him seriously ill (7.74–83). Just as at his

---

[24]   The discussion between Psellos and Isaac is a major element in the case made by A. Kaldellis for the underlying agenda of Psellos in the book. The analysis here does not invalidate Kaldellis' proposals, but will involve their restatement in a less direct form, along lines he has already foreshadowed: see A. Kaldellis, *The Argument of Psellos' Chronographia* (Leiden, Boston and Cologne, 1999), 167–8.

[25]   Ed. Sathas, *Mesaionike Bibliotheke*, IV, 368–9.

[26]   Attaleiates, *Historia*, 52.20–25; *Ioannes Skylitzes Continuatus*, ed. E. Tsolakes (Thessalonike, 1968), 108.1–10.

own father's death two decades before,[27] he took the emperor's pulse, disputing the doctor's diagnosis. Isaac grew worse, thinking of tonsure and abdication, for which the empress wrongly blamed Psellos. Isaac chose as successor Constantine X, a colleague from the civil war (7.84–7.a14). The *Chronographia* then describes how Psellos transferred symbols of rule to the new emperor, and presided over initial ceremonial. Isaac's brother John said nothing, or in one source refused an offer of the throne[28] – an unexpected reaction in the husband of Anna Dalassene and father of the young Alexios I, the single-minded refounders of the Comnenian dynasty, who may have been present.[29]

Let us read Psellos against Psellos over his relationship with Isaac. The first problem is that a passage in his speech prosecuting Keroularios describes as a failure the first embassy to Isaac, during which Psellos made his great speech.[30] In this it agrees with Skylitzes and the Armenian historian Aristakes, though Skylitzes' evidence is almost worthless, as it involves Katakalon Kekaumenos, whose role in Skylitzes is always suspect.[31] Another ambassador, Constantine Leichoudes, gained more of Isaac's favour than Psellos, winning a major secular post, then appointment as patriarch. This is stated in Psellos' funeral oration for Leichoudes[32] and confirmed by a letter of the time (S73), which calls Leichoudes the only route to Isaac. But the real problem arises from letters Psellos sent to Isaac, his family and entourage during his reign. In the corpus of letters they are conspicuous for humility, distance from their recipients, and ignorance of events. The picture given is utterly different from that discussed above, from the *Chronographia*.

S112, to Isaac's Bulgarian wife, laments that life was unbearable in Isaac's absence, and wonders if his current trip was for business or hunting. S70 and S191 were sent to imperial *notarioi*, on campaign with Isaac. Psellos

---

[27] 'Encomium on his Mother', in Sathas, ed., *Mesaionike Bibliotheke*, V, 38, translated by A. Kaldellis, *Mothers and Sons, Fathers and Daughters: The Byzantine Family of Michael Psellos* (Notre Dame, IN, 2006), 84.

[28] *Nicephori Bryennii Historiarum libri quattuor*, ed. P. Gautier (Brussels, 1975), 79–85.

[29] The most recent word on this difficult scene is V. Stankovic, *Komnini u Carigradu (1057–1185). Evolucija jedne vladarske parodice* (Belgrade, 2006), 12–16 [*The Komnenoi in Constantinople (1057–1185). The Evolution of a Ruling Family*].

[30] *Or. for.*, 51.

[31] Aristakes, *Récit des malheurs de la nation arménienne*, eds. M. Canard and H. Berbérian (Brussels, 1973), 104.112; Skylitzes, 497.1–11. See J. Shepard, 'A suspected source of Scylitzes' *Synopsis Historion*: the great Catacalon Cecaumenos', *BMGS* 16 (1992), 171–81.

[32] 'Encomium on Leichoudes', in Sathas, ed., *Mesaionike Bibliotheke*, IV, 388–421, here 409.

knows nothing of their location or activities, but pictures the scene from his knowledge of them and the emperor. S69 and S161 offer encomia to the emperor himself. In the first he refers only to Isaac's preparations before leaving the city, asking to be made a regular encomiast. The second explicitly complains that he cannot write encomia if, as at present, he is ignorant of what the emperor is doing. I have said that K–D156 provides sensitive advice for Isaac on dealing with the Pechenegs, especially Selte. However, it shows no knowledge of the situation beyond Selte's intransigence. Around that time he wrote S113 to Theodore Dokeianos, the emperor's nephew,[33] whom he did not know well. He hopes Theodore is enjoying hunting with Isaac, and says he has sent the emperor a letter: could Theodore please say how it was received, so he can decide whether to write again. S120 is also to Dokeianos, consoling him on the death of his father-in-law. Psellos adds that he has stopped sending the emperor little treats from the city, fearing to be called a flatterer. Finally K–D215 mentions a letter Psellos received from Isaac, after sending many of his own without reply. Unsophisticated delight and flattery lead to a promise to deposit the letter in his tomb.

In all this we are far from a philosopher-emperor asking a philosopher Psellos in the *Chronographia* how to rule well (7.39–43), or an amateur medic with whom the emperor was so familiar as to offer his wrist for him to take his pulse (7.74). In trying to reconcile the evidence of the two genres, I can reach only one conclusion: briefly stated, the letters, which show Psellos in a humble light, with a point of view limited to the time of writing, must be closer to the 'truth', while passages showing more glorious links of *parresia* with Isaac in the *Chronographia* must approach a kind of narrative fiction. I cannot imagine any scenario to explain the contrary assumption – that the level of contact implied by the dialogue of philosophers shown in the *Chronographia* is an accurate reflection of the links that existed between the two men, replaced by the humility, distance and unsophistication of the letters.

Constantine X Doukas

We may ask whether Psellos' references to himself should always be treated as fiction in the *Chronographia*, at least after Monomachos. I mentioned that the narrative of the abdication of Isaac made Psellos transfer imperial insignia to Constantine X. What do Psellos' letters say on their relationship? First, there are many letters accompanying small, symbolic gifts sent to Constantine, his wife Eudokia, his brother John, and their children,

---

[33] See K. Varzos, Ἡ γενεαλογία τῶν Κομνηνῶν (Thessalonike, 1984), I, 59–61.

apparently at festivals.[34] No such letters are datable to other reigns, suggesting unusual familiarity. Equally, soon after Constantine's accession Psellos wrote to reassure John, the caesar and the emperor's brother, that he still enjoyed Constantine's favour (G8), adding in support details from the past of the new imperial family, confirming his own statements that he was close to them. Many other letters to John are preserved.[35] They have been put in a suggested chronological progression in the *Prosopography of the Byzantine World*,[36] with Psellos losing intimacy and credibility first with Constantine and then with John himself. Here the *Chronographia*'s picture of closeness to Constantine at his succession is credible, though it did not last.

There are other letters about Constantine, maybe many of them. The main event at the start of his reign was a plot (in 1060 or 1061) to drown the imperial family as they returned from a festival at the Mangana complex in the north of the city. The *Chronographia* tells us that many conspirators were exiled, and shows Constantine weeping at table with Psellos, as the exiles cannot share their food (7.a22). There are more than 20 letters written by Psellos to named and unnamed exiles, datable or not, discussing the progress of their cases before the emperor, and others where it is unsure that the case has to do with exile. Some, apparently representative of the rest, name Constantine X as the emperor concerned, or speak of attempts to have the caesar John convince his brother.[37] Others do not name the emperor.[38] I have not so far in the *Prosopography* attributed all the cases without imperial names to Constantine X, but it is tempting to do so. The persona of the recalcitrant emperor, often pictured as a castle to be besieged to convince him to recall one exile or another, is familiar yet estranged, sympathetic yet obstinate, as we should expect of Constantine after the cooling of relations with Psellos I have described. This contrasts with the chapter on Constantine in the *Chronographia*, where Psellos remains the perpetual insider, and also with rhetorical texts. In a funeral speech

---

[34]   The list includes S48, S52, S74, S104, S132, S137, K–D234, K–D235, K–D236, K–D237, K–D238, K–D239, K–D271, K–D272, G26. Another letter, S68, addressed to the patriarch Constantine Leichoudes, is likely to belong to the same sequence.

[35]   They include S72, K–D40, K–D213, K–D231, K–D233, G1, G2, G4, G5, G7, G10, G11, G13.

[36]   At http://www.pbw.kcl.ac.uk/, accessed 15 June 2010.

[37]   Several of these are connected with the case of Nicholas Skleros, which is dated to the early 1060s by the common attachment of Nicholas and Psellos to Anastasios Lizix, who died tragically at that time: see K–D37, K–D44, K–D56, K–D63, K–D127. Others are K–D48 and K–D79.

[38]   Examples are S22, S93, S97, S98, S123, K–D41, K–D85 and K–D168.

for John's wife in 1064 or 1065,[39] Psellos pictures himself making similar medical interventions involving the imperial family as at Isaac's abdication in 1059. The letters make us doubt whether he would have been welcome.

We now have three different kinds of relationship for Psellos to the three emperors studied. With Constantine IX he was certainly close, an impression confirmed by the *Chronographia*. With Isaac I the intimacy shown in the *Chronographia* seems fictitious. With Constantine X he may have been very close at the beginning of the reign, but the relationship cooled later, with little indication of the change in the *Chronographia*. How do the other emperors fit these patterns?

Theodora

Her reign follows the death of Monomachos, and begins and ends in the *Chronographia* with Psellos enjoying great *parresia*. The empress confides in him both before and after accession, but intimacy breaks down through the jealousy of his rivals (6.a13–14). Then, as Theodora lies dying 20 months later, Psellos is present to see her ministers, mainly eunuchs, choose the nonentity Michael VI to succeed her, in the correct belief that he will leave them in power (6.a19–21). But other evidence raises doubts about the validity of the narrative.

First, we learn that Psellos' withdrawal to a monastery on Mt Olympos in Bithynia, glossed over in the *Chronographia* (6.189, 6.a13), lasted nearly a year. The best evidence is a couplet joking that Psellos-Zeus could not survive even a year away from his goddesses.[40] But if he had been away for much less than a year, the satire would be expressed differently. Some letters imply he left the capital to avoid Monomachos. But if he was consulted there by Theodora at her accession, he must have left after Monomachos' death. We also have a report, signed by Theodora, of a trial over Psellos' adopted daughter that would place him outside the monastery for at least the last two months or so of her reign.[41] Most awkward of all is a series of letters addressed to Theodora's chief eunuch, Leon Paraspondylos,[42] well

---

[39] E. Kurtz and F. Drexl, *Michaelis Pselli Scripta minora magnam partem adhuc inedita*, I (Milan, 1936), 155–89, here 176.

[40] *Poem.*, no. 21, p. 259.

[41] *Or. for.*, 143–55. See the fascinating suggestion of D. Jenkins in *Mothers and sons, fathers and daughters* (as in note 27), 139–46, that the report is another example of Psellian fiction. The Psellos who is a principal in the trial over his adopted daughter cannot legally equate with a Psellos who writes the official report of the trial; but it was plainly based on a real trial, which must have taken a good deal of his time.

[42] S7, S8, S9, S10, K–D72, K–D87, G32, Pap.

analyzed by Eva de Vries-van der Velden.[43] They begin under Monomachos, when Leon was out of favour and Psellos could be condescending. Then, at Theodora's accession, with Psellos tonsured, his friend Leon became her all-powerful minister. Psellos rejoiced, sent an encomium of Leon and a curriculum vitae, and waited for a post. Nothing came. His letters moved from sycophancy to complaint. Eventually he was offered what he called, disparagingly, the *trimenon* of Papa-Sabinos (S198 and S199: maybe an elementary teaching post?). Did this frustrated waiting for Leon occur in the capital, or on Olympos? Later, how did Psellos recover the *parresia* necessary to be present when Leon and his colleagues chose Theodora's successor? Historical scenarios may be written to explain everything, but they can only be rather strained: neither the diary of the reign nor the motivation of events is convincing.

Michael VI

Connections with this emperor are fewer. The *Chronographia* places Psellos at Michael's side at the tipping-point of his reign, when he denied promotions to eastern generals after giving them generously to civil functionaries (7.2–3). Michael and Leon Paraspondylos pushed the generals, led by Isaac, to revolt. At this point Michael consulted Psellos, apparently for the first time, and received detailed advice that he followed only in part (7.9–11). What was Psellos doing earlier at the emperor's side? The imperial and rebel armies met near Nicaea, and Isaac was victorious. In this emergency, Michael turned to Psellos for the embassy already discussed, leading to Isaac's reign.

Eudokia

Keroularios' niece and empress of Constantine X, she was twice briefly ruler in her own right. The first time, just after Constantine's death, the *Chronographia* saw her mainly as mother and guardian of the young Michael VII, of whom Psellos was tutor (7.b2–3). Psellos also heard her expressing a contempt for supreme power that impressed him (7.b4). The first report of close contact between them was when she asked him about breaking her solemn oaths by inviting Romanos IV to marry her and save the empire. Psellos argued against the plan, but discovered it was a *fait accompli*, with Romanos already in the palace. The *Chronographia* makes Eudokia take Psellos with her to inform the sleeping Michael VII.

---

[43] E. de Vries-van der Velden, 'Les amitiés dangereuses: Psellos et Léon Paraspondylos', *BSl* 60 (1999), 315–50.

She sat on Michael's bed with Psellos at her side, telling her son of her decision to remarry, adding unconvincing promises from Romanos that Michael's position would be respected. Michael listened impassively, then went downstairs to meet Romanos and begin ceremonies of marriage and coronation (7.b5–8).

Psellos was also involved in Eudokia's second interlude of rule. After Manzikert he claims he was the first to insist that Romanos, when unexpectedly freed, should not be accepted back as emperor (7.b27). This returned imperial power to Eudokia and Michael VII. But the Varangians soon insisted that Michael be freed from his mother's apron strings, and made a noisy coup in the palace (7.b28–30). The *Chronographia* claims Psellos was with Eudokia as she ran in terror to hide in a distant room, where he stood guard. After the coup she was deposed, tonsured, and shut in the monastery of Piperoudion.

The relationship to Eudokia shown in Psellos' other works is not inconsistent with the narrative of the *Chronographia*, though some of the scenes listed above imply a degree of intimacy not fully supported by other evidence. In a letter to Constantine X accompanying a gift, she is explicitly called Psellos' benefactor, and spiritual niece (S104, cf. *Chronographia* 7.b4). There is at least one speech to her after her wedding to Romanos, congratulating her on her choice of emperor.[44] Later in the reign of Romanos, Psellos wrote to encourage the exiled caesar John, saying that Eudokia and even Romanos often spoke of him at table, implying that Psellos often ate with the imperial couple: but this may be fiction to reassure John (S156). One letter describes a misunderstanding over a document Eudokia issued permitting Psellos to receive money: he thought it was for regular sums, to avoid constant requests, while she intended a one-off payment, and accused him of ingratitude when he used the document again. He sent her indignantly a long list of emperors he had served well without such accusations (G35). Years later, in 1078, the last year of his life, Psellos would write in a tragic letter (K–D214) that meetings with Eudokia, released from the monastery by Nikephoros Botaneiates, were his only consolation in the capital after losing both his natural and adoptive families.

---

[44]   *Or. paneg.*, 124–6.

Romanos IV

The situation over Psellos' relations with Romanos is more complex. As well as the need for *parresia* with the ruling sovereign, we must bear in mind that the last section of the *Chronographia* was finished in the reign of Michael VII,[45] the figurehead of the Doukai against Romanos in the civil war after Manzikert. Thus the *Chronographia* shows no sympathy for Romanos, as is well shown by Eva de Vries-van der Velden.[46] He is portrayed as an incompetent warmonger fighting the Turks without reason, marching in all directions with no overall plan and recklessly exposing himself to danger, making defeat at Manzikert inevitable. He is shown as ungrateful and vindictive towards Eudokia and her family. Psellos' good advice was always disregarded, especially during his personal participation in the second of Romanos' three campaigns (7.b16). How much of this derives from Romanos' reign, and how much was added for political reasons after the civil war? Again Psellos' other texts, particularly the letters, give a more nuanced picture. Here, as elsewhere, whole letters may have been suppressed, but I can see no signs of editorial interference with extant texts.[47]

It will be no surprise that Psellos displays a desire for *parresia* with Romanos, despite subsequent disapproval of all he did. This is shown by encomia, already mentioned, written for Romanos and Eudokia, admiring the new emperor and husband for his refusal to enjoy the comforts of office and marriage and his amazingly quick departure on campaign. There are several such speeches written for different occasions.[48] It is hard to decide whether they were commissioned by the authorities and delivered, or submitted as a portfolio of what he could produce if asked.

Romanos spent 1068 on a long campaign reaching Hierapolis in northern Syria. This was a difficult time for Psellos. He regretted the absence of five friends in the army, writing to them to reconcile two bishops in central Anatolia.[49] He complained to all correspondents of loneliness, reading lifeless books, sensing the loss of imperial favour. Even Eudokia was invisible, probably through pregnancy. He wrote to Romanos himself, listing the imperial virtues he missed, begging him to return (S6). In all these letters the predominant tone is positive towards the army's progress.

---

[45]   The two sections of the book, with their different implications for structures and motivations, are conveniently summarized by Pietsch, *Chronographia*, 4–5.

[46]   E. de Vries-van der Velden, 'Psellos, Romain IV Diogénès et Mantzikert', *BSl* 58 (1997), 274–310 (henceforth 'Mantzikert').

[47]   I have discovered, in personal discussion, that the future editor of Psellos' letters, Stratis Papaioannou, has a similar view.

[48]   *Or. paneg.*, 175–6 (four speeches).

[49]   S124, K–D146, K–D147, K–D148, K–D149, G25

Critical notes are rare: he praises the successes of the campaign, but questions why they were not properly advertised (G25), and complains that the army has marched a long way, wondering if they will stop before they reach India (S124).

As Romanos returned early in 1069, Psellos sent congratulations, requesting a bigger role in his propaganda machine, with another encomium (K–D5). As already mentioned, Romanos reacted by inviting, even pressing, him to go on that year's campaign. This has been judged a way to prevent Psellos from plotting in the capital – an unlikely suggestion not supported in any source.[50] Psellos did not complete the campaign, writing from Caesarea to friends still in the army that he was not fit enough (S176). In another letter to a friend in the capital he described the campaign in a way that persuades Eva de Vries-van der Velden that it was the campaign of 1071, placing him with the group sent off to Chliat when the army was divided before Manzikert.[51] Her arguments are detailed but not fully convincing. This letter confirms the message of the *Chronographia* (7.b16) that Psellos' value to the army was his expertise in the classicizing military *taktika*. Romanos (Psellos claims) enviously acknowledged inferiority to Psellos in this area, especially in siegecraft – a comment to be borne in mind while evaluating such manuals. After Psellos reached home, he told everybody of Romanos' bravery and devotion, making Eudokia's heart swell with pride. He told Romanos he whispered the news to the couple's baby son, who smiled, squirmed and squealed appropriately (S3).

Disregarding the unconvincing proposal of Eva de Vries, I know of no surviving letters of Psellos to Romanos datable to 1070 or 1071. I do not know if this is significant. A case could be made that anything written then had to be suppressed, but it would be a poor *argumentum ex silentio*. By the end of 1071 or early 1072, Psellos was writing to encourage Andronikos Doukas in the civil war *against* Romanos (S145). Finally there is the infamous message in 1072 virtually congratulating Romanos on being blinded, to achieve a divine inner light (S82). The point of that letter is to exonerate Michael VII from guilt over the crime. It will serve as a transition to Michael, Psellos' last significant emperor.

---

[50] De Vries-van den Velden, 'Mantzikert', 287–8 and *passim*, shows how this proposal is untenable.

[51] S186, cf. 'Mantzikert', 294–310. I see inadequate justification for her assumption that S186 is written from the point of view of the besieger of a city – an assumption that becomes crucial to her argument. I would date the letter rather to 1069.

Michael VII

I have found no conventional letters addressed by Psellos to Michael. This could mean that the tie between them was weak, or that they were so close that letters were unnecessary. Though evidence is slight, there may be truth in both explanations. We have seen Michael as Psellos' pupil, noting his presence when Eudokia told her son about her remarriage. There are two routine speeches composed for Michael, the more interesting of which concerns Psellos' own expulsion and return to court after a misunderstanding.[52] Among other texts written for him by Psellos, one is an art-historical review of an ancient carved relief,[53] another a chrysobull over the exchange of estates,[54] a third a collection of texts on the Incarnation for a sympathetic Turkish ruler,[55] and a fourth the collection of varied questions and answers called *De omnifaria doctrina*.[56] There is also a letter to Robert Guiscard, in which Psellos makes Michael recognize the bloodthirsty Norman as a fellow pacifist, and propose a marriage alliance.[57]

In all this there is a sense that Psellos now composes texts for others, not as an agent in his own right. The only exceptions have more private motivations: preserved speeches praise elderly colleagues before it is too late; preserved letters discuss family affairs with old friends, rather than dispensing advice to provincial judges as in previous reigns, justifying his earlier claims as the governor of the empire's governors (S95). The *Chronographia* on Michael VII is painfully adulatory, despite claiming the contrary, probably with a good deal of irony, reminiscent of its approach to Constantine IX.[58] Psellos has become a passive functionary, close to power yet rarely taking initiatives, waiting for the instructions of Michael and his ministers.

One group of his texts is in verse. Psellos wrote prose introductions to different subjects, religious, legal, rhetorical and others he judged necessary for emperors. Most were dedicated to Monomachos.[59] But these high-style compositions were difficult to read for half-educated princes, and he needed to find a more accessible medium. How could a writer whose career demanded regular display of the high style simplify this material to make it readable? The answer, paradoxically, was to write in verse. Fifteen-syllable verse, unlike other literary forms available to Psellos,

---

52   *Or. min.*, 6–10; *Or. paneg.*, 127–30.
53   *Or. min.*, 126–7.
54   *Or. for.*, 155–9.
55   *Theologica* II, 17–41.
56   *De omnifari doctrina*, ed. L. G. Westerink (Nijmegen, 1948).
57   *Or. for.*, 176–81.
58   See the intelligent proposals in Pietsch, *Chronographia*, 111–28.
59   *Poem.*, p. VII.

had no ancient models to follow, allowing more relaxed language and style than prose. Most of the poems were first written for Monomachos, while others were composed or updated for Constantine X and Michael VII.[60] One poem, on the Song of Songs, was one of the last texts on which Psellos worked. One manuscript sketches an introduction to Nikephoros III Botaneiates, who came to the throne just before Psellos' death.[61]

It is time for conclusions. First, on narrow positivist criteria of historical truth. Do not trust the *Chronographia* on Psellos without external confirmation, at least after Monomachos. Fictions may appear anywhere. These are not just distortions of genre, but the active rewriting of what 'happened', and its replacement by what needed to happen to achieve the author's purposes. But, surprisingly, it is from Psellos' own letters that help is at hand for those who wish to make the distinction. It is often possible to get behind the charming aesthetics of friendship characteristic of the epistle and concentrate on the communication of the moment, isolating useful nuggets of truth. Papaioannou's edition, when it appears, will force scholars to confront and use a surprising volume of hard information, not only for political historians but also on issues like imperial administration and land tenure. I expect it to be cited by future historians as much as the *Chronographia*. All this material is in fact available now, in rather less accurate and accessible form.

A decade ago Ruth Macrides wrote an article called 'The Historian in the History',[62] centring on Psellos. She showed that his presence in the *Chronographia* is far greater than could be justified by Thucydidean preference for eyewitness history. I would like to amplify the reasons she gave for this development. I assume that the narrative structure of the *Chronographia* began with the reign of Monomachos. For him, Psellos developed a discourse combining extreme closeness to the ruler with complex arguments over impartiality, allowing him to paint a lively but negative picture while escaping charges of ingratitude. The Monomachos framework was easily extended backwards by omniscient narration, with occasional dramatic foretastes of Psellos' own arrival on the scene. However, under subsequent rulers, after tonsure in 1054, his position close to the emperor was undermined, leaving him from time to time without *parresia*. As a result he faced a choice: either change his narrative methods and the horizon of expectations of his audience, or create a situation, false at times, in which intimacy was maintained with Monomachos' successors. Questions of ingratitude would again need to be addressed, especially with

---

[60] *Poem.*, esp. p. VII, discussed (with reference to inferior previous editions) by M. Jeffreys, 'The nature and origin of the political verse', *DOP* 28 (1974), 164–5.

[61] *Poem.*, pp. X–XI, 13–14.

[62] In Constantinides, *et al.*, eds., *ΦΙΛΕΛΛΗΝ*, 205–24.

Isaac I and Michael VII, due to the timing of the work's two editions.[63] He made the latter choice. The Historian entered Psellos' History because that is how the imperial secretary of Monomachos chose to narrate his reign. He stayed there because the method was so persuasive and successful in literary terms that a narrative position as close confidant to subsequent emperors had to be established, often fictitiously, in defiance of changing situations.

I do not wish to deny that Psellos was self-centred, that he dramatized events in which he was involved, or that he was interested in justifying himself and emphasizing his qualifications for writing the *Chronographia* through his closeness to the emperors portrayed. It is natural for works of fiction to show some attitudes that coincide with those of their authors. I do think, however, that his most fundamental purpose was none of the above, but to write a persuasive and engrossing narrative. I would suggest that he had found a formula that allowed his creative talents wide opportunities, and stuck to it.

I shall end by looking at Psellos' project in the *Chronographia*, using some simple vocabulary of literary criticism. The assumption is usually made that the narrator who may be heard in the text is, or approximates very closely to, the historical Michael Psellos, just as the British Prime Minister during the Second World War who appears in the various historical texts of Winston Churchill is Winston Churchill. The identity confirms the authenticity of the story in a Thucydidean way. We shall allow Psellos or Churchill to present themselves in the best possible light, but their names are a kind of guarantee of the basic factual framework of the text. If we found that Churchill has inverted the order of events or narrated a meeting that did not happen, we should feel cheated. Psellos is often accused of writing a memoir, not history,[64] and this accusation implicitly confirms him in the category of Churchill. The historical Michael Psellos is made morally responsible for the story that the narrator of the *Chronographia* tells, and this judgement has dominated all forms of criticism of the book.

This paper has found discrepancies between the narrator of the *Chronographia* and the epistolary voice of Psellos (which, it argues, is closer to that of the historical person). This seems to indicate failure on the part of the writer. But what if these differences are part of the programme of the book? It is obvious that Psellos is willing to experiment in the *Chronographia* with the narratorial voice: the famous tour of the living arrangements of Constantine IX, which is interrupted so as not to disturb the emperor with his mistress, must put us on our guard (6.65). Stratis Papaioannou, working from completely different premises, has come to conclusions about Psellos' idea of the self (including the self as narrator) that foreground flexibility,

---

[63]   See note 45 above.
[64]   Pietsch, *Chronographia*, 16–17.

even ambiguity.[65] Perhaps the most striking pieces of evidence have already been mentioned here: Efthymia Pietsch distinguishes a Psellos-narrator who falsely pretends to be fair to Monomachos from another who seeks to make him seem foolish and unreliable, while David Jenkins (over a different text) points out that the Psellos who is principal in a trial cannot legally equate with a Psellos who reports the trial, throwing the status of the narrative into serious doubt before it begins.[66]

I would like to suggest three ways forward for research:

1. More deconstruction of the *Chronographia* (and of other texts of Psellos with complex narrative patterns), widening and developing the attempts made here. Reinterpretation of influential texts can only begin by destructive penetration of their veneer of persuasiveness.

2. Extension of Pietsch's narratological analysis of the volume, and the selection of an appropriate framework in which to chart the results. The narrative focalization of the text is so central to the way that the story is told that I am tempted to suggest cinematic analysis, the writing of a *Chronographia* storyboard. It might be found, for example, that the Psellos who is the work's hero acts as its narrative lens and often as the stimulus that causes other characters to behave in an interesting way. Nearly all his interactions discussed above have a significant visual dimension. If that proves so, the conclusions above may be restated as follows: the character was given *parresia* in the book in some cases when the historical Psellos had lost it because it was essential for him to be brought within close camera range of the narrative's key agents, especially the emperors.

3. The *Chronographia* is steadily being uncoupled from the simple and literal role it has so far played in the modern writing of Byzantine history. The opinions it offers have always been suspect, but its events have been seen as guaranteed by the identity of the writer. Now they too must be under question. Historians, who are used to such complexities, must establish and apply more subtle criteria for the recoupling of eleventh-century Byzantine history to its most influential source.

---

[65] Particularly in S. Papaioannou, 'Michael Psellos's rhetorical gender', *BMGS* 24 (2000) 133–46.

[66] See notes 21 and 41 above.

5. 'Listen, all of you, both Franks and Romans': the narrator in the *Chronicle of Morea*

Teresa Shawcross

In the course of the late twelfth and early thirteenth centuries, large swathes of territory belonging to the Byzantine Empire fell to western invaders. This process of conquest and occupation was accompanied by the development in the regions in question of a tradition of historical writing different to anything that had preceded it. A key position within the new tradition came to be occupied by the *Chronicle of Morea*. Comprising a detailed account of the formation and government by the Villehardouin dynasty of the Principality of Morea, a crusader state of considerable longevity that had the Peloponnese as its heartland, the *Chronicle* was initially composed in the early decades of the fourteenth century, but then revised and updated on a number of occasions. This work is known in versions both in prose and in verse, and is extant today in a total of four vernacular languages: Greek, French, Spanish and Italian.

What is striking about these versions is the degree to which they feature in their fabric a complex, and highly modulated, series of interactions between orality and literacy. When approaching texts that, like the *Chronicle*, can be identified as having been generated in the vernacular, we may be inclined, as indeed were the first scholars who worked on the subject, to view these texts in terms of a dichotomy, categorizing them according to whether they are considered to be either records of the actual creation and simultaneous performance of improvised songs or stories given by illiterate artists, or, alternatively, fully literate products that originated with authors whose compositional method was determined by the practices of reading and writing.[1] In the one instance, a work is created and disseminated

---

[1] The point is discussed in G. Spadaro: 'Studi introduttivi alla Cronaca di Morea. Storia della scoperta del testo e problemi relative ad esso', *Siculorum Gymnasium* 12 (1959), 125–52; 'Studi introduttivi alla Cronaca di Morea, II', *Siculorum Gymnasium* 13 (1960), 133–76; 'Studi introduttivi alla Cronaca di Morea,

essentially by mouth and ear, and relies for its survival exclusively upon memory, while, in the other, the hand and the eye play a crucial part. This black-and-white classification is, however, not satisfactory with regard to medieval material, for the possibility should be raised of the existence, in an era that antedated the invention and widespread use of printing, of what may be referred to as 'intermediate' texts – of texts, in other words, that resist facile interpretation and taxonomy. In the Middle Ages, wherever the vernacular had begun to emerge as a medium appropriate to literature, replacing classicizing idioms, highly developed non-written forms can be argued to have preceded and in part predetermined the style of written works. Although writing was ultimately to transmute this legacy into a new aesthetic, earlier modes of thinking and of expression persisted. Most notably, epic poems, even after their passage into manuscript circulation, continued to be characterized by a fundamental debt to oral tradition. Other genres, such as historiography, also used – sometimes extensively, sometimes in more vestigial form – these inherited techniques, creating textual tensions not easily resolved.

The written text

All of the different versions of the *Chronicle of Morea* owe their existence to milieux that were far removed from the 'pristine' orality of cultures

---

III', *Siculorum Gymnasium* 14 (1961), 1–70; *Contributo sulle fonti del romanzo greco-medievale Florio e Plaziaflora* (Athens, 1966); 'Problemi relativi ai romanzi greci dell'età dei Paleologi, I. Rapporti tra Ἰμπέριος καὶ Μαργαρώνα e Φλώριος καὶ Πλατζιαφλόρε', *Hell* 28 (1975), 302–27; 'Imberio e Margarona e Florio e Plaziaflore', in *Miscellanea neograeca, atti del I Convegno Nazionale di Studi Neograeci* (Palermo, 1976), 181–6; 'Problemi relativi ai romanzi greci dell'età dei Paleologi, II. Rapporti tra la Διήγησις τοῦ Ἀχιλλέως, la Διήγησις τοῦ Βελισαρίου e Ἰμπέριος καὶ Μαργαρῶνα', *Hell* 29 (1976), 278–310; 'Sul Teseida neogreco', *Folia neohellenica* 2 (1977), 157–60; 'Problemi relativi ai romanzi greci dell'età dei Paleologi, III. Achilleide, Georgillàs, Callimaco, Beltandro, Libistro, Florio, Imberio e Διήγησις γεναμένη ἐν Τροίᾳ', *Hell* 30 (1977–78), 223–79; 'L'inedito Polemos tis Troados e l'Achilleide', *BZ* 71 (1978), 1–9; 'L'Achilleide e la Ἱστορικὴ ἐξήγησις περὶ Βελισαρίου di Gheorghillàs', *Diptycha* 2 (1980–81), 23–41; 'Ἡ Ἀχιλληΐδα καὶ ἡ Ἱστορία τοῦ Βελισαρίου', *Hell* 33 (1981), 82–97. See also A. F. van Gemert and W. Bakker, 'Ἡ Ἀχιλληΐδα καὶ ἡ ἱστορία τοῦ Βελισαρίου', *Hell* 33 (1981), 82–97; H. Eideneier, 'Leser- oder Hörerkreis? Zur byzantinischen Dichtung in der Volkssprache', *Hell* 34 (1982–3), 119–50; R. Beaton, 'The oral traditions of modern Greece: a survey', *Oral Tradition* 1 (1986), 110–33, and *idem*, 'Orality and the reception of late Byzantine vernacular literature', *BMGS* 14 (1990), 174–83; D. Holton, 'Orality in Cretan narrative poetry', *BMGS* 14 (1990), 186–98.

ignorant of writing.[2] The content of these versions is such that it provides a lengthy commentary upon the workings of a society that, instead of being preliterate, can, on the contrary, be shown to have valued the penned word *qua* artefact or witness, and consequently to have relied to a substantial degree upon that word in order to regulate and solemnize its affairs. References abound in the *Chronicle* to the importance not only of the written medium in general,[3] but of specific categories of writing, with mention being made of the role played in public business by letters of appointment, treaties, charters and proclamations of various sorts, property deeds, records of legal judgements, and, finally, by wills and testaments,[4] while – time and time again – attention is drawn to the ritual of the penning, sealing and dispatch or presentation of documents.[5] On a

---

[2]   See, for the Greek, J. Schmitt, ed., *The Chronicle of Morea (Τὸ χρονικὸν τοῦ Μορέως), A History in Political Verse, Relating the Establishment of Feudalism in Greece by the Franks in the Thirteenth Century, Edited in Two Parallel Texts from the MSS of Copenhagen and Paris, with Introduction, Critical Notes and Indices* (London, 1904); for the French, J. Longnon, ed., *Livre de la conquête de la Princée de Morée – Chronique de Morée (1204–1305), Publiée pour la Société de l'Histoire de France* (Paris, 1911); for the Spanish, A. Morel-Fatio, ed., *Libro de los fechos et conquistas del principado de la Morea compilado por comandamiento de Don Fray Johan Ferrandez de Heredia, maestro del Hospital de S. Johan de Jerusalem (Chronique de Morée au XIIIe et XIVe siècles publiée et traduite pour la première fois pour la Société de l'Orient Latin)*, Publications de la Société de l'Orient Latin série historique 4 (Geneva, 1885); for the Italian, C. Hopf, ed., *Chroniques gréco-romanes inédites ou peu connues* (Berlin, 1873), 414–68.

[3]   Schmitt, ed., *The Chronicle of Morea*, vv. 679, 1893, 2337, 2351, 3482, 4620, 8745; Longnon, ed., *Livre de la conquête de la Princée de Morée*, §§12, 14–15, 165, 257, 529, 605; Morel-Fatio, ed., *Libro de los fechos*, §§9, 10, 11–12, 14, 16, 20, 141, 149, 155, 174, 253, 291, 292, 294, 295, 314, 316, 360–61, 418, 428–30, 440–42, 451; Hopf, ed., *Chroniques gréco-romanes inédites ou peu connues*, 415, 416, 432, 440, 464, 466.

[4]   Schmitt, ed., The Chronicle of Moreα, vv. 316, 364, 365, 579, 1893, 2162, 2330, 2335, 2340, 2341, 2380, 2418–19, 2444; 2942, 2943, 3030, 7689, 7695, 7725, 7771, 7781, 8253, 8579, 8770; Longnon, ed., *Livre de la conquête de la Princée de Morée*, §§17, 32, 126, 165; 141, 164, 170, 526, 528, 533, 590, 605; Morel-Fatio, ed., Libro de los fechos, §4, 148, 166, 175, 177, 420–423, 418; Hopf, ed., Chroniques gréco-romanes inédites ou peu connues, 433, 440, 451, 459, 467.

[5]   Schmitt, ed., *The Chronicle of Moreα*, vv. 315, 579, 2381, 2427, 2445, 2941, 3031, 4571, 7695, 7750, 8125, 8745, 8753–4; Longnon, ed., *Livre de la conquête de la Princée de Morée*, §§126; Morel-Fatio (ed.), *Libro de los fechos*, §§4, 16, 314, 326; Hopf, ed., *Chroniques gréco-romanes inédites ou peu connues*, 415, 416, 440, 467. In addition to this, it may be noted that the literacy skills of a number of characters within the narrative is commented upon with approval, while even in instances where individuals cannot or chose not to read or write themselves, these individuals are nonetheless shown interacting with texts and performing literate tasks through recourse to a clerk or other intermediary. See, for example, Schmitt, ed., *The Chronicle of Morea*, v. 7535: 'μισὶϱ Λινάϱδον τὸ ὄνομα, ἀπὸ τὴν Πούλιαν ἦτον· /

different level, confirmation of the power of written communication was offered by the material existence of the *Chronicle of Morea* itself. When dealing with this work, one is, after all, dealing with a series of manuscripts that have resulted from the multiple activities of a small army of redactors, translators and scribes. Thus, it is possible to analyze the visual dimension – the structure of individual codices, the lay-out of the text on each page, the nature of the script or of the illustrations included. On opening one manuscript (Brussels, Bibliothèque royale de Belgique, MS 15702), you immediately encounter a linear table of contents whose presence is surely an indication of a concern to guide the reader and facilitate his or her task (fols. 1r–3v). Setting out to peruse another manuscript (Madrid, Biblioteca Nacional, MS 10131), you come across illuminated initials that visually divide the text into introduction, main body and conclusion (183r, 194r, 257v). As you turn the pages of yet another (Paris, Bibliothèque nationale de France, MS gr. 2898), you discover an entire paratextual apparatus, including rubrics or headings before individual sections of the narrative ('How they made the Count of Champagne captain of the host', fol. 112v.) and marginal glosses or notes ('Alexios, blood-brother of Isaac', fol. 117 v).[6] Each manuscript of the *Chronicle* is a physical object that came into being so that it might be possessed, handled and repeatedly scrutinized. Whereas the spoken word – the 'winged word', as it has been called since Homeric times – displays the tendency to vanish into thin air immediately after its utterance, these objects circulated, suffering damage from water and worm-holes, and acquiring greasy paw-marks or other unmistakeable signs of readership.

There were a variety of ways in which a reader might leave his mark – by using blank margins or folios to inscribe ownership,[7] do sums,[8] keep a record of a commercial voyage,[9] copy a prayer,[10] or practise calligraphy.[11] In moments of leisure or boredom, he might well draw a hunting scene,[12]

ἄνθρωπος ἦτον φρόνιμος, καλὰ γραμματισμένος' ('Sir Leonard was his name and he was from Apulia / a wise and well-educated man'; v. 3482: 'Ὁρίζει, γράφουν γράμματα, μαντατοφόρους στέλνει' ('He commands them to write letters, and sends messengers').

   6   'Πῶς ἔποικαν τὸν κόντε τῆς Τσαμπάνιας καπετάνιον στὰ φουσσᾶτα'; 'Ἀλέξιος αὐτάδελφος Ἰσάκου'.

   7   Copenhagen, Det Kongelige Bibliotek, MS Fabricius 57, fol. 1r.

   8   Turin, Biblioteca Nazionale Universitaria, B. II. I (LXVI), fols. 130r–v.

   9   Turin, Biblioteca Nazionale Universitaria, B. II. I (LXVI), fols. 129v and 132 r–v.

   10   Turin, Biblioteca Nazionale Universitaria, B. II. I (LXVI), fol. 129r.

   11   Turin, Biblioteca Nazionale Universitaria, B. II. I (LXVI), fol. 129r.

   12   Brussels, Bibliothèque royale de Belgique, MS 15702, fol. 182v.

the *Arma Christi*,[13] or a pentalpha,[14] producing doodles that are redolent, in turn, of secular preoccupations, religious fervour, and just possibly a certain interest in dabbling in the arcane. Treating the text in a somewhat more invasive fashion, he might give a different title to an existing exemplar of a work ('History of the Emperor of Constantinople, Baudouin, Count of Flanders'; 'Story in the Vernacular of how the Franks took / Jerusalem and Many Other Places in the Orient'),[15] or even produce a completely new exemplar himself, noting lacunae in the manuscript from which he was working: 'A page is missing here'; 'Here two pages are missing. For this reason I have left space'; 'Here a good six pages are missing, where the rebellion in the Escorta is narrated, which was against Prince Guillaume and in favour of the emperor's brother, the grand domestic.'[16] If aspects of the content of the text failed to meet with complete approval, the offending passages could be crossed or torn out, or, going still further, an extensive project of rewriting embarked upon.[17]

Because of their very nature as manuscripts, none of the extant texts of the *Chronicle of Morea* can be viewed as a genuine product of simultaneous processes of oral composition, performance and transmission. Nor, for that matter, should we imagine that, somewhere behind it all, there lurks an act of dictation by an illiterate person and the faithful recording or transcription of that act by an amanuensis. Nowhere in the *Chronicle of Morea* is there an admission, such as is sometimes found articulated in other historical narratives (e.g. 'arranged to have put into writing'; 'dictated this work'),[18] that an arrangement of this type ever existed. On the contrary, the *Chronicle* can be shown conclusively even in its earliest form to have been a compilation put together from a range of written sources, some of which

---

[13] Turin, Biblioteca Nazionale Universitaria, B. II. I (LXVI), fol. 1v.

[14] Copenhagen, Det Kongelige Bibliotek, MS Fabricius 57, fols. 27v–28r.

[15] 'Histoire de l'empeureur de Constantinople, Baulduin comte de Flandres' (Brussels, Bibliothèque royale de Belgique, MS 15702, fol. 1r); Ἱστορία βουλγάρε, πῶς οἱ φράγκοι ἔλαβον / τὴν Ἱερουσαλὴμ καὶ πολλὰ ἄλλα μέρη ἀνατολικά' (Paris, Bibliothèque nationale de France, MS gr. 2898, fol. 1r).

[16] 'Manca un foglio' (Venice, Biblioteca Marciana, Mss. Italiani Classe VII Cod. 712 coll. 8754, fol. 47r); 'Cy endroit faillent .ij. feuilles. Pour ce j'ay leissiée l'espace' (Brussels, Bibliothèque royale de Belgique, MS 15702, 182v); 'Cy endroit fault bien .vj. feuilles, la ou parole du revel de l'Escorta, qui contre le prince Guillerme fu, et se rendirent au frère de l'empereur, au grant domestic. Si ay leissié le espace' (Brussels, Bibliothèque royale de Belgique, MS 15702, fol. 61r).

[17] See, for example, Copenhagen, Det Kongelige Bibliotek, MS Fabricius 57, fols.18v–129r, for deliberate mutilation of the manuscript.

[18] See Robert de Clari, *La Conquête de Constantinople*, ed. J. Dufournet (Paris, 2004), §120 ('a fait metre en escrit'), or Geoffroi de Villehardouin, *La Conquête de Constantinople*, ed. J. Dufournet (Paris, 2004), §120 ('cest oevre dicta').

are openly acknowledged ('as the *Great History of the Kingdom of Jerusalem* tells us and bears witness to' and 'as we found written in detail in the *Book/ of Conquest*, which was written at that time in Syria'),[19] while others are identifiable from references of a more indirect nature.[20] It may be argued, therefore, that, at every stage in the genesis and life of the *Chronicle of Morea*, paper and ink played a vital part.

Yet, for all that, a fundamental distinction should be made between the physical means by which a work is composed and the type of discourse employed in that composition.[21] We turn now to an examination of the stylistic attributes of the *Chronicle of Morea*, focusing on one particular exemplar, Fabricius 57 of the Kongelige Bibliotek or Royal Library of Copenhagen, which, while it is not itself the original work preserved intact, can be shown to be that work's single most reliable witness.[22] The text contained in this manuscript is written in Greek in a fifteen-syllable line known as *political verse*, and will henceforth be referred to for the sake of convenience as the Χρονικὸν τοῦ Μορέως (*Chronikon tou Moreos*). It has hitherto been studied with regard to the manner in which the narrative is structured, with attention being given to two basic building-blocks, namely the phrase or formula, and the episode, an approach that has opened the way for further research.[23] In examining the influence of orality upon the text, my concern, rather than addressing every permutation of the question, is to look at a single aspect that can be argued to be of primary importance. The aim of the analysis that follows is to try to conjure up an image of the narrator who accompanies us, speaks out to us from the written page, as we leaf through our manuscript.

---

[19]   Longnon, ed., *Livre de la conqueste de la Princée de Morée*, §2 : 'selonc ce que la grant estoire dou reaulme de Jherusalem nous raconte et tesmoigne'; Schmitt, ed., *The Chronicle of Morea*, vv. 91–2: 'Καθὼς ἐγγράφως ηὕραμεν λεπτῶς εἰς τὸ Βιβλίο / τῆς Κουγκέστας, ὅπου ἔγινεν ἐτότες στὴν Συρίαν'.

[20]   See, for instance, Schmitt, ed., *The Chronicle of Morea*, vv. 7567–8, 7587, 7589, 7638; Longnon, ed., *Livre de la conqueste de la Princée de Morée*, §§519, 521, 522, 524.

[21]   The distinction is made most forcibly by F.H. Bäuml, 'Medieval texts and the two theories of oral-formulaic composition: a proposition for a third theory', *New Literary History* 16 (1984), 37.

[22]   T. Shawcross, *The Chronicle of Morea: Historiography in Crusader Greece* (Oxford, 2009).

[23]   M. Jeffreys: 'Formulas in the *Chronicle of Morea*', *DOP* 27 (1973), 163–95, and 'The *Chronicle of the Morea* – a Greek oral poem?', *Actes du XIV congrès international des études Byzantines*, eds. M. Berza and E. Stănescu (Bucharest, 1975), 153–8; T. Shawcross, 'Oral residue and narrative structure in the Chronicle of Morea', *Byz* 75 (2005), 310–33.

The singer of tales

Ἐν τούτῳ ἄρξομαι ἀπ'ἐδῶ κι ἀφκράζου τὰ σὲ λέγω' ('Now here I begin, so listen to what I have to say', v. 1356). To whom (or, indeed, to what) should these words be attributed? Such questions, concerning the entity in charge of telling the story, seem so banal as to require no discussion – until an attempt is made to answer them. The historical personage, the author responsible for the line just quoted, does not stand before us now, at this moment, in flesh and blood, but has in fact quitted the scene long ago, leaving behind what he has wrought. All that could have been transmitted of him is an empty name, a signature, if you will, claiming responsibility for the text. In this particular instance, that too is absent. While information regarding the individual answerable for the Χρονικὸν could conceivably once have been available either in the prologue or the epilogue, these sections have proven to be vulnerable, both because of their physical location as extremities of the text, and also because the data they contained was especially receptive to alteration or omission, a circumstance that has resulted in the handing down of the work to us as anonymous. Even had this not been the case, pseudonymity of various sorts – from the invention of a *nom de plume* to the appropriation of a pre-existing authorial identity – was so rife in medieval texts that the relation between person and onomastic would still necessarily have been equivocal. Thus, one finds the acrostic of the name of Romanos the Melode (e.g. 'THE PSALM OF ROMANOS'; 'POEM OF HUMBLE ROMANOS'; 'OF WRETCHED ROMANOS'; 'SONG OF ROMANOS'; 'THIS OF THE LOWLY ROMANOS'; 'THIS HYMN OF HUMBLE ROMANOS') woven into the writings of subsequent practitioners of the *kontakion*, a certain type of religious verse that he had made famous,[24] while a less flattering, but not entirely dissimilar, form of tribute to a master results from the attachment of the name of the imperial panegyricist Theodoros Prodromos to the titles (e.g. 'Verses of Theodore Prodromos the Poor to the Emperor Manuel Komnenos'; 'Other Verses of the Monk Hilarion Prodromos the Poor Addressed to the Most Noble Emperor Manuel') and text (e.g. 'and you will lose your Prodromos, your best encomiast'; 'Do not be fooled, most noble lord, by these antics of Prodromos the Poor'; 'Upon your soul, Prodromos, sit still!') of a group of especially shameless and outspoken

---

[24]   *Sancti Romani Melodi Cantica: Cantica Dubia*, ed. P. Maas and C. A. Trypanis (Berlin, 1970), 34: 'ΡΩΜΑΝΟΥ Ο ΨΑΛΜΟΣ'; 45: 'ΤΟΥ ΤΑΠΙΝΟΥ [sic] ΡΩΜΑΝΟΥ ΠΟΙΗΜΑ'; 52: 'ΤΟΥ ΤΑΛΑ ΡΩΜΑΝΟΥ'; 59: 'ΑΙΝΟΣ ΡΩΜΑΝΟΥ'; 71: 'ΤΑΥΤΗ Η ΩΔΗ ΤΟΥ ΕΛΑΧΕΙΣΤΟΥ ΡΩΜΑΝΟΥ'; 91: 'ΤΟΥ ΤΑΠΕΙΝΟΥ ΡΩΜΑΝΟΥ [Ο] ΥΜΝΟΣ [ΟΥΤΟΣΣ] [sic]'.

begging poems.[25] None of these practices, however, should be viewed as impeding an analysis of narrative voice in the *Chronikon tou Moreos* – for that voice can be shown to reside elsewhere, with the first-person narrator or narratorial 'I'.

Who, then, speaks to us? How are we to describe him? There is a certain resemblance between the narrator of the *Chronikon tou Moreos* and a real-life figure with which contemporaries in the fourteenth century would have been exceedingly familiar – that of the storyteller or singer of tales who, working within an oral medium, achieved professional or quasi-professional status. Encountered in a variety of guises in accounts of the medieval period dealing with the eastern Mediterranean, this individual was referred to by terms such as those of *juglars* and *menestreux*, of παιγνιῶται, of ἀγύρται or μηναγύρται, and, lastly, of ἀγείροντες and μυθολόγοι.[26] A number of such persons are recorded as participants in the Fourth Crusade. Of them, the person with the highest profile was Conon de Béthune, who was born in the region of Artois, and performed, while still in France, before both Philippe Auguste, the French king, and countess Marie de Champagne, the great patroness of literature,[27] before going on to hold important administrative posts in the Latin Empire, culminating, in 1219, with that of regent.[28] Conon was admired greatly by his fellow crusaders, who praised him as a 'good, wise and most eloquent knight'.[29] Others were *troubadours* and *trouvères*, many of whom had, already in Italy, flocked to Boniface de Montferrat, the future ruler of the Kingdom of Thessalonike, attracted by his reputation for culture and generosity.[30]

---

[25]   H. Eideneier, ed., *Ptochoprodromos: Einführung, kritische Ausgabe, deutsche Übersetzung, Glossar* (Cologne, 1991), Poem III, Title: 'Στίχοι Θεοδώρου τοῦ Πτωχοπροδρόμου πρὸς τὸν βασιλέα κὺρ Μανουὴλ τὸν Κομνηνόν'; Poem IV, Title: "Ἕτεροι στίχοι Ἱλαρίωνος μοναχοῦ τοῦ Πτωχοπροδρόμου πρὸς τὸν εὐσεβέστατον βασιλέα κύριον Μανουήλ'; Poem I, v. 274: 'καὶ χάσῃς σου τὸν Πρόδρομον, τὸν κάλλιστον εὐχέτην'; Poem II, v. 101: 'Μὴ σὲ πλανᾷ, πανσέβαστε, τὸ Πτωχοπροδρομάτον'; Poem I, v. 158: 'Διὰ τὴν ψυχήν σου, Πρόδρομε, καθίζου σιγηρός σου'.

[26]   Ramon Muntaner, *Crònica*, ed. M. Gustà, II (Barcelona, 1979), §244; C. D. F. du Cange (revised by J.-A. Buchon), *Histoire de l'Empire de Constantinople sous les empereurs français jusqu'à la conquête des Turcs*, II (Paris, 1826), 355; Tzetzes, *Historiae*, Chil. XIII, Hist. 474–5, vv. 232, 236–7, 246; Van Gemert and Bakker, 'Ἡ Ἀχιλληῖδα καὶ ἡ ἱστορία τοῦ Βελισαρίου', 96.

[27]   A. Wallensköld, ed., *Les Chansons de Conon de Béthune* (Paris, 1921), iv–v.

[28]   Du Cange (rev. Buchon), *Histoire de l'Empire de Constantinople*, I, 165.

[29]   De Villehardouin, *La Conquête de Constantinople*, §144: 'bons chevaliers et sages [...] et bien parlanz'.

[30]   Although George Akropolites and Robert de Clari refer to Boniface de Montferrat as 'king' of Thessalonike the ruler's name does not appear with the title in sources dating from his own lifetime; instead, he appears to have used

Four such men – Raimbaut de Vaqueiras, Elias Cairel, Gaucelm Faidit and Hugues de Berzé – not only chose to emulate their patron and take the cross, but, while on crusade, continued to compose verse either for him or for his family and wider entourage.[31] Indeed, following the partition of the Byzantine Empire, the Aleramici court at Thessalonike appears to have aspired to become a place famous, as one contemporary noted, for its 'viols and songs'.[32] For every one of these renowned master-craftsmen who appears in the historical record, there may well have been scores of individuals of lesser social rank or lesser skill, whose names were not considered by contemporaries to be worthy of preservation for posterity. What is certain is that, a hundred years or so after the conquest, performers of poems and songs continued to remain highly active in the occupied lands. At the court of the duchy of Athens, for instance, such performers seem to have been something of a fixture in the late thirteenth and early fourteenth centuries. Thus, at the dubbing of the young duke, Guyot de la Roche, guests attending the ceremony gave fine garments to the *jongleurs* who contributed to the festivities, while among the expenditure listed by a foreign envoy sent to Greece were sums paid to at least two minstrels in the employ of Gautier de Brienne, Guyot's successor, for their provision of entertainment at a wedding, and for other similar services.[33] Minstrels in the Principality of Morea proper are also attested, with three of them being taken in the late fourteenth century by the diplomat John Laskaris Kalopheros on a mission from the Peloponnese to the court of Amadeo di Savoia, Count of Piedmont, where, as part of attempts to persuade the count to come with troops to the aid of the crusader state, they were apparently expected to give a recital or to improvise before their host.[34]

---

the formula 'regni Thessalonicensis et Crete dominus'. See Akropolites, *History*, §8:13.11–12; De Clari, *La Conquête de Constantinople*, §110; L. Deslisle, 'Lettres inédites d'Innocent III', *Bibliothèque de l'École des Chartes* 34 (1873), 408; R. Macrides, George Akropolites, *The History* (Oxford, 2007), 126, n. 7.

[31]   J. Linskill, ed., *The Poems of the Troubadour Raimbaut de Vaqueiras* (The Hague, 1964), 216–344; G. Lachin, ed., *Il trovatore Elias Cairel* (Modena, 2004), 21–205; J. Mouzat, ed., *Les Poèmes de Gaucelm Faidit* (Paris, 1965), 482–89. See also J. Longnon, *L'Empire latin de Constantinople et la Principauté de Morée* (Paris, 1949), 139.

[32]   Linksill, ed., *The Poems of the Troubadour Raimbaut de Vaqueiras*, 'Epic Letter', vv. 103–5: 'viulas e chantar'. See also L.M. Paterson, 'Occitan literature and the Holy Land', in M. Bull and C. Léglu, eds., *The World of Eleanor of Aquitaine: Literature and Society in Southern France between the Eleventh and Thirteenth Centuries* (Woodbridge, 2005), 92.

[33]   Muntaner, *Crònica*, §244; Du Cange (rev. Buchon), *Histoire de l'Empire de Constantinople*, II, 355.

[34]   R. Cessi, 'Amedeo di Acaia e la rivendicazione dei domini Sabaudi in Oriente', *Nuovo Achivio veneto* 20 (1919), 7, n. 7, 44 (item 4).

Although these examples concern individuals among whom were recent arrivals in the eastern Mediterranean, and who, in some cases at least, are likely to have expressed themselves in various Romance tongues, it should not be thought that such activities were confined to the *langue d'oil* and *langue d'oc*, for Greek also appears to have been widely used in the region for comparable purposes.[35] There are indications that, after the Fourth Crusade, the indigenous vernacular was employed for the composition of ballads that praised the deeds of Henri de Flandres, the Latin emperor of Constantinople.[36] In any case, the phenomenon of the poet–performer was not a foreign import that first took root in the former Byzantine provinces in the wake of 1204, but, on the contrary, antedated the formation of the crusader states. Already in the twelfth century, Tzetzes described people going from door to door on certain feast-days with songs and speeches in return for which payment was solicited.[37] In the tenth century, Arethas of Caesarea commented on the activities of those 'who compose songs [...] and earn their living by going round houses and performing them'.[38] Earlier still, in the seventh century, it was noted by Theophylact of Simokatta that the garb and accoutrements peculiar to such persons had been assumed by foreign spies on a mission within the territory of the Byzantine Empire. The disguise was one that would hardly have been favoured had it not been thought to stand a good chance of achieving its objective, which was to allow its wearer to 'blend in' and thus have access to an environment that would otherwise have been completely denied him.

The fare offered by such performers ranged over different genres,[39] and apparently included narratives of heroic deeds of the past. One witness refers to 'songs about the ordeals undergone by great men', while another, recounting a diplomatic mission undertaken by him, tells us of passing through an area of deep ravines on a cloudy night, and of his companions' attempt to keep fear at bay by singing, as he puts it, about 'the deeds of men of whose glorious reputation we have heard many things but about

---

[35]   E. M. Jeffreys and M. Jeffreys, 'The oral background of Byzantine popular poetry', *Oral Tradition* 1/3 (1986), 508–9.

[36]   M. Manoussacas, 'Τὸ ἑλληνικὸ δημοτικὸ τραγούδι – γιὰ τὸν Βασιλιὰ Ἑρρῖκο τῆς Φλάντρας', *Laographia* 14 (1952), 3–52. However, it should be noted that the evidence here depends on the transcriptions of folk songs made in the nineteenth century by ethnographers.

[37]   Tzetzes, *Historiae*, Chil. XIII, Hist. 474–5, vv. 218–46.

[38]   S.B. Kougeas, 'Ἔρευναι περὶ τῆς ἑλληνικῆς λαογραφίας κατὰ τοὺς μέσους χρόνους α΄: αἱ ἔν τοῖς σχολίοις τοῦ Ἀρέθα λαογραφικαὶ εἰδήσεις', *Λαογραφία* 4 (1912/13), 239: 'οἱ κατάρατοι Παφλαγόνες ᾠδάς τινας συμπλάσαντες [...] καὶ πρὸς ὀβολὸν ᾄδοντες καθ'ἑκάστην οἰκίαν'.

[39]   See Theophanes Continuatus, ch. 20:72.15–22; *Vita Stephani Iunioris*, in *PG* 100.1116.

whom we know very little for certain'.[40] The audience, too, to whom these performances would appeal was varied. In the fourteenth century, the Patriarch Philotheos scolded a monk for neglecting his Bible and listening instead to 'beggars' and 'purveyors of fables', accusing him of paying too much attention to 'blind players who strum the lyre and go into raptures, composing songs mainly for that instrument – those piteous songs of the blind –, and who gather unhappy women together at crossroads, so that they eke out a living by turning into ordinary commercial intercourse the sorrows of grief-stricken old women, and of the poor, and of females with nothing better to do, constantly stirring up their audience's emotions through the music and singing'.[41] The implication of this rebuke was that such forms of entertainment were considered fit for secular people rather than for those who had dedicated themselves to God, and, even then, only for the masses and not for the more discerning. Yet despite the supposed inappropriateness of his reaction, the fact remains that the monk in question, Nikephoros Gregoras, was deeply moved by the performance and found solace in it.[42] Another contemporary, the emperor John Kantakouzenos himself, certainly seems not to have considered it beneath his dignity to take with him on a military campaign 'a creator of songs' who was able to cradle his lyre and produce a piece at a moment's notice.[43]

These are admittedly but scraps of information, from which we can assemble a picture that remains tantalizingly fragmentary. But then we know very little about many aspects of ordinary everyday life in the eastern Mediterranean. Indeed, when we look for evidence of oral storytellers and singers of tales, part of our problem is that we are searching for precisely those types of activity that were taken for granted and considered unexceptional by our sources. The evidence we do have, however, gives the overall impression of entrenched cultural practices that were intelligible to and appreciated by the majority of the indigenous population, irrespective of social standing. Our greatest insight into the degree to which the figure

---

[40]   Kougeas, Ἔρευναι περὶ τῆς ἑλληνικῆς λαογραφίας κατὰ τοὺς μέσους χρόνους α΄', 239 and Nikephoros Gregoras, *Byzantina Historia*, ed. L. Schopen, vol. 1 (Bonn, 1829), 377.7–8: 'ᾠδάς […] πάθη περιεχούσας ἐνδόξων ἀνδρῶν'; 'δ'ἆρα κλέα ἀνδρῶν, ὧν οἷον κλέος ἀκούομεν, οὐδέ τοι ἴδμεν'.

[41]   Van Gemert and Bakker, 'Ἡ Ἀχιλληΐδα καὶ ἡ ἱστορία τοῦ Βελισαρίου', 96: 'ἀγύρτας'; 'μυθολόγους'; 'τυφλῶν λυριζόντων ἢ παραληρούντων […] μέλη τινὰ ξυντιθέντων πρὸς λύραν συνήθως, αὐτὰ δὴ ταῦτα λέγων τὰ τραγικὰ τῶν τυφλῶν ᾄσματα, οἷς ἐκεῖνοι τὰ δυστυχῆ γύναια συναθροίζουσιν ἐπὶ τῶν ἀμφόδων, κοινὴν ἐμπορίαν τῶν ἀναγκαίων ποιούμενοι τὰ τῶν ἀλγούντων γραιδίων τε καὶ πενήτων καὶ ἀργῶν γυναικῶν ἄλλως πένθη, διὰ γε τὸ τοῖς μέλεσι καὶ ταῖς ᾠδαῖς ταῖς παρ'αὐτῶν προσερεθίζειν ἐκεῖνα'.

[42]   Van Gemert and Bakker, 'Ἡ Ἀχιλληΐδα καὶ ἡ ἱστορία τοῦ Βελισαρίου', 96.

[43]   Gregoras, II, 705.23–706.1: 'ᾀσμάτων δημιουργὸς'.

of the singer of tales was an integrated part of daily life in Greek-speaking lands is provided by a horoscope that was produced for the year 1336 in Trebizond and owes its chance survival to the reuse of the paper for an anthology of medical texts.[44] The horoscope offers prognostications for various people, beginning with the emperors themselves, and then going on to discuss categories such as those of the leading magnates, of civil servants and notaries, of prelates and clergy, of military commanders and soldiers, of noble old men, eunuchs and women, and of official messengers and envoys, ending, finally, with the common people. Among the last to be treated are 'merchants and peddlers'.[45] Here, certain comments are directed specifically to the sub-category of itinerant players, for whom the text, promising joy and prosperity, prophesizes that the New Year will bring superior compositional abilities and greater eloquence, leading not only to the improvisation of new poems, but also to more attentive and willing audiences.[46]

Narrator and narratees

Although the *Chronikon tou Moreos* should not be associated with an actual storyteller or poet who, at a public festival or before a private hearth, gathered an audience together and then, whether beating time with his hands or a staff, or alternatively strumming or sawing away at whatever string instrument he favoured, performed the narrative of the conquest of Constantinople and of the Peloponnese to general acclaim, a being of this type does seem to speak to us. Thus, the opening of the *Chronikon* takes the form of the following address: 'Θέλω νὰ σὲ ἀφηγηθῶ ἀφήγησιν μεγάλην· / κι ἂν θέλης νὰ μὲ ἀκροαστῆς, ὀλπίζω νὰ σ'ἀρέση...' ('I am going to recount a great tale for your benefit / and if you will listen to me, I trust you will like it', vv. 1–2).[47] A few lines further down, Latins and Greeks are encouraged to assemble and hear the tale: 'Ἀκούσατε οἱ ἅπαντες, Φράγκοι τε καὶ Ρωμαῖοι / ὅσοι πιστεύετε εἰς Χριστόν, τὸ βάφτισμα φορεῖτε, / ἐλᾶτε ἐδῶ νὰ ἀκούσετε ὑπόθεσιν μεγάλην.' ('Listen all of you, both Franks and Romans, / all you who believe in Christ and wear the tunic of baptism / gather round and listen to an important matter...', vv. 724–6). These two passages both contain phrases that would

---

[44]   Lambros, 'Τραπεζουντιακὸν ὡροσκόπιον', 33–50.

[45]   Lambros, 'Τραπεζουντιακὸν ὡροσκόπιον', 40: 'Τοῖς πραγματευταῖς καὶ τοῖς ἐμπόροις'.

[46]   Lambros, 'Τραπεζουντιακὸν ὡροσκόπιον', 40.

[47]   Paris, Bibliothèque nationale de France, MS gr. 2898 is cited here because the Copenhagen manuscript is missing the opening folio and is considerably damaged for the next four folios.

not have been out of place on the lips of a storyteller or singer of tales seeking, through the advertisement of his product, to drum up interest. At the beginning of the *Chronikon*, what is represented can be described as the initial moment at the commencement of an oral performance, when the singer steps forward, people gather round, and a hush of expectation falls. In subsequent passages, this scenario is elaborated upon, resulting in the consummate establishment of an illusion, with the singer in question (who, after all, is a literary construct – a persona – that is built into the narrative itself and can have no existence independent of that narrative) being made to seem 'present' to us while we are reading. His attributes, inscribed into every word and every line, and indeed definable as the result of the sum-total of pen-strokes found in the manuscript, are most obvious in those comments or asides that punctuate the narrative:

Ἀκούσατε, χάριν τοῦ Χριστοῦ, κἀνεὶς ἀπὸ τοὺς Φράγκους
κοντάρι οὐδὲν ἐπίασεν, κἀνεὶς οὐκ ἐλαβώθη
Listen! By the Grace of God none of the Franks
was touched by a lance, none was wounded
(vv. 4769–70)

κι ὅσοι τὸ ἀκούετε, λέγετε· «ὁ Θεὸς τοῦ συμπαθήσῃ»
And all of you who hear this, say: 'May God rest his soul!'
(v. 2755)

Κι ἂν μὲ ἐρωτήσῃ ὀκάποιος, «διὰ τί τρόπον τὸ ἐποῖκεν;»
ἐγὼ τοῦ ἀποκρένομαι· «διατί ὁρισμὸν τὸ εἶχεν»
If someone asks me: 'Why did he do this?',
I answer him: 'Because he had received orders.'
(vv. 6660–61).

Direct addresses, exhortations and rhetorical questions of this type are examples of devices that imitate the stock-in-trade of a performer seeking to maintain the interest of a public to whom a tale is in the process of being told. Such interventions act as the means by which interaction between an implied storyteller and an implied audience can be brought into the foreground. Indeed, a constant urge is displayed to bring narrator and narratees into each other's mental presence, for both the first and second grammatical persons may be fairly described as ubiquitous in the *Chronikon* with the former appearing on average once every nineteen lines and the latter once every twenty lines. One phrase of the type 'σὲ λαλῶ' ('I speak to you'), 'σὲ λέγω' ('I say to you'), 'εἶπα σε' ('I said to you'), or 'σᾶς ἀφηγοῦμαι' ('I tell you') is thus encountered on every single page of the manuscript or, if reading, approximately every five minutes or so. This really *is* very frequent. A fictitious oral storyteller or singer is depicted disporting himself with a fictitious audience throughout the narrative – it is these imaginary interlocutors, and not the protagonists of the story such as Guillaume de Villehardouin or Geoffroi de Briel, who, in a sense, are centre stage.

This persistent reminder of the exchange between narrator and narratees found in the *Chronikon tou Moreos* indicates, paradoxically, a certain uneasiness about the relationship between the composition and the reception of a text within a culture where scribes play an important role in transmission, and where texts circulate in manuscript form. After all, not everything can be transposed into writing. One has only to consider the archival material from the fieldwork carried out by Milman Parry and Albert Lord in the Balkans during the early twentieth century. In the case of Yugoslav oral epic, the transcriptions cannot adequately prepare us for the video footage, since reading and perusing the words spoken by Avdo Međedović, the most talented singer found by Parry and Lord, proves to be an entirely different – and indeed far less satisfactory experience – to watching and hearing the man himself perform.[48] The point has been stressed by the cultural anthropologist and expert on oral culture Ruth Finnegan, when discussing her research among the Limba of Sierra Leone in West Africa. She remarked: 'I was enormously impressed by hearing […] stories in the field – by their subtlety, creativity, drama and human qualities, and I recorded a large corpus of them. But when I came back and typed my transcriptions […] they seemed so lifeless'.[49] The manner in which words are uttered during an actual oral performance completely transforms their impact and meaning, since effective communication is inextricably dependent on delivery skills that include not only the speed and intonation with which the narrative is vocalized, but also the facial expressions and gestures employed by the storyteller, and even the mimicry of certain sounds. If these aspects are at all to be conveyed in writing, they have to be scripted into the text in question in a highly exaggerated manner.[50] This would seem to be precisely what has happened in the *Chronikon tou Moreos*. Over-insistence upon narratorial interventions should thus be seen here as a development connected to the decoupling of the process of composition from that of reception.

Whereas an oral linguistic exchange consists of the production of an utterance and its hearing within the same spatio-temporal context, this

---

[48]   See A. B. Lord, *The Singer of Tales* (Cambridge, MA, 2001), together with accompanying footage, and also the Milman Parry Collection of oral literature online, at www.chs.harvard.edu/mpc/gallery/avdo.html, accessed 18 June 2010.

[49]   R. Finnegan, 'What is orality – if anything?', *BMGS* 14 (1990), 135.

[50]   J. J. Duggan, 'Performance and transmission, aural and ocular reception in the twelfth- and thirteenth-century vernacular literature of France', *Romance Philology* 43 (1989), 51–2.

simultaneity, attributable to the material interaction of the interlocutors, is lost with the written word. It is in order to compensate for this loss that the *Chronikon* seeks to replicate, within the parameters of the text itself, the establishment and maintenance of a bond typical of orality. By being fictionalized, the communicative act has been immortalized: both narrator and narratees have been created and are fixed on the written page, as if in perpetual stasis, ready to re-enact, over and over again, whenever they should be called upon, the preordained roles that have been allotted to them. The practice is one that characterizes not only the *Chronikon tou Moreos*, but also later examples of historiography produced in the Greek vernacular. This is especially true where verse texts are concerned. In the *Χρονικὸν τῶν Τόκκο* (*Chronikon ton Tocco*), for instance, an early fifteenth-century chronicle in *political verse*, narratorial interventions can be identified that are similar in nature and in frequency to those already discussed:

Ἀκούσατε γάρ, ἅπαντες, μετὰ πληροφορίας,
τὸ πῶς ἐγίνη ἡ ἀρχὴ θαυμάσια μεγάλως.
Hear now, all of you, and be informed,[51]
of the marvellous manner in which things began.
(vv. 1–2)

Ἤκουσε δὲ νὰ σὲ εἰπῶ τὸ τότε τί ἐγίνη.
Hear me tell you what happened then.
(v. 43)

Καὶ ἄκουσε πρᾶγμα φοβερὸν καὶ ξένον· νὰ θαυμάσῃς.
And hear of a strange and fearful thing, and be amazed.
(v. 2668)

<Καὶ> ἄκο νὰ σὲ τὸ εἰπῶ λεπτὰ νὰ τὸ ἀκούσῃς.
<And> listen while I tell you this in detail so that you may hear it.
(v. 2678)

«Καὶ τί ἐγίνετον εὐθύς, σύντομα, εἰς τὴν ὥραν;»
Ἄκουσον, φίλε, τοῦ Θεοῦ δύναμιν τὴν μεγάλην
καὶ θαύμασον τὰ μέλλοντα συμβαίνειν τοῖς ἀνθρώποις.'
'And what thereupon happened, straightaway, without any time having passed?'
Hear, friend, of God's great power
and wonder at men's destiny'
(v. 1081)

---

[51] It is most likely that we are dealing with a present imperative and not an aorist indicative; however, a possible confusion over tense means that this should perhaps be translated as 'You have already heard and been informed'.

'ἐφαίνετόν σε· εἰς τὸ φαρὶ στέκεται καρφωμένος'
'And it seemed to you that he is glued to the saddle'
(v. 347).[52]

To some extent, a carry-over of the same pattern can be found preserved even in prose texts. Indeed, the] Ἐξήγησις τῆς γλυκείας χώρας Κύπρου (*Exegesis tes glykeias choras Kyprou*) by Leontios Machairas contains a number of familiar phrases and expressions: 'Ἀγροικήσετε πῶς...' ('Hear how...', §67);[53] 'Τώρα θέλω νὰ σᾶς πῶ ν'ἀγροικήσετε...' ('Now I want to tell you so you may hear...', §484); 'Τώρα νὰ σᾶς εἰπῶ τίντα ἐποῖκεν τὴν αὐτὴν ἡμέραν...' ('Now let me tell you what he did that day...', §562); 'ὡς γοιὸν σᾶς τὸ εἴπουν' ('as I have already told you', §688); 'Καὶ ἂν θέλης νὰ σοῦ πῶ πῶς ἡ Ἀμόχουστο ἐπάρτην, ἦτον παραχώρησις θεοῦ διὰ τὰς ἁμαρτίας μας' ('And if you wish me to tell you how Famagusta was taken, well, it was surrendered by God because of our sins', §482).[54]

The poet–performer, the oral storyteller, the singer of tales – this figure, however we wish to call him – became the persona of choice favoured by the writers of an entire branch of historiography composed in vernacular Greek in the late medieval eastern Mediterranean. Assigned the task of narrating the texts in which he appeared, this persona also acted as the guarantor of the same texts' accuracy and truth, with his comments or asides often containing assertions of his privileged position of knowledge. Illustration of this phenomenon may be found in the following passages from the *Chronikon tou Moreos*:

τὸ ἔτος τότε ἔτρεχεν τὸ ἀπὸ κτίσεως κόσμου
ἔξι χιλιάδες, λέγω σε, κ'ἑφτὰ ἑκατοντάδες,
καὶ δεκάξι μοναχοὺς χρόνους εἶχεν τὸ ἔ<τος>,
<οἱ> κόντοι ἐκεῖνοι ἐνώθησαν, ὅπερ ἐδῶ ὀνομ<άζω>,
<κι ἄ>λλοι μεγάλοι ἄνθρωποι ἐνῷ ἦσαν ἐκ τὴν Δύσιν·
ὅρκον ἐποίησαν ὁμοῦ καὶ τὸν σταυρὸν ἀπῆραν
In the year from creation
six thousand, I say to you, and seven hundred
and sixteen, that was the year,
those counts, whom I name here, gathered together,
and other great men too who were from the West;
they swore an oath together and took the Cross
(vv. 124–9)

---

[52] G. Schirò, ed., *Cronaca dei Tocco di Cefalonia* (Rome, 1975).

[53] This should perhaps be translated as 'You have heard how'.

[54] Leontios Machairas, *Recital Concerning the Sweet Land of Cyprus Entitled Chronicle'*, vol. 1, ed. R. M. Dawkins (Oxford, 1932).

Ἐτοῦτοι ὅλοι, ὅπου μὲ ἀκούεις καὶ λέγω κι ὀνομάζω,
εὑρέθησαν...
All these, whom you hear me tell of and name
were to be found...
(vv. 1962–3)

Λοιπὸν ἐκεῖνον τὸν καιρὸν κ'ἐκεῖνους γὰρ τοὺς χρόνους
ὁ Φρεδερίγος βασιλέας, ἐκεῖνος τῆς Ἀλλαμάνιας,
ἀφέντευεν τὴν Σικελίαν ἐκεῖνο τὸ ρηγᾶτο
σὺν τὰ τῆς Πούλιας, σὲ λαλῶ, εἶχεν τὴν ἀφεντίαν
So at that time and in those years
King Frederick of Germany
ruled over the Kingdom of Sicily,
and had, I tell you, the lordship of the lands of Apulia
(vv. 5955–8)

Ὁ κάποιος γέρων ἄνθρωπος εὑρέθη ἐκεῖ εἰς τὴν Πόλιν·
[...]
τὸ ἀκούσει πῶς ἠθέλασιν οἱ Φράγκοι νὰ τὸν ἔχουν κρίνει,
ἐκεῖνον τὸν πανάπιστον τὸν Μούρτζουφλον, σὲ λέγω,
ἔδραμε...
An old man was found there in the City
[...]
and upon hearing that the Franks wished to pass judgement on
that faithless Murtzuphlus, I tell you,
he ran...
(vv. 875–9)

Ἐν τούτῳ ἐσκόπησεν καλὰ ἔσω στὸν λογισμόν του
καὶ εἶπεν κ'ἐδιακρίσετον οὕτως, ὡσὰν τὸ λέγω·
ὅτι...
Thereupon, he pondered upon the matter
and said and decided the following, just as I say it,
namely, that...
(vv. 6272–4).

It is the narrator's job to reassure us, in passages such as these, that the relationship between the actual events of the past and their textual incarnation is straightforward and unproblematic. Of course, there were other solutions, other ways of securing credibility, available to an ambitious historian writing in Greek in the late Middle Ages. For example, such a historian could, instead, have traced his pedigree back to the acknowledged fathers of history, Herodotus or Thucydides, so that, standing on the shoulders of these giants and forebears, he also became a colossus. This is the strategy adopted by much of the extant historiography surviving from the Byzantine Empire – historiography largely composed in Constantinople.[55] In contrast, the *Chronikon tou Moreos* quite deliberately avoids this technique. Marking a stylistic break with imperial historiography that is also an ideological break, the *Chronikon* turns back the clock to a time before Herodotus or Thucydides, to a time when anonymous bards and professional entertainers fulfilled the role of guardians of memory. That era was one during which it had still been possible for a heroic ancestral past to be enshrined in epic discourse that expressed unquestioned collective truths. It was the age-old responsibility of the singer of tales as someone who knitted a community together and acted as its honoured mouthpiece that made this persona the perfect disguise to be assumed by a historian with an agenda. Moreover, when putting on his costume, the author assumed a specific role that was well known and accepted both by the conquering Latin knights and by the native Greek *archondes*, the two social groups that form the primary targets of the *Chronikon tou Moreos*. In other words, the singer of tales represented a point of contact and communality for these two ethnicities in the fourteenth century.

To us, however, today, the appearance of the same singer of tales within a work of historiography occasions little respect. On the contrary, any encounter with him causes distaste, for to us he is a figure of fun, a poor mountebank belonging to a time before science and reason, who is out of place in the modern progressive world, and whom it would be better by far to consign to oblivion. It is scarcely surprising that scholarship tends to ignore the Greek version of the *Chronicle of Morea* and to prefer instead to cite the French version, *Le Livre de la conqueste de la Princée de l'Amorée*, a version that most probably was in fact redacted later, but seems at a first glance more convincing because in it almost all traces of the first-person narrator have been removed and replaced by an impersonal narrating instance. In the *Livre de la conqueste*, we are dealing with discourse that is apparently unmediated and speaker-less – an act of enunciation that does not require an enunciator: 'Mais or se taist cil contes de parler…' ('But now this tale stops talking…', §474); 'tout ainxi que l'estoire le vous a conté ça arriers' ('as the story has narrated to you here at an earlier point',

---

[55] Extensive borrowings from ancient authors can be found in the prefaces of Byzantine historiographical writings. However, it should be noted that, while Byzantine authors might seek to draw attention to their indebtedness to a well-established tradition, they would often manipulate that tradition in order to fulfil very different objectives to those of the models they were ostensibly emulating. See, for instance, H. Lieberich, *Studien zu den Proömien in der griechischen und byzantinischen Geschichtschreibung*, vol. 2: Die byzantinischen Geschichtschreiber und Chronisten (Munich, 1900), and R. Scott, 'The classical tradition in Byzantine historiography', in Mullett and Scott, eds., *The Classical Tradition*, 61–74.

§440); 'tout ainxi comme il sera conté chi devant en cestui livre' ('as will be narrated later in this book', §75). Narrative that seeks to narrate itself is closer to our own sensibilities, our own understanding of the conventions governing historiography. As a result, we look askance at anyone who has the temerity to assert 'It is true because I, who am telling you this, guarantee it!', our distrust being especially great when our interlocutor would appear to be carrying some sort of folk instrument tucked under his arm, and can neither read nor write. Such a personage, we feel, cannot possibly be 'one of us', for illiteracy in our own society is considered incompatible with a discerning mind. Yet we should take care lest a smug sense of superiority should lead us to fall victims of what is, after all, merely another ploy. Although assertions of the type 'It is true because the narrative says it is true!' may appear to be of a weighty nature, the objectivity and dispassionateness suggested by such formulations cannot be substantiated. Ironically, though there is great divergence in the type of discourse used for the Greek and French versions of the *Chronicle of Morea*, and therefore in their literary fabric, their factual or raw content remains pretty much identical in both, so that, as an accurate record of the past, the one text is little better than the other.

SECTION IV
Story-telling

6. From propaganda to history to literature: the Byzantine stories of Theodosius' apple and Marcian's eagles

Roger Scott

The fifth-century stories of Theodosius' apple and Marcian's eagles illustrate several aspects of the significance of good stories in Byzantine culture: first, the initial recognition of their value for political propaganda and counter propaganda by the actual political participants, with each side recognizing the power of their opponent's fiction and hence the need for a rebuttal that silently acknowledges the strength of that fiction; then the use of the stories by the earlier chroniclers who, in recording them as history, adapt them for their own historical or literary purpose that differs from the original political use of the stories; finally, as the stories become accepted elements in popular memory of the 'national' past, the later telling of them involves further literary adaptation now far removed from the original political purpose. In the course of this process not only do these stories become part of Byzantine history, but their function in historical narrative enables us to observe how chroniclers adapt material for their own literary ends. This latter point is important because Byzantine chroniclers are sometimes still seen as simple-minded plagiarists, who simply copy what was in their source. Here by examining Theophanes' treatment in particular but also Malalas', we can watch how carefully these two chroniclers adapt the stories to suit their own narrative and interpretation of the past. Limitations of space permit also only a brief look at the later use of the stories in the eleventh and twelfth centuries where earlier competing strands of narrative are brought together but where, with their historical context now lost or insignificant, the stories are given instead a new moral interpretation suited to contemporary taste. Throughout the whole process, the awareness of an interested audience also helps draw attention to a remarkable feature of Byzantine culture, namely a popular interest in history as an important branch of literature.

The stories

In the first story Theodosius II is presented with an enormous apple, which he gives to his wife, Eudocia, who gives it to her boyfriend, Paulinus, who unfortunately gives it back to the emperor. As Theodosius is understandably suspicious about how Paulinus got the apple, he asks Eudocia what she had done with it, and she, also understandably, lies, saying, 'I ate it'. Theodosius promptly gets rid of Paulinus while Eudocia, in disgrace, asks to be sent to Jerusalem. The story has been used to help date Eudocia's journeys to Jerusalem and interpret political machinations in Theodosius' court. I argue below that the story, which first occurs in Malalas in the sixth century, was only invented after the synod of Chalcedon in 451 to counter slanderous Monophysite storytelling.

The second story gives two accounts of how portents involving an eagle foretold that the future emperor Marcian, when he was just a lowly soldier, would in fact become emperor as God had intended. In each case an eagle had spread its wings over Marcian while he was asleep, protecting him from the midday sun. Those who saw this recognized the obscure Marcian's destiny. In each case the eagle stories also allude to (and presumably helped answer criticism of) Marcian's undistinguished military record, one occurring when through illness he had failed to keep up with his regiment in Lydia, and the other as Gizerich's prisoner of war in Vandal Africa. They also helped justify both his promotion of friends and his failure to pursue war against the Vandals, in each case showing him loyal to his promises.[1]

The apple and eagle stories are told in chronicle after chronicle for the next millennium, with the eagle story also being revived and exploited by Basil I to demonstrate divine support for himself.[2] The eagle stories are part of a collection emanating from Marcian to justify his weak claim to the throne. These stories were evidently successful, winning Marcian a good reputation,[3] though only in the Greek tradition, which Marcian seems to have controlled. It is here that the apple story becomes important, because behind it lies a tradition of opposition to Marcian surviving in Syriac, which Marcian or his supporters managed to eliminate from the Byzantine Greek historical tradition.

Both stories in fact arise from attempts to deal with some awkward aspects of the last two years of Theodosius' reign and his succession by Marcian, in essence from August 449 to October 451. First there is the second ecumenical synod at Ephesos in August 449, the *latrocinium* or

---

[1]   Theophanes, AM 5943; Procopius, *BV* 1.4.10–11.

[2]   Skylitzes, 118.60–119.75. Cf. Philippikos' banishment for stating that he had dreamt of an eagle shadowing his head (Theophanes, AM 6194).

[3]   *ODB* 2, 1296.

'robber synod', which, with Theodosius' support, in effect pronounced Monophysitism to be orthodox; next, Theodosius' death in the following year on 28 July 450 at a youthful 49, after a hunting accident; third, his replacement a whole four weeks later on 25 August by the obscure Marcian, who, aged 58, promptly married Theodosius' 51-year-old sister, Pulcheria, despite her vow of virginity; and finally in 451 and most importantly, the fourth ecumenical synod at Chalcedon, at the instigation of the new emperor Marcian and more particularly Pulcheria, which overturned the decisions at Ephesos. This naturally resulted in both Marcian and Pulcheria becoming heroes among western orthodox catholic 'Chalcedonians' and being utterly detested among eastern orthodox Monophysites.

Marcian's eagles were obviously created to show that, despite his obscure and lowly background, he was the right and proper emperor and had God's support. Whether or not he had God's support, he had little claim to be emperor. On Theodosius' death, it was the right of the then western emperor, Valentinian, to appoint his successor. In the event Valentinian was not even consulted[4] and initially regarded Marcian as a usurper. How Marcian managed to be chosen is unclear, but he spread various stories to show that the empire was his God-given right. Of the eagle stories the version located in Vandal Africa first occurs in Procopius, while the version located in Lydia first appears in the ninth century in Theophanes, who also includes the story from Procopius.[5] Presumably both versions rely ultimately on Marcian's propaganda, which had then entered the historical tradition (very likely in Priscus and from him to Eustathius of Epiphaneia). Theophanes is quite specific that both eagle stories demonstrated that Marcian was God's choice. With this Procopius agrees obliquely, noting that Gizerich recognized this and so exacted a promise from his prisoner never to attack the Vandals should he become emperor; Procopius then comments that this failure to attack the Vandals was the one blemish on Marcian's reign.

Evagrius provides a further story that Marcian, on his way to enrol in the army, reported his discovery by the roadside of a dead soldier but then escaped execution for the soldier's murder only through divine providence. Subsequently, instead of taking the lowest rank at his enrolment, he was assigned the place of the dead soldier, whose name was, providentially, Augustus.[6] Malalas omits these stories but provides our earliest account of yet another, that Theodosius, just before his death, made a special trip to Ephesos to ask St John who would succeed him, and had been told

[4]   R. W. Burgess, 'The accession of Marcian in the light of Chalcedonian apologetic and Monophysite polemic', *BZ* 86–7 (1993–94), 47–68.

[5]   Procopius, *BV* 1.4.1–11; Theophanes, AM 5943.

[6]   Evagrius, *Ecclesiastical History*, 2.1.

in a vision that it would be Marcian.[7] That it took almost a month after Theodosius' death to appoint Marcian is enough to discredit this story. If Marcian really had Theodosius' support, his appointment as emperor would have taken a couple of days at most rather than four weeks. It is also highly unlikely that Theodosius would have been worrying about a successor. He was only 49 when he died; his death was the result of a riding accident, not illness; and the fact that it was a riding accident during a hunting expedition suggests he was an active and healthy 49-year-old with no reason to assume there would be any need for a successor for quite some time. The story of Theodosius' journey to Ephesos and vision, like the stories of the eagle and the dead soldier Augustus, was invented to shore up Marcian's dubious claim. What needs to be stressed, however, is Marcian's success in having all these stories enter the historical tradition, together with an overall favourable judgement on his reign.

In contrast is the wholly hostile tradition in Monophysite sources surviving in Syriac but (in at least some cases) written originally in Greek. Here it was Marcian's and Pulcheria's decision to summon the synod at Chalcedon that did the damage. Because of their opposition to Chalcedon, the Monophysites attacked both Marcian and Pulcheria as much as they could. So we get various stories in Syriac abusing Marcian and Pulcheria as servants of the devil.[8] The Monophysites claimed to be particularly outraged by their marriage, suggesting either that Marcian had seduced Pulcheria or that Pulcheria had abandoned her life of chastity to keep her position as empress. All the stories emphasize their sexual immorality. There is just one that needs to be noted, as follows. Pulcheria and Marcian were secret lovers. One day Theodosius was given a wonderful apple, which he gave to his esteemed sister, Pulcheria. Since she loved no one more than Marcian, she gave it to him, and then of course Marcian gave it back to Theodosius. When Theodosius asked how he got the apple, Marcian said a friend, who was a general (*stratelates*), had given it to him. Theodosius realized that Pulcheria burned with adulterous love for Marcian and so banished him with the pretext that he was a Nestorian but really to block his affair with Pulcheria.[9]

The Pulcheria version occurs in Theopistos' *Vita Dioscori*. Richard Burgess deserves the credit for reminding Byzantinists of it. Because his focus was on Marcian's appointment, Burgess buries in a footnote a suggestion that this version came first with the Eudocia story as a necessary response to it. This is virtually certain. Burgess errs, however, in stating

---

[7]   Malalas, *Chronographia*, 14.27:288.20–33.

[8]   Burgess, 'Accession', 50–54.

[9]   M. F. Nau, ed. and trans., 'Histoire de Dioscore, patriarche d'Alexandrie, écrite par son disciple Théopiste', *Journal Asiatique* 10/1 (1903), 5–108 (introduction and Syriac text), 241–310 (French translation), here 23–5 (Syriac) and 244 (French).

that this is the only occurrence of the story. In fact it also occurs in an Armenian version.[10] Since Theopistos' *Vita Dioscori* was written in Greek, its Syriac translation and the survival of the story in Armenian suggest strongly that the Monophysites were successful in spreading the Pulcheria version. This is further reinforced by Nestorius, who in Egyptian exile apparently 'knew' of Pulcheria's sinful behaviour.[11] That the propaganda of the Monophysites had reached their and Pulcheria's exiled archenemy testifies to their success and the need for a response to the story.

Theopistos' *Vita Dioscori* was written between 454 and 477,[12] at least half a century earlier than the first occurrence of the Eudocia story, though this could be just chance. More persuasive are the historical circumstances. It is simply much more likely that the Eudocia story was invented to counter Monophysite propaganda against Pulcheria rather than the other way round. Pulcheria had to be presented as chaste and virtuous because she was so influential in organizing Chalcedon, which is so important in catholic and orthodox theology. Slander about a dirty love affair could not be left unanswered. It is too powerful and memorable a story. So the same story was retained but applied instead to the emperor's unfortunate wife. Eudocia had to be sacrificed, at least for a while, in order to restore and ensure the holy Pulcheria's immaculate reputation. Various oddities in Eudocia's career could be exploited skilfully to make this version of the apple story seem credible, though these same oddities in fact show how unlikely it is that the story should apply to Eudocia.

The Eudocia story first appears in Malalas, presumably in his first edition and so written around 532 to 540. Malalas shows no interest in the theological background to the story, but that is characteristic of him. (His account, for instance, of Chalcedon, which one might have expected to receive considerable attention, only just reaches a second line of text. He covers the entire synod in twelve words.[13]) The story simply exploits the well-known fact that Eudocia had lived in Jerusalem and died there on her second stay. Eudocia, Paulinus and Theodosius had certainly been close friends early in the reign. The earliest and only credible source for Paulinus' execution is Marcellinus *comes*, who, writing under Justinian and following his Constantinopolitan source, dates it to 440. There is no reason

---

[10]   M. von Esbroeck, 'La pomme de Théodose II et sa réplique arménienne', in Sode and Takács, eds., *Novum Millennium*, 109–11.

[11]   E. W. Brooks, 'Some historical references in the Πραγματεία Ἡρακλείδου', *BZ* 21 (1912–13), 94–6; cf. *The Bazaar of Heracleides*, trans. G. Driver and L. Hodgson (Oxford, 1923), 96–7. Nestorius was also aware of Eudocia's supposed adultery: *Bazaar*, 379.

[12]   Nau, 'Theopistos', 11–13. Additional material was added *c.* 512.

[13]   For Malalas' lack of interest in theology, B. Croke, 'Malalas, the man and his work', in Jeffreys, *et al.*, eds., *Studies in John Malalas*, 14–15.

to doubt this date. Marcellinus also dates Eudocia's return from her first pilgrimage to Jerusalem to 439. The date of her second journey is disputed, but if it is linked to Paulinus' execution it cannot have been long after 440. The year 443 is quite likely or else 441/2, linked to the fall of Cyrus of Panopolis.[14] There is, however, no suggestion of a date anywhere close to Chalcedon in 451. That the Eudocia version of the apple story was either not linked to the Pulcheria version or that the two versions were separated by a decade is simply beyond belief, and the only plausible context for the Pulcheria version is the aftermath of Chalcedon. But since it would have been well known that Eudocia's friend Paulinus had been executed for whatever reason and that Eudocia had certainly left her emperor husband to live in Jerusalem possibly at about the same time, it made sense for a later storyteller to interpret Eudocia's journey to Jerusalem as a case of her being banished in disgrace as a result of an invented adultery, especially when a suitable context needed to be invented a decade later to help rebut the Monophysites' effective and scandalous rumour about the new emperor and his immaculate wife. Yet Eudocia's actual activities in Jerusalem are simply incompatible with any notion of her being there in disgrace.[15]

Eudocia's activities on her two visits are similar and sometimes difficult to distinguish. For both pilgrimages our ecclesiastical sources concentrate on her massive and pious building projects, such as founding or repairing monasteries and churches and building homes for the poor and for the elderly. It is, however, clear that on this second stay she also had access to huge amounts of cash that distinguish her projects from those of other wealthy patrons.[16] She does not merely build but provides income to support her projects. That is enough to make it clear that Eudocia was not in Jerusalem in disgrace. What puts this suggestion beyond doubt are her additional secular activities.[17] She had access to troops to use for her own purposes and also played an active if minor role in Jerusalem's administration. Secular works include a large cistern to improve water supply and the particularly expensive project of building the walls of

---

[14]   Theophanes' date of 449/50 (Theodosius' 42nd year) may reflect 443 based on Theodosius' official regnal year reckoned from 402. See *PLRE* 2.409 following J.B. Bury, *Later Roman Empire*, 2 vols. (London, 1923), I, 230 n. 5, although wrongly believing that Kedrenos and Zonaras were using the official regnal year when they simply follow their source Theophanes. For 441/42 see E. D. Hunt, *Holy Land and Pilgrimage in the Later Roman Empire AD 312–460* (Oxford, 1984), 234–6.

[15]   As first suggested to me by Annie Carter. A. L. Carter, *Juliana and her Female Lineage*, unpublished BA (Hons) thesis, University of Melbourne (Melbourne, 1997), 24–30.

[16]   Cf. Hunt, *Holy Land and Pilgrimage*, 230.

[17]   F. Nau, ed. and trans., 'Vita Barsauma', *Revue de l'Orient Chrétien* 19 (1914), 117–30.

Jerusalem enclosing much more than the surviving Ottoman walls. Eudocia must have had enormous funds at her disposal. Nikephoros Kallistos Xanthopoulos gives a figure of 20,480 pounds of gold.[18] Access to such funds, military power and such a public presence (including retention of the title of Augusta) are simply not consistent with the story of a woman banished for adultery. It is much more likely that a perfectly chaste Eudocia went to Jerusalem with the full support and authority of her husband on a pious mission to benefit the Holy City as best she could. This would fit the whole image of the reign (at least in its propaganda) of supporting sexual abstinence, so that even the royal palace could be presented as a kind of monastery. But by applying the apple story (and its implications of sexual impropriety) to Eudocia, not only would Pulcheria's reputation be saved but so too would Marcian's, and the orthodox tradition could get round the awkward fact that Theodosius had supported Ephesos II, which had favoured Monophysitism.

The Eudocia story was evidently effective, for the Monophysites reacted with their own Eudocia apple story preserved in John of Nikiu.[19] It absolves her of any guilt, stressing instead Paulinus' illness and his realization of being in danger and so plotting against Theodosius, for which he is executed. John's point is that Eudocia was not responsible for Paulinus' death. He further explains Eudocia's separation and move to Jerusalem as resulting from a holy man's warning that Theodosius' successor would be a heretic. To avoid being responsible 'they abandoned all conjugal intercourse and lived, by mutual consent, in befitting chastity',[20] which leads to Eudocia's request to visit Jerusalem 'to worship there in righteousness' and certainly not in disgrace. John makes absolutely clear that his account is a response to the Chalcedonian version. 'But lying historians who are heretics and abide not by the truth have recounted and said that Paulinus was put to death because of the empress Eudocia'.[21] So just as the Chalcedonians had found it necessary to create their own apple story to save Pulcheria from Monophysite slander, so the Monophysites needed to respond with one that imitated the Chalcedonian story as closely as possible. With story, counter-story and counter-counter-story, both sides clearly recognized not merely a story's effectiveness for propaganda but the necessity of adapting their fiction to their opponents' fiction and having it recorded as history.

---

[18]   Xanthopoulos, 14.50: *PG* 146, 1240, a huge sum but accepted as realistic by M. Avi-Yonah, 'Economics of Byzantine Palestine', *Israel Exploration Journal* 8 (1958), 39–51.

[19]   John of Nikiu, 87.1–22 trans. R. H. Charles, *The Chronicle of John, Bishop of Nikiu*, The Text and Translation Society (Oxford, 1916), 105.

[20]   John of Nikiu, 87.16; trans. Charles, 105.

[21]   John of Nikiu, 87.13; trans. Charles, 105.

John also reports that Theodosius gave the poor man not 150 *nomismata*, as stated by Malalas, but 100, a small point that helps identify the story's later influence.

Theophanes

The apple and eagle stories were created for political reasons. Theophanes' use of them in the early ninth century shows that the theological politics behind the stories still remained an issue over three centuries later. This use also illustrates history's importance in Byzantium, where aspects of the past could be revived to strengthen current arguments, a use that assumes the existence of an interested audience. We do not have the text of Theophanes' opponents, but his approach suggests that, as with the early use of the apple and eagle stories, his technique involved taking his opponents' material (and so in effect admitting popular recognition of their version) and turning it against them.

Throughout his chronicle Theophanes is determined to demonstrate both the correctness of the orthodox (and iconodule) version of history (and God's practical support for it in the form of military victories and other successes) and the errors of his heretical opponents, or perhaps, more particularly, to damn the iconoclast version. To achieve this he does infer, quite wrongly, a link between iconoclasm and Arianism. Parallel to the technique of adapting a story, Theophanes appears willing to take his opponents' material as a source and do his best to discredit it by adaptation. This is clearest in his use of an Arian source for much of the fourth century, which also suggests, surprisingly, that this Arian version still had some influence in the ninth century.[22] Likewise for the reigns of Theodosius and Marcian, Theophanes seems to have been acutely aware of the strength of the Monophysite version of their reigns with its attacks on the heroes of Chalcedon, namely Marcian, Pulcheria and Pope Leo in Rome, and its perfectly accurate claim that Theodosius had supported Monophysitism insofar as he had authorized Ephesos II. All of this was a version of history that Theophanes felt necessary to reject. So he produces a narrative that restores the reputation of orthodoxy's heroes. By the same token, he needed to undermine Monophysite praise for Valentinian's refusal to recognize Marcian. For most of Theophanes' narrative of the fourth to sixth centuries we have his sources. But for much of Theodosius' reign and especially for the final three years and for various other items involving the reputation of those involved in the theological disputes, Theophanes does not use any known source. Instead he appears to be 'correcting' the version of history

---

[22]   R. Scott, 'The image of Constantine in Malalas and Theophanes', in Magdalino, ed., *New Constantines*, 68–70.

presented in Monophysite sources[23] perhaps linked in argument (though scarcely in fact) to the contemporary big issue of Iconoclasm. His use of our stories is part of this process.

For this he mixes two techniques. He seems to have taken and adapted a Monophysite narrative of the main political events, into which he has interwoven his version of the apple story. This he separates into different stages across three years rather than repeating the continuous narrative of his source, which is clearly Malalas. So the basic apple story is given very briefly at AM 5940 (AD 447/48); Eudocia's departure for Jerusalem is at AM 5942 (AD 449/50); and Eudocia's death at AM 5947 (AD 454/55), where most notably Theophanes makes no mention of Eudocia's claim to innocence and her denial of any responsibility for Paulinus' death, which is reported in Malalas and almost every other version. Eudocia is left as guilty of adultery. Earlier, at AM 5911 (AD 418/19), Theophanes mentions Eudocia's background, baptism, beauty, intelligence and marriage to Theodosius on Pulcheria's advice, compressing all this information into a perfunctory three-and-a-half lines.[24] Paulinus and his friendship with Theodosius are not mentioned. Nor is there any mention of Eudocia not retaliating against her brothers for their greed over the inheritance but rather rewarding them with appointments – such generosity has to be reserved for the good Marcian. By depriving the account of its romantic elements Theophanes is careful to avoid any suggestion of a good story, since that would have been not merely irrelevant but contrary to his purpose. But it is in the next two stages that Theophanes' handling of the story is most complex, since these do not stand as simply part of the Eudocia story but are worked into a careful context of other material that underlies Theophanes' main aim.

That aim is to restore Theodosius' reputation as orthodox and then to reinforce Marcian's claim to be God's choice as the rightful ruler. Burgess perceptively noticed that Theophanes' account of Marcian's accession was based on and aimed at undermining Monophysite criticism.[25] This should, however, be extended to cover Theophanes' entire narrative of the reigns of both Theodosius and Marcian. Although Theophanes worked this theme right through his account of Theodosius' 42-year reign, it is most prominent in the years involving the Eudocia apple story. He achieves his picture by claiming that a perfectly orthodox but gullible Theodosius was tricked into supporting the Monophysite robber synod by the wicked eunuch Chrysaphius. The latter used his cunning as a eunuch to undermine the authority and influence of the orthodox patriarch, Flavian,

---

[23]   Reflected too in the frequency of his parallels here with Michael the Syrian.

[24]   Theophanes, AM 5911:83.19–22 is from Theodore Lector 316 (Hansen, 93.16–18) rather than Malalas.

[25]   Burgess, 'Accession', 61.

and also exploited Eudocia's feminine weaknesses. As a result Pulcheria lost her authority and retired from the palace. Then in the last year of his life Theodosius, realizing that he has been duped by Chrysaphius and Eudocia, in effect banishes the pair of them and recalls Pulcheria, who, in the final paragraph of the account of Theodosius' reign, arranges for Marcian to succeed. That leads to the eagle stories in the opening year of the pious Marcian, followed by Pope Leo asking for the *latrocinium* to be overturned and the council of Chalcedon to be summoned, which happens in the following year. So Theodosius is absolved, orthodoxy restored, and the Monophysite version of history overturned.

Although virtually every statement that Theophanes makes is taken verbatim from his sources, he nevertheless creates his own careful narrative.[26] He goes to some length to introduce his main characters at appropriate moments to prepare his readers for what is to come. We have already seen that, when Eudocia is introduced at AM 5911 (AD 418/19), the story of her rags-to-riches marriage to Theodosius is deprived of its romantic elements. So too Theophanes introduces Marcian as Gizerich's prisoner of war at the end of his narrative of the Vandals' arrival in Africa at AM 5931 (AD 438/39) only because he is conscious of the weight he will later be placing on the eagle stories, even though they will not be introduced for another twelve years. Both this and the omission of Eudocia's romance must be Theophanes' own deliberate narrative ploys. Likewise he takes advantage of a minor matter to make his audience quite unnecessarily aware of Chrysaphius at AM 5938 (AD 445/46), a couple of years ahead of his crucial role as the key villain in causing (and hence exculpating) Theodosius' various lapses. Theophanes also points out in this introduction that 'justice caught up with Chrysaphius not much later', so ensuring a happy ending (for his audience) that Theophanes later creates by a small distortion, while Malalas' robust statement that Theodosius was Chrysaphius' lover is notably omitted,[27] as had been Paulinus' friendship with Theodosius earlier. All this narrative preparation can then culminate at AM 5940–44 (AD 447/48–451/52) in the crucial final three years of Theodosius' 42-year reign and the first two of Marcian's supposedly blessed

---

[26]   Since I may appear to be challenging Cyril Mango's interpretation of Theophanes as a dossier of passages, I do stress that the success of Theophanes' manipulation depends precisely on his sticking closely to the wording of his sources. So his text in effect remains a dossier despite the alterations. His approach is parallel to adaptation in propaganda stories that rely on staying as close as possible to the original. I have discussed this further in '"The events of every year arranged without confusion": Justinian and others in the chronicle of Theophanes Confessor', in Odorico, *et al.*, eds., *L'écriture de la mémoire*, 49–65.

[27]   Malalas, *Chronographia*, 14.19:283.

rule. What is clear is that Theophanes has taken some trouble to organize this narrative rather than simply reproduce his source.

The first of Theodosius' final three years, AM 5940 (AD 447/48), begins with 'Chrysaphius, a eunuch, who exercised power over the palace and the Emperor Theodosius' and who 'being impious and not suffering to see harmony among the churches made it his purpose to disturb them.' The horror of this Monophysite attempt to gain control is the central issue for Theophanes. So Chrysaphius creates trouble for the good patriarch Flavian and then manipulates Eudocia, which leads to Pulcheria, the heroine of orthodoxy and only stabilizing force on Theodosius, being in effect driven from the palace. Then with 'Eudocia directing the Empire' Theophanes tells the apple story with remarkable brevity. His is the only account not to mention that the apple came from 'a poor man' (he is simply 'someone') and that Theodosius gave him 150 *nomismata*; he omits other details as well.[28] The romantic story, as earlier with the rags-to-riches marriage, has instead become a simple chronicle entry following Pulcheria's retirement and Eudocia's grab for power. Theophanes then provides a paragraph narrating the events leading to Ephesos II. These involve Chrysaphius, 'who controlled the palace', working on behalf of the Monophysite archimandrite Eutyches against Flavian, and using Eudocia, who despite the apple incident is still around and needed for Theophanes' narrative, until 'the pair of them pressed the emperor into decreeing that a second synod be assembled in Ephesos' with Dioscorus, the evil Alexandrian patriarch, as president, assisted by a large army. So the briefly told apple story has been presented in the context of the build-up to Theodosius' great mistake of calling and endorsing Ephesos II, which is dealt with in AM 5941 (AD 448/49). Here Theophanes can expound on the further villainies of Chrysaphius and Dioscorus, including their physical assault on the excellent Flavian that resulted in his death. At the end Theophanes emphasizes again that 'Theodosius was easily swayed' with the story of his signing papers unread so that he mistakenly ceded Eudocia to slavery 'for which he was severely reproached by Pulcheria'. So, too, the climax and denouement in AM 5942 (AD 450/51), the third of the three years involving the apple story. Here Theodosius, in the final year of his life, 'after collecting his thoughts, realized that he had been deceived by Chrysaphius' villainy' and 'then inveighed severely against Eudocia, naming her as responsible for all the evils and in particular for driving Pulcheria from the palace and also reproaching her over the affair with Paulinus.' It is only at this point that Theophanes has Eudocia asking 'to be sent away to Jerusalem', some two years after the apple incident. The reader perhaps does not bother to reflect on the improbability of this, but the delay does enable Theophanes to use the story further as part of his

---

[28] Location; occasion; 'Phrygian' apple; senate's amazement; Paulinus' illness.

final exculpation of Theodosius for causing Ephesos II. He then provides a happy ending for his readers with the restoration of Pulcheria and her translation of Flavian's relics to Constantinople; and ending the year with her proclamation of Marcian, who, perhaps in contrast to her brother, was 'distinguished by his prudence and dignity and now very old and capable', and who in marriage would guard her virginity. The Monophysite slur on her dirty affair with Marcian has been well and truly buried.

That leads to Marcian's first two years. Theophanes begins with Pulcheria 'handing over the universally detested Chrysaphius to Jordanes', who murders him (AM 5943, AD 450/51), although this requires some alteration to his sources' dating and personnel. More importantly Theophanes devotes Marcian's first year largely to the two eagle stories, demonstrating him as God's choice. Notably, Theophanes is our earliest source to provide both eagle stories, so he presumably has gone to some effort to find them three-and-a-half centuries later. He devotes the second year of Marcian's reign to Chalcedon, which is the crucial issue in Theophanes' battle with a Monophysite tradition and for which the previous narrative has been a preparation.

After that Theophanes works in various items on Pulcheria's and Marcian's good deeds, which are contrasted with Valentinian's reign in Rome. For the Monophysites, Valentinian had remained something of a hero because of his initial refusal to recognize their villain Marcian. Theophanes accepts that Valentinian himself remained orthodox, but draws attention to his depraved immorality. He also suggests that events in the west under Valentinian were in a bad way (which they were), but contrasts this with the east, where, he claims, the people 'enjoyed complete peace, justice and happiness during Marcian's rule' and that 'those were indeed golden years because of the emperor's goodness.' For this the only evidence will have been Marcian's own propaganda; but whatever the truth, the claim suited Theophanes as it revealed the benefits that flowed from the champions of Chalcedonian orthodoxy, Marcian and Pulcheria, whose goodness Theophanes keeps mentioning. In contrast he pointed to the western emperor Valentinian, who, he asserts, though theologically orthodox, had a bad history of sexual transgressions. 'He cohabited with other women in a demonic fashion despite having a beautiful wife and continually conversed even with those who practiced magic. So he was given over to a most shameful death', which Theophanes relates enthusiastically with extra moralizing for good measure. 'For where anyone sins, there will he be punished.' Just as the Monophysites had used sexual innuendo as a key element of their criticism of Marcian and Pulcheria, Theophanes now counters this with a similar emphasis on sexual transgressions by his opponents and a stress on the moral purity of his heroes. So that feature of Byzantine chronicles of countering opponents by using their methods against them becomes Theophanes' final riposte to the Monophysite slur on Pulcheria and Marcian with their version of the apple story.

Malalas

A recognition of how Theophanes manipulates his account of Eudocia and the apple story makes it easier to appreciate the different approach of his source Malalas. Malalas' account is really the conclusion of a story of the life of Eudocia. His Book 13 had opened with, for Malalas, the most important event in history apart from the Incarnation and Resurrection, namely Christian victory with Constantine (and to some extent the threat to this victory under Julian). For the remainder of Book 13, extending to the death of Honorius, Malalas had been struggling with his chronology of events and the succession of emperors (or else was simply not much interested), and gets confused between east and west. Book 14 allowed a new start with Theodosius II, for which Malalas has in effect two separate narratives: first the Eudocia story, and then everything else, with no attempt at interrelating the two. So the Eudocia story begins with Theodosius' boyhood friendship with Paulinus, then an adolescent Theodosius pestering his virgin sister to find him a beautiful wife, next the engaging account of Eudocia's Athenian pagan background and being left destitute, her being paraded privately for Theodosius' delectation as if in a brideshow with Theodosius and Paulinus hiding behind a screen, Eudocia's generosity to her greedy brothers, the apple story in full detail, and finally Eudocia's death and her deathbed claim of innocence. It is a wonderful narrative, full of lively romantic detail. It is, however, quite separate from the second narrative that follows, though that narrative covers the same chronological period, opening with a new introduction of Theodosius and without a single mention of Eudocia or Paulinus and with Pulcheria only mentioned once at the very end with Theodosius' endorsement to her of Marcian as his successor. She belongs to Marcian's narrative rather than Theodosius'. That is, Malalas sees the whole Eudocia story, in which Pulcheria and Paulinus have major roles, as an isolated narrative with no other relevance to its contemporary context, and then provides a separate narrative on Theodosius' reign in which Pulcheria, Eudocia and Paulinus are simply irrelevant. Presumably the Eudocia story comes from a source distinct from his normal chronicle material. We can only guess at why he has given it precedence, but throughout his chronicle Malalas does show his fondness for a good story, particularly something where sexual morality is an issue.[29]

---

[29]   R. Scott, 'Malalas' view of the classical past', in G. W. Clarke, ed., *Reading the Past in Late Antiquity* (Canberra, 1990), 148–64.

Malalas' source presumably goes back, directly or indirectly, to the same propaganda aimed at saving Chalcedon's heroes, Pulcheria and Marcian. That Malalas' version is oblivious to theological issues is not surprising. Malalas simply was not interested in theology, so it would not be odd if he, rather than any intermediary source, removed the theological content and context. Nor can we tell if the suggestion of Eudocia's innocence would have been already admitted in the Chalcedonian propaganda version, but this is possible, however unlikely, since it is Theophanes alone who does not allow it; the rejection of her innocence is clearly Theophanes' own construct.

It is just possible that the stories of Eudocia's earlier life could also go back to the same Chalcedonian propaganda that created the Eudocia version of the apple story and so provided Malalas with his complete narrative. Perhaps, too, the eagle stories are likewise absent simply because they had not been created into a single narrative for a lazy Malalas along with the rest of Marcian's propaganda.[30] But, equally, the one element that Malalas does include from this propaganda – St John's revelation to Theodosius at Ephesos – was sufficient for showing Marcian's right to rule and was more in keeping with Malalas' predilection for prophetic dreams and oracles than the symbolic portents of the dead soldier Augustus and the eagle stories. Likewise his emphasis on the significance of Paulinus for both Theodosius and Eudocia throughout their lives and his later references to Theodosius' erotic love for Chrysaphius are difficult to reconcile with Chalcedonian propaganda. Whatever his source, there is no need to deprive Malalas of the credit for creating his Eudocia narrative. But whether he created it or simply preserved it, Malalas has left us a colourful and engaging narrative to enjoy. It remains one of the delights of Byzantine history as literature, but it also underlines the extent of Theophanes' later manipulation of it.

Later versions

Evagrius, writing his *Ecclesiastical History* at the end of the sixth century, is the first writer after Procopius to mention an eagle story, but only the Gizerich one that he got from Procopius. He provides a detailed account and devotes an amount of space to Eudocia's two pilgrimages to Jerusalem and her money, but does not include the apple story though he is aware

---

[30]   The only occurrence of the complete set of Marcian's propaganda demonstrating his divine selection (i.e. St John's revelation to Theodosius, the dead soldier Augustus, and both eagle stories) is in Nikephoros Kallistos Xanthopoulos, 15.1: *PG* 147.9–12. He, however, is an underrated historian who was certainly capable of compiling this from various sources rather than lifting it from elsewhere.

of rumours about her, which he rejects.[31] The *Chronicon Paschale* of about 630 follows Malalas in reporting Theodosius' apple, but naturally has no eagles, which must wait till Theophanes' research, though still omitted in the tenth century by George the Monk. George, however, does follow Malalas to create a narrative of Eudocia's life, including naturally the apple story where he particularly stresses Eudocia's esteem for Paulinus because of his role in bringing about her marriage, and by implication a suggestion of Eudocia's innocence in the affair. George uses this account to conclude his Theodosius narrative, in effect a collection of half a dozen highlights of popular history from the reign without any indication of chronology.

So despite Theophanes, it is not until the eleventh century that the two eagle stories occur again together; this happens in the chronicles of Symeon Magister[32] and Pseudo-Symeon.[33] Yet though both these chroniclers must thus have been aware of Theophanes' account, they both reveal signs of also being influenced by the other traditions. The two Symeons offer linguistically similar but not identical accounts of the apple story, though not drawn precisely from any known source. Both do have Theodosius giving the poor man 100 rather than 150 *nomismata*, which suggests the survival of the Monophysite counter-counter-story together with at least a hint in each of their acceptance also of Eudocia's innocence. Symeon *magister* covers both eagle stories very briefly in just thirteen lines, with a further thirteen for Eudocia's life. Yet despite his awareness of Theophanes for the two eagle stories, he has still clearly relied on Malalas (presumably via George the Monk) rather than Theophanes for the apple. He draws attention twice to Paulinus' influence in arranging Eudocia's marriage in contrast to Paulinus' exclusion in Theophanes, and he also includes Eudocia's deathbed protest of innocence and other details that are absent from Theophanes. Pseudo-Symeon, in contrast, is very much more detailed and essentially follows Theophanes almost verbatim for almost all of Theodosius' 42-year reign and also for Marcian's, including the narrative of both eagle stories. Yet despite his close reliance on Theophanes he also restructures that narrative in small but significant ways. It would be out of place to consider here all the details of this, but for our purposes his most dramatic alteration is to transfer the apple story from Theodosius' fortieth year to his seventeenth, where he also avoids using Theophanes' version. The transfer is certainly quite deliberate, since he follows Theophanes for that crucial fortieth year almost verbatim up to the point where the apple story should appear and continues verbatim from where it ended

---

[31]   Evagrius, *Ecclesiastical History*, 1.21.

[32]   Symeon Magister, *Chronicon*, ed. S. Wahlgren, CFHB 44/1 (Berlin 2006), 124–5 (Eudocia), 129 (eagles).

[33]   Paris. gr. 1712, fol. 103v, line 34 to fol. 104r, line 5 (apple), fol. 108v, line 14 to fol. 109r, line 13 (eagles).

in Theophanes.[34] It almost looks as if he had copied Theophanes verbatim for the whole of that long year of narrative and then simply excised the apple story. The insertion of the story in Theodosius' seventeenth year (at the expense of Theophanes' narrative for that and the following year) is the only place where Pseudo-Symeon deviates from Theophanes' order of narrative. The inserted apple story, being almost identical with that in Symeon *magister*, is thus, though brief, also more informative than Theophanes' version. The combination of a different, more informative version in a different place has the effect of destroying Theophanes' careful arrangement and interpretation, and so producing instead, despite being otherwise almost totally reliant on Theophanes, an interpretation that rather resembles Malalas and George. So the two Symeons are our earliest witnesses to use both Malalas and Theophanes. But their accounts also suggest that the pro-Monophysite counter-counter-story had some success even if the Monophysite Pulcheria story had lost, and that success is also quite evident in the *Patria*'s strangely different version where both Eudocia and Paulinus are innocent, with the latter kept safe from Theodosius by the *Anargyroi* until he finished building their church.[35]

The twelfth century's literary confidence produced new treatments. Zonaras and Glykas pointedly avoid their sources' language and arrangement. Glykas has both eagles as well as the whole Eudocia story[36] from Malalas, including the deathbed denial, so the mixture of Theophanes and Malalas is now established. Zonaras' account of Eudocia is divided up in a similar way to Theophanes, but he also used much of Malalas' material, including, too, Eudocia's literary achievements, which others omitted.[37] Kedrenos' account of the two eagle stories is based closely on Theophanes and needs no further comment, but his use of the apple story shows twelfth-century predilections.[38] Possibly following Pseudo-Symeon he places it in Theodosius' fourteenth year, a year he introduces with a famine and its almost certainly anachronistic result for the fifth century of Paphlagonians turning their children into eunuchs for sale.[39] He then tells the story of Eudocia's background and marriage, but without mentioning Paulinus. The apple story is told next as a kind of moralizing appendix, but with greater emphasis than he gave to the marriage story. What is

---

[34]   The story should occur at Paris. gr. 1712, fol. 107r, line 33.

[35]   Ed. Th. Preger, *Scriptores originum Constantinopolitanarum*, 2 vols. (Leipzig, 1901–1907, repr. 1989), I, 261.1–263.3.

[36]   Glykas, 487.4–17 (eagles); 484.1–485.4 (Eudocia story).

[37]   Zonaras, *Epitome*, III, 100.18–102.12 (marriage); 110.8–111.10 (apple); 113.10–115.4 (eagles).

[38]   Kedrenos, I, 590.7–591.24 (apple); 603.11–604.13 (eagles).

[39]   Though an established practice in Kedrenos' time. Kedrenos is the only source for this famine.

intriguing is that Kedrenos, although following Malalas closely in terms of language, uses the story to illustrate envy, a characteristic twelfth-century literary theme, just as he and his contemporaries also do for Belisarius. He also turns the apple's donor into a 'poor man from Asia' to compensate for deleting the apple's epithet of 'Phrygian'. He also has to introduce Paulinus here specifically, having presumably omitted him from the background marriage story deliberately, as this now enables him to highlight his theme of envy. That links his account with that of Manasses' verse chronicle where both apple and eagle stories are treated with greater complexity.[40] Manasses both links Eudocia's apple to another apple episode, the judgement of Paris, and employs a range of contemporary literary techniques to produce an entertaining and instructive narrative. The stories are now literature rather than propaganda, essential items in Byzantine memory of its distant past, equivalent to Canute and the waves or George Washington's cherry tree, far removed from the original Chalcedonian political response to Monophysite slander or Marcian's advertising his rule.

The stories continued to be told: they are present, for instance, in Nikephoros Kallistos Xanthopoulos' fourteenth-century *Ecclesiastical History* and in Pseudo-Dorotheos' *Biblion Historikon*, which, though composed about 1570, became in 1631 the first printed book of Greek history with over thirty editions by the nineteenth century. But despite the seeming conservatism of the chronicle tradition over a millennium or more, it is worth remembering that the stories did evolve considerably from their origins as effective religious and political propaganda in a society that knew how to exploit a good story.[41]

---

[40] I. Nilsson and E. Nyström, 'To compose, read, and use a Byzantine text: aspects of the chronicle of Constantine Manasses', *BMGS* 33/1 (2009), 42–60.

[41] This paper was first drafted for a seminar on Byzantine chronicles in Athens in November 2006 organized by Athanasios Markopoulos. Thanks are owed to him and the other speakers: John Burke, Ingela Nilsson, Eva Nyström and Paul Tuffin.

7. Dream narratives in historical writing. Making sense of history in Theophanes' *Chronographia*

George T. Calofonos

Back in 1990, at the height of the Kuwait crisis that led to Operation Desert Storm, the world was awaiting Saddam Hussein's reply to the ultimatum delivered to him by the allied forces. On 23 March of that year, a piece of news dominated bulletins and newspaper articles around the world.[1] The night before, Saddam Hussein had a dream. In his dream the Prophet had appeared before him and proclaimed that Iraq's missiles were pointed in the wrong direction. The story was accompanied by extensive analysis by Middle East experts. The dream clearly indicated that Saddam was preparing Iraqi public opinion for a withdrawal from Kuwait. In other words, having couched his resistance to Western demands in terms of Holy War, he would present his forthcoming compliance as obedience to God's Will: the Prophet, undoubtedly, did not sanction hostility to the allied forces, some of whom were fellow Muslims.

Eventually, this interpretation was proved wrong. Assuming that the story was put into circulation by the Iraqi side, its purpose must have been to intensify, rather than de-escalate, Holy War pressure: not only did the Prophet endorse Saddam's policy – since he honoured him with an appearance in his dream – but he was an active participant in his war strategy, fine-tuning the positioning of Iraqi missiles.

Whatever the case might have been, Iraq was eventually defeated – twice –, Saddam has been executed, and the story has been forgotten. It sounds a bit naive today, out of tune with the pragmatic approach of contemporary international policymaking. In our post-Freudian times, the socio-cultural dimension of dreaming, which is rooted in tradition and has a prominent political function, is alien. To our mind it is a sad,

---

[1]   See e.g. M.L. Wald, 'Record Fall Puts Oil Below $30', *The New York Times*, 23 October 1990, at http://www.nytimes.com/1990/10/23/business/record-fall-puts-oil-below-30.html, accessed 19 June 2010.

fossilized survival of a world long past, but it is still very much alive, it seems, in present-day Islam.

Dreams of this sort function on a historical rather than a psychological level. Their scope is public rather than private; they point to the future rather than past. It is exactly this kind of dream that often occurs in the historiographical sources of Late Antiquity and Byzantium. In this paper, I shall be looking at ways in which such dream-reports were incorporated in historical narrative, and particularly in chronography. I shall use as an example the ninth-century chronicle of Theophanes the Confessor, a highly esteemed Byzantine historiographical work, which never ceased to provide subsequent writers of historical accounts with material for their own narratives. Theophanes, therefore, is a good starting point for a general survey of dream narratives in Byzantine historical writing.[2]

Under the heading of Byzantine dreaming, I also include reports of experiences or phenomena that we would classify today as 'visions'. Both visions and dreams were thought in Antiquity and Byzantium to belong to the same mode of perception: they were normally classed 'dreaming', with visions sometimes occupying the top level of hierarchical classifications of dream types. This lack of discrimination between dreaming, daydreaming or visions in Byzantine sources was amply illustrated by Margaret Kenny in one of the past Spring Symposia.[3] For the sake of convenience I shall, therefore, be referring to this whole range of phenomena as 'dreams', even if 'dreams/visions' would obviously be a more accurate choice of terminology.

Theophanes' chronicle includes thirteen dreams. These belong to the wider repertoire of the bizarre and the supernatural, which informs

---

[2]   This task will become considerably easier to undertake upon the completion of the database 'Dreaming in Byzantium', which Christine Angelidi, Katerina Nikolaou, Stamatis Busses and I are presently compiling at the National Hellenic Research Foundation in Athens. Historiographical sources are a priority, and all dream reports in historical sources from the seventh to the twelfth centuries will, we hope, soon be available online. Study of Byzantine dreaming has advanced considerably in recent years: this was evident in the conference on 'Dreams and Visions in Late Antiquity and Byzantium' (Athens, 23–4 May 2008), the first international conference dedicated entirely to the study of Byzantine dreams. It included three papers on historiography: the first on Procopius by Ilias Anagnostakis, the second, on Middle Byzantine historiography, by Paul Magdalino, and the third on the Continuation of Theophanes, a paper by me, which follows on from this one. The proceedings will be published soon by Ashgate.

[3]   M. Kenny, 'Distinguishing between dreams and visions in ninth-century hagiography', communication at the 30th Spring Symposium of Byzantine Studies, 'Byzantium Dead or Alive', Birmingham, March 1996, published online in *Gouden Hoorn / Golden Horn. Journal of Byzantium* 4.1 (Summer 1996), at http://www.isidore-of-seville.com/goudenhoorn/41margaret.html, accessed 19 June 2010.

historical writing in Late Antiquity. Together with prophecies, earthquakes, comets, abnormalities and other signs, dreams were viewed as bearers of messages from the divine world. What sets dreams apart is that they are an everyday experience common to all humanity: an intriguing and perplexing experience, but often alien and threatening.[4] They appear to be windows to a different realm of reality, their rich imagery being always open to interpretation.

Communication with the divine was not the only function attributed to dreaming in Antiquity and Byzantium.[5] Some dreams were also thought to have an inherent prophetic value arising from the divine element of the soul, while others were considered to be insignificant – the outcome of psychological and physiological procedures, or even demonic deception. It was significant dreams, however, that were deemed important enough to be recorded in history. Viewed as vehicles of divine intervention, they possessed a legitimizing function, and were very useful in historical writing for *making* a story.

On the other hand, dream-reports are narratives by themselves: small narratives that show an impressive uniformity in terms of structure over time. As John Hanson has observed about Hellenistic and Roman dreaming, 'it is … difficult to distinguish the evidence of these periods from what preceded them',[6] and this holds true to a great extent with regard to what followed them. As we shall see, their well-defined, framed narrative form – the outcome of long-established convention, as well as a trait inherent in the dreaming experience – also makes them useful narrative devices for *telling* a story.

To give an example of the form of dream narratives, I shall turn to Theophanes' text. In his section on the year 6146, the thirteenth year of Constans II, Theophanes gives an account of the sea battle at Phoinix:[7]

> This man [Abulauar] arrived at Phoinix (as it is called) in Lycia, where the Emperor Constans lay with the Roman fleet, and engaged him in sea battle. As the emperor was about to fight on sea, he saw in a dream that

---

[4]   Cf. P. L. Berger and T. Lackman, *The Social Construction of Reality* (Harmondsworth, 1967): dreams, like sickness, injury or death, are marginal situations expressing a threat to the paramount reality of everyday life. They need to be invested with meaning in order to cease to be threatening.

[5]   See G. T. Calofonos, 'Ὀνειροκριτική και οραματική γνώση στην ύστερη αρχαιότητα και τον πρώιμο Χριστιανισμό', in D. Kyrtatas and C. Balla, eds., *Η μετάδοση της γνώσης στην αρχαιότητα, Topika*, 5 (Athens, 1999), 79–88.

[6]   J. S. Hanson, 'Dreams and Visions in the Graeco-Roman World and Early Christianity', *Aufstieg und Niedergang der Römischen Welt* II 23/2 (1980), 1394–427.

[7]   Theophanes, 345–6; Mango and Scott, *The Chronicle of Theophanes*, 482, with a more literal rendering of the phrase 'Θὲς ἄλλῳ νίκην'.

night that he was at Thessalonike. When he was awakened, he related his vision to an interpreter of dreams, who said, 'Would, O emperor, that you had not fallen asleep or seen a dream, for your being in Thessalonike is interpreted as (Θὲς ἄλλῳ νίκην) "place on another the victory", (that is) victory will go to your enemy.' Now the emperor, who had taken no measures to draw up his battle line, ordered the Roman fleet to fight, and when the two sides engaged, the Romans were defeated and the sea was dyed with Roman blood.

Before entering into a discussion of this dream narrative as a story, I shall first consider its form.[8] The core dream experience itself, whether real or fictional ('He finds himself in Thessalonike'), is explicitly framed by a report of its coordinates: *what* it is, to *whom* and *how* it occurs, *what* it means and *what* follows it. The dreamer's name and status are given, as well as place and time (although this is normally part of the dream-narrative frame, here it has already been stated in the wider narrative of the historical record in which the dream-report is integrated). The emotional state of the dreamer is another important factor, and the shift in his state of consciousness ('in a dream that night' meaning 'asleep') is also noted. These markers of time, status, place and state of consciousness signal the onset of the dreaming experience. Its outset is signalled with further markers: shift in the state of consciousness ('he was awakened'), actions taken ('related his vision to an interpreter of dreams'), and meaning. Most of these markers, but not necessarily all, are normally present in such narratives. In this particular dream narrative, for example, the marker indicating emotional state, usually placed at the outset of the dreaming experience, is missing. Dream frame is an integral part of the dream narrative – and hence the dreaming experience reported: without it, the description of dream content – that is, the dream proper – would be incomprehensible. The phrase 'He was in Thessalonike' hardly reveals to the reader a reference to a dream or anything significant for that matter. Sometimes, however, the frame can be minimal. This is the case in another dream narrative from Theophanes involving a soldier named Constantine, who fought during the Arab siege of Nicaea, in the time of Leo III.[9] The soldier threw a stone at one of the icons of the Virgin Mary, which were set up on the city wall as a means of defence, and broke it. Thereafter, the Virgin appeared to him and told him, 'See what a

---

[8]   This dream narrative's function is being examined here at three levels: the textual, the contextual and the intertextual. A similar tripartite analysis of Mayan dreams – from an anthropological perspective – has been proposed by B. Tedlock: 'Quiché Maya dream interpretation', *Ethos* 9/4 (1981), 313–30, and 'The role of dreams and visionary narratives in Mayan cultural survival', *Ethos* 20/4 (1992), 453–76, esp. 468.

[9]   Theophanes, 406.

brave thing you have done to me? Verily you've done it against your head'. Needless to say, in the battle on the next day, the wretched man's head was shattered by a stone thrown by an enemy catapult. Here the phrase 'the Virgin appeared to him' does not need the state of consciousness marker 'in a vision': Theophanes nevertheless includes it in his text, proving the tenacity of literary convention in dream narrative.

Dream narrative frame is sometimes used in a much more creative manner in other kinds of Byzantine writing such as epistolography or hagiography: in some instances, after the hero of the story finds him- or herself involved in strange or threatening situations, he or she is suddenly awakened, to discover – together with the reader – that what had happened was only part of a dream.[10] While a frame of markers of some sort is essential for the function of the dream narrative, the description of the dream proper is not always so. The statement 'He was commanded to do such and such a thing in a dream' may well retain the fundamental functions of the dream narrative, both on the level of *narration* and that of the *story*, without disclosing the actual dream content to the reader. In Theophanes a good example is a story about the foundation of Constantinople:[11] while Constantine had decided to build his city on the plain of Troy, no one less than God Himself commanded him in a dream to build Constantinople in Byzantium. Theophanes discloses nothing further about this important dream.

Both in prophetic and instructive dreams, one of the main components of the narratives is dream fulfilment. In this sense the dream narrative integrates the historical events to which it refers, and which are normally narrated immediately after it. Thus, in the case of the Constantinople story, the ensuing account, which describes the actual building of the city, is incorporated entirely within the frame of Constantine's dream.[12] Furthermore, one could argue that, on a second level, from this point in the *Chronographia* onwards, every future reference to the city is coloured by this dream narrative: in the mind of the reader from now on, 'Constantinople' is 'the divinely ordained city'.

To go back to the dream of Constans, the dream narrative subsumes the short text that follows and gives a more detailed account of the sea battle.[13] Fearing for his life, Constans dresses up a soldier, actually a war hero, with the imperial robes and flees the scene. The soldier bravely puts

---

[10] See e.g. *The Miracles of Saint Artemios*, ed. A. Papadopoulos-Kerameus, *Varia Graeca Sacra* (St Petersburg, 1909), and *The Miracles of Saint Demetrios*, ed. P. Lemerle, *Les plus anciens recueils des Miracles de Saint Démétrios* (Paris, 1979), for numerous such examples.

[11] Theophanes, 23.

[12] Ibid., 23–4.

[13] Ibid., 346.

up resistance and dies instead of the cowardly emperor. The inclusion of this short paragraph within the dream narrative frame will, I hope, help illustrate how this dream episode functions as a story within the wider narrative frame of Theophanes' work.

Before proceeding, however, it may be useful to keep in mind the way in which Theophanes' chronography is structured. Two scholars have recently attempted to discern some order and organization behind the chaos of what Cyril Mango has aptly called 'the scissors and paste technique' of Theophanes,[14] and what the late Alexander Kazhdan has called 'the endless monotony of annalistic chronography'.[15] Roger Scott has demonstrated that Theophanes' scissors were busy unscrupulously rearranging chronology in ways that would prove God's partiality to the pious and the orthodox. He even suppresses any reference to Constantine I and his successors' connection to Monophysitism, among other things.[16] Alexander Kazhdan, on the other hand, in his posthumous *History of Byzantine Literature*, detects in Theophanes' work the idea that the empire, after the Golden Age of Constantine, had entered a process of gradual decline.[17] Furthermore, Kazhdan draws our attention to Theophanes' use of episodes. These are larger narrative units, which tell an actual story, thus breaking the monotony of the chronographer's endless list of events arranged by year.[18] These themes and techniques are clearly present in the work of Theophanes. The two ways of looking at the chronicle – in terms of the themes of orthodoxy and decline respectively – are not mutually exclusive. They are alternative explanatory ways that, in a both contrasting and complementary manner, serve to turn the amorphous and monotonous record of events into a more meaningful text for its contemporary reader.

Dreams, long-established agents of the supernatural, are well-tested sources of meaning. I shall return to the sea battle of Phoinix, to Constans and his dream of Thessalonike, in order to suggest how this dream narrative would have been understood by a reader of the *Chronographia*. A first-level 'innocent' reading would be that this narrative is about divination and destiny. The emperor had an inauspicious dream, which was explained to him by an expert. The decipherment was carried out by

---

[14]   C. Mango, 'The availability of books in the Byzantine Empire, A.D. 750–850', in *Byzantine Books and Bookmen* (Washington, DC, 1975), 36, n. 300; see also his 'Who wrote the Chronicle of Theophanes?', *ZRVI* 18 [1978]), 578–87 (both reprinted in *Byzantium and its Image* [London, 1984], as studies VII and XI respectively).

[15]   Kazhdan, *A History of Byzantine Literature (650–850)*, 226, 229.

[16]   R. Scott, '"The events of every year, arranged without confusion": Justinian and others in the Chronicle of Theophanes', in Odorico, *et al.*, eds., *L'écriture de la mémoire*, 49–65.

[17]   Kazhdan, *A History of Byzantine Literature (650–850)*, 216–24, esp. 221.

[18]   Kazhdan describes these episodic units as 'novelettes': ibid., 227–9.

means of *paronomasia* – a standard oneirocritical method.[19] At first Constans tried to ignore it, but on realizing that it was true, he fled to save his life. The story offers no indication of any opportunity the emperor might have had to avoid battle altogether and thus to save the lives of his men. Any suspicion of irresponsibility is enhanced by what the dream interpreter told the emperor: 'Would, O emperor, that you had not fallen asleep…'. Though this appears initially to be a rhetorical device, expressing the interpreter's despair, it may also reflect popular belief in the existence of a magical homoeopathic relation between the dream and its meaning.[20] In other words, if the emperor had not dreamed of Thessalonike he would not have lost the battle. The reader, however, realizes that, on the eve of this crucial sea battle and while surrounded by an enemy fleet, rather than planning his defence line, the emperor went to bed and slept like a baby, quite irresponsibly on his part – some people would have said 'criminally'.

In the second layer, a less innocent reader would read this episode in the context of similar accounts of dreams that generals had before battles, which in most cases portend victory.[21] Byzantine manuals of military strategy, following Roman ones, advise generals to announce to their armies

---

[19]   Interpretations based on phonetic or etymological analogies are quite common in Byzantine dreambooks. For example, being chased in a dream signifies persecution, a pun based on the double meaning of the word διώκω (*Dreambook of the Prophet Daniel*, line 38, ed. F. Drexl, 'Das Traumbuch des Propheten Daniel nach dem cod. Vatic. Palat. gr. 319', *BZ* 26 [1926], 290–314); a fox (κερδώ) in a dream signifies future profit (κέρδος) (*Dreambook of Patriarch Nikephoros*, v. 51, ed. G. Guidorizzi, Pseudo-Niceforo, *Libro dei sogni* [Naples, 1985]); standing in a church (ἐκκλησία), a lawsuit (ἔγκλησις) (v. 32); milk (γάλα), serenity (γαληνοὺς τρόπους) (v. 18); and so forth. On the Byzantine oneirocritic tradition and its methods see S. Oberhelman, *Dreambooks in Byzantium: Six* Oneirocritica *in Translation with Commentary and Introduction* (Aldershot, 2008), and his introduction to the translation of Achmet's dreambook, *The Oneirocriticon of Achmet: A Medieval Greek Treatise on the Interpretation of Dreams* (Lubbock, TX, 1991); G. Guidorizzi's introduction to his edition of *Nikephoros*; also Calofonos, 'Ονειροκριτική και οραματική γνώση'; and the excellent study of Achmet's Arabic sources by M. Mavroudi, *A Byzantine Book on Dream Interpretation: The Oneirocriticon of Achmet and Its Arabic Sources* (Leiden, 2002), with extensive bibliography.

[20]   On these magical practices see S. Eitrem, 'Dreams and divination in magical ritual', in C. A. Faraone and D. Obbink, eds., *Magika Hiera: Ancient Greek Magic and Religion* (New York and Oxford, 1991), 175–87; also M. K. Stephanides, 'Ονειροπομποί', *Laographia* 7 (1923), 259–65.

[21]   There is a strong ancient Near Eastern tradition of such dreams reflected in the vision of Joshua (5:13–15). The famous Dream of Scipio also belongs to this genre.

before battle that they had dreams that foretold victory.[22] Thus, Constans' dream of defeat is highly untypical in terms of literary convention as well as cultural norm.

An educated reader would have read the dream as a parody of the well-known dream experienced by Alexander the Great before the capture of Tyre in Phoenicia (which suggestively evokes Constans' Phoinix). While besieging the city, Alexander dreamt of a Satyr dancing on a shield. When he related his dream to the famous dream-interpreter Aristandros of Telmessos, who accompanied him on his campaigns, the latter told him that the Satyr (Σάτυρος) was to be interpreted Σὰ Τύρος, 'Tyre is yours'. The story is to be found in Plutarch,[23] but also in the *Oneirokritika* of Artemidoros,[24] the second-century pagan handbook of dream interpretation that enjoyed wide circulation in Byzantium.

A less learned reader need not have looked any further for a good dream of victory. The very first dream narrative Theophanes records is Constantine's dream before the battle of the Milvian Bridge.[25] In his account of this famous story, he follows the version of Eusebius' *Life of Constantine*.[26] On the eve of the crucial battle with Maxentius, having observed the sign of a cross made of light with the inscription 'In this conquer', the founding father of the Byzantine Empire received a visit of Christ in a dream, who instructed him to construct the *labaron*, a golden cross that would ensure victory. The *labaron*, the narrator of the chronicle remarks, was still in existence during his time. What Constantine's dream and the *labaron* represent is a pact with God, which assures the Byzantine emperor of victory as long as he is Christian – that is, a *pious* and *Orthodox* Christian, as Theophanes implies.[27] But Constans was neither of the two. Read against the account of Constantine's dream – as it was in fact read – the dream narrative of Constans takes on extremely negative implications for its protagonist. Through this – and the strong allusions to the dream of Alexander – the emperor stands in contrast to two paragons of Byzantine imperial ideology. The dream and its interpretation, combined with the description of Constans' behaviour during the battle, make the dream narrative a libel at the expense of the heretical emperor. Its effect

---

[22]   Cf. Leo VI the Wise, *Tactica*, 177, PG 107.1061; also 78–80, PG 107.1033–6.

[23]   Plutarch, *Alexander* 24.8–9, Loeb 7 (London, 1971).

[24]   Artemidorus of Daldis, *Onirocriticon libri V*, 4.24, ed. R. A. Pack (Leipzig, 1963).

[25]   Theophanes, 13–14.

[26]   Eusebius of Caesaria, *Life of Constantine*, 1.28–31, ed. F. Winkelmann, *Eusebius Werke, Band 1.1* (Berlin, 1975), 3–151.

[27]   On Constantine see R. Scott, 'The image of Constantine in Malalas and Theophanes', in Magdalino, ed., *New Constantines*, ed., 57–71; also Kazhdan, *A History of Byzantine Literature (650–850)*, 227.

becomes more apparent as the historical narrative progresses and further evidence of his cruelty and his unreliability is brought out. His defects are epitomized by the narrator in the account of his assassination in a bath at Syracuse.[28] People hated him because of his cruelty: he had executed his brother Theodosius; he had deceived Pope Martin and sent him into exile; he had cut off the hand and the tongue of Maximus the Confessor. In this way, the dream and its outcome – that is, the dream *narrative* of defeat – are linked to the assassination account, framing Constans' reign, and infusing it with an aroma of divine disapproval.[29]

Another theme of dream narratives in the chronicles related to divine disapproval is that of the condemnation of emperors to death. There are two such narratives in Theophanes. In the first, a double dream, dreamt by the aging emperor Anastasius and Amantius his *praepositus*,[30] a terrifying man crossed out fifteen years from the life of the 90-year-old emperor to punish him for his erroneous – i.e. heretical – beliefs. At the same time a wild boar knocked down a helpless Amantius in his own dream. When the dream interpreter Proclus was urgently brought in, he proclaimed that they would both die soon. And die they did, if only to facilitate the ascent to the throne of the 'orthodox' Justin I, the founder of Justinian's dynasty.

---

[28]   Theophanes, 351–2.

[29]   This dream narrative is part of a section of the Chronicle, thought to be derived from lost Syrian sources that, for religious reasons, would be much more sympathetic to Constans than the orthodox Theophanes. A very similar account of Constans' dream can be found in the reconstituted chronicle of Dionysius of Tel-Maḥrē, a work of the ninth century: ed. and trans. A. Palmer, *The Seventh Century in West-Syrian Chronicles* (Liverpool, 1993), 179–80. Unfortunately, the evidence from this chronicle's version of the dream narrative cannot support such a view any further. Its meaning cannot be stretched to sustain positive undertones for the heretical emperor any more than Theophanes' account does. By this evidence alone, it would appear that it was the Syrian chronicle that copied Theophanes' account of the dream or some other orthodox source. Furthermore, the dream's interpretation is based on a pun in Greek, which also suggests a Greek source for the dream narrative. Fortunately, the endeavour of determining the chronicle's sources is irrelevant to my argument in this paper, as I try to interpret the text of Theophanes in its own terms: as a piece of literature read and perhaps enjoyed by a contemporary audience who, surely, were not interested in its supposed dependence on Syrian sources.

[30]   Theophanes, 163–4, also 165–6 for the death of Amantius. Cf. G. T. Calofonos, 'Dreaming at the End of Time. Eschatology and propaganda in sixth-century historiography' (forthcoming), and 'Το ιστορικό όνειρο στο τέλος της αρχαιότητας', in D. Kyrtatas, ed., ὄψις ἐνυπνίου: Χρήσεις των ονείρων στην αρχαιότητα (Herakleion, 1993), 283–322, esp. 302–6, where I analyze extensively the same dream episode's functions in the chronicle of John Malalas. In Theophanes, however, the story is stripped of its eschatological context.

The second dream narrative marks the onset of a traumatic and perplexing development for society of the times. Shortly before his deposition and execution by the tyrant Phocas, his predecessor Marcian was offered a choice by a mysterious voice issuing from the icon of Christ that allegedly stood on top of the Chalke Gate of the imperial palace – a highly symbolic icon in Theophanes' chronicle. It was the reported destruction of this icon by Leo III that in turn signalled the onset of iconoclasm.[31] The speaking icon asked Marcian in his dream whether he would prefer to pay for his sins 'here and now' or 'in the life hereafter'.[32] Needless to say, Marcian chose to pay in this life, making the way for the tyrannical reign of Phocas, which never ceased to shock the Byzantines. St Anastasius of Sinai, a near contemporary, quotes a story where a perplexed pious monk asks God why he allowed a monster like Phocas to become the ruler of the Christian empire. After days of intense prayer, the monk heard a supernatural voice, not unlike the one in Maurice's dream, answering: 'Because I could not find anyone worse'.[33]

It is not possible to cover here in full the implications and function of those two deadly dreams. In order to demonstrate further not only the way dream narratives relate to a wider historical narrative, but also how they manifest their inherent political power, I shall turn briefly to another – lighter – theme: that of dreaming of becoming an emperor – and sometimes succeeding!

One might suppose that a certain Philippikos had read his Theophanes, were it not for the fact that he actually is a character in Theophanes. He was banished to the island of Cephalonia by the Emperor Tiberios Apsimar for announcing that he had dreamt that an eagle flying above him had provided him with shade and that he was therefore destined to be the next emperor.[34] Still, he might have read Theophanes' sources, because, as a careful reader of the chronicle would certainly know at this point of the narrative, enjoying the shade of an eagle in real life was the sign that had already predicted that another nobody, a common soldier by the name of Marcian, was to become emperor. This earned Marcian two sponsors who

---

[31] Whether Leo III was indeed an iconoclast remains an open question: the current consensus seems to be that he really was not, although the argument is not always entirely convincing. Furthermore, the existence of the famous image of Christ above the Chalke Gate in the times of Leo has also been disputed. There is, however, no need to address these two arguments in this paper, as they are irrelevant to my analysis. What is important to the understanding of the function of such dream narratives is how they are presented by Theophanes and how they were perceived by his readers.

[32] Theophanes, 284–6.

[33] Anastasius of Sinai, *Interrogationes et responsiones*, 16, *PG* 89.476.

[34] Theophanes, 372.

financed the first steps of his impressive military career that led eventually to his marriage to the Empress Pulcheria and to accession to the imperial throne.[35] Dreaming of becoming an emperor was a serious offence; hence dream interpretation was forbidden by imperial Roman law from the very beginning, in the time of Augustus.[36] However strange, this story was not unheard of: a similar story occurs in Ammianus Marcellinus.[37] What would come as a surprise, at least to the ignorant reader, is that nine years and several pages later, Philippicus resurfaces, still an exile – this time in Cherson. He stages a coup, overthrows Justinian II, who was then emperor, and occupies the imperial throne.[38]

Eight out of thirteen dream narratives in the *Chronographia* pertain to royalty; though the dreams were not necessarily dreamt by the rulers themselves, they nevertheless refer to them.[39] They serve as channels for the Christian emperor's privileged interaction with the divine. At the same time they are vehicles of political power, agents of imperial propaganda, or personal claims to power. They usually appear at the outset of dynastic changes and in effect legitimize political developments either in a positive or even a negative way. Some of the narratives of royal dreams, like other dream narratives in Theophanes that betray an affinity to hagiography, serve also to legitimize religious attitudes and views.[40]

---

[35]   Ibid., 104.

[36]   Cf. *Codex Theodosianus*, 9.16.6 (358), ed. T. Mommsen and P. M. Meyer (Berlin, 1903). Cf. A. A. Barb, 'The survival of magic arts', in A. Momigliano, ed., *The Conflict between Paganism and Christianity in the 4th Century* (Oxford, 1963), 102–3; also G.T. Calofonos, 'Dream interpretation: a Byzantinist superstition?', *BMGS* 9 (1984–85), 215–20; S. Troianos, 'Ἡ μαγεία στὰ βυζαντινὰ νομικὰ κείμενα', in Ἡ Καθημερινὴ ζωὴ στὸ Βυζάντιο. Τομὲς καὶ συνέχειες στὴν ἑλληνιστικὴ καὶ ρωμαϊκὴ παράδοση. Πρακτικὰ τοῦ Α´ διεθνοῦς συμποσίου, Ἀθήνα, 15–17 Σεπτεμβρίου 1988 (Athens, 1989), 549–72.

[37]   Ammianus Marcellinus, *Res Gestae*, 19.12.10, ed. W. Seyfarth, *Ammiani Marcellini Rerum gestarum libri qui supersunt* (Leipzig, 1978).

[38]   Theophanes, 379f.

[39]   These are the two dreams of Constantine, a dream of Pulcheria and a dream of Theodore Lector related to Anastasius' death (both discussed in the following footnote); Anastasius' dream of the Book of Life and Amantius' dream of the wild boar; Maurice's dream of the Chalke icon; and last but not least, the dream Constans had before his defeat.

[40]   A well-known relic hunter, the pious Empress Pulcheria is informed in a dream by St Stephen himself that his right arm has arrived in Constantinople (Theophanes, 86–7); also, Patriarch Macedonius, right after Anastasius has him killed, dictates the following message to the church historian Theodore Lector in his dream: 'Take this down. Go and read it out to Anastasius and say, "I am going to my fathers, whose faith I have preserved. But I shall not cease importuning the

A third type of dream narrative explains and legitimizes cruel events in terms of divine retribution, such as a devastating earthquake in Antioch,[41] an epidemic of demonic possessions in Alexandria,[42] or, indeed, the heartless execution by Phocas of the Emperor Maurice and all of his family – including his baby son – that the narrative presents as an act of divine mercy, for they were said to have gained thereby eternal life.

As I have tried to demonstrate in this paper, dream narratives tend in a number of ways to take root in historical texts, connecting with one another, as well as with other narrative blocks that feature prophecy, natural signs, even factual accounts that may seem irrelevant at first sight. They form a tight network of meaning, which attempts to explain and legitimize an often harsh and sometimes incomprehensible reality in even harsher, but perfectly comprehensible terms.

I would like to close this paper by going back to the cruel point where it started: October 1990 and Saddam Hussein's dream. News bulletins at the time included another interesting item: the White House spokesman, when asked to comment on the Saddam dream story, replied: 'No comment on dreams, I have enough problems dealing with reality'.[43]

Byzantines in the time of Theophanes had also their share of difficulty in comprehending reality. The only difference is that for them dreams were always part of their way of dealing with it.

Lord until you have arrived, and we go to be judged together''' (Theophanes, 161–2; Mango and Scott, *The Chronicle of Theophanes Confessor*, 245).

[41] Theophanes, 177–8: A prescriptive dream, reminiscent of dream cures, that reveals to a pious Antiochian a way to stop the devastating earthquakes. All the survivors had to write on the lintels of their houses the phrase 'Christ is with us. Stand', which reportedly worked, allowing the restoration and rededication of the city with the new name 'Theoupolis'.

[42] Theophanes, 162: An unnamed person is informed by a terrible spectre in his dream that the Alexandrians are suffering because of the anathemas pronounced against the synod of Chalcedon. This is one of the four dreams in the chronicle expressing divine disapproval of Anastasius and his policies.

[43] Quoted in T. L. Friedman, 'The World; A Dreamlike Landscape, a Dreamlike Reality', *The New York Times*, 28 October 1990, at http://www.nytimes.com/1990/10/28/weekinreview/the-world-a-dreamlike-landscape-a-dreamlike-reality.html, accessed 20 June 2010.

8. The Venice *Alexander Romance*: pictorial narrative and the art of telling stories

Nicolette S. Trahoulia

With a total of 250 illustrations, Venice Hellenic Institute Gr. 5 contains the only fully illustrated copy of the Greek *Alexander Romance* to have survived to the present day.[1] Each illustration is accompanied by rubrics written in red ink, as well as Turkish notes that were added at some later date when the manuscript came into Turkish hands.[2] Since Andreas Xyngopoulos first published the manuscript's illustrations in 1966, the codex has been firmly connected with fourteenth-century Trebizond on the basis of the title given the emperor in the frontispiece illustration (Fig. 8.1).[3] This Trapezuntine emperor, clearly the book's patron, is in all

---

[1]   Only one other illustrated version of the Greek text survives. Oxford Bodleian Library Barocci 17 is a small book with 31 illustrations done in a summary and rough manner, and spaces for an additional 89 illustrations that were never carried out. The illustrations are published in I. Hutter, *Corpus der byzantinischen Miniaturenhandschriften* II/2 *Oxford, Bodleian Library* (Stuttgart, 1978), 33–6, 116–23. The author wishes to thank Deree College – the American College of Greece – for providing funds for reproductions.

[2]   The Turkish notes to a number of illustrations are translated into English in N.S. Trahoulia, *The Venice Alexander Romance, Hellenic Institute Codex Gr. 5: A Study of Alexander the Great as an Imperial Paradigm in Byzantine Art and Literature* (PhD dissertation, Harvard University, 1997), 221–6. Translations of a selection of the Turkish notes into Italian can be found in G. Bellingeri, 'Il "Romanzo d'Alessandro" dell'Istituto Ellenico di Venezia: Glosse Turche "Gregarie"', in *Turco-Veneta* (Istanbul, 2003), 31–60.

[3]   Λ. Xyngopoulos, *Les Miniatures du Roman d'Alexandre le Grand dans le codex de l'Institut Hellénique de Venise* (Athens and Venice, 1966); for the identification of the imperial patron as a Trapezuntine emperor see L. Gallagher, 'The Alexander Romance in the Hellenic Institute at Venice. Some notes on the initial miniature', *Thesaurismata* 16 (1979), 170–205.

From *History as Literature in Byzantium*, ed. Ruth Macrides. Copyright © 2010 by the Society for the Promotion of Byzantine Studies. Published by Ashgate Publishing Ltd, Wey Court East, Union Road, Farnham, Surrey, GU9 7PT, Great Britain.

Fig. 8.1   Folio 1r.

likelihood Alexios III Komnenos (1349–90), an emperor who was compared to Alexander the Great in imperial panegyric.[4] In the dedicatory inscription accompanying the emperor's portrait, he addresses Alexander: 'I, O brave emperor Alexander, most excellent of all crowned men and ruler of all the world, having contemplated your great labours and [deeds], and your all-triumphant kingship, I had the desire…'.[5] Because the remainder of the inscription is missing, the nature of the emperor's desire must remain enigmatic, a matter for speculation. Evidence suggests that the emperor's portrait originally faced an image of Alexander, now missing, and that the rulers may have been shown as if engaged in dialogue.[6] This would explain the emperor's gaze and gesture to the right, presumably directed towards the image of Alexander.

A similar instance of dialogue is seen in the manuscript of Hippocrates (Paris Bibliothèque Nationale Gr. 2144) commissioned by Alexios Apokaukos between 1341 and 1345.[7] Hippocrates and Apokaukos face each other in frontispiece portraits with dialogue in verse surrounding the miniatures.[8] As in Gr. 5, Apokaukos addresses Hippocrates in the first person and expresses a desire, in this case to read the works of the author. Hippocrates responds by praising Apokaukos' skills as a commander and

----

[4]   For the association with Alexios III see Trahoulia, *The Venice Alexander Romance*, 53–64; and N. S. Trahoulia, *The Greek Alexander Romance: Venice Hellenic Institute Codex Gr. 5* (Athens, 1997), 33–5.

[5]   'ἐγώ, βασιλεῦ Ἀλέξανδρε γεννα[ιε] στεφηφόρων ἄριστ[ε] καὶ κοσμοκράτ[ωρ] τοὺς σοὺς κατὶδ[ων] καμάτους καὶ τὰ [ἔργα], ὑπερνικώς[αν] τῶν ὅλων βασιλε[ίαν] ἔσχον πόθον.' All translations are the author's.

[6]   The emperor folio has been rebound as a recto, but was originally a verso as is indicated by the wide inner margin with Turkish inscription; on the other folios, the wider margin is the outer one and the Turkish inscription is written on the outer margin. In the original arrangement, this folio would have formed a bifolio, with the recto image of Alexander in the familiar diptych arrangement of frontispiece portraits. Confirmation of this is found in the Turkish inscription accompanying the surviving frontispiece. This inscription labels the emperor as Alexander's grandfather, presumably because when the Turkish was written there were two imperial images, Alexander and the emperor. See Trahoulia, *The Greek Alexander Romance*, 39; Gallagher, 'The Alexander Romance', 180–85; Xyngopoulos, *Les miniatures*, 15; and Bellingeri, 'Il "Romanzo d'Alessandro"', 58.

[7]   Cited in Gallagher, 'The Alexander Romance', 182–4.

[8]   The illustrations are reproduced in H. Omont, *Miniatures des plus anciens manuscrits grecs de la Bibliothèque Nationale du VIe au XIe siècle* (Paris, 1929), pls. 128 and 129. See also Joseph A. Munitiz, 'Dedicating a volume: Apokaukos and Hippocrates (Paris gr. 2144)', in Constantinides, *et al.*, *ΦΙΛΕΛΛΗΝ*, 267–80.

his wish to acquire the knowledge contained in his writings.[9] Based on this
example, it is quite possible that the emperor's stated desire in Gr. 5 was to
read about and see images of Alexander's great triumphs and adventures,
to which he alludes in the surviving inscription. The facing illustration of
Alexander may then have been accompanied by an inscription in which he
replies to the emperor in a manner similar to Hippocrates. This imagined
conversation suggests a special relationship between the great ruler of the
past and the present ruler, perhaps expressing the unspoken desire of the
emperor to be a 'New Alexander', or an 'emulator of Alexander', as the
court panegyrist Stephanos Sgouropoulos proclaimed Alexios III in at
least one encomium.[10]

Elsewhere I have demonstrated that the text of Gr. 5, known as the
γ recension, combines two earlier recensions, the ε and the β, choosing
the most byzantinizing and glorifying descriptions from each to create
a truly Byzantine Alexander.[11] At the same time, the illustrations not
only depict Alexander in the guise of a Byzantine emperor acting in a
Byzantine environment, but enliven the story in such a way as to draw
the viewer into the action. Paging through the book, one is struck by the
extensiveness of the illustration. Text and image appear to share equally
the task of communicating the narrative. In order to illustrate the text so
completely, the majority of full-page illustrations are divided into two
frames to accommodate two scenes. These may be separate episodes or
different moments of a single episode. Furthermore, within a single frame
consecutive and simultaneous actions within an episode are often depicted.
The extent to which the narrative is dissected and illustrated in all its fine
detail produces a particularly dense pictorial narrative. Various pictorial
devices are used to express temporal development so that the illustrations
do more than just illustrate key moments in the narrative; they perform the
narrative over space and time. The overtly performative character of the
pictorial narrative in the Venice *Alexander Romance* suggests that using the
book was meant to provide a particular kind of experience.

In this essay, I shall argue that the illustrations of Gr. 5 are structured for
performance, so that the images are most effective if viewed while listening
to an oral recitation of the narrative. The audience could be composed of

---

[9]   The text is published in I. Boivin, *Nicephori Gregorae Historiae Byzantinae* II
(Paris, 1702), 777–8; and Gregoras, II, 1256–8.

[10]   'Μιμητὴν τοῦ Μακεδόνος/Ἀλεξάνδρου', in T. Papatheodoridou, ed., 'Τοῦ
πρωτονοταρίου Τραπεζοῦντος Στεφάνου τοῦ Σγουροπούλου πρὸς τὸν βασιλέα
κυρὸν Ἀλέξιον τὸν Κομνηνὸν στίχοι ἐγκωμιαστικοί', *Ἀρχεῖον Πόντου* 19 (1954),
280 vv. 188–9.

[11]   For a detailed analysis of the γ recension and the elements taken from ε
and β see Trahoulia, *The Venice Alexander Romance*, 76–96, and *The Greek Alexander
Romance*, 42–6.

the emperor alone, or with members of the court gathered in the emperor's *theatron*. The codex and its mostly full-page illustrations are large enough that, if the book were displayed on a bookstand, the illustrations would be legible to a number of people gathered for a performance.[12] I believe the performance of the narrative would have played a crucial role in the ultimate function of the book: situating the emperor in proximity to his imperial paradigm in a symbolic literary space. Historians and philologists have increasingly addressed the performative nature of Byzantine texts and the issue of orality.[13] However, in the study of illustrated manuscripts little attention has been given to the function of text and image within a context of performance and what it might mean for images to be accompanied by the spoken word.[14]

---

[12] The codex measures 32cm by 24cm. For the assumption that lavish illustrated manuscripts in the West were meant to be displayed to an audience rather than privately read, see M. Camille, 'Visual signs of the sacred page: books in the *Bible moralisée*', *Word and Image* 5 (1989), 117.

[13] The term 'orality' as it is used in this essay encompasses both reading aloud as well as reciting from memory. Guglielmo Cavallo believes that silent reading in private was rare in Byzantium, an activity confined to intellectual circles: G. Cavallo, 'Le rossignol et l'hirondelle: lire et écrire à Byzance, en Occident', *Annales: Histoire et Sciences Sociales* 4 (2001), 854–5. Herbert Hunger presents evidence suggesting that reading aloud, whether in public or private, continues into the time of Joseph Bryennios (*c.* 1350–1430): H. Hunger, *Schreiben und Lesen in Byzanz. Die byzantinische Buchkultur* (Munich, 1989), 126. Also see G. Cavallo, 'Trace per una storia della lettura á Bisanzio', *BZ* 95 (2002), 423–44; M. Mullett, 'Writing in early mediaeval Byzantium', in R. McKitterick, ed., *The Uses of Literacy in Early Mediaeval Europe* (Cambridge, 1990), 159–60; E. M. and M. J. Jeffreys, 'The oral background of Byzantine popular poetry', *Oral Tradition* 1/3 (1986), 504–47; M. Mullett, 'Rhetoric, theory and the imperative of performance: Byzantium and now', in Jeffreys, ed., *Rhetoric*, 151–71. Paul Magdalino writes of the importance of 'rhetorical theatre' in twelfth-century Byzantium: P. Magdalino, *The Empire of Manuel I Komnenos* (Cambridge, 1993), 335–6, 426–30; G. Cavallo, 'Alphabetismi e letture a Bisanzio', in B. Mondrain, ed., *Lire et écrire à Byzance* (Paris, 2006), 97–109; P. A. Agapitos, 'Writing, reading and reciting (in) Byzantine erotic fiction', in Mondrain, ed., *Lire et écrire*, 125–76; and see Brian Croke, Athanasios Angelou and Teresa Shawcross for their discussions of orality in this volume.

[14] See J. Burke, 'The Madrid *Skylitzes* as an audio-visual experiment', in Burke, *et al.*, eds., *Byzantine Narrative*, 137–48. Burke proposes that the text of the Madrid Skylitzes was intended for oral performance but finds it difficult to conceive how the reading aloud of the text could have coincided with the viewing of the pictures. Also see C. Barber, 'In the presence of the text: a note on writing, speaking and performing in the Theodore Psalter', in E. James, ed., *Art and Text in Byzantine Culture* (Cambridge, 2007), 83–99. The examination of orality, in general, and its manifestation in illustrated manuscripts has been more fully explored in the western medieval context. The seminal works are P. Saenger, 'Silent reading:

Pictorial devices

A number of creative pictorial devices are used in Gr. 5's illustrations to give the viewer a sense of movement and temporal progression. First, the direction of narrative flow for most illustrations is left to right. In particular, when Alexander leads his army, the direction of movement is almost always from left to right. And while Alexander's army advances rightwards, opposing armies march leftwards. The illustration on folio 173r (Fig. 8.2) shows Alexander leading his army to the right against Evrymithres. Turning the page, one encounters on its verso (Fig. 8.3) Evrymithres leading his army in the opposite direction to meet Alexander. The distance separating the armies is experienced as the page is turned. Appropriately, the direction of movement is reversed only in the rare instances when Alexander and his army retreat, as in the upper scene on folio 52r (Fig. 8.4) where the Macedonians flee the Tyrians following a defeat. Alexander's consistent left to right movement means that as the pages are turned there is a sense of Alexander's steady progression through time and space. Additionally, the main premise of his expeditions – his determined march eastwards – is reinforced.

Another device is to represent independent yet related events side by side in the same picture field, what is commonly called 'continuous narrative.' This method can be seen on folio 20v (Fig. 8.5), where the young Alexander is informed that the Olympic Games will take place in Rome. In the upper frame we see him conversing with a group of men at left, receiving this news. Next he goes to Philip to ask permission to participate. He stands before his father and then falls to his knees, kissing his father's hand. In the lower register, Alexander approaches again at right, having been granted permission. At left he sets off on his journey. His elaborate dress is explained in the romance text, where we read that Philip gives Alexander jewel-encrusted robes as a token of his blessing.[15] The red

---

its impact on late medieval script and society', *Viator* 113 (1982), 376–414; *idem, Space between Words: The Origins of Silent Reading* (Stanford, CA, 1997); B. Stock, *The Implications of Literacy: Written Language and Models of Interpretation in the Eleventh and Twelfth Centuries* (Princeton, NJ, 1983); W. J. Ong, 'Orality, literacy, and medieval textualization', *New Literary History* 16 (1984), 1–12; and M. T. Clanchy, *From Memory to Written Record* (Cambridge, MA, 1979). Sylvia Huot has discussed in great detail 'the performative quality of the medieval book': S. Huot, *From Song to Book: The Poetics of Writing in Old French Lyric and Lyrical Narrative Poetry* (Ithaca, NY, 1987), 2, 3. Sandra Hindman writes of a 'culture of orality' evoked by the manuscripts of Chrétien de Troyes, which she believes were read aloud while the pictures were shown to the listeners: S. Hindman, *Sealed in Parchment: Rereadings of Knighthood in the Illuminated Manuscripts of Chrétien de Troyes* (Chicago, IL, 1994), 91 and 94.

[15]   U. von Lauenstein, ed., *Der griechische Alexanderroman Rezension Γ*, I (Meisenheim am Glan, 1962), 46, vv. 10–15.

rubric at the top reads: 'Here Alexander came to Philip and asked that he be allowed to go to Rome.'[16] And below: 'Philip refused, but when he saw his eagerness, he assented.'[17] As this example demonstrates, while the red rubrics provide a brief description of the main action of the scenes, they are not always enough to understand the pictures fully. The illustrations are so packed with sequential and simultaneous actions that further explanation is needed.

A similar instance is seen on folio 16v (Fig. 8.6), where the rubric to the illustration reads at top: 'Philip leaves for Delphi to receive an oracle concerning who will rule after him.'[18] And below: 'He is told that the one who is able to tame [the horse] Bucephalus will rule after you.'[19] In the upper portion of the illustration we see Philip talking to a group of men. He then turns to an architectural structure with nude statues standing in arcades, meant to represent the site of Delphi. In the middle ground a figure stands before the now enthroned Philip, and below we see Alexander approaching Bucephalus and ultimately riding him to the right. A fuller understanding of this illustration comes from reading the romance text, where Alexander is said to release Bucephalus from a special enclosure in which Philip kept the horse (the domed structure we see in the illustration), and news of Alexander's taming the horse is subsequently brought to Philip (the action in the middle ground).[20] Presumably this additional information would be available to the viewer who has either read the text or who listens to the narrative while looking at the pictures.

Often, actions that take place over a relatively narrow period of time are combined in what appears at first glance to be an illustration of a single moment. We can see this temporal layering in the illustration on folio 89v (Fig. 8.7). The rubric to the upper scene tells us that the image depicts the reply of Darius' wife, mother and daughter to Alexander's letter.[21] For the scene below, the rubric states that Alexander wrote to his mother, Olympias, asking her to send him the things necessary for his wedding.[22]

---

[16]   'ἔνθα ἀλέξαδρος προς φίλιππον ἀπελθών, ἤτησε τοῦ ἀπελθεῖν ἐν ρώμη.'

[17]   'ὁ δὲ φίλιππος οὐκ ἠνέσχετο, ἀλλ' ἐπειδὴ εἶδεν αὐτὸν προθυμοποιούμενον, κατένευσε καὶ αὐτός.'

[18]   'ἀπελθὼν δὲ φίλιππος εἰς δελφοὺς χρησμοδοτηθῆναι τὸ ποῖος ἄρα μετ' αὐτὸν βασιλεύσει.'

[19]   'ὃς καὶ χρηματισθεὶς ὡς ὁ δυνάμενος τὸν βουκέφαλον ὑποτάξαι, ἐκεῖνος μετὰ σὲ βασιλεύσει.'

[20]   Von Lauenstein, ed., *Der griechische Alexanderroman*, 44, vv. 8–18.

[21]   'ἀντίγραμμα τῆς γυναικος δαρείου, τῆς μητρός καὶ τῆς τῆς θυγατρος αὐτοῦ προς ἀλέξανδρον τον βασιλέα.'

[22]   'ἔγραψε δὲ ἀλέξανδρος καὶ εἰς τὴν μητέρα αὐτοῦ ὀλυμπιάδα τοῦ ἀποστεῖλαι αὐτῷ τὰ πρὸς ἑτοιμασίαν τῶν γάμων αὐτοῦ.'

The upper scene shows the three women seated on the right. Outside the palace wall two men approach; one hands a letter to a third figure in front of him. This letter is then shown to the three women by a fourth figure. Within the palace, the three women dictate a reply to a scribe sitting at their feet. The letter is then handed to a messenger, who sets off together with another figure to deliver the letter on the far left. A similar scene occurs in the lower register, where Alexander receives the letter from Darius' family, then dictates and dispatches a letter to his mother. These illustrations repeat only the figures that are moving, in this case the messengers. The same messenger appears twice, once being dispatched, and a second time setting off on his journey. Alexander and the three women appear only once, and so seem to be doing three things simultaneously – receiving a letter, dictating a reply, and dispatching it with a messenger. The result is a complex scene that maximizes the number of moments depicted while maintaining an economy of figures. At the same time, movement is suggested by the repeated figure of the messenger, whom the viewer's eye would follow while listening to a description of the various actions.

Perhaps the most compelling temporal device employed in the illustrations involves the use of repeated figures that may even overlap to suggest physical movement. On folio 140r (Fig. 8.8) Alexander, now in India, consults two oracular cypress trees on how many years he has yet to live. We see him at the far left with his companions, then consulting with a priest, and a third time as he kneels slightly and places his hand on one of the trees. Three overlapping figures of Alexander move from left to right, performing the narrative. The repetition of a figure within a frame in order to accommodate a series of actions is not uncommon in Byzantine manuscripts.[23] However, the extent to which this device is used in Gr. 5 is not seen elsewhere. Often, the repetition of figures has been amplified to represent moments so closely related in time as to produce the effect of overlaid film stills. This almost cinematic quality of the illustrations would be activated by the oral performance of the narrative, the figures viewed as if coming to life and moving before the viewer's eyes.

One of the more dynamic instances of this acting out of the narrative can be seen on folio 76r (Fig. 8.9), where Alexander makes his escape after infiltrating Darius' camp in disguise. The rubric to the upper register describes a series of actions: 'Having removed his god-like costume, Alexander put on Persian dress. And striking the sentry on the head, he

---

[23]   This method is used, for instance, in the ninth-century Vatican manuscript of the *Christian Topography* of Cosmas Indicopleustes (Rome Vat. Gr. 699). Paul appears four times in the scene of his conversion (folio 83v): witnessing the lightning from heaven, falling to his knees, standing frontally, and being led to Damascus. K. Weitzmann, *Illustrations in Roll and Codex: A Study of the Origin and Method of Text Illustration* (Princeton, NJ, 1970), pl. XXXIX, 130.

Fig. 8.2   Folio 173r

Fig. 8.3   Folio 173v

Fig. 8.4   Folio 52r

Fig. 8.5   Folio 20v

Fig. 8.6   Folio 16v

Fig. 8.7   Folio 89v

Fig. 8.8   Folio 140r

Fig. 8.9   Folio 76r

fled.'[24] In the illustration Alexander sheds his clothes, dons Persian dress, hits a guard over the head, and flees on his horse, all within the same scene. At the far left two Alexanders overlap each other in the process of changing disguises. Similarly, the bottom register shows Darius asking a guard about Alexander's whereabouts. The guard then turns to interrogate two other figures, one of whom finds the injured guard to tell him his story.

Many more examples could be presented of the performative nature of the illustrations. The pictorial narrative is depicted as a continuous temporal flow, leaving few gaps. With 163 out of 193 folios bearing illustration on one or both sides, the illustrations play a significant part in the storytelling process. Accompanied by the oral component of the performance, the illustrations would animate the events and bring them into the present in as vivid a way as possible.[25] Furthermore, the pictorial devices in Gr. 5 would encourage the viewer to identify with the characters, particularly of course with Alexander, and experience the narrative with them. It seems, then, that the illustrations of Gr. 5 are evidence of the kind of interface between orality and literacy that we find in residually oral societies.[26] They were designed to offer optimal pleasure when viewed in conjunction with an oral performance of the story. Thus the nature of the text, meant to be performed in some manner before an audience, has dictated the nature of the illustrations.

In a society where texts were constantly being read or recited to the emperor, as in panegyric, the reading of the *Alexander Romance* before the emperor may have constituted a similar event. However, in Gr. 5 the text describing a particular episode seldom occurs on the same or facing page as the illustration of that episode. This poses a problem if we are to suppose the text was read aloud while the emperor and possibly others viewed the illustrations.[27] But it is possible that, while the text may have

---

[24]   'ὁ δὲ ἀλέξανδρος ἀποδυσάμενος τὴν θεϊκὴν στολήν, τὴν δὲ περσικὴν ἀμφιασάμενος καὶ τὸν φρούραρχον κατὰ κεφαλῆς κρούων, ἐξέφυγεν. ὁ δὲ δαρεῖος ἤρξατο ἐπιζητεῖν τὸν ἀλέξανδρον καὶ οὐχ εὑρίσκετο.'

[25]   For the importance of visualization on the part of the medieval orator in order to elicit vivid mental images in his listeners see L. James, 'Art and lies: text, image and imagination in the medieval world', in Eastmond and James, eds., *Icon and Word*, 61–2.

[26]   Walter Ong uses the term 'residually oral' to refer to societies that are literate but still maintain elements of 'oral mindsets and ways of expression': Ong, 'Orality, literacy, and medieval textualization', 1. See also J. Goody, *The Interface between the Written and the Oral* (Cambridge, 1987) for discussion of 'mixed modes' in residually oral societies.

[27]   Such an instance is seen in a thirteenth-century French manuscript of the *Life of Saint Edward* where illustrations with red rubrics are carefully aligned

been read on certain occasions, the illustrations could also be viewed while the story was recited from memory, allowing for even greater flexibility in the use of the book.[28] We could imagine the story recounted via the pictures and the mnemonic device of the prominent red rubrics, and punctuated with comparisons with the emperor and current events, a kind of imperial panegyric woven into the Alexander narrative, producing a meta-narrative. In this scenario, the illustrations may have functioned independently to focus attention on a particular episode of the story, even eliciting comment from the audience.[29] In fact the illustrations do maintain the narrative structure of the text by being organized in clusters, so that an episode is shown in a group of illustrations placed on consecutive pages without more than one side of a folio with text separating them. Thus illustrations and rubrics form a discursive unit, the red of the rubrics matched by the red frames of the illustrations and the script used for the rubrics differentiated from that of the text in its more compact style. This aspect of the manuscript is underlined if we compare Gr. 5 to the manuscripts of the Octateuchs, for example. Although these manuscripts have extensive illustration, the illustrations are usually integrated into a

---

with the relevant text, leading Michael Camille to propose that a clerk would read the text aloud while the manuscript's owner looked at the pictures: M. Camille, 'Seeing and reading: some visual implications of medieval literacy and illiteracy', *Art History* 8 (1985), 41–2.

[28]   Vitz asserts that in the West romance as a genre was strongly oral, and that at festive court events, such as weddings, it was usually recited from memory, rather than read aloud: E. B. Vitz, *Orality and Performance in early French Romance* (Cambridge, 1999), 165 and 200. The text of Gr. 5 does not appear to be written with any special provision to facilitate reading aloud. Although large red initials are usually placed at or near the beginning of a chapter, they also occur elsewhere for no apparent reason.

[29]   In illustrated saints' lives, Cynthia Hahn believes that rubrics to the illustrations that summarize the text indicate that 'performance was intended'. Furthermore, since these texts were well known to the audience, she argues that the performance of these lives would have allowed 'comment and interaction between performer and audience' so that certain points in the narrative could be further discussed: C. Hahn, 'The limits of text and image? Matthew Paris's final project, the *Vitae duorum Offarum*, as a historical romance', in D. S. Areford and N. A. Rowe, eds., *Excavating the Medieval Image: Manuscripts, Artists, Audiences: Essays in Honor of Sandra Hindman* (London, 2004), 48. Also see C. Hahn, *Portrayed on the Heart: Narrative Effects in Pictorial Lives of Saints from the Tenth through the Thirteenth Century* (Berkeley, CA, 2001). For a contrasting study that interprets innovative pictorial narratives in late medieval French picture books as more suited to silent reading in private see K. Maekawa, *Narrative and Experience: Innovations in Thirteenth-Century Picture Books* (Frankfurt am Main, 2000), esp. 155–69.

text page and do not always have rubrics, making it necessary to read the accompanying text as well as look at the pictures.[30]

Whether or not explicit comparison was made with the emperor, the performance of the text before him, both verbally and visually, would be a highly charged 'narrative event' that would invite identification of the emperor with Alexander, inscribing the past onto the present.[31] Ruth Finnegan writes of court poets in general: 'The primary audience may be the ruler, but the poems are given meaning and effect by the wider audience of those present during his [the poet's] performance.'[32] In addition, while the text of Gr. 5 has been composed from earlier recensions in order to create a Byzantine Alexander acting in a Byzantine imperial setting, the telling of the story orally could have further accentuated these aspects, thereby uniting emperor and imperial model in the symbolic literary space of the performance.[33]

Let us also not forget the facing frontispiece portraits of Alexander and the emperor that, I argue, originally opened the book and, in all likelihood, presented them engaged in dialogue. As well as amplifying the relationship

---

[30]   J. Lowden, *The Octateuchs: A Study in Byzantine Manuscript Illustration* (University Park, PN, 1992); and K. Weitzmann and M. Bernabò, *The Illustrations of the Manuscripts of the Septuagint*, II: *The Byzantine Octateuchs* (Princeton, NJ, 1999).

[31]   The term 'cultural performance' could also be used here in the sense that Victor Turner uses it to designate 'plays, concerts, and lectures … [but] also prayers, ritual readings and recitations' that make manifest some set of fundamental values for a particular group: V. Turner, *The Anthropology of Performance* (New York, 1988), 24–5.

[32]   R. Finnegan, *Oral Poetry: Its Nature, Significance and Social Context* (Cambridge, 1977; repr. 1992), 227. While the text of Gr. 5 is not written in verse, Finnegan also notes medieval examples of mostly prose being recited from memory, such as the Turkish *Tale of Dede Korkut*: *Oral Poetry*, 119. For a version of the *Alexander Romance* in verse see the fourteenth-century Marciana Gr. 408: S. Reichmann, ed., *Das byzantinische Alexandergedicht* (Meisenheim am Glan, 1963). For references to itinerant poet performers in Trebizond see the Trapezuntine horoscope of 1336: Lambros, 'Τραπεζουντιακὸν ὡροσκόπιον', 40, 42, 44, 45, 46.

[33]   Examples of this type of narrative flexibility can be found in primary oral cultures (cultures with no knowledge of writing). As Ruth Finnegan notes with the Sunjata epic in West Africa, each performer 'adapted his version to the situation in which he performed – when leading persons present in the audience, for instance, could trace their descent from figures in the Sunjata story' – *Oral Poetry*, 76. Walter Ong says something similar about primary oral cultures in general: 'Narrative originality lodges not in making up new stories but in managing a particular interaction with this audience at this time – at every telling the story has to be introduced uniquely into a unique situation … Praise poems of chiefs invite entrepreneurship, as the old formulas and themes have to be made to interact with new and often complicated political situations' – W. J. Ong, *Orality and Literacy* (London, 1982, repr. 1988), 41–2, and see 48–9.

of the two by showing the emperor conversing with his exemplum, this placement demonstrates the manner in which the book is viewed as a device that enables the speech act and makes the exchange possible.[34] The emperor gestures with one hand towards his words written in red ink (and also towards the now-missing image of Alexander whom he addresses). In fact, throughout the manuscript's illustrations hand gestures are used to indicate speech, the words spoken by the figures often contained in the rubrics. Many rubrics report the characters' words in the third person (e.g., 'Alexander reproaches Darius, saying that if he delays going to battle, he is not a brave king'[35]). But for a number of illustrations the rubrics quote the characters' words directly (e.g., 'Alexander says: What favour can I do for you, O Diogenes?'[36]). Indeed, the romance text itself is full of dialogue expressed in the first person. Thus a viewer would not only see the figures acting out the narrative, he would hear them speak, whether in the voice of a court performer or as he himself read the words aloud. In the latter case the viewer speaking these words would be drawn even further into the fictive space of the narrative and the identities of the characters.

*   *   *

For emperors who claimed, rather optimistically, to be rulers of 'all the East', as the Trapezuntine imperial title did, Alexander must have had special appeal as an imperial paradigm. By the fourteenth century, Trebizond was surrounded on all sides by Turkish emirates. Although the Trapezuntines gave their princesses to Turkoman princes in diplomatic marriages, they could not always avoid military confrontation. Trapezuntine texts commonly referred to the Turks as 'Persians', a standard Byzantine equation that recalled not only the ancient enemy of the Greeks, but Alexander of Macedon who had vanquished the Persians centuries earlier.[37] Having taken the throne as a young boy, Alexios III was called upon to be a military leader at an early age, much as Alexander had been. It has been asserted that the majority of the Trapezuntine victories against the Turks occurred during his reign.[38] Indeed, many of the events related in the

---

[34]   The concept of a book as a means to connect with people of the past is illustrated by Chaucer's account that he wrote *The Parliament of Fowls* because after reading about Scipio Africanus Major, the latter appeared to him in a dream and conversed with him: Ong, 'Orality, literacy, and medieval textualization', 2.

[35]   Folio 74v: 'ἐνταῦθα προσονειδίζων ἀλέξανδρος δαρείῳ, ὡς ὅτιγε ἐὰν βραδύνων εἰς μάχην βασιλεύς, οὐκ ἀνδρείος ἐστίν.'

[36]   Folio 39r: 'φησὶ ὁ ἀλέξανδρος: τί σοι χαρίσομαι, ὦ διογένες'

[37]   As in Constantine Loukites' funerary panegyric for Alexios II Komnenos (1297–1330): A. Papadopoulos-Kerameus, ed., Ἀνάλεκτα Ἱεροσολυμιτικῆς Σταχυολογίας (St Petersburg, 1891), 421–30.

[38]   R. Shukurov, 'Between peace and hostility: Trebizond and the Pontic Turkish periphery in the fourteenth century', *Mediterranean Historical Review* 9

Alexander Romance and illustrated in Gr. 5 must have resonated with the Trapezuntine present: Alexander enthroned receiving foreign embassies, leading his army, or the marriage of Alexander with the Persian princess Roxanne. In addition to the diplomatic marriages of Alexios III's daughters to Turkoman princes, the Trapezuntines were also engaged during this period in establishing diplomatic relations with the Persians.[39] So returning to the subject of the emperor's desire, if in the words of Northrop Frye, 'the quest-romance is the search of the libido or desiring self for a fulfillment that will deliver it from the anxieties of reality but will still contain that reality',[40] I believe Hellenic Institute Gr. 5 with its lively pictorial narrative fulfilled just such a desire for the emperor.

(1994), 67; and see E. Janssens, *Trébizonde en Colchide* (Brussels, 1969), 112–23.

[39]   S. Lambros, 'Τὰ ὑπ' ἀριθμόν Α καὶ Β κατάλοιπα', *NE* 15 (1921), 332–6.

[40]   N. Frye, *Anatomy of Criticism* (Princeton, NJ, 1957), 193.

SECTION V
The Classical Tradition Reinterpreted

9. A historian and his tragic hero: a literary reading of Theophylact Simokatta's *Ecumenical History*

Stephanos Efthymiadis

The *Ecumenical History* of Theophylact Simokatta has ever since Photios been deplored as a work difficult in style, with successive shifts in narrative focus, few and not always reliable chronological indications, repetitive insertions of apophthegmatic sentences, rhetorical speeches and other devices.[1] In addition to severely testing its modern readers' patience, this rather rambling reconstruction of twenty years of Roman history cannot completely satisfy those seeking sound historical information and is a disappointment to those in search of deeper ideas and philosophical messages. By common scholarly consent, Theophylact largely failed to be a reliable reporter of the reign of Maurice and moreover, for all his high-minded pretensions, he hardly succeeded in endowing his account with the profundity and breadth of classical historiography.[2]

---

[1]   *Theophylacti Simocattae, Historiae*, ed. C. de Boor; repr. P. Wirth; English trans. by Michael and Mary Whitby, *The* History *of Theophylact Simocatta: An English Translation with Introduction and Notes* (Oxford, 1986). Unless otherwise stated, passages cited in English translation are the Whitbys'. It should also be noted that, in accordance with the manuscript tradition, I adopt *Ecumenical History* (henceforth *EH*) as the title of Theophylact's work, being, however, conscious that *Historiae* (as in Photios' *Bibliotheca*) may have been the original one. For critical comments on this paper I thank Anthony Kaldellis.

[2]   Derogatory comments on Theophylact's arrangement of historical material and style start with Photios' *Bibliotheke*, cod. 65, I. 79–80, and culminate in modern times with N. Wilson, *Scholars of Byzantium* (London, 1982), 59–60; Whitby and Whitby, *The* History *of Theophylact*, xxv–xxviii; repeated by Michael Whitby, in the chapter entitled 'Historiographer vs. historian' of his monograph *The Emperor Maurice and his Historian: Theophylact Simocatta on Persian and Balkan Warfare* (Oxford, 1988), 49–50: 'Granted these limitations, as well as the fact that Th. seems to have had no geographical knowledge or experience of military matters which could help him to make sense of the available source information, his significance

However, a different evaluation emerges if we adopt a literary perspective. Writing from a distance in time about events that could have reached him only by hearsay, the last classicizing historian of antiquity followed in full the method of literary re-adaptation of his sources, and supplemented them in several identifiable cases with 'literary invention'. Paradoxically, all criticisms that have heavily shaken his value as a historian–reporter can serve as counter-arguments and enhance his evaluation as a writer.[3]

The last in a long tradition, Simokatta's *History* is unquestionably a good candidate for a literary study. To begin with, this is a narrative in which, for the first time, a Christian interpretation of historical events merges with the principles and rhetorical means of classical historiography. Hagiography and apocalyptic literature alternate with rhetorical speeches and descriptions of battles.[4] In introducing these novelties in his literary reconstruction of historical reality, Theophylact clearly deviates from Procopius and Agathias, but, as will be shown below, he somehow joins them in choosing to be allusive with regard to political, religious and military developments both in the reign of Maurice (582–602) and the reign of his own contemporary Heraclius (610–41). By embedding a

---

as a historian might be questioned'; and *idem*, 'Greek historical writing after Procopius: variety and vitality', in A. Cameron and L. I. Conrad, eds., *The Byzantine and Early Islamic Near East, v. I: Problems in the Literary Source Material* (Princeton, NJ, 1992), 46: 'Th. was basically a secondhand compiler who created a historical narrative by reworking, integrating, and sometimes interpreting the narratives of earlier writers'; similar characterizations are found in W. Treadgold, *The Early Byzantine Historians* (Hampshire and New York, 2007), 337–40. More balanced are the comments of Karpozilos, Βυζαντινοὶ Ἱστορικοί, I, 475–81. The modest evaluation of Simokatta as a historian, especially if compared to Procopius and Agathias, has also been underscored by D. Brodka, *Die Geschichtsphilosophie in der spätantiken Historiographie. Studien zu Prokopios von Kaisareia, Agathias von Myrina und Theophylaktos Simokattes*, Studien und Texte zur Byzantinistik 5 (Frankfurt am Main, 2004), 235–6.

[3] Despite being fully conscious that Th. proceeded to a free literary re-adaptation of his sources, Michael and Mary Whitby prefer to treat him as a second-rate historiographer; see *The History of Theophylact*, xxvii: 'as a classicizing historiographer, Th. was undoubtedly more interested in the artistic packaging than in the factual content of his narrative'; Michael Whitby reprimands him for his 'feebleness of ideas' and absence of a strong personal interpretation: see *The Emperor Maurice*, 322–3. Conversely, closer to a literary reading of Th. are the studies by I.V. Krivushin, 'Theophylact Simocatta's conception of political conflicts', *BF* 19 (1993), 171–82; and 'Théophylacte Simocatta peintre du chaos', *Études Balcaniques* 1 (1994), 115–33.

[4] In this belief in *omina* and miracles of any kind Hunger saw the mark of a change in historical writing; see Hunger, *Literatur*, I, 319.

variety of literary genres into his narrative, modifying his style in several instances and introducing secondary characters, he creates the effect of both a polyphonically voiced but also well-hidden truth about political and other developments occurring in his own time. In writing about the days and deeds of the ill-fated Maurice and in denouncing the tyranny of Phocas (602–10), who was overthrown by the reigning emperor Heraclius, Simokatta was in an advantageous position compared to his predecessors Procopius and Agathias, who chose to write about a reigning emperor. Nonetheless, in contrast to the epic and encomiastic discourse of the court poet George Pisides, his was a sad, not to say depressing, story.

In other words, if, as is believed, he indeed wrote in the early 630s, i.e. soon after the final defeat of the Persians and Heraclius' triumphal return to the Byzantine capital, he would have been in marked contrast to the spirit of an otherwise heroic age.[5] This 'heroic spirit' is discernible only in the Dialogue between Philosophy and History that introduces us to the main text of the *Ecumenical History*. Therein words of praise and panegyric are reserved for the 'descendants of Heraclius' (Ἡρακλεῖδαι) who expelled the repudiated Calydonian tyrant Phocas from the palace. Whether this Dialogue, unparalleled in classical and post-classical historiography, was an integral part of Theophylact's initial composition or a separate text (earlier or later, by his own hand or that of a scribe) inserted in Vaticanus gr. 977 – in essence the *codex unicus* to the History – is debatable.[6] For our present purposes, we must underscore that it is only in this Dialogue and

---

[5] For such an early dating of *EH* see Whitby, *Emperor Maurice*, 39–40; and Treadgold, *The Early Byzantine Historians*, 333–4.

[6] That the Dialogue was not an integral part of the History was first suggested by T. Olajos, 'Contributions à une analyse de la genèse de l'Histoire Universelle de Théophylacte Simocatta', *Acta Antiqua Academiae Scientiarum Hungaricae* 29 (1981), 417–18. Whitby (*The Emperor Maurice*, 40–41) objected to this view. P. Schreiner also endorsed the idea that the dialogue was not an inherent part of Theophylact's initial composition, 'Photios und Theophylaktos Simokates. Das Problem des "Inhaltsverzeichnisses" im Geschichtswerk', in Constantinides, *et al.*, eds., *ΦΙΛΕΛΛΗΝ*, 391–8. For a description of the manuscript preserving *EH* and its possible association with the *Excerpta* of Constantine VII Porphyrogennetos see P. Schreiner, 'Die Historikerhandschrift Vaticanus graecus 977: ein Handexemplar zur Vorbereitung des konstantinischen Exzerptenwerkes?', *JÖB* 37 (1987), 1–29. Cf. also *Theophylaktos Simokattes. Geschichte*, trans. and intro. by P. Schreiner (Stuttgart, 1985), 22–4; and T. Olajos, 'Remarques sur la tradition manuscrite de l'*Histoire Universelle* de Théophylacte Simocatta', *Revue d'Histoire des Textes* 9 (1979), 261–6. P. Speck also argued in favour of the Dialogue's early date and autonomy; see 'Eine Gedächtnisfeier am Grabe des Maurikios. Die *Historiai* des Theophylaktos Simokates: der Auftrag; die Fertigstellung; der Grundgedanke', *Varia IV*, Poikila Byzantina 12 (Bonn, 1993), 212–17.

not in the History itself that words of praise and panegyric are pronounced in favour of the 'dynasty of Heraclius'.

Be that as it may, the proem of the History proper, which follows the Dialogue, contains a different encounter, that between History and Poetry.[7] Theophylact picks up the introductory scene of the *Odyssey* and brings his listeners/readers into the palace of Alcinous. It was at the court of the king of the Phaeacians that the stranger Odysseus 'with his body bruised after the shipwreck' was granted freedom of speech and storytelling.[8] No doubt Theophylact saw himself in the guise of that foreigner who made Phaeacians cease drinking and prick up their ears to what, in his words, was 'a long and gloomy account'. Unlike the Homeric hero, however, who contrived false stories, he opted for the teaching of History that 'advises what should be undertaken and what should be ignored as disadvantageous'. History, we are told, can make generals wiser; not only can it instruct them how to arrange their forces in battle, but also 'through the disasters of others make them more provident, guiding them by means of the earlier mistakes of others'.[9] In sum, then, it was at a friendly court that this foreign servant of History came to follow the example of the *Odyssey* and relate stories about the disasters of the past. From this proem it is legitimate to infer, therefore, that the court of Alcinous was none other than that of Heraclius, but also that the tone of the *Ecumenical History* was not expected to be panegyrical, but didactic. Conforming to Thucydidean tradition, Simokatta presents himself as a constant adviser and reminder for all who wish to know about the past and the recurrence of similar situations in the future.[10]

It was Joseph Frendo who first interpreted Theophylact's History as a work fulfilling a threefold function; it was couched in a panegyrical tone and was meant for recitation performed by an author personified as

---

[7]   The discussion concerning the relationship between History and Poetry occurs in Aristotle's *Poetics* (ch. 9) and recurs in Theophylact's predecessor Agathias; see A. Kaldellis, 'Agathias on History and Poetry', *GRBS* 38 (1997), 295–305.

[8]   Proem 8:37; trans. Whitby and Whitby, 17–18. On the Homeric allusions of this proem see T. Olajos, 'Quelques remarques sur les réminiscences homériques chez Théophylacte Simocatta historien', in I. Tar, ed., *Epik durch die Jahrhunderte. Internationale Konferenz Szeged 2–4. Oktober 1997*, Acta antiqua et archaeologica XXVII (Szeged, 1998), 207–8.

[9]   Proem 13–14:38; trans. Whitby and Whitby, 18. This is a borrowing from Diodoros Siculus' *Bibliotheca historica*, I 1.1–5; cf. H. Lieberich, *Studien zu den Proömien in der griechischen und byzantinischen Geschichtsschreibung*, II. Program des Kgl. Realgymnasiums München für das Schuljahr 1899/1900 (Munich, 1900), 16–18, and Th. Nissen, 'Das Proemium zu Theophylakts Historien und die Sophistik', *BNJ* 15 (1939), 4–6.

[10]   Nissen, 'Das Prooemium', 12, regards Theophylact's text as a work combining the flattery to Heraclius and the invective against Phocas.

Odysseus and 'addressing an audience'.[11] In response, Michael Whitby considered this theory to be 'based on an excessively literary interpretation of Theophylactean imagery'.[12] More recently, Anna-Maria Taragna explored all references and allusions in the *Ecumenical History* to the concept of the *theatron* and analyzed how this performance of History shaped the act of writing. Expanding further this approach, she made a good case for the theory that the various kinds of theatrically staged scenes were inserted in the narrative and orchestrated by an author who, as 'le nouvel Ulysse', was, in fact, a 'metteur en scène'.[13] Indeed, far from being informative in a strict sense, Theophylact's work was chiefly performative, inscribing historical truth within a dramatic context. Unlike Procopius and Agathias, he does not introduce himself in the opening lines but has we Phaeacians, i.e. his listeners/readers, wait until the end of Book VII before he briefly alludes to himself; nonetheless, he is an omnipresent author conducting the audience from intense emotions to whispered truths and from thematic rotations to recurrent themes. Signs of his endeavour to guide his audience are spread throughout his narrative, be they apophthegmatic statements or phrases introducing a shift in focus. To be sure, with his self-identification as a foreigner (ἔπηλυς) Theophylact inserted the first autobiographical allusion in his narrative, hinting both at his Egyptian (i.e. non-Constantinopolitan) origins and independence from the imperial court.[14] Simokatta is not an objective observer from a distance but an author who frequently adopts the view endorsed by his positive heroes, intentionally introduced in his narrative, such as the ideal ruler Tiberius in Book I, an anonymous war veteran on the Persian front in Book II, and Domitianus, bishop of Melitene, in Book V. Their speeches – this critical weapon that grants narrative advantages to any historian who follows the classicizing tradition – enshrine political ideas shared by the 'playwright' and author.[15] Their main function is to dramatize a situation, not to depict a personality. Yet

---

[11]   See J. D. C. Frendo, 'History and panegyric in the age of Heraclius: the literary background to the composition of the *Histories* of Theophylact Simocatta', *DOP* 42 (1988), 143–56 (esp. 147–51). Speck drew similar conclusions holding that *EH* is a work of propaganda for Heraclius in 'Gedächtnisfeier am Grabe des Maurikios', 182–5 and 244–52.

[12]   Whitby, 'Greek historical writing', 49, n. 104.

[13]   A. M. Taragna, 'Il me revêtit d'un habit resplendissant: l'écriture de l'histoire chez Théophylacte Symocatta', in Odorico, *et al.*, eds., *L'écriture de la mémoire*, 67–84.

[14]   This possible double hint at his Egyptian origins and independence from the imperial court, which passed unnoticed by Frendo and Taragna, is in fact the first autobiographical allusion that Th. inserts in his narrative.

[15]   *EH* includes twenty-two orations and seven letters; see A. M. Taragna, *Logoi historias: discorsi e lettere nella prima storiografia retorica bizantina*, Hellenica 7

what were these ideas? And by what rhetorical means were they literarily achieved? It is worth noting them, keeping these questions in mind as we proceed through a brief but sequential reading of Theophylact's text.

Mostly devoted to a sole emperor, Maurice, the *Ecumenical History* was by no means meant to be his biography or eulogy. He is no doubt the central figure of the drama, without, however, steadily attracting narrative focus. The author never feels sanguine about him, and the few positive portraits of Maurice are immediately followed by negative ones.[16] Thus, rather pompously introduced right after the proem, Maurice is cautiously reminded right afterwards by the dying Tiberius that those 'who possess abundance of power are likely also to be attended by more numerous faults' (I.1.6); and his end was envisioned in a dream that his predecessor saw as he lay dying. A critical reader of this section, Photios was fairly right in seeing in this a foretelling (προαγόρευσις) of a tragedy.[17] Tiberius' death caused a deep mourning among the population, for, in the words of the author, 'subjects are accustomed to suffer upon the untimely decease of those who have ascended to power, at any rate if they began their rule in a winning and popular manner'.[18] Things were thus left at an ideal standpoint, but dramatic developments were about to ensue.

In Book I we receive a clear view of what troubles lay in store. We first hear that on the Balkan front peace was disrupted by the Avars and an attempt was made by Maurice to restore it by dispatching to the khagan all kinds of gifts: but neither an elephant, whom the barbarian either feared or scorned, nor a golden bed, nor a generous amount of tribute, sufficed to prevent barbaric aggression. Singidunum was lost, and at this point Theophylact's criticism is targeted against the sluggishness of the Thracian army that was occasioned by the long-lasting peace. Sent as an ambassador on a peace mission, the *scribon* Comentiolus delivers a long

---

(Alessandria, 2000), 185–7 and 239–41 (where a table with their distribution by book and a more detailed one with orators and addressees).

[16] *Contra* P. Allen, *Evagrius Scholasticus the Church Historian* (Louvain, 1981), 14–15 (who speaks of Th.'s encomiastic exaggeration towards Maurice); and A. M. Taragna, 'Osservazioni sul προοίμιον delle *Historiae* di Teofillato Simocatta', *Quaderni del Dipartimento di Filologia, Linguistica e Tradizione classica dell'Università degli Studi di Torino* 11 (1998), 264, who considers that *EH* is a text much concerned with the *Bios* of the emperor; cf. *eadem*, *Logoi historias*, 198. By contrast, I. V. Krivushin cautiously speaks of a multicoloured portrayal of Maurice: 'Les personnages dans les Histoires de Théophylacte Simocatta', *BSl* 55 (1994), 12.

[17] Photios' full citation as in his *Bibliotheke*, cod. 65, I, 80.34–6: 'ἦν δ' ἄρα ταῦτα ἐκεῖνα τραγῳδίας τινὸς προαγόρευσις τῆς ἀνὰ τὸν παλαμναῖον Φωκᾶν ἀνοσιουργοῦ τυραννίδος.'

[18] Whitby and Whitby (p. 23) wrongly translate δεινοπαθεῖν as 'to show great grief'; for a similar meaning of the word but in a different context see *EH* 3.1.15:112,13.

speech defending the rights of the Romans. Like other orators who will be introduced in the narrative, be they Byzantines, Persians or Avars, Comentiolus will gain his point not in the short- but in the long run. What Simokatta parenthetically states in Book VI, namely that 'the might of the tongue can rule nature, impose laws on necessity, re-channel processes of thought, change fortune, and transform, mould, and fashion everything in obedience',[19] is mostly justified in the hortatory harangues pronounced by generals, lower-ranking officers, or bishops addressing the troops. In many instances in Theophylact's account the course of events is redirected, reoriented or subverted through this kind of speech.

By the same token, stories (διηγήσεις, ἀφηγήσεις or ἀφηγήματα) fulfil a symbolic purpose. Until his eighth and last book, Theophylact favours contrasting imagery in which negative situations alternate with positive counterpoints. Thus, in Book I, we are transferred from the Persian war front to the wedding of Maurice, then to the fire that broke out in the Forum in Constantinople, then to the episode of Paulinus. This was a magician who put a silver basin in the service of his abominable practices, but whose act of treachery was unveiled after some time. Brought to the palace to be judged by the emperor, he almost managed to win a pardon. Nonetheless, succumbing to the persistent demands of the patriarch John the Faster (Νηστευτής), Maurice condemned the man to capital punishment. Before suffering impalement, we are told, Paulinus was forced to witness the cruel execution of his son, who had joined his father in evil practices. Now, the same episode is recorded in the *Coptic Chronicle* of John of Nikiu, with the patriarch appearing strongly intransigent and criticism directed against 'those who followed Paulinus in his evil practices' and 'sought to save him'; as the same chapter has it, even Maurice himself was said to have followed 'heathen practices'.[20]

Commenting on this passage on two different occasions, Joseph Frendo drew attention to the role of the patriarch and the emperor as well as to the attitude of Simokatta towards both of them.[21] There is no doubt that,

---

[19]   See *EH* 6.8.2:234; trans. Whitby and Whitby, 170.

[20]   See ch. 98, ed. E. H. Charles, *The Chronicle of John (c. 690AD) Coptic bishop of Nikiu, being a history of Egypt before and during the Arab conquest*, trans. H. Zotenberg's edition of the Ethiopic versions (London, 1916; repr. Amsterdam, 1982), 161–2. The story resembles one narrated in ch. 42 of the Life of St Theodore of Sykeon; see A. J. Festugière, ed. and trans., *Vie de Théodore de Sykéon*, Subsidia Hagiographica 48 (Brussels, 1970), 36–8.

[21]   Frendo, 'History and panegyric' (as in note 11), 155; and, more extensively, *idem*, 'Three authors in search of a reader: an approach to the analysis of direct discourse in Procopius, Agathias and Theophylact Simocatta', in Sode and Takács, eds., *Novum Millennium*, 123–35. For a discussion of the device of execution see P. Speck, 'Eine Quelle zum Tod an der Furca', *JÖB* 42 (1992), 83–5.

embedding as he did this story in his main narrative, Simokatta's primary purpose was not just edifying and entertaining; nor did he aim at redeeming the posthumous reputation of Maurice, as Frendo suggests.[22] Notably, in the *Coptic Chronicle* the detail about the son who was executed before his father's eyes is missing, thereby raising suspicion. Why has Theophylact rounded off his narration by adding this particular detail? The answer could be sought further down in his account, where we encounter two similar events. First, in Book IV, the Persian Hormisdas (Hormizd, Hurmazd), the son of Chosroes I (Khusro, Khusrau), witnessed both the slaughter of his son and the more cruel execution of his wife; Theophylact comments, 'such destruction of his wife's life before a public audience, together with his wretched son's, constituted the material of tragedy'.[23] As it happens, Hormisdas is absolutely denigrated in Theophylact's account, being the first in the *Ecumenical History*'s narrative upon whom the attribute τύραννος is bestowed, regardless of the fact that he was the legitimate successor to the Persian throne. It was the inescapable culmination of this tragedy that the tyrant met a violent death that, in turn, was followed by the establishment of another τύραννος, his son Chosroes II. More interestingly, the culmination of what happened at the barbarians' court and, before that, to the magician Paulinus, emerges in Book VIII: a touching description of Maurice's own execution by the tyrant Phocas also has him witness to the cruel death of his two sons. It is thus not accidental that he introduces the episode of the execution of Paulinus and his sons in Book I, where a historiographer sets forth his basic ideas and ultimate goals. Apart from a tinge of tragic irony, it must have conveyed a broader message that we cannot fully grasp. Did this somehow carry an implicit criticism of Maurice for being submissive to the patriarch?

In Book II we lose sight of Maurice. The stage is occupied by his generals Philippicus, Comentiolus and, most notably, the elder Heraclius or 'Heraclius the father of the emperor Heraclius', as he is repetitively styled.[24] Moving away from the Persian to the Avar battlefront, Theophylact inserts a pair of speeches in opposition addressed to the Roman troops by his favourite 'secondary characters': the first is by a χιλίαρχος of Comentiolus

---

[22]   Frendo surmises that this source is likely to have been the *vita*, now almost completely lost, of the patriarch John the Faster by Photeinos; see 'History and panegyric', 156. For arguments against this hypothesis and in favour of the possible dependence of Th. on the Copt chronicler see Whitby, 'Greek historical writing', 51, n. 111.

[23]   See *EH* 6. 6.2–4:160; trans. Whitby and Whitby, 111.

[24]   Although it is true that the elder Heraclius is the only general directly praised by Th. (III 6.2:120.6–9), Frendo's contention ('History and panegyric', 151) that these references to Heraclius Senior's exploits imply a kind of 'panegyric by indirection' is hardly convincing.

and aims both at discouraging the soldiers from fighting in a risky cause and at persuading them to retreat; the second is by a war veteran who, echoing the Periclean Funeral Oration, defends the greatness of Rome and the courage of its soldiers. Maurice is nowhere named yet implied and implicated by both. 'These relatively small successes', says the first, 'delude the emperor, and he will not dispense additional allied assistance for us, since he has not yet learned of the more recent ill fortunes'; 'I am amazed if the barbarians are rushing around near the Long Walls', says the other, 'and the emperor has not been aroused, when such great confusion is surging in the city'.[25]

In Book III, entirely set on the eastern frontier, we first detect the emergence of a Christian element. The bishops of Damascus and Edessa were needed to encourage and appease an army on the verge of rebellion. The scene is characterized by feelings of disharmony among the Roman army and rivalry among its generals. Philippicus, *magister militum per Orientem*, is blamed by Priscus as Maurice's adviser for reducing the soldiers' stipends (III 2–3) and is finally replaced (III 5.16). The situation at the Persian court, which Theophylact relates immediately after, is not pleasant either: the death of Chosroes I raises sentiments of defection and the question of tyranny comes to the fore. This context of general chaos and instability offers a pretext for Theophylact to insert a long excursus, his own 'Archaeology' (III 9–18), and refer to the outbreak of the war and its causes. He offers his readers/listeners a brief chronicle from Justinian to Justin II and from Tiberius to Maurice, but the historian's eye is not so much turned to the past as to the future. Once again, we hear the voice of the emperor in a 'mirror-of-princes'-like speech now pronounced in a brief moment of lucidity by the mentally ill Justin II. At variance with Procopius and Agathias, Simokatta grants the 'privilege' of speech to emperors, yet not to the reigning emperor, namely Maurice, but to his predecessors; their words are words of advice to their successors.[26]

Indeed, in his short speech, composed in short sentences reminiscent of the Psalms, Justin warns his successor Tiberius 'not to delight in bloodshed', 'not to be party of murders', 'not to repay evil with evil', and concludes with such words of advice as 'pay attention to your army', 'do not entertain slanderers', 'do not let men say to you that your predecessor behaved thus'.[27] Contrasting the long speeches of a *chiliarchos* or a war

---

[25]   *EH* 2.13.12 and 14.9: 96 and 98; trans. Whitby and Whitby, 62–3.

[26]   On this issue see Kaldellis, *Procopius of Caesarea*, 48: 'one could even say that Justinian is relatively absent from the work, despite being its alleged protagonist'. On the speeches of Justin II to Tiberius and of the latter to Maurice as 'mirrors of princes' integrated in the historical narrative see G. Prinzing, 'Beobachtungen zu "integrierten" Fürstenspiegeln der Byzantiner', *JÖB* 38 (1988), 6–12.

[27]   *EH* 3.11.9–11: 133; trans. Whitby and Whitby, 89–90.

veteran that are fully adjusted to the requirements of *Kunstprosa*, the naked exposition of the emperor's words, as the historian explains, was prompted by the need for veracity. What mattered was not only a naked exposition of an emperor whom Theophylact consistently portrays in negative terms, but immediacy and foresight of the danger generated by a policy lacking in prudence. The 'Archaeology' is rounded off with a long speech of genuine crusading inspiration where personal heroism is praised and Persian religion is reprimanded. Delivered by the general Justinian, a distant cousin of Justin II, it is again given in a succession of short sentences, some in metre, yet cast in a higher style than that of Justin.[28]

Book IV is devoted to regime change in Persia and the ensuing contacts with Constantinople. Implicit words of advice and prophecy are now put in the mouth of the enemy. Following the Herodotean tradition, Theophylact sets his second antithetical pair of speeches by bringing the internal affairs and problems of the Romans into the Persian palace;[29] yet, in fact, the oppositional speeches of the fallen tyrant Hormisdas and the Persian noble Bindoes have an accumulative rather than a dialectical effect, for they both converge on how the problem of tyranny can be treated. Taken from prison, Hormisdas warns his spectators about the fall of the Persian kingdom that might be caused 'because of tyranny' (διὰ τὸ τύραννον). 'Unless you winnow out the tyrants, you will lead the kingdom into servitude and be a plaything for the nations (ἔθνη) when you have acquired vulnerability through the discordant conduct of life'.[30] In the place of his son Chosroes, a 'belligerent warmonger', Hormisdas in vain proposes his other son as his successor. In his antilogy the Persian Bindoes derogatorily denies him the rights of counselling and admonition, concluding his speech with the words: 'let the destruction of one man be a lesson in prudence and let this be a most equitable law, a salvation for those to come'. Together with his son and his wife, Hormisdas is driven to a most violent death hinted at above, and the empire passes to another tyrant, Chosroes. To be sure, Hormisdas' aversion towards his son Chosroes is also that of Theophylact

---

[28]   Notably, some clauses of this speech are in a twelve-syllable metre; see *EH* 3.13.11–12:137.8–14.

[29]   Herodotus in his *Historia* III 80–82 was the first to have presented the case for democracy, oligarchy and monarchy, a debate purely Greek in conception, in a trilogy of speeches exchanged between Persian nobles. For the representation or misrepresentation of the Persian events in question in the *EH* see D. Frendo, 'Theophylact Simocatta on the revolt of Bahram Chobin and the early career of Khusrau II', *Bulletin of the Asian Institute*, n.s. 3 (1989), 77–88.

[30]   *EH* 4. 4.13: 157; trans. Whitby and Whitby, 108.

and his times, but this contemporary echo does more than merely generate a hostile attitude.[31]

In what comes next, the words of the speakers delve into much more significant issues. Confronted with the difficulties derived from his conflict with the usurper Bahram and seeking assistance from Constantinople, Chosroes sends to Maurice first a letter, then an embassy to the Great Palace to restate and reinforce the previous arguments about the 'two eyes', i.e. the greatest powers by which 'the disobedient and bellicose tribes are winnowed'.[32] It is from the most distinguished of the ambassadors who, as a means of *captatio benevolentiae*, mixed words with tears that we hear about the impossibility of a single nation coping with the innumerable cares of the organization of the universe. 'Even though the Persians were to be deprived of power, power would immediately transfer to other men', Theophylact warns us, and adduces such conspicuous examples of the past as the Medes being taken over by the Persians and the latter succumbing to the Parthians; or the ambitious Alexander who yearned for Indian power and threatened to subjugate Libya, but, instead of becoming a single unitary rule, his kingdom was divided up into a leadership of multiple tyranny (τὴν πολυτύραννον ... ἡγεμονίαν). And through the Persian ambassador, Simokatta exclaims: 'what prosperity would events devolve upon Romans if the Persians are deprived of power and transmit mastery to another tribe?'[33]

This mention of successive empires and rules that subvert one another harks back to the Archaeology of Book III (chs. 9–10) and the root of all contemporary evil. Yet which tribe is this that might overthrow Persian

---

[31] T. Olajos, *Les sources de Théophylacte Simocatta historien* (Budapest and Leiden, 1988), 61.

[32] *EH* 4.11.2–3:169; trans. Whitby and Whitby, 117 and n. 40 (for a parallel in Peter the Patrician's lost History, fr. 12). Note that, later on, in the patriarch Nicholas Mystikos' correspondence, the polity of the Abbasids was, like that of the Sassanians, paired with the Roman empire as 'constituting the two eyes of the universe': see L. G. Westerink and R. J. H. Jenkins, eds. and trans., *Nicholas I Patriarch of Constantinople: Letters*, CFHB 6, Series Washingtonensis (Washington, DC, 1973), 2–3. On the question of the authenticity of the letters exchanged between Chosroes II and Maurice see Cl. A. Ciancaglini, 'Le "lettere persiane" nelle *Storie* di Teofilatto Simocatta', in *La Persia e Bisanzio*, Atti dei convegni Lincei 201 (Rome, 2004), 639–49; for a presentation of the ideas prevailing in the letter of Chosroes see Brodka, *Die Geschichtsphilosophie*, 196–8 and 203–9.

[33] *EH* 4. 13.13: 175. Unlike Whitby and Whitby (p. 122), I translate φῦλον as 'tribe' and not as 'nation'. Schreiner translates it as 'Stamm' [*Theophylaktos* (note 6 above), 132]. This passage was interpreted as ironic rather than a prophecy to the expansion of the Arabs by R. G. Hoyland, *Seeing Islam as Others Saw it: A Survey and Evaluation of Christian, Jewish and Zoroastrian Writings on Early Islam* (Princeton, NJ, 1997), 54–5.

rule, and, like Alexander, reach as far as India and threaten Libya? What is the chronological scope of the prophecies enshrined in these speeches, which are undoubtedly Theophylact's own literary inventions and personal concerns? Being clear allusions to the expansion of the Arabs, as I believe, and pointers to a dating of the *Ecumenical History* in the period from c. 638 to 642, these words of the Persian ambassador can account for the dramatic change in the narrative that we observe from the end of Book IV onwards.[34]

When in Book V war against the usurper Bahram is brought to a glorious conclusion, Simokatta returns, once again, to the idea of the 'succession and end of empires', highlighted here by mutual and intersecting prophecies: as he was well-versed in the 'vain wisdom' of the Chaldean astrologers, Chosroes predicted that the gods would send troubles back to the Romans and that the Babylonian race would get hold of the Roman empire for *a threefold cyclic hebdomad of years* and that the Romans would enslave the Persians on the *fifth hebdomad of years*.[35] This astrological type of prophecy

---

[34]   In a casual aside T. Olajos implies a later date of composition: 'que son activité ait duré jusqu'au début de la conquête arabe et que cet événement d'une importance historique universelle ait influencé son opinion, reste encore à prouver bien que d'après quelques passages (par exemple 3.9,11; 17,7; 4.11,2–3; 13,6–13) on puisse le supposer'; see *Les sources de Théophylacte*, 11. In a similar vein, Schreiner is inclined to endorse the same view: see *Theophylaktos*, 2–3 and esp. n. 591: 'Die prophetischen Worte dieser Rede haben sich als wahr erwiesen, und es bleibt die Frage, ob sie nur "prophetisch" waren oder *post festum*, d.h. nach 636 niedergeschrieben wurden. Ich möchte letzteres für wahrscheinlicher halten. Dies würde bedeuten, daß Th. seine Geschichte endgültig erst kurz vor dem Tod des Herakleios redigiert hat'. Cf. also W. Kaegi, *Heraclius, Emperor of Byzantium* (Cambridge, 2003), 84.

[35]   *EH* 5.15.6–7: 216–7. Different interpretations have been put forward as to the exact calculation and meaning of these puzzling expressions; Whitby and Whitby, 153, n. 80 reckon that the *threefold cyclic hebdomad of years* points to the years before 622, whereas the *fifth hebdomad of years* hints at the years of Heraclius' campaign (622–28). The hebdomad missing from this calculation must both have been one of peace and have preceded the Persian conquest. For Schreiner the starting year was 591, i.e. when peace was interrupted, and the *fifth hebdomad* coincided again with the years of Heraclius' Persian campaign: *Theophylaktos*, 160 and 320 n. 784. While rejecting the interpretation of M. and M. Whitby, G. J. Reinink suggested that Chosroes' prophecy intended to show the relativity and the short-term impact of both Persian and Roman military successes; see 'Heraclius, the new Alexander: Apocalyptic prophecies during the reign of Heraclius', in Reinink and B. H. Stolte, eds., *The Reign of Heraclius (610–641): Crisis and Confrontation*, Groningen Studies in Cultural Change II (Louvain, 2002), 86–9. Yet, as Th. clearly speaks of enslavement of the Persians, the *fifth hebdomad* could be no other than the one following 628; cf. Treadgold, *The Early Byzantine Historians*, 332. On the whole prophecy and its relationship to contemporary belief in the imminence of world's

found response to the episode that is related immediately afterwards: dispatched as an ambassador to the Persian king, the bishop of Chalcedon, Probus, was asked to show to him an image of the Mother of God; once he venerated it, Chosroes said that its archetype appeared to him and revealed that the victories of Alexander of Macedon would be granted to him. Simokatta comments that the prophecy was already fulfilled because Chosroes had returned to his palace and overpowered the tyrants 'through the strength and the power of the emperor' (meaning Maurice).[36]

The cycle of Persian events thus concluded, Theophylact turns attention back to Europe and, at long last, to the Roman emperor. How is Maurice presented in the three last books, which correspond to the second half of his reign and ten years of Byzantine history (592–602)? The overall impression is that the emperor is simply a passive actor, unable to embark on righteous initiatives or proceed to justified decisions. The attempts of the senate, the patriarch and the empress to dissuade him from campaigning against the Avars in Anchialos are altogether fruitless. Having been discouraged by the human representatives of power, he is then averted from launching his Thracian expedition by the elements of nature: a great eclipse of the sun, violent gusts of wind, and a boar threatening to throw him from his horse's seat. Omens further militate against his presence in Thrace, as a woman in Herakleia is reported to have given birth to a monster, and a herd of deer attack him while he is marching.

It is after this last episode with the deer that a crime story unfolds in detail. Although it was a Gepid soldier who murdered an imperial attendant, the emperor imposed the death penalty upon a peasant who discovered the victim's dead body. Split into two sections that are placed at distant points in the narrative, this detective story has its mystery finally solved with an emblematic phrase: 'it is not beside the point to describe as well the causation of the active Providence which daily traverses the whole world, watches over mortal affairs with its untiring eye, and always administers to mankind retribution for acts of violence'.[37] To be sure, these words do not involve solely the infamous Gepid soldier but the emperor

---

end see P. Magdalino, 'The history of the future and its uses: prophecy, policy, and propaganda', in R. Beaton and C. Roueché, eds., *The Making of Byzantine History: Studies dedicated to Donald M. Nicol* (Aldershot, 1993), 18–19; and *idem, L'Orthodoxie des astrologues. La science entre le dogme et la divination à Byzance (VIIe–XIVe siècle),* Réalités byzantines 12 (Paris, 2006), 39. On the medieval idea of the succession of the four kingdoms echoing the biblical dream of Daniel as in *The Book of Daniel* ch. 7 see H. Guenée, *Histoire et culture historique dans l'Occident médiéval* (Paris, 1980), 148–54.

[36]   *EH* 5.15.9–11: 216–7; trans. Whitby and Whitby, 154.

[37]   The story is first inserted in *EH* 6. 2, then resumed and rounded out in 6.10: 222–3 and 239–42; the saying is in 6.10.4: 239, trans. Whitby and Whitby, 174. For

himself who, once again after the episode of Paulinus, had, through his own judicial decisions, stained his hands with blood.

Kaiserkritik is intensified in the context of the Balkan campaign against the Avars. The reluctance of the army to fight comes gradually to the fore, and Simokatta undermines the justification of this war through various rhetorical means: speeches of the Avar ambassador Koch (VI 6.7–12) and of the Avar Khagan (VII 10 and 15), the narration about Sesostris by the ambassador Theodore (styled as a man with a free tongue), and the accusations of inertia brought by the emperor against his brother Peter, recently appointed general in the Balkan front and seriously wounded by a boar while hunting (VII 2.11–14). Notably, the picture of Maurice drawn up here is markedly different from the one in Evagrius.[38] The profile of a pious emperor, so conspicuously promoted in the last book of the ecclesiastical historian's work, is symbolically discarded in Simokatta's report on the death of John the Faster. In a clear flicker of irony the two roles are masterfully crossed by mutual transposition of vocabulary; for we are told that the patriarch owed his nickname to his ability to resist pleasure through his philosophy (καταφιλοσοφῆσαι τῶν ἡδονῶν), master passions as would a tyrant (τυραννῆσαι τῶν παθῶν), and become master of the belly (αὐτοκράτορά τε τῆς κοιλίας γενέσθαι), whereas the emperor passed his nights during Lent on the priest's wooden bedstead, 'as if he thought that he would partake of divine grace thereby'.[39] Notably, this is the second mention of the patriarch John the Faster in the whole narrative, and the obvious meaning of this passage is that the emperor failed to emulate him in virtue. Yet was Simokatta's irony directed towards something further? Did he insinuate, as in the case of Paulinus, that the patriarch did eventually win over the emperor?

As a land of trouble and the starting-point of the rising tyrant, Thrace is the next-to-last stage in the drama but, all of a sudden, Theophylact retreats, now by means of a geographical transposition, to Egypt. Coming from the other end of the empire and the author's place of origin, the epiphany of anthropomorphic and other animals of the Nile brings a last omen into the narrative (VII 16). Clearly, both the animals attacking humans in Thrace

---

the question as to where Th. may have borrowed this story from see Olajos, *Les sources de Théophylacte*, 138–9.

[38] Evagrius, *Ecclesiastical History*, ch. VI, 222–41; for the panegyrical way Maurice is treated by Evagrius see M. Whitby, *The Ecclesiastical History of Evagrius Scholasticus*, Translated Texts for Historians 33 (Liverpool, 2000), xlvii–xlix.

[39] *EH* 7.6.1–5: 254–5. This example alone suffices to discard Michael and Mary Whitby's contention that 'Th.'s use of a similar ornate style for the most rhetorical passages of the *History* indicates that he was not parodying, but imitating, Christian rhetoric, which provided a stylistic ideal to be set alongside the Greek of classical writers'; see *The History of Theophylact*, xxviii.

and the awe-inspiring human monsters in Egypt function as omens. Yet prophecy cannot explain history and human political responsibility, as this derives from the acts of the men of power; first and foremost, animals and monsters emerge in the narrative in order to suggest how frail and vulnerable a king can be. The Christian Simokatta uses them throughout his narrative with an ironical and not an apocalyptic intention.

What we have read so far in the seven books of the *Ecumenical History* are rather vague anticipations of the culmination of Simokatta's narrative. What was kept in store is brought to the surface in Book VIII, now set in Constantinople, with the tragic hero Maurice and all other major figures of the plot (Priscus, Peter, Comentiolus) coming to centre stage. Neither speeches nor stories can any longer be of any use, and the narrative unfolds in short sentences creating an atmosphere of suspense.[40]

In spite of the army's reaction, Maurice urged his reluctant brother Peter to move ahead with his army and cross the Danube. The crowds disobeyed, and Phocas was proclaimed their leader. For once, as the messenger brought the bad news, we gain sight of the palace and its prominent dweller who, however, proved inferior to critical circumstances. There is no point in retelling the tragic conclusion of the story. One after another all the protagonists of the *Ecumenical History* meet a violent end and Simokatta for the first time casts a sympathetic eye upon his tragic hero: besides revealing to his murderers where his child was hiding, Maurice asked, by his letters to the most venerable churches of the inhabited world, that the Lord Christ would punish him in this and not the afterlife. This is part of the so-called hagiography of Maurice that developed soon after his death. It is inserted here to confirm the author's conviction that the emperor had a great deal of responsibility for meeting this tragic ending.[41]

But what was wrong with Maurice? Was he guilty of any sins? And, if so, which ones? With *Kaiserkritik* constantly creeping into his account, Simokatta blamed the ruler for lack of political shrewdness, inability to cope with or understand the shaken military morale, sluggishness, and consideration of military and political developments from a distance. By

---

[40]   The only speech inserted here is Th.'s own funeral oration for Maurice (8.12.5), of which only a few sentences survive in Vaticanus gr. 977; Whitby held that by so doing 'Th. did not want to interrupt the narrative' (*The Emperor Maurice*, 49). On stylistic grounds, basically the use of I-person in the narrative, Speck suggested that the speech was an interpolation by a later redactor who, however, copied it down from an oration delivered by Th. after Phocas' fall in 610: see 'Gedächtnisfeier am Grabe des Maurikios', 199–212.

[41]   Judging from *EH*, the 'hagiography' must have developed not much after Maurice's death; see J. Wortley, 'The Legend of the Emperor Maurice', *Actes du XV* *Congrès international d'études byzantines. Athènes Septembre 1976*, IV. Histoire, Communications (Athens, 1980), 382–91.

contrast, private sins and vices were not serious grounds for criticism, since knowledge of them derived from the rumours of the anonymous mob.[42] Maurice's faults were secular, not religious. However, having thus decided to conform to the classical tradition according to which the protagonists of history are responsible for their own acts, Theophylact had to further contribute his own Christian views on causation;[43] for him, predestination was another factor that might determine human life. In his extant short treatise on this particular subject, he set forth arguments both in favour and against those who maintain that human life is predestined by quoting relevant passages from the Bible. Taking a different stance himself from both parties, neither did he accept predestination, as this was a Greek concept typical of a tyrannical Deity, nor did he uphold indeterminacy since infinity may be attributed to God alone. He concluded that 'both length of life and its curtailment arising from death are of our own free choice' and that 'supplementation of life and bringing on of death are literally mortised to the human race through virtue or vice'.[44] By laying emphasis on prophecies, omens and rhetorical warnings in his *Ecumenical History*, Theophylact assigned to *tyche* a new, Christian meaning, making it contingent upon God's response to human virtue or vice.[45]

The tragic end of Maurice in 602 may seem to us a remote event, but it was not so to the author Theophylact, although the time of composition of his History at least postdated the Persian defeat in 628. Paradoxically, in the concluding pages of his Book VIII and in an oft-quoted passage, we are told that a kind of prophecy had to be fulfilled before the Persians of Chosroes could be defeated. It was during the final battle against them on 12 December 627 that Heraclius found out that there were two soldiers alone left from the army that marched with Phocas to Constantinople, 'even though the intervening years had not been numerous'.[46] This

---

[42]   See the words inserted in defence of Maurice in 2.17.5 and 8.9.9:103–4 and 301. For a detailed account of the events see D. M. Olster, *The Politics of Usurpation in the Seventh Century: Rhetoric and Revolution in Byzantium* (Amsterdam, 1993), 52–60. However, I disagree with him when he states that for Maurice's fall Th. puts the blame on the demes and the mob's frenzy, *ibid.*, 53.

[43]   Whitby, *The Emperor Maurice*, 323–4, prefers to consider it 'haphazard'.

[44]   See *Theophylactus Simocates: On Predestined Terms of Life*, Greek text and English trans. by C. Garton and L. G. Westerink, Arethusa Monographs VI (Buffalo, NY, 1978), 24–5.

[45]   The whole question requires further discussion, which cannot be undertaken here. For the function it acquires in Procopius' *Wars* see Kaldellis, *Procopius of Caesarea*, 165–221.

[46]   *EH* 8.12.12:308: '… δύο καὶ μόνους στρατιώτας τῆς φιλοτυράννου πληθύος ὑπολελειμμένους ἐξεῦρεν, καίτοι μὴ πολλῶν μεσολαβησάντων τῶν χρόνων'; trans. Whitby and Whitby, 230. Speck suggested that this sentence derived from

generation of murderers had to be exterminated to achieve a sort of *catharsis*. Significantly and contrary to what one might have expected, the twenty-five years that separated the death of his main hero from the victorious end of Heraclius' campaign were not seen by Theophylact as many, nor had they extinguished memories. Persons, stories, situations and ideas related to Maurice's gloomy story were not yet dead and buried. Writing thus not long after, as he thought, the years of tyranny, Simokatta wove a kind of protracted history with a clear projection into the future. Maurice's calamities were a serious and wise warning for the present emperor, namely Heraclius. The problem of tyranny and the idea that the ruler should provide happiness and not cause troubles to his subjects were too diachronic and universal to be confined to the reign of Maurice and his mongrel barbarian (μιξοβάρβαρος) successor.[47]

---

the hand of a redactor that intervened after the death of Th.: 'Gedächtnisfeier am Grabe des Maurikios', 186–98.

[47]   The expression μιξοβάρβαρος τύραννος referring to Phocas occurs in *EH* 8.10.4: 303.

10. Envy and Nemesis in the *Vita Basilii* and Leo the Deacon: literary mimesis or something more?

Martin Hinterberger[*]

Like other genres of Byzantine literature, historiography also was permeated by the principle of *mimesis*, or the imitation of linguistic and stylistic models.[1] The imitation of models manifests itself on various levels. It begins with the usage of 'atticistic' vocabulary, employing words found in the model texts, and culminates in the incorporation of slightly adapted passages into a new textual environment. The latter phenomenon has given rise to doubts concerning the veracity of accounts that borrow whole passages from other texts, but in general these doubts have proved to be unfounded. For example, only recently D.R. Reinsch offered a brilliant analysis of how John Kantakouzenos, writing on the plague of 1347, bases himself linguistically on Thucydides, but gives the linguistic material a new sense.[2] Another difficulty is the conceptual confusion produced by the interference of different linguistic layers that stretch over

---

[*] I would like to thank my colleague Chris Schabel for improving my English.

[1] On *mimesis* in Byzantine literature in general see H. Hunger, 'On the imitation (ΜΙΜΗΣΙΣ) of Antiquity in Byzantine literature', *DOP* 23 (1968), 17–38; in historiography in particular: Gy. Moravcsik, 'Klassizismus in der byzantinischen Geschichtsschreibung', in P. Wirth, ed., *Polychronion. Festschrift für F. Dölger zum 75. Geburtstag* (Heidelberg 1966), 366–77. On the substantial differences that, despite intensive *mimesis*, exist between ancient and Byzantine historiography, see esp. R. Scott, 'The classical tradition in Byzantine historiography', in Mullett and Scott, eds., *The Classical Tradition*, 61–74, and W. J. Aerts, 'Imitatio and aemulatio in Byzantium with classical literature, especially in historical writing', in H. Hokwerda, ed., *Constructions of Greek Past: Identity and Historical Consciousness from Antiquity to the Present* (Groningen, 2003), 89–99.

[2] D. R. Reinsch, 'Byzantine adaptations of Thucydides', in A. Rengakos and A. Tsakmakis, eds., *Brill's Companion to Thucydides* (Leiden and Boston, 2006), 755–78, esp. 775–6.

many centuries. Thucydides and Procopius were separated by more than 900 years. Obviously, the meaning of words changed over such a length of time. Did Procopius, when he imitated Thucydides, use the words in the sense Thucydides did, or in the sense current in his time? What was the current sense, given the fact that most texts obey the principle of *mimesis*? Furthermore, Byzantine authors usually did not rely on just one model, but imitated more than one author at the same time, with the result that several linguistic and stylistic forms were mingled. We know that Byzantine authors frequently used outdated terms even when they referred to their actual present times. Thus, for instance, they spoke about Scythians and Persians when they actually meant Bulgarians and Turks. Normally the context provides sufficient information so that the meaning of the text is nevertheless clear. In some cases, however, interpretation can become difficult, especially when we have to do with abstract terms that also form part of the linguistic and cultural heritage. How can we grasp their actual meaning in a specific text? Let us recall that for Byzantine Greek we have no dictionary at our disposal; we rely on dictionaries of ancient Greek.[3] So far this question has not received much attention. In this paper I shall attempt to deal with the meaning of some abstract notions by reading two texts closely, establishing their literary tradition and investigating the usage of the terms in question in texts contemporary to them.

My presentation is going to focus on the meaning of the words *phthonos*, (*baskanos*) *nemesis* and *baskanos tyche* respectively (conventionally rendered as envy, envious revenge/retribution and envious fate), and I shall investigate these terms in two historiographical works of the tenth century, the so-called *Vita Basilii* (=*VB*), the biography of the emperor Basil I (r. 867–86), which constitutes part of the collection of historiographical works known as the Continuation of Theophanes, and the History of Leo the Deacon (=*HLD*), which, roughly speaking, covers the reigns of Nikephoros Phokas and John Tzimiskes (r. 963–69 and 969–76 respectively).[4] Whereas

---

[3]   The *Lexikon der byzantinischen Gräzität* by E. Trapp and his team (= *LBG*, so far fascicles 1–6, Vienna 1994–2007) records exclusively new words not recorded in H. G. Liddell, R. Scott and H. Stuart Jones, *A Greek–English Lexicon* (Oxford, 1925–40⁹) and G. W. H. Lampe, *A Patristic Greek Lexicon* (Oxford, 1961–68), or words insufficiently testified in these lexica. At the present stage, the recording of specific Byzantine usages of old words, especially of abstract terms, is, justifiably, beyond the scope of the *LBG*.

[4]   Theophanes Continuatus, *Chronographia*, 211–353; Leo the Deacon (ed. Hase). I am indebted to the late Professor Ihor Ševčenko for allowing me to consult a provisional version of his forthcoming edition of the *VB* accompanied by an English translation (as already announced by De Gruyter). A. Markopoulos, ʼΚύρου παιδεία καὶ Βίος Βασιλείου. Ἕνας πιθανὸς συσχετισμόςʼ, *Symmeikta* 15 (2002), 91–108, esp. 91–5, provides a rich bibliographical overview. On both texts see Karpozilos, Βυζαντινοὶ Ἱστορικοί, II, 352–8 and 476–508 (bibliography at 365–6

phthonos, *nemesis* and *baskanos tyche* appear as superhuman powers also in other historiographical works, it is in these two texts that they are allotted an especially crucial role in the explanation of historical developments.

In the *VB* these metaphysical powers appear in four passages, presented here in the order of their appearance in the text (chs. 34, 50–51, 64–6 and 100).

(1) *Phthonos* appears for the first time after Basil's attempt to reform the legal system. The passage refers to events of the year 867 and follows the description of Basil's reforms:

> Since, however, *phthonos* tends to attach itself to good things as worms mostly do to sweet-tasting wood, and since bad demons (φαῦλα δαιμόνια), begrudging (βασκαίνοντα) the well-being (εὐετηρία) and flourishing of the universal state, attempt through evil people to disturb the flow of good things, because of all this, Symbatios and George, too, planned and contrived a plot against the emperor.[5]

(2) In chs. 50–51 the author relates the events that led to the disastrous Byzantine defeat at the hands of the Arabs at Tarsos in 883. At the end of this episode he concludes: 'Such was the outcome of the foolish campaign that *phthonos* had adjudicated to the disadvantage of the Romans and such was the trophy that *baskanos* (envious) *nemesis* set up against the formerly prospering Romans.'[6] With these words the author leaves the eastern part of the empire behind and turns thereafter to events in the West. The bitter ending of the episode is already hinted at when, at the beginning, the virtuous general Andreas *ek Skython*, after a series of splendid victories, is said to have refrained from advancing further out of fear that 'the envy of nemesis (τὸ τῆς νεμέσεως ... φθονερόν), as often happens, might destroy what he already had attained'.[7]

(3) A few chapters further down (chs. 65–6), the author describes the Byzantines' struggles to regain control of southern Italy. The Byzantines engaged both navy and land forces in the battle and thus drove back the Arabs in Calabria and Langobardia. After this success the author comments: 'In this fashion the naval forces overcame treachery, *phthonos* and *nemesis*, and returned to the emperor with rich spoils and with wreaths of victory

---

and 489–91), as well as Kazhdan, *A History of Byzantine Literature (850–1000)*, 137–44 and 273–90. *IILD* has recently been translated and commented on by Talbot and Sullivan, *The History of Leo the Deacon* (= Talbot–Sullivan). My English rendering of passages of *VB* and *HLD* follows closely the respective translations of Ševčenko and Talbot–Sullivan (with slight adaptations).

[5] *VB* ch. 34: 263.3–8.
[6] *VB* ch. 50: 288.6–9.
[7] *VB* ch. 51: 286.4–7.

... But the land forces, on the other hand, were not quite able to escape *phthonos*.[8] In another encounter, *c*. 880, the Byzantine troops are defeated because of strife between two generals.

(4) *Phthonos* appears for the last time towards the end of Basil's life (ch. 100). The passage is preceded by a description of the pains Basil took in order to protect the common people from unfair taxation. Thereafter we read:

> Then *phthonos* once again aroused another storm and another tempest in the imperial palace, for it threw bonds of nature into confusion and stirred it up against itself. As Constantine, the most beloved son of the emperor, had recently departed this life, the emperor's affection and hopes were transferred to his second son Leo; but the envious tribe of demons could not bear this meekly, for in all likelihood they had noticed the mild, peaceful, pious and harmonious character of the one who was to succeed to the imperial throne and concluded that because of all this his subjects would prosper ($εὐετηρίαν$) and would increase in all kinds of laudable qualities during his reign. The demons therefore girded themselves for the contest against him and battled him in the following fashion.[9]

What follows is an account of Theodore Santabarenos' intrigues against Leo, which led to Leo's alienation from his father and subsequent imprisonment.

Though in some of the above-mentioned cases *phthonos* may also allude to the human emotion of a specific person involved in the event, it is clear that in the context of these passages the word means something that transcends the human sphere and is essentially different from envy, the emotion, and much more powerful. If we compare these four passages, we observe the following: Passages 1 and 4 closely correspond, as do passages 2 and 3. Each time *phthonos* appears, the story takes a negative turn. What precedes the appearance of *phthonos* is military success or a positive development in the administration of the state. In the first case, where victory is followed by defeat, *phthonos* appears in combination with envious *nemesis*; in the second case, where the emperor's care for justice is followed by internal strife, *phthonos* is accompanied by envious demons. Each time an ideal, utterly positive, situation is reversed into its opposite and thus destroyed. From a narratological point of view we also observe that each mention of *phthonos* functions as a transition from one narrative unit to the next. Whereas in chs. 51 and 64 the author refers to *phthonos* at the end of a narrative unit, in chs. 34 and 100 *phthonos* marks the beginning

---

[8]   *VB* chs. 65–6: 305.13–18.

[9]   *VB* ch. 100: 348.10–20.

of a new subject. In all four passages, the narrator's words integrate the events he comments on into a causative and interpretive framework. He explains where these developments come from, that they are bad, and who is to blame, namely *phthonos*.

Two passages in Leo the Deacon's nearly contemporary History present several lexical and structural similarities with the above-mentioned passages in the *VB*.

(1) In the year 964 (or 965)[10] Nikephoros Phokas launched a major naval operation against Sicily. The events in Sicily are narrated as follows:

> They (the Byzantine forces) enjoyed such good fortune (εὐετηρία) at the beginning that they captured the renowned and celebrated cities of Syracuse and Himera at the first assault and in addition subdued Tauromenium and Leontini without any bloodshed. But in the end envious fate (ἡ βάσκανος τύχη) was not to send them a favourable breeze, but blew fiercely and violently against them and submerged them.[11]

In what follows Leo relates the subsequent disastrous events in Sicily that led to the destruction of the whole army. This passage reminds us clearly of the account of the defeat at Tarsos in ch. 51 of *VB*. But here, instead of *phthonos* and *nemesis* we find 'envious fate'. Furthermore, whereas *phthonos* in ch. 51 of *VB* is referred to at the end of the passage, in Leo's account the mention of the final cause, *baskanos tyche*, marks the beginning of the story. The motive that provokes *phthonos* and *baskanos tyche* respectively in Leo's account is *eueteria*, good fortune, the very same word used in chs. 34 and 100 of the *VB*.

(2) The second time we see the envious powers in action in *HLD*, they appear in connection with Nikephoros Phokas' violent death in 969 (ch. 5.3 and ch. 5.8). Leo first announces Nikephoros' death when he refers to the affairs in Bulgaria and the Bulgarian embassy to the Byzantine Empire. He uses this occasion for a first attempt to explain Nikephoros' unexpected end, which thwarted the Bulgarians' initiative to obtain Byzantine support against the Rus:

> But human fortunes are raised up by a small shift of the scale and are as if suspended from a slender thread, and wont to turn also in the opposite direction. For some people rightly believe that a certain divine *nemesis* and human *phthonos* attack the most prominent and valorous, tripping them up, overthrowing them, and driving them to extinction. This is the sort of fate that then befell the Emperor Nikephoros, when his fortunes were prospering, more so than for any of those who ruled before him.

---

[10]   On the date of this event see Talbot–Sullivan, 115, n. 63.
[11]   *HLD* end of ch. 4.7: 66.7–12; cf. Talbot–Sullivan, 116.

And I will say this: that it is through the unfathomable forethought of
the Almighty that mankind's prospering affairs change to the opposite,
so that they thus be taught that they are mortal and ephemeral beings
and should not puff up more than is fitting. For already certain men, who
have met with success and have distinguished themselves in battle, have
not hesitated to declare themselves gods, insulting Providence itself.[12]

Leo gives some examples of this behaviour (Otos and Ephialtes,
Nebuchadnezzar, Alexander), before he concludes:

Thus it is understandable that men's fortunes are subject to changes and
reverses. This is what then happened to the Romans, who soon lost their
ruler, a man the likes of whom the Roman Empire had not had before.
For if their fortunes had not been reversed through his murder, then
nothing would have prevented them, if he had lived, from establishing
the boundaries of their territory where the sun rises in India, and again
where it sets, at the very end of the world.[13]

These words seem to prepare the audience for the events to come.
Subsequently, as if wanting to increase suspense, Leo first relates in
great detail the conquest of Antioch, before turning to the arrival of John
Tzimiskes in Constantinople and the denouement itself, the horrible
murder of Phokas by Tzimiskes. After a final appraisal of Nikephoros
Phokas' personality, the author resumes the argumentative thread of ch. 3,
repeating its essential message:

But I say that, if some envious fate had not begrudged (βάσκανος
νεμεσήσασα τύχη) his prospering affairs and suddenly snatched away
this man's life, the Roman Empire would have obtained greater glory
than ever before. But Providence (πρόνοια), which abhors harsh and
overweening spirits in men, curtails and checks them and reduces them
to nothing, with its incomprehensible decisions steering the transport
ship of life on an expedient course.[14]

Like the author of the *VB*, Leo the Deacon refers to *phthonos* and envious
fate in order to explain why things happen in the way he describes them.
What becomes even clearer in Leo's text than in the *VB* is that the blow of
the envious powers comes according to a certain rule that governs human
life: 'Human fortunes are wont to turn in the opposite direction', says
Leo, whereas we read in the *VB* (ch. 34) that 'envy tends to attach itself to

---

[12]   *HLD* ch. 5.3: 80.7–21; cf. Talbot–Sullivan, 131–2.
[13]   *HLD* ch. 5.3: 81.2–10.
[14]   *HLD* end of ch. 5.8: 90.5–11; cf. Talbot–Sullivan, 140.

good things'. Nevertheless, this rule, the reversal of good fortune into bad fortune, is explicitly declared to serve Providence, although this does not mean that divine providence and the said envious powers are identical; rather the envious powers appear to be subordinated to Providence, which, without doubt, is to be identified with God.

Let us now investigate the significance of *mimesis* for the construction of the passages mentioned above. Since the studies of R. Jenkins, C.B. Hase and others it has been common knowledge that both the *VB* and *HLD* draw extensively on works of ancient and early Byzantine literature (esp. Xenophon [4th cent. BC], Plutarch [40–120 AD], Libanius [4th cent.] for the *VB*, Agathias [6th cent.] for *HLD*).[15] In particular, βασκαίνοντα τὰ φαῦλα δαιμόνια (the mean and envious demons) of the *VB* ch. 34 are to be found in the proem of the twelfth book of Plutarch's *Parallel Lives*, on Dion and Brutus, where Plutarch subscribes to the belief that 'mean and envious spirits (τὰ φαῦλα καὶ βάσκανα δαιμόνια), begrudging good men and hindering their noble deeds, try to confound and terrify them, causing their virtue to rock and totter, in order that they may not continue erect and inviolate in the path of honour and so obtain a better portion after death than the spirits themselves' (2.6 [94.9–13]).[16] Agathias Scholasticus (6th cent.) has been regarded as the main model for *HLD*, and Agathias' influence is clearly observed on several occasions.[17] The passage in 5.3 on the reason for Nikephoros Phokas' death, however, for the most part consists of a verbatim quotation from Dionysius of Halicarnassus' *Roman Antiquities* 8.52.1 (end of 1st cent. BC),[18] and obviously it is Dionysius to whom Leo refers when in the same passage he says, 'some people rightly believe'. The 'slender thread' (λεπτῆς κρόκης),[19] inserted into the longer quotation from Dionysius, is taken from Lucian of Samosata's (120–80 AD) dialogue Πλοῖον ἢ εὐχαί (ch. 26).[20] Interestingly, in this dialogue the words quoted by Leo mark the beginning of a longer passage on the contingencies of human life that threaten the rich. The context of the model-

---

15   R. J. H. Jenkins, 'The classical background of the Scriptores post Theophanem', *DOP* 8 (1954), 13–30; Hase, ed., *Leonis diaconi Historiae*, xx; Markopoulos, 'Κύρου παιδεία', *passim*.

16   Cf. the English translation by B. Perrin, *Plutarch's Lives in Eleven Volumes* (London, 1914–26), vi. See on this passage also T. Rakoczy, *Böser Blick, Macht des Auges und Neid der Götter. Eine Untersuchung zur Kraft des Blickes in der griechischen Literatur* (Tübingen, 1996), esp. 114–16.

17   Karpozilos, Βυζαντινοὶ Ἱστορικοί, II, 492–501.

18   Cf. Talbot–Sullivan, 18 and 131, n. 34.

19   *HLD* ch. 5.3: 80.8.

20   Ed. M.D. Macleod (Oxford, 1987), IV 109.16–18. For the reception of Lucian's work in ninth- to tenth-century Byzantium see Kazhdan, *A History of Byzantine Literature*, 295–7.

text thus matches perfectly Leo's argument concerning the instability of human fortune. This is no coincidence, of course, but is due to the author's careful choice of quotation, and in all probability it impressed his learned audience.[21]

Finally and most importantly, the very idea of superhuman, abstract powers (other than God), which underlies all passages in the *VB* and *HLD* noted above, is a feature that most scholars connect directly with ancient beliefs and pagan religion. Nemesis is a well-known goddess venerated from the sixth century BC on, with a widespread cult during the imperial period.[22] Envy especially is usually identified with the well-known 'envy of the gods' and directly associated with views found in Herodotus.[23] It is these very meanings of the words *nemesis* and *phthonos*, Goddess of Revenge or Retribution and Envy of the Gods, that are evoked when in translations of Byzantine texts, as the *VB* and *HLD*, we read Envy (with capitals) and Nemesis.[24] But *phthonos* as a universally destructive power appears alone (and not as *phthonos ton theon*) in funeral inscriptions of Hellenistic and imperial times. And it is in writers of these periods that we find closer connections to *phthonos*, *nemesis* and *tyche* as they occur in our two Byzantine texts than in classical authors of the fifth and fourth centuries BC. Envious fate is an important concept in Polybius (1st cent. BC); divine *nemesis* and human *phthonos* (as a fixed combination as in Leo) is to be found in the historiographical works of Dionysius of Halicarnassus (end of 1st cent. BC) and Appian (2nd cent. AD).[25] At the time of the composition

[21]   Hunger, 'Imitation' (as in note 1), esp. 29–30.

[22]   H. Herter, 'Nemesis', *RE* 16/2 (1935), 2338–80. For the veneration during the imperial period see esp. B. Lichocka, *Nemesis en Égypte romaine* (Mainz, 2004).

[23]   E.g., Rakoczy, *Böser Blick*, esp. 247–70. D. R. Reinsch, 'Die Palamedes-Episode in der Synopsis Chronike des Konstantinos Manasses und ihre Inspirationsquelle', in M. Hinterberger and E. Schiffer, eds., *Byzantinische Sprachkunst. Studien zur byzantinischen Literatur gewidmet W. Hörandner zum 65. Geburtstag*, Byzantinisches Archiv 20 (Berlin and New York 2007), 266–76, esp. 269. Talbot–Sullivan, 18, n. 62, and 131, n. 34.

[24]   For instance, in the German translation of the *VB*, L. Breyer, *Vom Bauernhof auf den Kaiserthron. Das Leben des Basileios I.* (Graz, 1981), 99 (and 101), we read 'Nemesis' (explained as Rachegöttin and with a further annotation, 165–6: 'Nemesis' = Rachegöttin: Personifikation des gerechten des gerechten Unwillens über unverdientes Glück anderer Menschen). I. Ševčenko, in the translation of *VB* that accompanies his forthcoming edition, always writes Envy and Nemesis without further explanation.

[25]   On *phthonos* in Polybius see G. J. D. Aalders, 'The Hellenistic concept of the Enviousness of Fate', in M. J. Vermaseren, ed., *Studies in Hellenistic Religions* (Leiden, 1979), 1–8. E.g., Dionysius of Halicarnassus, *Roman Antiquities*, ed. C. Jacoby (Leipzig, 1885–1925; repr. Stuttgart, 1967–85), 2.35.3, 8.52.1, 8.80.2, cf. also 3.5.1. Appian, *Roman History*, ed. L. Mendelssohn, I. P. Viereck and A. G. Roos

of *VB* and *HLD* these authors were well known and read, as is testified by their ample usage in the Constantinian excerpts.[26]

Besides these close parallels with ancient and Late Antique texts, there are also considerable differences. Plutarch adduces the 'bad and envious demons' merely in connection with the frightful visions announcing to Dion and Brutus their imminent death. The quotation of Dionysius does not consist of the narrator's words, but is part of the direct speech of one of the protagonists (Veturia speaking to her son Gaius Marcius Coriolanus); this means that Leo did not borrow the historian's concept of causation, but uses the phrasing in order to express his own ideas.[27] Furthermore, nowhere in ancient literature is *phthonos* given the importance it has in our tenth-century texts, nor does its mention have the narrative function we have observed there. These differences, however, are consistent with the principle of *mimesis*, according to which traditional features are combined in order to create something new and are thus given a new sense. It is our task as historians to investigate this new sense

It has thus become clear that the passages under scrutiny are influenced by older (ancient and Late Antique) model-texts. Yet this has not brought us any nearer to their actual meaning. Often, statements in Byzantine literature that clearly reflect the world of pagan antiquity are regarded as insignificant for the texts' ideology. When Byzantine authors use words like *phthonos*, *nemesis* and *tyche* referring to superhuman powers, it is supposed that they employ antique phrasing in order to connect their writing explicitly with their ancient models, without, however, attaching any meaning to these statements. These statements, it is argued, are mere linguistic embellishment, classicizing 'seasoning', so to speak, that is added to the circumstances described, because in ancient texts this phrasing, the causation of such events by *phthonos*, for example, is associated with circumstances similar to the ones described in the Byzantine texts. According to this opinion, Byzantine authors employ a model-causation (*phthonos* etc.)

(Leipzig, 1905), Sam 4.2.9, Lib 57 (§250) and 62 (§ 276). It is not clear to me what *theia nemesis kai anthropinos phthonos* mean exactly in Dionysius and Appian. I have the impression that these words have more to do with the concept of Latin *invidia* than with the old belief in *phthonos theon*. It also seems to me that at least in Appian *phthonos* and *nemesis* have a positive meaning that the Byzantines could not understand as such because for them *phthonos* was a thoroughly negative concept. Further investigation into the topic is still needed. On Latin *invidia* see R. A. Kaster, *Emotion, Restraint and Community in Ancient Rome* (Oxford, 2005), 84–103.

[26]   On the texts used for the *excerpta Constantini* see the recent study by B. Flusin, 'Les excerpta Constantiniens. Logique d'une anti-histoire', in S. Pittia, ed., *Fragments d'historiens Grecs. Autour de Denys d'Halicarnasse* (Rome, 2002), 537–59.

[27]   Scott, 'The classical tradition in Byzantine historiography', esp. 64, pointed out that, despite the manifold borrowings from ancient historiography, Byzantine historiography exhibits essential differences with regard to the concept of history.

for the explanation of a certain set of facts, namely great success followed by downfall into utter misery, as a mere stylistic device.[28]

If we do not dismiss the idea of superhuman powers as a mere literary device, opting rather to take it seriously, we cannot but observe that there exists a certain contradiction between such beliefs and the Christian faith. Therefore, the occurrence of *tyche* and *phthonos* (not so much *nemesis*, because it is used rather seldom) in other Byzantine historiographical texts has evoked some lively discussions concerning the orthodoxy of the authors who employ such concepts in order to describe and explain historical events. The most famous case is probably Procopius, where *phthonos* plays just a minor role beside *tyche* (esp. *BG* II. 8.1). The problem of the compatibility of Procopius' statements with Christian orthodoxy has been discussed at length by Averil Cameron in her classic study and again more recently by D. Brodka and A. Kaldellis, the first two ascribing the usage of *tyche* (and *phthonos*) to the literary tradition, the last interpreting *tyche* as a dominant feature of Procopius' non-Christian world-view.[29] In the framework of Byzantine literature, however, Procopius is a special case, because he wrote during a period when pagan beliefs were still alive and Procopius' adherence to the old creed is a plausible possibility. Therefore, we cannot easily compare Procopius' case with that of authors of the middle Byzantine period, when the survival of paganism seems rather improbable. Recently two scholars, independently from each other, questioned the orthodoxy of the twelfth-century author Constantine Manasses on grounds that in his *Synopsis Chronike* he presents *phthonos* as a driving force in history. P. Magdalino concluded that Manasses has a 'secular, semi-pagan outlook on life'.[30] D. R. Reinsch conceded that Manasses is a Christian, but emphasized that his world-view (as the world-view of many Byzantines) is contradictory. According to Reinsch, Manasses fears God and Providence, but he also fears *phthonos* and *tyche*, which he regards as metaphysical powers. Only fundamentalists have a totally consistent world-view, says Reinsch.[31] Leo the Deacon's seemingly contradictory statements also have provoked remarks (without further

---

[28] For examples of this approach see the following notes.

[29] A. Cameron, *Procopius and the Sixth Century* (London, 1985; repr. 1996), ch. 7: 'Procopius and Christianity'; *eadem*, 'The "Scepticism" of Procopius', *Historia* 15 (1966), 466–82, esp. 477; D. Brodka, *Die Geschichtsphilosophie in der spätantiken Historiographie. Studien zu Prokopios von Kaisareia, Agathias von Myrina und Theophylaktos Simokattes*, Studien und Texte zur Byzantinistik 5 (Frankfurt am Main, 2004); Kaldellis, *Procopius of Caesarea*: both Brodka and Kaldellis without special reference to *phthonos*.

[30] P. Magdalino, 'In search of the Byzantine courtier: Leo Choirosphaktes and Constantine Manasses', in Maguire, ed., *Byzantine Court Culture*, 141–65, esp. 163.

[31] Reinsch, 'Palamedes-Episode', esp. 269–70.

investigation, however). As it is expressed in the introduction to the new English translation, 'Leo's approach to historical causation seems to reflect a conflict between his classicizing style and his Christianity'.[32] Here again, the existence of metaphysical powers other than God in a Byzantine text is interpreted as a mere stylistic feature. It seems, however, quite improbable that either the author of the *VB* or Leo the Deacon was a pagan or had pagan inclinations. From their texts it becomes sufficiently clear that according to their *Weltanschauung* the stream of historical events is guided by divine providence. *Mimesis* without doubt is one important aspect in their choice of *nemesis* and *phthonos* in their texts. Yet it might prove fruitful to investigate whether there are other reasons than mere literary *mimesis* for the occurrence of such terms as *phthonos* in our texts. If neither paganism nor *mimesis*, what do these authors mean when they refer to *phthonos*?

Let us have a closer look at the key words of our passages. In the history of the Greek language *nemesis*, *phthonos* and *baskania* are closely related cognate terms and for this reason difficult to distinguish as concerns their meaning. All of these words express 'ill will felt because of another person's well-being'. In the fifth-/fourth century BC we observe a shift from *nemesis* to *phthonos*, which becomes the dominant term, being substituted for the first in most cases; *nemesis*, however, continues to be used in connection with the sphere of the divine.[33] *Baskanos* and *baskania* are rather new words in the Greek vocabulary, and from the beginning they are closely connected to *phthonos*.[34] By the time of the Cappadocian Fathers of the Church *phthonos* and *baskania* are used more or less as synonyms, whereas *nemesis* no longer belongs to the current vocabulary.[35] Given the situation sketched at the beginning, with Late Antique and Byzantine classicizing authors writing their texts with a constant look back at their textual past, confusion with the terms was inevitable and is indeed reflected in several texts.[36]

---

[32]   Talbot–Sullivan, 16.

[33]   For the semantic development of these words see D. Konstan, *The Emotions of the Ancient Greeks: Studies in Aristotle and Classical Literature* (Toronto, 2006), ch. 5 ('Envy and indignation'), esp. 123–4.

[34]   Cf. Rakoczy, *Böser Blick*, esp. 123–5. The original meaning of *baskanos* seems to be 'slanderous, accusing', as the active expression of an envious disposition.

[35]   In his famous treatise on *phthonos* (*PG* 31.372B–385C) Basil the Great makes parallel use of both *phthonos* and *baskania*; as an adjective, however, he prefers *baskanos* (as do other Late Antique authors, e.g. Ailios Aristeides). According to the TLG database *nemesis* is not used at all by Basil and Gregory of Nyssa, whereas it occurs only once in Gregory of Nazianzus, namely in the stereotypical phrase *ou nemesis*; see http://stephanus.tlg.uci.edu, accessed 12 July 2010.

[36]   Cf. Rakoczy, *Böser Blick*, esp. 118, n. 362, and 127–8. In this respect, scholia and commentaries on classical texts bear especially telling witness to the terminological confusion. According to scholia on Homer Il. 507 (D scholia, ed.

Can we establish the exact meaning of these key words (*phthonos, nemesis, baskania*) in the tenth century? Let us have a look at some texts used in tenth-century Byzantium that provide explanations and definitions of certain terms. In the dictionary ascribed to Photios as well as in the tenth-century encyclopaedic dictionary Suda we read: *nemesis* means reprimand, justice, hubris, envy, fate (*mempsis, dike, hybris, phthonos, tyche*).[37] Furthermore, from ancient times on *phthonos* and *nemesis* were frequently used in the expressions *phthonos oudeis* and *ou nemesis* respectively. In Byzantine times these expressions had become nearly synonymous, both meaning 'there is no reason for indignation or reprimand'. Also, in the apotropaic phrase *phthonou belos me se/me baloi*, *phthonou* can be substituted with *nemeseos* or *baskanias*.[38] On the other hand, in tenth-century treatises on envy and in pertinent chapters of anthologies, *phthonos* and *baskania* are used interchangeably.[39] There are also differences, but, in general, these three terms, *phthonos, baskania* and *nemesis*, as well as the corresponding adjectives and verbs, to a considerable extent converge semantically, *phthonos* being most frequently used.

C.G. Heyne [Oxford, 1834]) the verbs *nemeso, phthono* and *baskaino* are synonyms. Scholia to Pindar Ol. 13.35.1 (ed. E. Abel [Berlin, 1891]) declare: '*Phthonos* and *nemesis* do not differ'. Scholia in Aeschylum Pers. 362 (ed. W. Dindorf [Oxford, 1851]) explain *phthonos theon* with *nemesis*.

[37]   Ps.-Photios, *Lexicon*, ed. R. Porson (Cambridge, 1822), s.v.; *Suda*, ed. A. Adler (Leipzig, 1928–38; repr. Stuttgart, 1967–71), s.v.

[38]   E.g. Libanius uses *phthonou belos* in Ep. 563.5.7 and Ep. 1185.1.2, but *nemeseos belos* in Or. 1.1.10. Cf. also Michael Psellos, Letter to Michael Keroularios, 207, ed. Sathas, *Mesaionike Bibliotheke*, V, 507.6–7; ed. U. Criscuolo, *Michele Psello, Epistola a Michele Cerulario* (Naples, 1990), 59 (*phthonou*); *Chronographia* 3.c 8 (*baskanias mede nemeseos*) and Or. paneg. 17.356 (*belos nemeseos*).

[39]   E.g., in the so-called *Eclogai* (excerpts) from John Chrysostom (a compilation ascribed to Theodore Daphnopates), ch. 17 (*On Envy*, PG 63.670–682), as well as in the excerpts from Basil the Great on several topics (a similar compilation, ascribed to Symeon Metaphrastes), ch. 18 (interestingly, the title consists of a combination of both words: *Peri phthonou kai baskanias*, PG 32.1336–1345). In the approximately contemporary florilegium of Ps. Maximus Confessor (ed. S. Ihm [Stuttgart, 2001]), ch. 47 (54), *Peri phthonou*, nine out of fifty-one lemmata have *baskania* (or one of its derivates). Also in the so-called vita A of Theodore the Studite (dating to the tenth century and by some manuscripts ascribed to Theodore Daphnopates), the verb *nemeso* appears as a synonym of *baskaino* (PG 99.224B). In the same way *nemeso* is used by Niketas Stethatos in the preface to his edition of Symeon the New Theologian's hymns (l. 286, ed. J. Koder [Paris, 1969] p. 132), as well as in his treatise 'Against the Accusers of Saints' (ll. 67–8, ed. S.A. Paschalides, Ὁ ἀνέκδοτος λόγος τοῦ Νικήτα Στηθάτου Κατὰ ἁγιοκατηγόρων καὶ ἡ ἀμφισβήτηση τῆς ἁγιότητας στὸ Βυζάντιο κατὰ τὸν 11ο αἰώνα', in E. Kountoura-Galake, ed., *The Heroes of the Orthodox Church: The New Saints, 8th–16th c.* [Athens, 2004], 493–518, esp. 517).

In the light of this information let us re-examine the meaning of the passages in the *VB* and *HLD* and try again to establish the actual meaning of the words. In Book V of *HLD*, *baskanos nemesesasa tyche* (ch. 8) corresponds to *nemesis theia* (ch. 5). Whereas the latter is part of the quotation from Dionysius, the first repeats the meaning in Leo's own words, in a more independent fashion. I therefore conclude that in Leo's text the concept of *nemesis* is identical with *baskanos tyche*, *nemesis* being an expression of the latter. Circumstances and events as described in the *VB* and *HLD* are similar. In both cases we have a pair of words designating metaphysical powers, *phthonos* and *baskanos nemesis/baskana daimonia* in the first, *phthonos* and *nemesis/baskanos tyche* in the latter. Since *baskanos* is a (well-established) synonym of *phthoneros*, the predominant characteristic/trait of these pairs is *phthonos*, envy. Therefore, the concept central to all passages cited above is *phthonos*.[40]

The *VB* was composed by an author working under the guidance of Constantine VII Porphyrogennetos, according to I. Ševčenko, or, less plausibly, by Constantine himself.[41] In any case the work dates to the middle of the tenth century and does have some connection with Constantine Porphyrogennetos and the learned men around him. The History of Leo the Deacon is about one generation younger and again connected to the imperial court, insofar as Leo was a member of the palace clergy during the first years of Basil's II reign (after 976), although he composed his History later.[42] In the following I shall compare the use of *phthonos* in other non-historiographical Byzantine texts contemporary with the *VB* and *HLD*.

Phthonos is mentioned several times in the correspondence between Constantine Porphyrogennetos and Theodore, metropolitan of Kyzikos.[43] Though the historical background of these letters is somewhat opaque, we may presume that when Constantine speaks of '*phthonos*, the bitter tyrant

---

[40]   It is interesting to note that John Skylitzes, when he incorporates parts of *VB* in his History, renders *phthonos and nemesis* (in *VB* 50–51 and 64–5) the first time as *phthonos* and the second time as *baskanos nemesis* (Basil 25 and 34 respectively, 144.44 and 156.65–6) and *phthonos and baskana daimonia* (in *VB* 100) as *phthonos* (Basil 46:168.81).

[41]   On the question of the authorship of the *VB* see Markopoulos, 'Κύρου παιδεία', 92–3, esp. n. 9, and Karpozilos, Βυζαντινοὶ Ἱστορικοί, II, 352–3. I find Ševčenko's stylistic arguments that support the identification of the author of *VB* with the anonymous author of the *De imagine Edessena* convincing. See I. Ševčenko, 'Re-reading Constantine Porphyrogenitus', in J. Shepard and S. Franklin, eds., *Byzantine Diplomacy* (Aldershot, 1992), 167–95, esp. 185, n. 46.

[42]   Talbot–Sullivan, 9–10. Karpozilos, Βυζαντινοὶ Ἱστορικοί, II, 482–3.

[43]   J. Darrouzès, *Épistoliers byzantins du Xe siècle*, Archives de l'Orient chrétien 6 (Paris 1960), VIII, 317–32, letters 1–18.

who separates the loving ones and implacable enemy',[44] he refers to the Russian assault on Byzantium under Igor in 941.[45] Constantine's phrase is taken over by Theodore as the 'raw and envious (baskanos) demon who inhibited participation in the feast'.[46] In letter 8 Theodore blames 'man-slaughtering envy and envious oppression (anthropoktono phthono kai te baskano epereia)'[47] for excluding Constantine from higher education, probably referring to the unfavourable circumstances created by Romanos Lekapenos and his clique.[48] Again Constantine's ill-fortune is meant when in another letter Theodore laments, 'bitter envy (pikros phthonos) prevents the world from gathering the fruits of the good and fruitful tree' (for 'tree' read 'Constantine').[49]

However, phthonos appears not only in notoriously classicizing genres as historiography and epistolography, but also in other texts less influenced by ancient models: at least on the surface this seems to be the case. Constantine Porphyrogennetos is credited with some hagiographical texts, among them an oration on the translation of the relics of John Chrysostom.[50] In this text, phthonos is held responsible for Chrysostom's exile, after he had become bishop of Constantinople, because 'phthonos was unable to bear meekly the good fortune of the inhabitants of Constantinople'.[51] Later on in the same text it is said that 'phthonos seemed to set up the trophy of his malice'.[52] Phthonos also appears frequently in the Menologion of Symeon

---

44   Darrouzès, Épistoliers, ep. 5: 322.13–14.
45   Darrouzès, Épistoliers, 322, n. 3. Darrouzès says, however, that 'dans la phrase précédant "envie, ce cruel tyran" est une simple personification dans le style des rhéteurs'.
46   Darrouzès, Épistoliers, ep. 6: 623.11–12.
47   Darrouzès, Épistoliers, ep. 8: 325.8–9.
48   Cf. ep. 1:319.33–5, and Darrouzès, Épistoliers, 318, n. 2; cf. Ševčenko, 'Re-reading Constantine', esp. 179 (on the identification of phthonos).
49   Darrouzès, Épistoliers, ep. 11: 328.10–11.
50   Ed. K. I. Dyobouniotes, 'Κωνσταντίνου Πορφυρογεννήτου Λόγος ἀνέκδοτος εἰς τὴν ἀνακομιδὴν τοῦ λειψάνου Ἰωάννου τοῦ Χρυσοστόμου', Ἐπιστημονικὴ Ἐπετηρὶς Θεολογικῆς Σχολῆς Πανεπιστημίου Ἀθηνῶν 1 (1926), 303–19. Cf. B. Flusin, 'L'empereur hagiographe. Remarques sur le rôle des premiers empereurs macédoniens dans le culte des saints', in P. Guran, ed., L'empereur hagiographe. Culte des saints et monarchie byzantine et post-byzantine (Bucharest, 2001), 29–54, esp. 50. S. A. Paschalides, Νικήτας Δαβίδ Παφλαγών. Τὸ πρόσωπον καὶ τὸ ἔργον του. Συμβολὴ στὴν μελέτη τῆς προσωπογραφίας καὶ τῆς ἁγιολογικῆς γραμματείας τῆς προμεταφραστικῆς περιόδου (Thessalonike, 1999), 113, considers this speech to have been composed by Niketas Paphlagon.
51   Ed. Dyobouniotes, 308.4–6.
52   Ed. Dyobouniotes, 309.18–20.

Metaphrastes, which dates to the end of the tenth century.[53] In this collection of hagiographical texts *phthonos* appears primarily as a power opposing the saint in his struggle for holiness, but *phthonos* is also referred to as the cause of historical events.[54] Interestingly, in the Metaphrastic Menologion *phthonos* often functions in the very same way as in the historiographical texts, namely as a marker for a turn in the plot.

Obviously, the metaphysical power *phthonos* is not restricted to 'secular' historiography, but appears to be a common feature of hagiography as well. In the context of hagiography, however, any doubts about the author's orthodoxy are of course inappropriate, especially in the case of the Metaphrastic Menologion, which intended to propagate the 'correct' veneration of saints. It is clear that in hagiographical texts *phthonos* corresponds to the devil, even if the range of his actions seems to be broader than we would expect. The strong connection between the devil and *phthonos* goes back to the early Christian period, and at the time of the Cappadocian Fathers it was already fully fledged. When the devil is connected to envy, he usually appears as *phthoneros* or *baskanos daimon*, but also merely as *phthonos*.[55] From Eusebius of Caesarea's historiographical works on, the envious demon assumes a role significant for historical events.[56] Along with the developing identification of the Christian Church with the Christian State, one observes the envious demon's development from an agent hostile to the Church to an historical agent hostile to the Christian State in general. Michael Attaleiates, writing about one hundred years after the author of the *VB*, speaks about the aggression of the 'one/demon who envies the good ones' when he refers to rebellions against the emperor that are related to circumstances (ἡσυχίαν, εὐδαιμονίαν) more or less identical with those found in the *VB*.[57] Judging from the examples

---

[53]   On Symeon Metaphrastes and his Menologion see Ch. Høgel, *Symeon Metaphrastes: Rewriting and Canonization* (Copenhagen, 2002).

[54]   E.g. Life of Theodora of Alexandria 9 (*PG* 115.676C); Life of John Chrysostom 2 (*PG* 114.1052A); *ibid.*, 46 (1173C–D); Life of Daniel the Stylite 16 (ed. H. Delehaye, *Les Saints Stylites* [Brussels, 1923], 117); Life of Loukas Steiriotes 4 and 41 (ed. D. Z. Sophianos [Athens, 1993], 127 and 148).

[55]   Cf. G. Bartelink, 'Baskanos, désignation de Satan et des démons chez les auteurs chrétiens', *OCP* 49 (1983), 390–406. Rakoczy, *Böser Blick*, 118–19 (with further bibliography).

[56]   See especially *Ecclesiastical History* (ed. G. Bardy [Paris, 1952–58; rcpr. 2001]), 8. 1.6; 5. 21.2; 10. 4.14.1 and 10. 8.2.2; *Life of Constantine*, ed. F. Winkelmann (Berlin, 1975; 2nd rev. edn, 1992), I 49.2 (41.5–6); II 73 (79.9–10); III 1.1 (80.2–3); III 59.1 (111.26–28); IV 41.1 (136.6–8).

[57]   Attaleiates, *Historia*, 17.8–18.2 (rebellion of Leo Tornikes against Constantine IX in 1047, after legal reforms) and 210.23–211.2 (rebellion of the palace guards against Nikephoros Botaneiates). In particular 18.2 ('But the one who always

cited above, we can conclude that the concept of *phthonos*/devil had also assumed the meaning and competence of 'envious fate'.

The identification of *phthonos*, bad luck, and the devil is vividly illustrated in a letter ascribed to Theodore Daphnopates (died after 961).[58] In this letter the author attempts to console his correspondent, John Koitonites, concerning a recent blow of fate that deprived him of his eminent position at the imperial court. The originator of the incident is subsequently referred to as βάσκανος τύχη καὶ δαίμων πονηρὸς ἀεὶ βασκαίνων τοῖς ἀγαθοῖς, φθόνος (several times) and βασκανία.[59] In the following section of the letter, the author compares his miserable friend, who had fallen prey to *phthonos*, with Job.[60] The comparison of the unfortunate John Koitonites with Job reveals the characteristic nature and mode of action of *phthonos*. The first part of Job's story, as it is told in the *Septuagint*, is the prototype of the narrative that is also found in all passages cited above: good fortune abruptly turned into its opposite. Whereas in the *Septuagint* the devil acts without explicit motive, according to the Byzantine version of the Story of Job, Satan attacks Job out of envy. In Niketas Paphlagon's praise of Gregory of Nazianzus (first half of tenth century), the story of Job begins as follows: 'Job, because of his virtue, one day became an object of envy to the devil, and upon demand was given over to him ... He received double in return for what Envy had destroyed'.[61] Not only had the Christian devil assimilated the characteristics as well as the names of the Late Antique envious demon, but *phthonos*, destructive envy, as Satan's main characteristic, stands for the devil, in the same way as in the texts, e.g., *pronoia*, providence as one of God's eminent features, often is used instead of God (e.g. in Leo's history discussed above).

The *mimesis* of ancient literature in Byzantine historiography must not prevent us from examining the actual meaning of Byzantine texts or from investigating parallels in other non-historiographical works. Originally, *phthonos* and envious fate are ancient concepts, but in Byzantine texts they assume a new meaning. In the guise of personified envy, *phthonos*, or the 'envious one' Satan stirs human affairs. What we observe here is not an

---

envies the good stirred up another internal strife ...') is a close parallel to *VB*, ch. 100: 348.10–11.

⁵⁸ J. Darrouzès and L. G. Westerink, *Théodore Daphnopatès correspondance* (Paris, 1978), 214–25 (no. 38). For Daphnopates see also Kazhdan, *A History of Byzantine Literature*, 152–7.

⁵⁹ Darrouzès and Westerink, *Théodore Daphnopatès correspondance*, 217.5–6, 217.11–16; 219.37–40, 219.46–8.

⁶⁰ Darrouzès and Westerink, *Théodore Daphnopatès correspondance*, 219.49–53.

⁶¹ J. J. Rizzo, *The Encomium of Gregory Nazianzen by Nicetas the Paphlagonian*, Subsidia Hagiographica 58 (Brussels, 1976), 109. Cf. also Symeon Metaphrastes, Life of Eustathios 7 (73.17–74.6, ed. G. van Hooff, *AnBoll* 3 [1884] 66–112).

appropriation of an ancient concept, but a reinterpretation. This 'osmosis of Byzantine concepts into ancient ones', as Herbert Hunger dubbed it, speaking of other genres of Byzantine literature as well,[62] must also be taken into consideration for historiographical texts as part of the literary production. Historiography is literature and displays many characteristics common to other branches of literature. We see this in the narrative strategies and concepts that are the normal tools of historiography and of other narrative genres, when we think of the role that *phthonos* plays as a marker for a turning-point in the narrative both in historiography and in hagiography. I do not maintain that in the texts discussed above *phthonos* (and *nemesis*) are used as full synonyms of *diabolos* or *Satanas*, but I do suggest that the Byzantine concept of *phthonos* is closely related to the concept of the devil, and that, also in classicizing historiographical texts, both concepts, to an important extent, overlap.[63]

---

[62] H. Hunger, 'Antiker und byzantinischer Roman', *Sitzungsberichte der Heidelberger Akademie der Wissenschaften, Phil. hist. Klasse* 1980, 3. Abh. (Heidelberg, 1980); repr. in *Epidosis. Gesammelte Schriften zur byzantinischen Geistes- und Kulturgeschichte* (Munich, 1989), study XIII, esp. 30.

[63] In a similar way *phthonos* appears in numerous other historiographical writings, esp. Pachymeres and Gregoras. Further details will be available in my book on *phthonos* in Byzantine literature and society, which I hope will be completed soon.

SECTION VI
Sources Reconfigured

11. The story of the patriarch Constantine II of Constantinople in Theophanes and George the Monk: transformations of a narrative

Dmitry Afinogenov

The dreadful fate of the Patriarch Constantine II (754–65) has been a subject of discussion for some time.[1] From Theophanes' *Chronographia* it may be gathered that the Emperor Constantine V became enraged against his namesake and appointee, adduced false witnesses who testified that the patriarch threw abuse at the emperor, swearing by the Holy Cross. He then banished the wretch, then recalled him from exile, subjected him to torture and humiliation, and finally had him decapitated.

Although everything seems quite clear, I believe the issue has to be re-examined, since researchers have concentrated on the historical veracity of the account, completely disregarding its literary aspect. However, if my hypothesis is correct,[2] the entire story was borrowed from the *Historia Leonis* (though it is dispersed in the *Chronographia* in keeping with the latter's annalistic structure).[3] The *Historia Leonis* was a biography of Leo III and his son Constantine V, highly polemical (i.e. anti-iconoclast), but written as a history in the ancient terms of that genre, in learned Greek, between 775 and 787. Large chunks of it survive in Theophanes and George the Monk as well as in the *Breviarium* and the *Antirrheticus III* by the Patriarch Nikephoros. The first two writers, while borrowing from the *Historia Leonis* independently of each other, mostly reproduce their source almost verbatim, although George the Monk is far more concise. Comparison of the various accounts about the caliph Yazīd and his

---

[1]   See, e.g., S. Gero, *Byzantine Iconoclasm during the Reign of Constantine V, with Particular Attention to the Oriental Sources* (Louvain, 1977), 129–35.

[2]   D. Afinogenov, 'A lost 8th century pamphlet against Leo III and Constantine V?', *Eranos* 100 (2002), 1–17.

[3]   Theophanes, 428.2–6; 438.28–439.5; 441.7–442.7; 442.8–13.

decree against Christian images, which is claimed to be the origin of the Byzantine iconoclasm through mediation of a certain Bisir (later one of Leo III's closest aides) or a certain Jew,[4] shows clearly that, in their common source, which must have been none other than the *Historia Leonis*, the story was well structured and balanced and made perfect sense from the point of view of both the plot and the underlying message. This means that the *Historia Leonis*, insofar as it can be reconstructed, must be treated as a work of literature, and that its author abided by certain rules of the narrative technique, which, unfortunately, were mostly irrelevant for the compilers who have preserved the *membra disiecta*; the changing propagandistic aims also added to the confusion. The version of the above-mentioned story undoubtedly closest to the lost original survives in the first and genuine version of the chronicle of George the Monk.[5] This is probably no accident. I believe that George was more conscious of those rules of narrative, most likely because of his penchant for edifying stories that do require a clear and well-organized plot.[6] Admittedly, the structure of Theophanes' work generally does not favour good preservation of self-contained narrative pieces if the action described therein happens to extend over several years. In such a case the narrative is perforce cut into chunks of varying sizes separated by unrelated text.

It must also be stated from the start that the aim of this article is not to reconstruct the *real* course of events. Rather, it is an attempt to restore the underlying narrative upon which our surviving sources are based. This is, in my opinion, a necessary stage in the historical enquiry so often left out by scholars. As a result, sympathies and antipathies, political or personal, and other inclinations of the original author's bias get substantially distorted and create more confusion than necessary.

The main questions that can be asked of the version of the story preserved by Theophanes are the following: (1) what was the actual reason for the emperor's rage and why is it not disclosed?, and (2) why did the imperial officials, before sending the deposed patriarch to death, want to hear from him that their faith was true and their council (Hieria, 754) blameless? There is no mention in Theophanes of the patriarch Constantine questioning in any way the legitimacy of the council of Hieria or any other dogmatic propositions by the emperor or his retinue.

Now let us see if George the Monk and, specifically, the original version of his chronicle, represented by codex Coislinianus 305 and the fourteenth-

---

[4]   Theophanes, 401.29–402.18; *Narratio Ioannis monachi*, Mansi, XIII, 197B–200B; *Nicephori Antirrheticus III*, PG 100, 528D–532A.

[5]   Coislinianus 305, f. 326v–327, first published in Afinogenov, 'A lost 8th century pamphlet against Leo III and Constantine V?', 1–17.

[6]   Cf. J. A. Ljubarskij, 'George the Monk as a short-story writer', *JÖB* 44 (1994), 255–64.

century Slavonic translation called *Letovnik*, can offer help in restoring the sequence and logic of the narrative. It should be noted here that the so-called *vulgata*, that is, the only version available in print, is a different text compiled in the last quarter of the ninth century on the basis of the real George the Monk and several other sources.[7] Therefore it cannot be used for the purposes of any investigation involving the relationship, in particular, of George and Theophanes. Since in the absence of the much-wanted edition of the original version my conclusions can be verified only with great difficulty (especially as Church Slavonic is not accessible to all) I feel obliged to publish here the corresponding fragment from the manuscript in question, having consulted the translation of *Letovnik*:

Cod. Coisl. 305, fols. 334–5 (11th cent.)

[334] ἀλλ' ὅ γε τύραννος ὄντως καὶ αὐθάδης ταῦτα παραγραψάμενος καὶ τὸν ὁμώνυμον αὐτοῦ χειροτονήσας, ὡς ᾤετο, δεινῶς ὕστερον ἐξεμάνη κατ' αὐτοῦ ὡς τὸ μυστήριον τῆς βλασφημίας αὐτοῦ θριαμβεύσαντος. μαθὼν γὰρ ἀκριβῶς, [334v] ὅτι κρατήσας[1] τὰ τίμια ξύλα πολλοὺς ἐπληροφόρησε λέγων· μὰ τὸν προσηλωθέντα εἰς ταῦτα κύριον, οὕτως μοι εἶπεν ὁ βασιλεύς, ὅτι· οὐκ ἔστι θεὸς ὁ Χριστός, διὰ τοῦτο οὐδὲ τὴν Μαρίαν ἔχω θεοτόκον. διὸ τοῦτον ὁ μιαιφόνος μετὰ πολλῶν ἐμπαιγμῶν καὶ μαστίγων ἐπὶ λαοῦ καὶ ἱπποδρομίου ἐκπομπεύσας, ἀποστέλλει πρὸς αὐτὸν πατρικίους καί φησιν· τί λέγεις ἄρτι περὶ τῆς πίστεως ἡμῶν καὶ τῆς συνόδου ἧς ἐποιήσαμεν; ὁ δὲ ματαιωθεὶς ταῖς φρεσὶ καὶ οἰόμενος αὐτὸν πάλιν ἐξευμενίσασθαι, καλῶς, ἔφη, πιστεύεις καὶ καλῶς τὴν σύνοδον ἐποίησας. οἱ δὲ ἀποκριθέντες εἶπον· ἡμεῖς τοῦτο καὶ μόνον ἠθέλομεν ἀκοῦσαι παρὰ τοῦ μιαροῦ σου στόματος. ἀπὸ δὲ τοῦ νῦν ἄπελθε εἰς τὸ ἀνάθεμα καὶ εἰς τὸ σκότος. ὃν καὶ παραχρῆμα καρατομήσαντες τὴν μὲν κεφαλὴν αὐτοῦ ἐν τῷ Φόρῳ ἐκρέμασαν, τὸ δὲ σῶμα ἐκ τῶν ποδῶν σχοινίῳ σύραντες ἔρριψαν εἰς τὰ Πελαγίου, ἔνθα ἦν ὁ τοῦ ἁγίου μάρτυρος Πελαγίου ναός, ὃν ὁ θεομισὴς καταλύσας καὶ τάφον καταδίκων ποιήσας ἐκάλεσε τὰ Πελαγίου. Πολλοὶ γὰρ τῷ φόβῳ τοῦ δυσμενοῦς ἐπαμφοτερίζοντες μετὰ διπλόης τὴν ὁμολογίαν τῆς πίστεως εἶχον... [335] οὕτως οὖν τὸν ὑπ' αὐτοῦ χειροτονηθέντα καὶ δοξασθέντα φατριάρχην τιμήσας ἀντιχειροτονεῖ πάλιν τὸν εὐνοῦχον Νικήταν καὶ Σκλάβον. ἀλλ' ὦ τῆς ἐσχάτης ἀπονοίας καὶ ἀπανθρωπίας τοῦ αὐθάδου. πῶς οὐκ αἰδέσθη[2] τὴν ἁγίαν κολυμβήθραν; δύο γὰρ αὐτοῦ τέκνα δεξάμενος ἦν ἐκ τῆς τρίτης γυναικός.

---

    7   See D. Afinogenov, 'Le manuscrit Coislin gr. 305: la version primitive de la Chronique de Georges le Moine', *REB* 62 (2004), 239–46.

¹ Vzĭmša na ruku = κρατήσας ἐν χερσὶν Let ² Ita cod.

The truly arrogant tyrant, having ignored this and ordained
(as he presumed) his namesake, later became fiercely enraged
at him, since the man had divulged the secret of his blasphemy.
For he learnt precisely that he [the patriarch] had assured
many people, holding the venerable Cross, and saying: 'By
the Lord Who was nailed to this, thus did the emperor say
to me: "Christ is not God, therefore neither Mary do I deem
Mother of God."' For that reason the murderer, after parading
him at the hippodrome with much scorn and flogging in
the presence of the people, sent to him patricians
who said: 'What do you say now concerning our faith and
the synod we have held?' Having become foolish in his mind,
hoping to make him [the emperor] well disposed again, he replied:
'You believe rightly and you have held the synod rightly.'
They replied: 'This is just what we wanted to hear from
your foul mouth. Henceforth depart under anathema
and into the darkness.' The man was immediately beheaded
and his head hung up in the Forum, while his body they dragged
by the feet by a cord and threw it at the place of Pelagios,
where there had been a church of the holy martyr Pelagios,
which the god-hated one tore down and made a burial place
for condemned criminals, calling it 'the place of Pelagios'.
Many people, behaving ambiguously out of fear of the
foe, made their profession of faith with duplicity … So having
thus honoured the *phatriarch* whom he had ordained
and glorified, he ordained[8] in his place Niketas, eunuch and Slav.
      Oh, the extreme folly and inhumanity of the arrogant one! Did he
      not feel any respect for the holy font – for Constantine baptized his
      two children by his third wife.

George, unlike Theophanes, says that Constantine V became enraged
against his namesake patriarch because the unfortunate ecclesiastic
betrayed the 'secret of his blasphemy', having sworn by the True Cross
that the emperor shared with him his opinion of Christ as a mere man.
Interestingly, a very similar passage does figure in Theophanes, but it refers
to the public pronouncements allegedly made by the patriarch Anastasios

---

8   George consciously stresses that it was the emperors who 'ordained'
iconoclast patriarchs who were consequently illegitimate (hence ὡς ᾤετο). See
D. Afinogenov, *Konstantinopolskii patriarchat i ikonovorcheski krizis v Bizantii, 784–
847* (Moscow, 1997), 142–3. This is especially evident in the unpublished original
version.

at the time when Constantinople was in the hands of Artabasdos.[9] It was
not difficult for scholars to do Theophanes' job for him and to find out why
Constantine V turned against his patriarch: apparently the latter participated
in the formidable conspiracy against the emperor detected in August 765,
the so-called conspiracy of Podopagouros.[10] This may be perfectly true, but
it does not save the balance of the narrative. From the text of Theophanes
it is clear that participation in the conspiracy was, according to the author
of the source excerpted by the chronicler, just a pretext invented by the
emperor in order to bring the patriarch down. Whatever the real reason
behind Constantine V's wrath, in the depiction of the author of the *Historia
Leonis* it certainly was not the patriarch's association with the plotters. Yet
without such a reason, no matter how fictitious, the story falls apart. If,
however, George's version is accepted, everything returns to normal. It
becomes clear why immediately before Constantine's execution officials
were sent to ask him what he thought about the emperor's faith and the
council of Hieria.[11] The word 'now' (ἄρτι) is preserved only by George the
Monk, who apparently realized that the question was supposed to refer to
the patriarch's earlier denunciation of Constantine V's impiety.

Let us now look at the already-mentioned episode with the patriarch
Anastasios. At first sight it is very much in place where it stands. Indeed,
public exposure of Constantine's impiety would have been a good means
of propaganda in favour of the pretender Artabasdos. However, there are
several problems connected with this passage, which, to my knowledge,
have never been pointed out.

First, Theophanes makes Anastasios, in direct speech, call Constantine
V 'emperor'. This seems strange if the patriarch recognized Artabasdos in
that capacity and regarded Constantine as deposed. Another word, such
as 'tyrant', or at least a reservation (e.g., 'false' or 'former'), would have
been expected.

Second, Anastasios' active involvement on Artabasdos' side, extending
to extremely grave public insult of Constantine, is difficult to reconcile with
the comparatively mild punishment to which he was subjected after the
latter's victory. In 719 Constantine's father Leo did not hesitate to execute the
occupant of the second most important see of the empire, the archbishop of

---

[9]   Theophanes, 415.24–30. There are verbal coincidences: Ἀναστάσιος δέ, ὁ
ψευδώνυμος πατριάρχης, κρατήσας τὰ τίμια καὶ ζωοποιὰ ξύλα ὤμοσε τῷ λαῷ,
ὅτι μὰ τὸν προσηλωθέντα ἐν αὐτοῖς, οὕτω μοι εἶπε Κωνσταντῖνος ὁ βασιλεύς,
ὅτι μὴ λογίσῃ υἱὸν θεοῦ εἶναι ὃν ἔτεκε Μαρία.

[10]   Cf. recently I. Rochow, 'Konstantinos II', in R.-J. Lilie, ed., *Die Patriarchen der
ikonoklastischen Zeit: Germanos I.–Methodios I. (715–847)*, Berliner Byzantinistische
Studien 5 (Frankfurt, 1999), 37–44.

[11]   Cf. Theophanes, 442.2–3; Mango and Scott, *The Chronicle of Theophanes
Confessor*, 610.

Thessalonike, for his participation in Artemios' coup.[12] Anastasios, on the contrary, could even keep his see. The patriarch could mitigate the main accusation against him, namely that he crowned Artabasdos and his sons emperors, by claiming that he acted under duress, but if he did pronounce from the pulpit of St Sophia what Theophanes puts in his mouth, it is hard to imagine an apology that would let him escape blinding and exile or even death.

Third, Constantine V was indeed an amateur theologian and there is nothing impossible in his communicating some not-quite-orthodox ideas of his to the patriarch. However, Constantine is in all respects a much better candidate for this role than Anastasios. Actually, the emperor Constantine had but a few months of 741 at his disposal to share his views with Anastasios before Artabasdos took possession of the capital, and one could not think of a more inopportune time for such utterances. Moreover, Theophanes relates an episode when the emperor summoned the patriarch Constantine (not Anastasios!) and enquired why the Virgin Mary should be called Theotokos and not Christotokos.[13] This is exactly the same issue on which Constantine V allegedly held his impious opinions. Again, according to the inner logic of the narrative it would have been much more natural if the emperor confided his thoughts to Constantine of Syllaion, whom he had handpicked, rather than to Anastasios, who was much older and ostensibly not very close to the young heir of the throne. All these considerations make me believe that in this case it is George the Monk who has better preserved the account of his and Theophanes' common source from the point of view of the narrative logic.

If there are any doubts about the existence of the *Historia Leonis*, or George the Monk's independent use of that work, the question can be formulated like this: did George assemble his short story from scattered elements he found in Theophanes, or did he just make a short summary of a considerably more extensive narrative structure already present in the source that Theophanes excerpted earlier? If the first proposition is accepted, George must be credited with remarkable creative capabilities. Why, then, did he not mention that the emperor actually confided 'his blasphemy' to the patriarch; that, therefore, the latter was telling the truth? There are many episodes that prove the chronicler's clumsy approach to the texts he incorporates into his own work in abbreviated form. For instance, under AM 6274 (AD 781/82) Theophanes relates how Byzantine generals blockaded the Arabs, who asked for peace. The Byzantines went forth on that mission without taking care to receive explicit promises and take the children of the Arab leaders (τέκνα τῶν πρωτευόντων) as hostages.[14]

---

12   Nikephoros, *Short History*, §57.31–33 (126).
13   Theophanes, 435.8–14.
14   Theophanes, 456.17.

When George abbreviates this passage for his chronicle he says that the *logothete* Staurakios, the *magistros* Peter and the *domestikos* Anthony as well as the children of the leaders (τέκνα τῶν πρωτευόντων) went forth on the peace mission.[15] Obviously, he hardly understands what it was all about. Examples like this make it highly unlikely that George was able to compile the story about Constantine II himself, given its state of preservation in the chronicle of Theophanes.

The scarcity of information provided by George the Monk, whose main purpose, as always, was to produce an edifying story – to which he apparently himself supplied a moral conclusion – compels us to attempt a restoration of the original account on the basis of the information available in both chronicles, now more confidently proceeding from the assumption that they used one common source where the narrative was organized into self-contained pieces.

So, in my view, the account both chroniclers read in the *Historia Leonis* was as follows: Constantine V confided in his namesake patriarch some unorthodox opinions concerning the status of Christ and the Virgin Mary, with strict warning that the conversation should not go beyond the two of them (ἕως δὲ ἰσοῦ ὁ λόγος).[16] Judging from Theophanes, Constantine simply wanted to consult, not to postulate. The patriarch apparently did not keep his mouth shut and informed a select group of his friends (μύστας αὐτοῦ καὶ φίλους)[17] about the emperor's views. This he did, swearing by the True Cross, which unequivocally meant a conscious hostile action against the emperor. The latter probably had spies among the patriarch's audience, and became understandably enraged upon learning about the matter. However, he naturally could not punish the real offence without compromising his own orthodoxy and thereby his legitimacy as the sovereign of the Christian empire. Therefore, Constantine made his false witnesses accuse the patriarch of subversive speeches in association with the conspiracy of Podopagouros. At this point (August 765) Constantine II was banished first to Hieria and then to the Princes' Islands. On 6 October 766 he was recalled and subjected to various kinds of torture and humiliations and finally decapitated after giving the imperial delegation the confession they wanted from him, namely that their (i.e. the emperor's) faith was right and the council fully legitimate.

Now it is possible to discuss the propagandistic aim that could stand behind this kind of story. It is hardly doubtful that Constantine II was in

---

[15] George the Monk, 767.11.

[16] Theophanes, 435.14. Insinuations about Constantine V's denial either of veneration of the Theotokos or even of the divinity of Christ became very common in iconophile polemics. Cf. 'Theostericti Vita Nicetae Medicii', in AASS, April, vol. I, XXII–XXXII, cap. 28.

[17] Theophanes, 438.29.

reality involved in the conspiracy of Podopagouros, which was extremely dangerous for the Emperor Constantine because the participants belonged precisely to the group of the Byzantine aristocracy that had been promoted by the ruling dynasty. Yet this time the adversaries of the emperor apparently took over the ideological weapon already current among members of the Byzantine élite who opposed the Isaurians from the very beginning. The question of icon worship, to be sure, could not play any significant role here, since the conspirators of Podopagouros were undoubtedly loyal iconoclasts. So another propaganda trick was invented, 'Constantine's secret blasphemy/impiety', which could cater both for the old (iconophile) opponents of the emperor and the new ones. The author of the *Historia Leonis* therefore tried hard to demonstrate that the 'blasphemy' was an extremely serious subject for the emperor, where he felt himself particularly vulnerable (presumably because there was a good deal of 'truth' in it), so that even one of the emperor's closest friends, who had baptized two of his children, had to pay with his life for divulging that secret.

To illustrate how the results obtained here by literary analysis may help to advance our understanding of Byzantine history, I shall give just one example that does not require any special explanation in the perspective of the narrative structure but is of substantial interest for reconstruction of real historical events. The important thing is that the one-year exile of the patriarch Constantine that preceded his dreadful demise is completely irrelevant for the plot (George the Monk does not mention this exile at all) and therefore must be regarded as an adequate reflection of reality. One may wonder what happened during this period that prompted the emperor to take such harsh measures. A tentative explanation might be that the propaganda tactics adopted by the followers of Constantine Podopagouros did actually work so well[18] that the emperor's wrath against his namesake patriarch could no longer be kept in check. And yet again, this propaganda can only be adequately perceived and described if we realize what kind of source stands behind Theophanes' text, in what circles it originated, and where its political topicality lay. Not much, in my view, can be done here without literary approaches.

---

[18]   This could be because the tactics were eagerly supported by those Byzantine aristocrats who already held a grudge against Constantine V and who used the question of icon worship to accuse him of impiety; hence the mention of the council of 754 in the patrician's question.

12. Engaging the Byzantine past: strategies of visualizing history in Sicily and Bulgaria

Elena N. Boeck[*]

The two manuscripts under examination here are well known, but their strategies for visualizing history are poorly understood. Owing to its unambiguous Bulgarian identity, the Vatican Manasses manuscript (Vat. slav. 2) has evaded the infatuation of Byzantinists. In contrast, the Sicilian illustrated Skylitzes manuscript (now housed in Madrid, B.N. Vitr. 26-2) has been embraced at times by both scholars and popular imagination as an authentic vision of Byzantium. Mined by designers of book jackets for scenes of life in Byzantium, scholars have often treated Skylitzes' images as eyewitness snapshots of Byzantine life rather than as sophisticated political and cultural constructs (See Fig. 12.1.) Though both manuscripts engaged in the visualization of Byzantine history and drew to an extent on Byzantine artistic forms, each created a partisan and outlandish vision of Byzantium.

The two manuscripts carry a cumbersome analytical burden, since they constitute the most extensive surviving evidence for illuminated histories in Byzantium. For Kurt Weitzmann they stood as lone exemplars of a 'widespread genre' and 'a type of illustrated text which could be traced back to the late classical period.'[1] Formal analysis reveals that the Byzantine hands of the Madrid Skylitzes and the illustrators of the Manasses display similarities in representing stock images, such as combat scenes, cavalry

---

[*] I would like to thank Maria Georgopoulou, my dissertation adviser, who has provided immeasurable encouragement over the years. I would also like to express my appreciation to Leslie Brubaker for her thoughtful advice and insightful comments on my previous work. The Biblioteca Nacional de Espana and the Vatican Library kindly granted permission to publish images from their collections. The University Research Council of DePaul University generously underwrote the cost of the photographs from the Vatican Library.

[1] K. Weitzmann, 'The selection of texts for cyclic illustration in Byzantine manuscripts', in *Byzantine Books and Bookmen* (Washington, DC, 1975), 83.

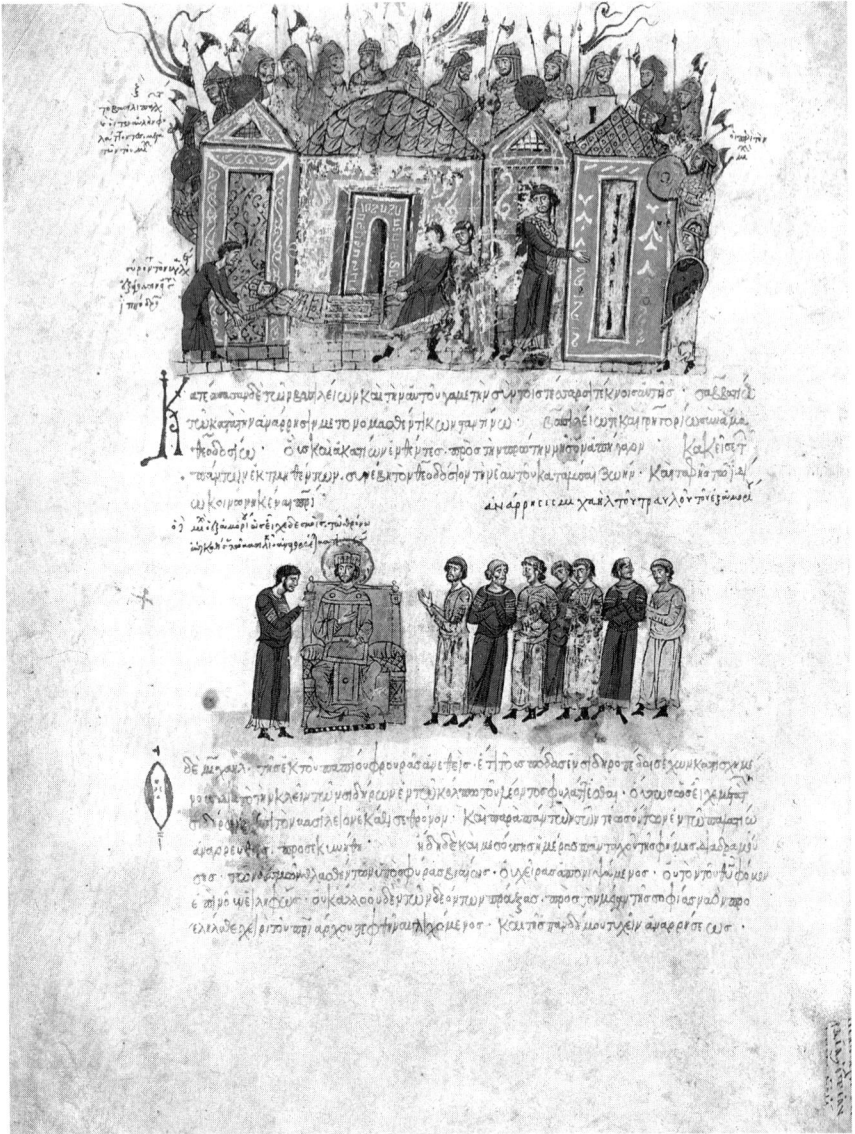

Fig, 12.1   Madrid Skylitzes Manuscript, Biblioteca Nacional, Madrid, Vitr. 26-2, fols. 26v

Fig. 12.1   fol. 27r

charges, and certain imperial poses and gestures.[2] Notwithstanding these surface similarities, scholars of both manuscripts have underestimated the utility of engaging in extensive comparison of their respective visual programmes.[3]

Rather than revisit considerations of style that have dominated discussions of this peculiar pair for decades, this study outlines some strategies, both subtle and transparent, that shaped their visual narratives. In analyzing the politics of visualization in the two manuscripts, I employ Hayden White's definition of narrative: 'the narrative is not merely a neutral discursive form that may or may not be used to represent real events in their aspect as developmental processes but rather entails ontological and epistemic choices with distinct ideological and even specifically political implications.'[4] Four case studies presented here will evaluate how the ideological strategies of their pictorial narratives diverge.

Partisanship and the politics of intervention

Since the Manasses is acknowledged as a partisan visual narrative, one that promotes a view of Byzantine history favourable to Bulgaria, it provides a valuable reference point for analyzing the politics of representation in the seemingly neutral visual narrative of the Skylitzes. After all, the most recent study of the Madrid manuscript by Vassiliki Tsamakda played down the visual programme's connections to Sicily and concluded that it 'does not reveal any intention to call attention to specific themes.'[5] While the Manasses establishes a clear visual agenda to elevate Tsar Ivan Alexander's Bulgaria, the messages of the Skylitzes have remained elusive. The Skylitzes visual narrative does not insert a Sicilian patron and his family into the programme or repeatedly weave his name and portraits into the fabric of the manuscript. As I suggest below, the lack of overt promotion of patronage does not necessarily constitute absence of partisan intervention in the production of the visual narrative.[6]

---

[2]   See A. Bozhkov, *Bulgarskata istoricheska zhivopis* (Sofia, 1972); A. Bozhkov, *Miniatiuri ot Madridskiia rukopis na Ioan Skilitsa* (Sofia, 1972).

[3]   T. Velmans, 'Three notes on the miniatures in the Chronicle of Manasses', *Macedonian Studies* 1 (1983), 27; V. Tsamakda, *The Illustrated Chronicle of Ioannes Skylitzes in Madrid* (Leiden, 2002), 264.

[4]   H. White, *The Content of Form: Narrative Discourse and Historical Representation* (Baltimore, MD, 1987), ix.

[5]   Tsamakda, *The Illustrated Chronicle*, 264.

[6]   For the prominence of patronage politics in shaping a visual programme, see L. Brubaker, *Vision and Meaning in Ninth-Century Byzantium: Image as Exegesis in the Homilies of Gregory of Nazianzus* (Cambridge, 1999).

The Byzantine text of the *Chronicle* of Constantine Manasses, originally written in Constantinople in the twelfth century, was translated into Bulgarian for Tsar Ivan Alexander in the mid-fourteenth century.[7] As a world chronicle, the span of this text reaches from the Creation to the accession of Alexios I Komnenos in 1081. The visual narrative, however, brought the past into the fourteenth-century present to bolster Ivan Alexander's claim to the Byzantine legacy. This vast time-span is illustrated with only sixty-nine images (clustering most densely towards the end of the book in sections that intersect with Bulgarian history).[8] Images embedded within the text (often placed following the conclusion of a reign) have been traditionally associated with a hypothetical Byzantine illustrated prototype.[9]

The Madrid Skylitzes, the earlier of the two manuscripts, is the only surviving illustrated chronicle in Greek from the Byzantine period.[10] Over 500 images guide the viewer through the lives and deaths of the Byzantine emperors who reigned between 811 and 1057, calling attention to the upheavals and insecurities of their reigns, and engaging to a lesser degree with their ecclesiastical and foreign relations.[11] The images display

---

[7]   The accepted date for the Vatican Manasses manuscript is 1344–45. See I. Dujčev, *The Miniatures of the Chronicle of Manasses* (Sofia, 1963), 32. This idiosyncratic manuscript has received attention from various scholars, including Bogdan Filov, Ivan Dujčev, Tania Velmans, Ioannis Spatharakis and Barbara Zeitler. For bibliography and further discussion of the Vatican Manasses, see E. Boeck, 'Displacing Byzantium, disgracing convention: the manuscript patronage of Tsar Ivan Alexander of Bulgaria', *Manuscripta: A Journal for Manuscript Research* 51/2 (2007), 199–207.

[8]   For a summary of the discussion see T. Velmans, 'La Chronique illustrée de Constantin Manassès: particularités de l'iconographie et du style', in *Byzance, les slaves et l'Occident: études sur l'art paléochrétien et médiéval* (London, 2001), 206, 227.

[9]   Dujčev, *The Miniatures of the Chronicle of Manasses*, 127.

[10]   The English translation by John Wortley will be used in this article, *John Scylitzes, a Synopsis of Histories (811–1057 A.D.): a provisional translation*, trans. J. Wortley (Winnipeg, 2000) (hereafter 'Wortley'). For an extensive introduction to the text and the critical edition see I. Thurn, ed., *Ioannis Scylitzae Synopsis historiarum* (Berlin and New York, 1973).

[11]   The bibliography on the images of the Madrid Skylitzes is extensive. See Tsamakda, *The Illustrated Chronicle*; A. Grabar and M. Manoussacas, *L'illustration du manuscrit de Skylitzès de la Bibliothèque nationale de Madrid* (Venice, 1979); S. Cirac Estopañan, *Skyllitzes Matritensis. Reproducciones y Miniaturas* (Barcelona and Madrid, 1965). The dissertation by B. Bjornholt, 'The Use and Portrayal of Spectacle in the "Madrid Skylitzes" (Bibl. Nac. Vitr. 26-2)' (PhD, Queen's University of Belfast, 2002), was not available to me for consultation.

an unparalleled variety of styles, usually referred to as 'Byzantine' and 'western'.[12]

The layout of the manuscript points to careful planning and design, but the density of images is uneven. The original beginning and the final sections of the manuscript do not survive.[13] Except for 28 un-illustrated pages out of the 226 surviving folios, every page contains one or more illustration: 222 pages contain one illustration, 164 have two, and 8 pages contain three illustrations. Narrative threads that were of particular interest to the designer of the visual narrative unfold across two or more images.

Since Ihor Ševčenko's 1984 article, which employed both visual and palaeographic observations to argue for a mid-twelfth-century Sicilian provenance of the manuscript, scholars have debated whether the manuscript's visual programme can be traced to Constantinople or Palermo.[14] The cultural distance of the visual narrative from Constantinople is exemplified in its imaginative representations of Hagia Sophia.[15] The most outlandish of these visualizes the church as an elongated building with a tall tower at the west end surmounted by a cockerel weather-vane (fol. 158va).[16] (See Fig. 12.2) I have argued elsewhere that a combination of visual, structural and narrative patterns indicate that the Madrid Skylitzes

---

[12]   André Grabar postulated a total of four 'manners' and up to six artists involved in the production. See A. Grabar, 'Les illustrations de la Chronique de Jean Skylitzès à la Bibliothèque Nationale de Madrid', *Cah Arch* 21 (1971), 191–211. Most recently Tsamakda identified seven artists. See Tsamakda, *The Illustrated Chronicle*, 373–9.

[13]   In its current condition the manuscript contains 226 parchment folios and 574 illustrations. There are 29 surviving quires (quire 16, between fols. 126 and 127, is missing; four other folios are missing from the body of the manuscript), and the back of the manuscript is mutilated. For a detailed description of the manuscript and its condition see Cirac Estopañan, *Skyllitzes Matritensis*, 16–17.

[14]   G. Cavallo, 'Scritture italo-greche liberarie e documentarie: Note introduttive ad uno studio correlato', in *Bisanzio e l'Italia: Raccolta di studi in memoria di Agostino Pertusi* (Milan, 1982), 35–6. This attribution was confirmed by I. Ševčenko, 'The Madrid manuscript of the Chronicle of Skylitzes in the light of the new dating', in *Byzanz und der Westen: Studien zur Kunst des Europäischen Mittelalters* (Vienna, 1984), 117–30.

[15]   Ihor Ševčenko has used this example to argue for ad hoc production of the visual narrative in Sicily: 'The Madrid manuscript', 127. Even earlier, Cyril Mango commented on the 'arbitrary' nature of architecture in the manuscript: *The Brazen House: A Study of the Vestibule of the Imperial Palace of Constantinople*, Arkaeologisk-Kunsthistoriske Meddelelser 4/4 (Copenhagen, 1959), 106.

[16]   I intend to treat this subject in a separate study. For inconsistent visualization of the Great Church see fols. 16va, 52, 79, 80 b, 144b and 158va.

Fig. 12.2   Madrid Skylitzes Manuscript, Biblioteca Nacional, Madrid,
                 Vitr. 26-2, fol. 158v

manuscript was produced ad hoc at the court of Roger II of Sicily.[17] While
recognizing that the complex question of patronage cannot be resolved
within the limited confines of a single article, I shall nonetheless draw
attention to some provocative narrative interventions that could constitute
evidence of a Sicilian agenda.

Strategic, even personal, structuring of narratives is widely acknowledged
in various disciplines. In her stimulating analysis of medieval historical
texts Gabrielle Spiegel noted: 'At work in shaping a literary text is a host of
unstated desires, beliefs, misunderstandings, and interests which impress
themselves upon the work, sometimes consciously, sometimes not, but
which arise from pressures that are social and not merely intertextual.'[18]
From this perspective narrative strategies need not be overt to be effective.
The Madrid Skylitzes reflects its Sicilian context in ways that are subtle,
selective, and embedded in the structure of the visual narrative.

---

[17]   See E. Boeck, 'The art of being Byzantine: history, structure and visual
narrative in the Madrid Skylitzes manuscript' (PhD dissertation, Yale University,
2003).

[18]   G. Spiegel, 'History, historicism, and the social logic of the text in the Middle
Ages', *Speculum* 65/1 (1990), 84.

The politics of space and place

The two manuscripts manifest vastly distinct strategies for visualizing defining engagements between each kingdom and Byzantium. The Vatican Manasses modifies the Byzantine historical framework by strategically increasing the visibility of Bulgarians, who were marginal in the Greek original. The Skylitzes, on the other hand, tactfully tiptoes across the 'ideological log-jam' that T. S. Brown believes kept Norman rulers from 'resting their claims to rule on the ancient past of the Greek tyrants or stressing continuity with the Lombard, Arab or Byzantine past of their territories'.[19] Rather than the consistent Manasses strategy of insertions, the visual narrative of the Madrid Skylitzes manifests its sensitivity to place in a strategic omission.

The transformation of the Greek chronicle of Constantine Manasses into a book for Tsar Ivan Alexander not only involved translation of the Greek text into Slavonic but also, as Ivan Dujčev noted, the addition of nineteen passages concerning Bulgarian history that were conceptualized from a Bulgarian perspective.[20] The bold choice of red ink for these insertions signaled to the viewer the particular importance of these passages as a self-conscious supplement to the original. Furthermore, the Bulgarian textual additions were regularly illustrated with full-page miniatures.[21] (See Figs. 12.3 and 12.4) These overt editorial interventions elevated Bulgaria onto the world stage, integrated its history into a Byzantine framework, and highlighted Bulgarian engagements with Byzantium.

Eschewing symbolic insertions, the Skylitzes visual narrative disengaged the origins of Norman rule in Sicily from their Byzantine foundations. The chronicle text recounted in detail (over fifty lines in the manuscript) the contentious inception of Norman interaction with the Byzantines in Sicily, which occurred during the campaign of general George Maniakes in 1038. Maniakes, who was dispatched to aid one of the local Muslim contenders embroiled in a civil war, was joined in Sicily by 'Frankish' mercenaries who arrived from Gaul. Skylitzes tells his reader that, after Maniakes was recalled to Byzantium, the Franks were denied pay, mutinied, and conquered most of southern Italy.[22] This episode was excluded from the visual narrative because it recalled an un-prestigious, mercenary past for

---

[19]   T.S. Brown, 'The political use of the past in Norman Sicily', in P. Magdalino, ed., *The Perception of the Past in Twelfth-Century Europe* (London, 1992), 207.

[20]   All but one (fol. 124r) are in red ink. See Dujčev, *The Miniatures of the Chronicle of Manasses*, 28.

[21]   See for instance fols. 145, 145v, 178, 178v, 183, 183v.

[22]   Fols. 223–223v; Skylitzes, 425–7; Wortley, 227–8.

Fig. 12.3   Vatican Manasses Manuscript, Biblioteca Apostolica Vaticana,
             Vat. Slav. 2, fol. 145r

Fig. 12.4   Vatican Manasses Manuscript, Biblioteca Apostolica Vaticana,
               Vat. Slav.2, fol. 145v

the Norman rulers in contested southern Italy.[23] An entire page was left un-illustrated, which would suggest this visual void was the result of a deliberate strategy.

Politicizing divine protection: the personal as political

Both manuscripts engage in a confrontational, visual dialogue with the Byzantine relationship to the divine. Both challenge the close relationship between the empire and God that was consistently reinforced in Byzantine imagery.[24] For Ivan Alexander's history, appropriating Byzantine forms for visualizing divine favour was paramount. The Madrid Skylitzes, on the other hand, regularly eliminates divine benediction from Byzantine history.

Five prominent images in the Manasses blur the personal, political and religious by employing universal history as a frame for immortalization and commemoration. Ivan Alexander is represented in full imperial splendour on folio 1r (discussed in depth below). (See Fig. 12.5) He mourns the death of his son Ivan Asen on folio 2r. The latter enters paradise on folio 2v. The tsar is addressed by King David and crowned by an angel on folio 91v. The book concludes on folio 205r with a depiction of Ivan Alexander and his sons. (See Fig. 12.6)[25] The last image appears as a pendant to the textual conclusion of the chronicle on folio 204v that is accompanied by representations of the final eight Byzantine emperors discussed by Manasses. Thus Ivan Alexander not only advances claims to the Byzantine

---

[23]   For a discussion of Roger's battle for legitimacy, see H. Wierszowski, 'Roger II of Sicily, Rex-Tyrannus, in twelfth-century political thought', *Speculum* 38/1 (1963), 46–78; V. von Falkenhausen, 'Komis, dux, prinkips, rex, basileus. Zu den griechischen Titeln der normannischen Herrscher in Süditalien und Sizilien', *Paleoslavica* 10/1 (2002), 79–93.

[24]   A. Grabar, *L'empereur dans l'art byzantin* (Paris, 1936), 263. See also P. Magdalino and R. Nelson, 'The emperor in Byzantine art of the twelfth century', *BF* 8 (1982), 123–83; C. Joliet-Levy, 'L'image du pouvoir dans l'art byzantin à l'époque de la dynastie macédonienne (867–1056)', *Byz* 57 (1987), 441–70; I.S. Chichurov, 'Teoriia i praktika vizantiiskoi imperatorskoi propagandy', *VV* 50 (1989), 106–15; H.P. L'Orange, *Studies on the Iconography of Cosmic Kingship in the Ancient World* (Oslo, 1953).

[25]   For the most recent discussion of these images see Velmans, 'La Chronique'; for a more extensive discussion of the latter image see J. Andreev, 'Ivan Alexandar et ses fils sur la dernière miniature de la Chronique de Manasses', *Etudes Balkaniques* 4 (1985), 39–47.

Fig. 12.5   Vatican Manasses Manuscript, Biblioteca Apostolica Vaticana, Vat. Slav. 2, fol. 1v

Fig. 12.6   Vatican Manasses Manuscript, Biblioteca Apostolica Vaticana,
              Vat. Slav. 2, fol. 205r

legacy, but also demonstrates a visual genealogy that makes his family the culmination of a sacred historical process.[26]

While previous studies emphasized formal analysis and potential sources of these compositions, their function within the historical narrative concerns us here. The glorious life of Ivan Alexander and the early death of his son repeatedly evoke powerful divine involvement in the affairs of the Bulgarian ruler. When on folio 2r Ivan Alexander mourns his son, the emotional representation (patterned on the Dormition of the Virgin),[27] includes the ruler's family, court, and the heavenly host. An angel stands at the foot of the bier, while another one ascends to heaven with the soul of the deceased.

The following folio (2v) epitomizes the visualization of the parental desire. The young tsar is represented twice: entering Paradise to be eagerly received by two angels and the Mother of God, then subsequently greeted by the Patriarch Abraham. An angel ushers the deceased to his father and brothers also in the final image of the manuscript, while Christ blesses them all from above.

The visual narrative of the Madrid Skylitzes consistently diminishes divine involvement in Byzantine affairs. Several saints who help the Byzantines in the text disappear from the visual narrative: St Gregory of Nazianzus, St Demetrios, St Theodore and St Peter.[28] These visual absences are notable, since in each case the text recounts at some length saintly manifestations and particular miracles.

The case of St Demetrios is an informative example of this pattern. On folio 217 the text narrates how St Demetrios led the Byzantine army to victory over the Bulgars at Thessalonike. After the residents of the city prayed at the tomb of St Demetrios, 'they flung open the gates and went out against the Bulgars … [The Bulgars] were not in the least willing to offer a sustained or courageous resistance for the Martyr was leading the Roman army and smoothing a path for it. This was attested with oaths by some Bulgars who were taken prisoner. They said they had seen a young horseman leading the Roman ranks, exuding a fire which burnt up the enemies.'[29] The generic image (fol. 217b) merely represents a cavalry group leaving a fortified enclosure in pursuit of another cavalry group. St Demetrios, the most important protagonist of the passage, is conspicuous in his absence.

---

[26]   The genealogical focus of the visual narrative is also underscored by representations of groups of successive rulers. Sometimes as many as six at a time stand in for their era, such as on fol. 89r.

[27]   Velmans, 'Three notes', 34.

[28]   Fol. 28 (St Gregory); fols. 66v, 79 (St Peter); fol. 171v (St Theodore); fol. 217 (St Demetrios).

[29]   Wortley, 221; Skylitzes, 413–14.

It strikes me as consequential, rather than coincidental, that the visual narrative of the Madrid Skylitzes omits a saint who became a public symbol of Norman power in Sicily and whose providential preference was repeatedly sought by Roger II. In an unusual move for a Latin ruler, but in standard Byzantine practice, Roger II issued a coin bearing images of himself and his expected successor, his son Roger. The chosen iconography was based on a coin of Alexios I Komnenos, which announced Alexios' successor John II, and represented him together with St Demetrios. On Roger's coin, King Roger appeared as an emperor, while his son, Duke Roger, was represented as a heroic military figure in the guise of St Demetrios.[30] Roger's affinity for St Demetrios is further attested by coins bearing the bust of the saint that commemorate a victory over the Byzantines in 1147.[31] Since Roger II appropriated this saint for Norman coins in celebration of his own victory over the Byzantines, the omission of a revered warrior saint is less surprising. In this case his absence was more ideologically useful than his presence.

Crowning achievements: the visibility of virtue

In Byzantium, representation of an emperor constituted a political act, since 'the person of the emperor … [was] the embodiment of Byzantine ideology'.[32] Byzantine imperial images were expected to conform to established ideological and iconographic conventions. In official images executed in different media and ranging from codices to coins to crowns, the emperor is regal and static; in the words of Henry Maguire, a nearly iconic 'diagram of imperial power'.[33]

---

[30]   M. Hendy discussed the similarity of the two coin types in *Coinage and Money in the Byzantine Empire 1081–1261* (Washington, DC, 1969), 42–3.

[31]   For discussion of the coin issue, see P. Grierson and L. Travaini, *Medieval European Coinage*, vol. 14: *Italy* (Cambridge, 1998), 123, cat. entry 226. For these historical events see H. Houben, *Roger II of Sicily: A Ruler between East and West*, trans. G. Loud and D. Milburn (Cambridge, 2002), 84–5; P. Magdalino, *The Empire of Manuel I Komnenos, 1143–1180* (Cambridge, 1993).

[32]   A. P. Kazhdan and A. Wharton Epstein, *Change in Byzantine Culture in the Eleventh and Twelfth Centuries* (Berkeley, CA, 1985), 110.

[33]   H. Maguire, catalogue entry 143, in H. Evans and W. Wixom, eds., *The Glory of Byzantium: Art and Culture of the Middle Byzantine Era A.D. 843–1261* (New York, 1997), 207–9.

Byzantine court rhetoric stressed that the emperor was divinely chosen for his virtue and derived his power from God.[34] For instance, Theophylact of Ochrid in his Mirror of Princes wrote: '[the king] does not acquire authority by force, or steep his robes in blood: his basis is the good will of the masses and the concurrence of the people, with his own moderation and mercy. He receives his crown as the reward of his virtue, and all men readily concede the best of things to the best of men.' [35] Robin Cormack stressed the centrality of virtue in imperial imagery: 'all Byzantine emperors were to be regarded as a "likeness" of God and must demonstrate their corresponding virtues – Philanthropy, Piety, Intelligence and Judgement.'[36] How, then, do the Vatican Manasses and Madrid Skylitzes visualize the nexus between power and virtue?

The Manasses aggressively appropriates imperial iconography and even surpasses Byzantine visual rhetoric in its audacious preface miniature. Ivan Alexander's ultimate elevation to holiness materializes on folio 1r in an image of 'symbolic investiture' (see Fig. 12.5).[37] The haloed and crowned ruler, who is about to be crowned by a heaven-descending angel, is flanked by Jesus (on his proper right) and Constantine Manasses (on his proper left). Needless to say no surviving Byzantine imperial representation allowed a ruler to display visible superiority to the Son of God.

In her analysis of the image, Tania Velmans found that this arrangement 'imparts an absurd aspect to the composition as a whole'.[38] Her argument is rooted in a mode of formal analysis that gives precedence to discovering deviation from the authentic (i.e. Byzantine) forms over analyzing the agency of the individual patrons. I would suggest that this potent image should neither be dismissed as 'absurd', nor categorized as a warped reflection of a Byzantine original. Rather it should be viewed as an attempt to use Byzantine artistic forms to usurp the imperial mystique. Building

---

[34]   Anon., 'Advice to the emperor', in *Cecaumeni Strategicon, De officiis regiis libellus*, eds. B. Wassiliewsky and V. Jernstedt (Amsterdam, 1965), 93; trans. E. Barker, *Social and Political Thought in Byzantium: From Justinian I to the Last Palaeologus* (Oxford, 1957), 126. See also H. Maguire, 'Style and ideology in Byzantine imperial art', *Gesta* 28/2 (1990), 223; A. Kazhdan, 'Certain traits of imperial propaganda in the Byzantine empire from the eighth to the fifteenth centuries', in *Prédication et propagande au Moyen Age. Islam, Byzance, Occident* (Paris, 1983), 14; G. Dennis, 'Imperial panegyric: rhetoric and reality', in Maguire, ed., *Byzantine Court Culture*, 139.

[35]   Theophylact of Ochrid, 'Paideia Basilike', *PG* 126. 273 BC; trans. E. Barker in *Social and Political Thought in Byzantium*, 147.

[36]   R. Cormack, 'The emperor at St. Sophia: viewer and viewed', in A. Guillou and J. Durand, eds., *Byzance et les images* (Paris, 1994), 234.

[37]   Velmans, 'Three notes', 27.

[38]   Velmans, 'Three notes', 29.

upon the Byzantine rhetoric of imperial *Christomimesis*, Ivan Alexander goes a step further and usurps the place of God.[39] The emulation of imperial ideology expressed in costume and style is fused with an aggressive claim of possession to the Byzantine Empire itself. The Bulgarian ruler titles himself 'Tsar and autokrator of all Bulgarians and Greeks', signalling a Bulgaria-centred reordering of the political world. This grandiose glorification of Ivan Alexander anchors his political claims, lineage, and special place within Christian history consistently developed in the manuscript.

In keeping with its worldly frame of reference, the Skylitzes visual narrative dispenses altogether with divine coronations. Instead, usurpation of imperial power is consistently highlighted as the norm. Although aspects of individual accession images, such as raising on a shield, have attracted the attention of scholars, the manuscript's treatment of tyranny has been studiously ignored in historiography.[40] Repeatedly, rulers are represented for what they are – usurpers, who climb to the throne by rebelling or murdering their predecessors.[41]

In fact, the visual narrative of the Skylitzes leaves little room for imperial virtue. It regularly diverts attention from imperial accomplishments highlighted in the text. Careful examination reveals consistent exclusion of a topic that at once exemplifies various imperial virtues: munificence.[42] Although imperial buildings, including religious structures, new foundations and restorations, are extolled in the text frequently and verbosely, they are consistently absent from images.[43]

For instance, an extensive and detailed narrative (57 manuscript lines) on the munificence of Basil I in rebuilding and restoring numerous churches in and around Constantinople was transformed into a visual void. This was not the result of lack of space, but of conscious intervention. On fol. 102r multiple images illustrate a mere 13 lines of text concerning the long-term relationship of the rich widow Danielis from the Peloponnesos with Emperor Basil I and his son. Danielis was Basil's benefactress when he was but a lowly servitor, and she left her fortune to Basil's son Leo VI. Her visits to Constantinople with gifts for the rulers are carefully represented in an extremely rare set of three images on a single page; only eight pages

---

[39]   For a discussion of uses and limitations of *Christomimesis* in Byzantine imperial imagery, see E. Kitzinger, 'On the portrait of Roger II in the Martorana in Palermo', *Proporzioni: Studi di Storia dell'Arte* III (1950), 30–35.

[40]   C. Walter, 'Raising on a shield in Byzantine iconography', *REB* 33 (1975), 133–75.

[41]   Boeck, 'The art of being Byzantine', 69–133.

[42]   On munificence, see M. McCormick, 'Legitimacy, political', in *ODB* II, 1203; D. Constantelos, *Byzantine Philanthropy and Social Welfare*, second edn. (New Rochelle, NY, 1991), 33–42.

[43]   These include fols. 46v, 101v, 102v, 103, 106v, 110v, 154, 180, 203v, 205v, 206.

in the entire manuscript contain three images. The miniatures are laid out in a careful and iconographically consistent manner: in all three Danielis appears along the planned vertical axis. While the upper composition highlights her luxurious mode of travel in a litter accompanied by numerous servants, in the following two images (which are nearly identical) she approaches an enthroned emperor from the left with attendants bearing costly gifts, to be greeted first by the bearded Basil I, and subsequently by the beardless Leo. There is no unequivocal explanation for the decision to foreground this episode, but the decision to de-emphasize the imperial munificence bestowed on the Byzantine capital is undeniable.[44]

Getting ahead: scrutinizing de-capitation

Although Byzantine historians regularly produced verbal invectives against rulers and often lingered on the bloody particularities of imperial successions,[45] verbal descriptions did not translate into visualization. Only subtle variations within established iconography communicated critiques of emperors, and even these images are sufficiently polyvalent that not all scholars recognize them as veiled messages.[46] In the surviving corpus of Byzantine images, not a single one displays the graphic demise of an emperor. Since political order, ideology and legitimacy converged in the imperial body, visualization of desecration was unthinkable. The Manasses and Skylitzes manuscripts dramatically diverge in their visual execution of imperial beheadings. While the Manasses exercises visual restraint, in the Skylitzes an emperor can be transformed from the head of

---

[44] These images are consistent with the visual narrative's fascination with paths to the throne and powers behind it. For a brief consideration of this page see also J. Burke, 'The Madrid Skylitzes as an audio-visual experiment', in Burke, *et al.*, eds., *Byzantine Narrative*, 141.

[45] A. Eastmond recently commented: 'The official status of the emperor and his image was often at odds with the personal nature of imperial rule, the capriciousness of imperial policy, and the ability to sin and commit foul deeds. Emperors were all too human. This is what gives Byzantine chronicles their force and interest': 'Between icon and idol: the uncertainty of imperial images', in Eastmond and James, eds., *Icon and Word*, 78. See also P. Magdalino, 'Aspects of twelfth-century Byzantine *Kaiserkritik*', *Speculum* 58/2 (1983), 326–46 (repr. in P. Magdalino, *Tradition and Transformation in Medieval Byzantium* [Aldershot, 1991], study VIII); F. Tinnefeld, *Kategorien der Kaiserkritik in der Byzantinischen Historiographie von Prokop bis Niketas Choniates* (Munich, 1971).

[46] I. Kalavrezou, N. Trahoulia and S. Sabar, 'Critique of the emperor in the Vatican Psalter gr. 752', *DOP* 47 (1993), 195–219; N. Oikonomides, 'Leo VI and the narthex mosaic of Saint Sophia', *DOP* 30 (1976), 151–72.

the Byzantine body politic into a bloody severed head offered on a pole for public inspection.

A particularly triumphant episode of ninth-century Bulgarian history was inserted into the Manasses translation. According to the Bulgarian text, Khan Krum captured the Byzantine emperor Nikephoros I, had him decapitated, and transformed the imperial skull into a drinking vessel. The original Greek text only briefly mentioned Nikephoros' demise on the battlefield in a conflict with Bulgars.[47]

The Bulgarian interpolation was extensively illustrated on two pages (fols. 145r and 145v). On folio 145r, two crowned rulers come face to face following the Byzantine invasion of Bulgaria at the top of the page (see Fig. 12.3). Khan Krum's superiority to Emperor Nikephoros is made immediately apparent in costume: although both figures are clad in imperial costume, Krum alone wears a *loros*. Body language and gestures amplify the Bulgarian ruler's upper hand in the situation: he rests his right hand on the shoulder of Nikephoros and raises his left hand towards the emperor's head. The Byzantine ruler's hands are bound.

In a full-page miniature on folio 145v Krum, again clad in imperial garments, holds a victory feast (see Fig. 12.4). The seated ruler is represented on the left side of the composition at the head of the table, while a servant enters from the right with a filled drinking vessel, which bears no traces of an anatomical provenance.[48] Although the Bulgarian text unambiguously informs the reader that Krum had the imperial head enchased and used it to drink to the Bulgarians' health, the visual narrative omits this imperial decapitation. For Ivan Alexander, getting ahead in his personal competition with Byzantium did not require a Bulgarian visual violation of an imperial body. His eagerness to claim an uncompromised Byzantine legacy might also explain this omission.

A different de-capitation inspired one of the most vivid and ruthless visual images in the entire Skylitzes manuscript. The chronicle develops at length a gruesome sequence of events that accompanied the regicidal imperial accession of John Tzimiskes. It narrates Tzimiskes' tryst with the empress, her betrayal of the emperor to the conspirators, the attack of multiple assailants upon the sleeping Emperor Nikephoros II Phokas, his agonizing wounds and beheading culminating in the display of his severed head as a deterrent to his supporters.

On folio 157va the viewer is confronted with the spectacle of the emperor's severed head projecting on a spear from a palace window to his distraught supporters. (See Fig. 12.7) Although the image also contains a figure of an enthroned emperor, John Tzimiskes depicted dressed in purple

---

[47]   Manasses, 4535–8.

[48]   Scholars have previously described this image, but they have not analyzed the absence of imperial decapitation.

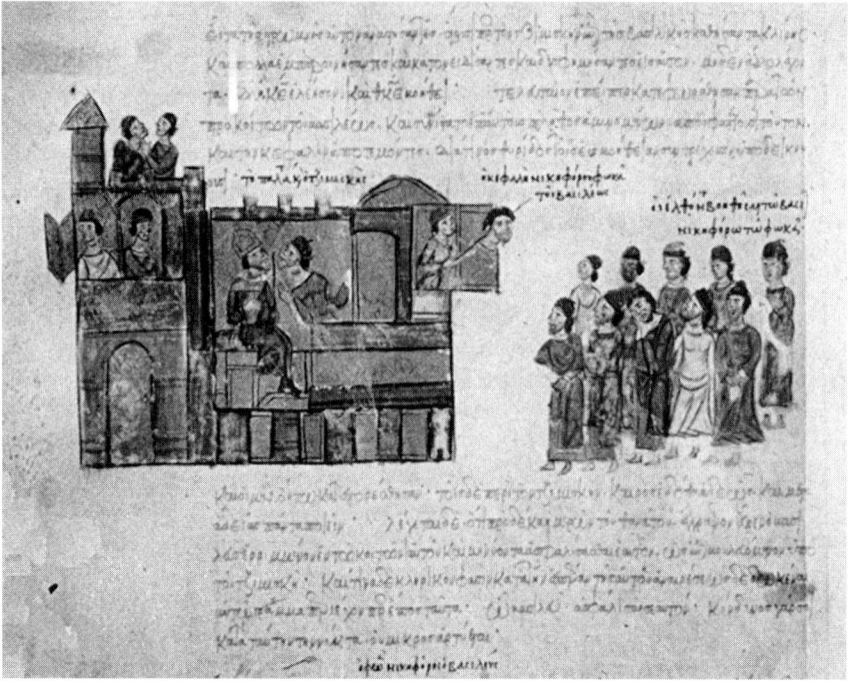

Fig. 12.7   Madrid Skylitzes Manuscript, Biblioteca Nacional, Madrid, Vitr. 26-2, fol. 157va

and wearing red shoes, the focal feature of the composition is the lifeless head of his royal victim. This is the most graphic and public re-presentation of a dismembered, formerly imperial, body in the entire manuscript. The casual transfer of legitimacy to Tzimiskes stands in stark contrast to the chronicler's response to the homicidal usurpation.[49]

The visual narrative's peculiar fascination with paths to the throne and the violent politics of imperial accessions is remarkably unrestrained. Visualizing Byzantine history as a series of violent actions by self-made men who challenged imperial authority and captured the throne could even serve Sicilian interests. After the invention of an upstart kingdom and the highly contentious coronation of Roger II in 1130 CE, international

---

[49]   Neither the text nor the captions accord him imperial legitimacy. The text continues to call him simply Tzimiskes and the captions above the crowned emperor read 'the palace and Tzimiskes'. Instead, legitimacy is retained by Nikephoros Phokas, whose protruding head is identified in the captions as 'the head of the emperor Nikephoros Phokas'.

opinion pronounced Sicily an age-old hotbed of tyranny.[50] Drawing attention to skeletons, or, in this case, skulls, in the Byzantine imperial closet had the potential to even the playing field between the Sicilian kings and their imperial rivals. An unvarnished visual guide to the intrigues and intricacies of Byzantine politics blurred the distinctions between rightful kings (*rex iustus sive rex a recte agendo*) and unjust tyrants (*rex iniustus sive tyrannus*).[51]

Conclusion

Even a brief comparison of the two manuscripts suggests that engaging the Byzantine past constituted a partisan pursuit. As Gabrielle Spiegel has argued, 'patronage of contemporary chronicles can be seen as a form of political action, an attempt to control the subject-matter of history'.[52] Visualization necessitated numerous political choices in the process of framing and claiming the Byzantine past. Neither manuscript offers an impartial parallel to its text.

This pair of manuscripts serves as a reminder that medieval narratives could be creative, contentious, prejudiced and political. Each manuscript presents a dynamic interplay between text and image, visualization and politics. It is fruitless to view either manuscript as a window into a lost Byzantine world, since each is a world of its own. However, by tracking how both manuscripts were attracted or repelled by Byzantium, we might better understand the changing contours of the empire's cultural orbit.

The new facsimile publication of the Vatican Manasses manuscript (Constantine Manasses, Synopsis chroniki: Codex Vaticano Slavo 2, 1344–45 [Athens: Globul Cosmote Group, 2007) became available to me too late to be incorporated into the notes of this article.

---

[50]   Wieruszowski, 'Roger II of Sicily, Rex-Tyrannus', 54; *The Letters of St. Bernard of Clairvaux*, trans. B.S. James (London, 1953), 201–2, 210–11, 348–9.

[51]   On political terminology, see Wieruszowski, 'Roger II of Sicily, Rex-Tyrannus', 54; R. W. Carlyle and A. J. Carlyle, *History of Medieval Political Theory in the West* (Edinburgh, 1903–36), I, 161 ff., III, 126 ff.

[52]   G. Spiegel, 'Medieval canon formation and the rise of royal historiography in Old French prose', *Modern Language Notes* 108/4 (1993), 641.

13. The *Synopsis Chronike* and hagiography: the presentation of Constantine the Great

Konstantinos Zafeiris

'Constantine was *the* emperor for the Byzantines', Alexander Kazhdan writes in '"Constantin Imaginaire" – Byzantine legends of the ninth century about Constantine the Great'.[1] Notwithstanding the criticism that aspects of Kazhdan's study have received,[2] the main premise – the great appeal and significance of Constantine for the Byzantines – does not appear to be debatable. Constantine was a seminal figure, with a strong and controversial impression that was central throughout the Byzantine era. His name and image were constantly used, associated with, conveniently overlooked, reinvented, manipulated and venerated, and the Society for the Promotion of Byzantine Studies has devoted a Spring Symposium on the subject that has provided a wide range of studies on the subsequent reception and usage of the 'idea' of Constantine.[3] This paper intends to look at the treatment of the legend in a chronicle of the thirteenth century, the *Synopsis Chronike*, and to explore the presentation of the reign of Constantine the Great, particularly in regard to the uncommon, almost unique, use of hagiographical material and style in the presentation of the narrative.

The *Synopsis Chronike*[4] (or *Synopsis Sathas*, as it is often called after its editor, Constantine Sathas) was written in the second half of the thirteenth century, after the recapture of Constantinople from the Latins,

---

[1] A. P. Kazhdan, '"Constantin Imaginaire" – Byzantine legends of the ninth century about Constantine the Great', *Byz* 57 (1987), 196–250.

[2] See Magdalino, ed., *New Constantines*, 3, n. 4; R. D. Scott, 'The image of Constantine in Malalas and Theophanes', in Magdalino, ed., *New Constantines*, 57–71. Also see Kazhdan, *A History of Byzantine Literature (650–850)*, 127–35.

[3] Magdalino, ed., *New Constantines*.

[4] *Synopsis Chronike*, ed. K. N. Sathas, *Mesaionike Bibliotheke* (Venice, 1872–94; repr. Athens, 1972), VI (hereafter, *SynChron*).

by an unknown author. It has traditionally been accepted as the work of
Theodore Skoutariotes, bishop of Kyzikos.[5] Internal evidence suggests that
the author was indeed a cleric,[6] but the identification with Skoutariotes
is problematic, and further research suggests that it should not be taken
for granted.[7] The text is usually labelled as a chronicle, but its distinctive
structure – namely the peculiar division of the material into two parts –
does not allow us to categorize it exclusively under either the history or the
chronicle genre.[8] On the one hand, the first part[9] forms a typical Byzantine
chronicle, and relates the events from the Creation of the world until the
enthronement of the emperor Alexios Komnenos, starting from Adam and
the biblical patriarchs and covering the history of the Roman Empire with
a sequence of its emperors and their deeds. On the other hand, the second
part of the work[10] is an extensive historical narrative, which describes in
detail the events following Alexios' accession to the throne in 1081, up to
the recapture of Constantinople by the Byzantines in 1261.[11]

The section on the reign of Constantine is found in pages 41 to 54 of
Sathas' edition, its substantial length confirming its significant position
within the text, which is enhanced by the use of additional narrative
devices. The section does not follow the usual structure of presentation of

---

[5]   The identification was first suggested in A. Heisenberg, *Analecta: Mitteilungen
aus italienischen Handschriften byzantinischer Chronographen* (Munich, 1901), 3–16.

[6]   Namely, the personal interventions of the author in the last part of the
text, especially in regard to his close relationship to the patriarch Arsenios and
his recurrent focus on ecclesiastical and religious matters. Also see R. Macrides,
George Akropolites, *The History* (Oxford, 2007), 70.

[7]   For a more detailed discussion of the subject, see K. A. Zafeiris, 'The *Synopsis
Chronike* and its place in the Byzantine chronicle tradition: its sources (Creation–1081
CE)' (PhD thesis, University of St Andrews, 2007), 22–9. Cf. R. Tocci, 'Zu Genese
und Kompositionsvorgang der Σύνοψις χρονική des Theodoros Skutariotes', *BZ*
98 (2005), 551–69.

[8]   Interestingly, Hunger used the example of the *SynChron* to depict the vague
distinction between the genres of history and chronicle (Hunger, *Literatur*, I, 253–
4). Scholarship now questions the validity of such a distinction; see particularly
Beck, '"Mönchschronik"', 188–97, J. N. Ljubarskij, 'New trends in the study of
Byzantine historiography', *DOP* 47 (1993), 131–8, and E. M. Jeffreys, 'The attitude
of Byzantine chroniclers towards ancient history', *Byz* 49 (1979), 199–200. In this
paper, the term 'chronicle' is used in its traditional meaning only as a convention,
as it does not always correspond to the characteristics of the different texts that are
customarily placed under this title.

[9]   *SynChron*, 3–173.

[10]   *SynChron*, 177–556.

[11]   For this part, the text follows closely the histories of Niketas Choniates
and George Akropolites, with only a few – but often significant – modifications or
additions.

imperial reigns, which are always introduced with the name of the emperor and the duration of the reign. In this case, the narrative starts from within the section devoted to Constantius Chlorus, in a rather short segment,[12] supplementary to the section on the reign of Diocletian and Maximianus; its narrative role is to introduce the reign of Constantine, by conveying the events that led to Constantine becoming the sole ruler of the Roman Empire, namely a first vision of the Cross and the ensuing victory against Maxentius in the battle of the Milvian Bridge. By doing this, the narrator breaks with his usual practice of relating the events within the reign of the emperor, thus indicating Constantine's distinctive place in the imperial sequence. This is also stressed by the subsequent passage[13] that describes – and defines – the chronological significance of the reign, and divides not only the narrative of the deeds of Constantine, but the narrative of the entire text. The passage conveys significant chronological points of the history of the world and their connection to Constantine: the time from the Creation of the world up to the Incarnation (5500 years, at the forty-second year of Augustus), the span of the life of Jesus Christ (thirty-three years), the time from the Ascension (at the eighteenth year of Tiberius' reign) to the first year of Constantine's reign (297 years), in total 5830 years. Such passages are not very common in the chronicle, at least in the post-biblical part of the text.[14] In this case, the passage connects Constantine to Jesus Christ, by drawing attention to the parallel of the significance of the birth of the latter to the reign of the former. Interestingly, the chronological division is complemented by the presence of a rubric in the main manuscript of the text (and also in the manuscript that holds the related chronicle *Synopsis Lambros*[15]), and hence the narrative is divided not only internally, but also externally. Following the chronological summary, the narrative continues with a passage that is written in the usual format of introducing imperial reigns. In the case of the reign of Constantine, it is a detailed (and not common in other sources)[16] chronological summary of his reign, preceded by the title ΠΡΩΤΟΣ ΒΑΣΙΛΕΥΣ ΕΥΣΕΒΩΝ ΚΩΝΣΤΑΝΤΙΝΟΣ.[17] Then, the section begins with Ὡωνσταντῖνος ὁ μέγας καὶ ἅγιος καὶ ἰσαπόστολος, καὶ πρῶτος τῶν χριστιανῶν βασιλέων, ὁ καὶ κτήτωρ τῆς Κωνσταντίνου

---

[12]   *SynChron*, 41.20–42.25.

[13]   *SynChron*, 42.26–43.4.

[14]   They do appear, though, in a few occasions in the first section of the chronicle (*SynChron*, 1 19), in order to describe the chronology of major biblical events, such as the Exodus of Israel from Egypt (*SynChron*, 8.12–7).

[15]   *Synopsis Lambros*, ed. S. Lambros, Lambros Archive, Department of History and Archaeology, University of Athens (Athens, [1917]; unpublished).

[16]   The only other text that presents the information in a similar form is George the Monk, 525.11–13.

[17]   *SynChron*, 43.4.

πόλεως...' ('Constantine the Great, Saint and Equal to the Apostles, the first of the Christian emperors, and the founder of Constantinople...').[18]

The Constantine section includes a wide range of events that took place in different times during his reign, not always in a coherent chronological order. It seems that the compiler was more interested in incorporating different events from the life of the emperor, drawing material from a wide range of texts, rather than using a specific earlier pattern or a sole source. The practice is evident in the muddled and often confusing presentation. It is telling that the texts of John Malalas and Theophanes Confessor, two of the most commonly used sources of the *SynChron*, are consulted only sporadically for the reign of Constantine. In general, the section has no easily recognized sources. This may be due to the multitude of accounts – often diverse and contradictory – about Constantine, which is also reflected in the hagiographical tradition. Speaking of the different versions and traditions of Constantine's life, Kazhdan rejected the existence of a *Vorvita* behind the corpus of hagiographical versions, and suggested that they probably took shape as oral tales dedicated to individual episodes in the story of Constantine.[19] The *SynChron* seems to reflect this situation; the compiled account derives from a broad pool of information, but does not follow directly or consistently a unique source.[20] It also tends to reproduce or imitate elements that are more often found in hagiographical texts than in chronicles or histories.

Influences of hagiography are not rare in the *SynChron* as a whole; on the contrary, they seem to be more prominent than in other chronicles. In addition to the numerous references to hagiographical themes, such as persecutions, martyrdoms, miracles, translation of relics of apostles and saints to Constantinople, most of which are usually accessed through earlier chronicles and histories rather than saints' lives, the text appears to draw its material from hagiographical texts in numerous other cases, such

---

[18]   *SynChron*, 43.5–7.

[19]   Kazhdan, '"Constantin Imaginaire"', 274. Also see F. Winkelmann, 'Ein Ordungsversuch der griechischen hagiographischen Konstantinviten und ihren Überlieferung', in J. Irmscher and P. Nagel, eds., *Studia Byzantina II* (Berlin, 1973; repr. *Studien zu Konstantin dem grossen und zur byzantinischen Kirchengeschicthen* [Birmingham, 1993]), 267–84.

[20]   The use of multiple sources is confirmed by incidents and events that are mentioned twice in the course of the narrative. More specifically, there are two passages on the vision of the cross (*SynChron*, 42.7–15, 44.1–22), attributed to different times in the life of the emperor; two contradictory passages on the chronology of the First Ecumenical Council (*SynChron*, 50.12–5, 50.23–5; the first passage puts the council in the fifteenth year of Constantine's reign, whereas the second one – only eight lines later – puts it in the twentieth year of the reign); and two separate passages dealing with the death of the emperor (*SynChron*, 53.17–23, 54.6–9).

as the attempt of the Emperor Tiberius to proclaim officially the divine status of Jesus Christ, the persecution of St Eustathios and his family, or the translation of the relics of St Gregory during the reign of Constantine Porphyrogennetos.[21] Nevertheless, the use of hagiographical elements in the *SynChron* is nowhere else more evident than in the extensive section on the reign of Constantine the Great.

The *SynChron* covers all the main aspects of Constantine's legend, as presented in hagiography and codified systematically by Kazhdan,[22] although not always extensively. For example, the issue of the birth and early years of Constantine, which other authors discuss in detail,[23] is only summarily mentioned in the *SynChron*, without any further references to its potential significance. Other elements of the legend, however, are given prominent attention, namely the vision (or visions) of the cross by Constantine, the foundation of Constantinople, the campaign against the Persians, the conversion of the emperor to Christianity and his baptism by the Pope Sylvester, and the discovery of the Holy Cross by his mother Helen. The bulk of the material used in the composition of the respective sections is largely drawn from hagiographical texts, and the *SynChron* is unique in its use of such sources, as well as in literary elements, which are influenced more by hagiography than historiography.

The vision of the cross and the foundation of Constantinople are aspects of the Constantinian legend with particular interest for our discussion, especially as the *SynChron* is one of a small number of texts that link the two events, the other two being Pseudo-Symeon and the Patmos Life of Constantine. According to them, when Constantine saw the vision of the Cross, he was also instructed by Jesus Christ to build a city in honour of the Virgin. At a later time, following his subsequent victory over Maxentius, Constantine recalled Jesus' command, and proceeded with the task. The three texts (and also Kedrenos, who does not include the first passage in the section of Constantine's vision of the Cross) share not only the same content, but more or less the same language:

Εἰς μνήμην δὲ ἐλθὼν τῆς πρὸς αὐτὸν φωνῆς τοῦ Κυρίου καθ' ὕπνους λεγούσης, Ἐγείρεις τῇ μητρί μου πόλιν ἐν ᾧ ὑποδείξω σοι τόπῳ.[24]

And he recalled the utterance of the Lord to him in his sleep, saying: 'You should found a city in honour of my mother, in the place that I will show you.'

---

[21] *SynChron*, 28.1–3: divine status of Christ; 31.13–14: persecution of St Eustathios; 153.3–12: translation of St Gregory's relics.

[22] Kazhdan, '"Constantin Imaginaire"', 212–40.

[23] See Kazhdan, '"Constantin Imaginaire"', 212–17.

[24] *SynChron*, 46.21–3.

Ἐν ταύταις ταῖς ἡμέραις εἰς μνήμην ἔρχεται τοῦ γενομένου ὑπὸ τοῦ κυρίου πρὸς αὐτὸν κατὰ τοὺς ὕπνους προστάγματος λέγοντος οἰκοδομεῖν τῇ θεοτόκῳ πόλει 'ἐν ᾧ τόπῳ αὐτὸς ὑποδείξω σοι'.[25]

In those days, he recalls the command given by the Lord to him in his sleep, saying that he should build a city in honour of Theotokos, 'in the place that I will show you myself'.

Ἐν ταύταις ταῖς ἡμέραις εἰς μνήμην ἔρχεται τοῦ γενομένου πρὸς αὐτὸν πλησίον Ῥώμης ὑπὸ τοῦ κυρίου κατὰ τοὺς ὕπνους προστάγματος, ὅπερ ἦν οἰκοδομῆσαι τῇ θεοτόκῳ πόλιν 'ἐν ᾧ τόπῳ αὐτὸς ὑποδείξω σοι' λέγοντος.[26]

In those days, he recalls the command given by the Lord to him in his sleep close to Rome, which was saying that he should build a city in honour of Theotokos, 'in the place that I will show you myself'.

ἐν ταύταις ταῖς ἡμέραις εἰς μνήμην ἔρχεται τοῦ γενομένου πλησίον Ῥώμης ὑπὸ τοῦ κυρίου πρὸς αὐτὸν κατὰ τοὺς ὕπνους προστάγματος, ὅπερ ἦν λέγοντος οἰκοδομῆσαι τῇ θεοτόκῳ πόλιν ἐν ᾧ τόπῳ αὐτὸς ὑποδείξω σοι.[27]

In those days, he recalls the command given by the Lord to him in his sleep close to Rome, which was saying that he should build a city in honour of Theotokos, 'in the place that I will show you myself'.

Similar parallels continue to appear throughout the section, not least in the structure of the narratives. The texts proceed by describing the search for the appropriate place for the building of the city, which is eventually decided to be the city of Chalcedon, in Bithynia. However, a divine sign appears: several eagles disrupt the building by raising the stones and carrying them to a different place, the city of Byzantium. A servant of the emperor, Euphratas, another significant figure in the hagiographical presentation of Constantine,[28] realizes the meaning of the sign and explains it to the emperor; then the place of the city is duly moved to the new position, but the narrative is sharply interrupted with the description of the campaign of Constantine against the Persians.

An objection could be raised in regard to this first example, that it may not be a case of influence from hagiography, but the consequence of the use of a version of the chronicle of Symeon the Logothete. Although this possibility cannot be discarded outright, the similar structure of the

---

[25]   Pseudo-Symeon, 10.1–4.

[26]   F. Halkin, 'Une nouvelle Vie de Constantine dans un légendier de Patmos', *AnBoll* 77 (1959), 63–107 (here at §8.1–5[83]).

[27]   Kedrenos, I, 495.22–496.2.

[28]   Kazhdan, '"Constantin Imaginaire"', 237–8.

sections of the *SynChron* and the Patmos Life of Constantine seems to support the existence of a link between them. Furthermore, the following passage, which describes the campaign of Constantine against the Persians, and the rarely mentioned episode of his subsequent capture and escape, suggests that the *SynChron* presents stronger similarities to the hagiographical tradition than to any historiographical texts; the episode of the capture of the emperor Constantine by the Persians is only hinted at by Pseudo-Symeon and Kedrenos.[29] On the contrary, the *SynChron* presents an extensive account of the event, with great similarities to the various *vitae* of Constantine, as well as to another hagiographical text, the *vita* of St Eusignios,[30] both in content and in language. The narrative of the *SynChron* focuses on the capture of the emperor, and describes in detail (although not to the same extent as the *vitae*) the different stages of the event that led to the eventual escape; it stresses with bold invocations the role of divine providence throughout the incident, both in the instigation of the capture (ὦ τῶν κριμάτων σου, Κύριε[31]), and in its happy resolution: τῆς θείας συνάρσεως ἐπιρρωσάσης τὰ τούτων φρονήματα,[32] and τις λαλήσει τὰς δυναστείας σου, Κύριε, ἀκουστὰς ποιήσει πάσας τὰς αἰνέσεις σου![33] Such manifestations seem to be the influence of hagiographical sources, which use similar expressions in their treatment of the event: τῆς μεγάλης σου ἀνοχῆς, Χριστέ μου,[34] writes one life of Constantine, and another ἀλλὰ σκοπεῖτε τὴν τοῦ Θεοῦ ἀγαθότητα, πῶς ἐν ἀπόροις πόρους δίδωσι.[35]

For the conversion of Constantine to Christianity, the text follows the pattern of its *Epitome* sources, and presents (in an extensive narrative) the version of Constantine's baptism by Pope Sylvester in response to his severe sickness. But in addition to the *Epitome*, the material of the *SynChron* seems to derive from hagiographical texts, namely the previously mentioned lives of Constantine as well as a *vita* of Pope Sylvester. A case in point is Constantine's vision of Peter and Paul,[36] in which the two apostles reveal that the emperor would be restored to health if he were to be baptized by

    [29]   Pseudo-Symeon, 18.18–20; Kedrenos, I, 496.15–17.

    [30]   P. Devos, 'Une recession nouvelle de la passion grecque BHG 639 de S. Eusignios', *AnBoll* 100 (1982), 209–28.

    [31]   *SynChron*, 47.2.

    [32]   *SynChron*, 47.15–16.

    [33]   *SynChron*, 47.20–21.

    [34]   M. Guidi, 'Un "bios" de Constantino', *Rendiconti della Reale Accademia dei Lincei*, Classe di Scienze Morali, Storiche et Filologiche 16 (1907) (repr. Rome, 1908), 304–40, 637–62 (here at 316.26–317.1).

    [35]   Halkin, 'Une nouvelle Vie de Constantine dans un légendier de Patmos', §9.13–14.

    [36]   *SynChron*, 45.10–15.

Sylvester. The passage is presented in a similar manner in three texts.[37] The *SynChron* shows a stronger connection to Kedrenos than to the *vita* of Sylvester, a possible indication of the origin of the material. Nevertheless, the presence of the passage in the *SynChron* may still denote the programme of the author to present a more idolized and hagiographical image of the emperor; this is supported further by a rare intervention by the narrator, who interrupts the sequence of the narrative to express his admiration for the attitude and actions of Constantine: ὦ χριστομιμήτου φωνῆς! ὦ ψυχῆς ἁγίας τε καὶ βασιλικῆς![38] Although the proclamation is more linked to rhetoric than hagiography – there is a very similar phrase in a panegyric speech of Euthymios Tornikes in honour of the Emperor Alexios Komnenos[39] – its inclusion here seems to suit the hagiographical tone of the section as a whole.

The possibility that the *SynChron* drew the material from hagiographical sources is supported further by the passage that describes Constantine's baptism,[40] which presents stronger similarities to the respective sections of the lives of Sylvester and Constantine.[41] Such a passage is not present either in Pseudo-Symeon or Kedrenos. Then again, the use of either *vita* by the *SynChron* cannot be easily confirmed. For example, the *SynChron* writes ὡς χεὶρ ἀπὸ οὐρανοῦ πεμφθεῖσα ἥψατό μου, which is clearly related to the two texts: the *vita* of Sylvester writes ὅτι χεὶρ τις ἥψατό μου, while the Guidi *vita* has χειρὸς ἠσθόμην ἁπτομένης μου. From the two, the use of almost identical phraseology and syntax seems to advance the possibility that the *SynChron* follows the *vita* of Sylvester. In the beginning of the passage, however, the phrase ἦχος ἐγένετο ὥσπερ τηγάνου πυρὶ καιομένου of the *SynChron* seems to resemble more the life of Constantine (καὶ ἦχος ἐγένετο ὡς χαλκοῦ δονουμένου) than the one of Sylvester (καὶ ἦχος μέγας ἐγένετο). It seems, then, that neither of the two texts could have been the direct source of the *SynChron*. Nevertheless, the strong similarities between the three texts can only suggest that the material of the *SynChron* originates from another hagiographical source, with strong connections to both the *vita* of Sylvester and the Guidi *vita* of Constantine, that does not survive.

---

[37] *SynChron*, 45.10–15; *Vita Silvestri*: F. Halkin, ed., 'Vita sancti Silvestri papae Romae (Cod. Baltimor. 521)', in *Le ménologe impérial de Baltimore* (Brussels, 1985), 20–33 (here at 4.34–7); Kedrenos, I.475.17–21. The incident is also present in Pseudo–Symeon (6.15–19), but its similarities to the other texts are weaker.

[38] *SynChron*, 45.6–7.

[39] 'Ὦ χριστομιμήτου βασιλέως ἐπιβατήρια', in J. Darrouzès, 'Les discours d'Euthyme Tornikès', *REB* 26 (1968), 1§8.6 (p. 63).

[40] *SynChron*, 45.20–25.

[41] *Vita Silvestri*, 4.85–90; *Vita Constantini (Guidi)*, 328.20–28.

The hagiographical influence is further supported by the inclusion of another rare incident of Constantine's life at the end of the section. After the baptism, and his immediate cure from the sickness, Constantine issues a directive that condemns blasphemy,[42] and founds a church at the location of the baptism.

Θέλων δὲ πᾶσι δεῖξαι τὴν οἰκείαν εὐσεβείαν, αὐτός οἰκείαις χερσὶ λαβὼν δίκελλαν πρῶτος ὀρύττειν ἤρξατο, προστάξας ἐκκλησίαν γενέσθαι ἐν ὀνόματι τοῦ δεσπότου ἡμῶν Ἰησοῦ Χριστοῦ τοῦ θεοῦ.[43]

And as he wanted to demonstrate to all his own piety, he himself took in his own hands a two-pronged fork, and was the first to begin digging, and ordered the building of a church in the name of our Lord Jesus Christ the God.

Ἵνα δὲ πᾶσιν ἡ αὐτοῦ πίστις φανερωθῇ, λαβὼν δίκελλαν μέσον τοῦ παλατίου αὐτοῦ ὀρύσσειν ἤρξατο· καὶ διαγραφὴν ποιησάμενος προσέταξεν ἐκκλησίαν οἰκοδομηθῆναι ἐπὶ τῷ ὀνόματι τοῦ κυρίου ἡμῶν Ἰησοῦ Χριστοῦ.[44]

And for his faith to become apparent to all, he took a two-pronged fork and started digging in the centre of his palace; and he made an outline, and ordered the building of a church in the name of our Lord Jesus Christ.

The similarities to the respective passage of the *vita* of Sylvester are evident, and the hagiographical link is stressed further by the *SynChron* being the only other chronicle that recounts the incident. The lack of other related texts prevents us from reaching a definitive conclusion about the specific sources of the *SynChron*, as the earlier reservations about the existence of a direct link between the texts cannot be easily discarded; nevertheless, there is little doubt of their hagiographical origin. In this case, the incorporation of the passage by the *SynChron* demonstrates the piety of the emperor, but also the hagiographical influence it had received, both in its choice of sources and in its choice of content. Interestingly, the only other text that relates the event is the *Ecclesiastical History* of Nikephoros Kallistos Xanthopoulos;[45] the parallel between the *SynChron* and the later ecclesiastical history is a further indication of the motive of the author in

---

[42]   *SynChron*, 45.26–46.1.

[43]   *SynChron*, 46.1–4.

[44]   *Vita Silvestri*, 4.93–7.

[45]   Xanthopoulos 7.34.3–10: *PG* 145,1284 C–D. Also see F. Winkelmann and G. Gentz, *Die Kirchengeschichte des Nicephorus Callistus Xanthopulus und ihre Quellen, Texte und Untersuchungengen zur Gesichte der alteristlichen Literatur*, 98 (Berlin, 1966), 76.

his persistent use of such material, namely his great interest in matters religious and ecclesiastical.

Such an interest is consistent with the clerical background of the author, and the use of hagiographical sources (instead of the more frequently used historiographical texts) in the presentation of ecclesiastical matters is telling. A good example of this practice can be found in the narrative of the First Ecumenical Council, which is also in the section of the reign of Constantine. In this case, one of the sources of the *SynChron* seems to be a rarely used hagiographical text, a *vita* of the bishops of Constantinople Metrophanes and Alexander,[46] or – most probably – a different version of the text that was in circulation in the thirteenth century. We can find a first indication of its use in the passage of the presidents of the Council.[47] Although it was traditionally accepted that the bishop of Constantinople at the time was Metrophanes, the *SynChron* is one of the few historiographical texts that refers to Alexander as one of the presidents of the Council of Nicaea. The two other texts that convey the same information are Pseudo-Symeon and Gelasius. However, the former mentions that Alexander was the bishop of Constantinople at the time of the council, but was not able to attend due to old age,[48] and the latter includes Alexander as bishop in the catalogue of the participants.[49] In neither text is the reference given in the same instance or setting as in the *SynChron*; furthermore, there are no other indications that Gelasius' *Ecclesiastical History* was the source of the *SynChron*, and there is no reason to assume that the reference to Alexander was an exception. The references do confirm, however, the existence of a different tradition for Alexander as bishop,[50] which did not survive in any other later sources apart from the *SynChron*.

In contrast to most historical sources, the Life of Metrophanes and Alexander conveys that Alexander was at the council representing Metrophanes, who was not able to attend because of sickness and old age.[51] The similarities between the *vita* and the *SynChron* in this instance may not be strong enough to confirm a direct link between the two texts. However, the parallels do not stop there; the material of the long section of the *SynChron*[52] with the circumstances surrounding the succession of

---

[46]   F. Winkelmann, 'Vita Metrophanis et Alexandri', *AnBoll* 100 (1982), 147–83.

[47]   *SynChron*, 50.6–12.

[48]   Pseudo-Symeon, 10.54–60.

[49]   Gelasius of Cyzicus, *Anonyme Kirchengeschichte*, ed. G. C. Hansen, Griechischen christlichen Schriftsteller der ersten Jahrhunderte, Neue Folge, 9 (Berlin, 2002). Here at 2.38.13.

[50]   Cf. F. Winkelmann, 'Die Bischöfe Metrofanes und Alexandros von Byzans', *BZ* 59 (1966), 56–7, 59.

[51]   *Vita Metrophanis et Alexandri* (as in note 46), 12.4–7.

[52]   *SynChron*, 51.3–52.10.

Metrophanes (his old age, the search for a suitable successor, the problems presented by the candidacy of Alexander, the involvement and concerns of the Emperor Constantine, and the eventual resolution of the matter) is present only in hagiography,[53] namely the above-mentioned *vita*, and also a shorter Life of Metrophanes in a Menologium.[54] And although the parallels are mainly confined to the content and structure of the two texts, we can also discern similarities in their language, albeit not to the same extent.[55] Nevertheless, it would be reasonable to accept that a link between the *SynChron* and the *vita* does exist, though whether it is a direct one is far from certain. Even so, the consistent employment of hagiography by the *SynChron* is confirmed yet again.

The relationship between the *SynChron* and the later chronicle of Theodore of Kyzikos[56] presents us with a helpful example of this practice, especially in regard to the respective sections discussed above. The two texts present great similarities, which led to the assumption that they should be identified as one and the same text.[57] But this does not seem to be the case, and it is more possible that they both derive from a common archetype;[58] and although they often convey the same material and share a common (but not identical) structure, they also use different sources, and treat them in a different manner, ultimately producing two distinct compilations. Their respective presentations of the reign of Constantine are of special interest for this study, for, as they both draw from the same source, we can explain any changes by attributing them to motives and ideas specific to the composition of each text.

---

[53] Gelasius (2.38.13) refers to the issue of the old age of Metrophanes, as the reason for the initiation of the succession process. However, this is a brief passage, without the details of the *SynChron* and with no reference to an intervention by Constantine.

[54] 'Vita S. Metrophanis', in *Menologii anonymi byzantini saeculi X quae supersunt*, ed. B. Latysev, 2 vols. (St Petersburg, 1911–12), 2, 12–5.

[55] *Vita Metrophani et Alexandri*, 14.1–15.4.

[56] The chronicle of Theodore of Kyzikos is a text with close links to the *SynChron*; see K. Krumbacher and G. Soteriades, Ἱστορία τῆς Βυζαντινῆς Λογοτεχνίας (Athens, 1900), 788–92. A critical edition of the text, based on the chronicle of the sixteenth-century manuscript *Athonensis 3758 (Mon. Dionysiou 224)*, was prepared by Spyridon Lambros (hence its conventional title *Synopsis Lambros*) in 1917, but remains unpublished. The draft can be found in the Library of the Department of History and Archaeology of the University of Athens (Lambros Archive); see F. Euaggelatou-Notara, 'Καταλογράφησις τοῦ ἀρχείου Σπ. Λάμπρου', Ἐπιστημονικὴ Ἐπετηρίδα Φιλοσοφικῆς Σχολῆς Ἀθηνῶν 25 (1974–77), 267, and G. Charitakis, 'Σπυρίδωνος Π. Λάμπρου – Τὰ μετὰ θάνατον εὑρεθέντα', *NE* 14 (1920), 205.

[57] Heisenberg, *Analecta*, 12–13; Hunger, *Literatur*, I, 477–8.

[58] Zafeiris, 'The *Synopsis Chronike*', 187–202.

On the one hand, the section on the conversion of Constantine is presented by both authors in a similar manner: the structure is the same, and the language and content are almost identical, with only small differences in the description of the healing of Constantine[59] and of Constantine's vision of Peter and Paul.[60] The two texts, though, do not treat the other incidents in a similar manner. For example, with regard to the first vision of the cross by Constantine and its link to the foundation of Constantinople, the two texts share the first reference,[61] including the phrase οἰκοδομήσεις δὲ πόλιν τῇ μητρὶ μου; but in the place of the passage that describes the foundation of Constantinople, for which – as we saw earlier – the *SynChron* is associated with hagiography, the *Synopsis Lambros* draws its material from Zonaras, in a section that does not contain any references to a link between Constantine's vision of the cross and the foundation of Constantinople. As for the campaign against the Persians, the previously discussed section of the *SynChron* on the subject[62] does not seem to have a corresponding passage in the *Synopsis Lambros*, although the latter mentions that Constantine's death occurred at the onset of such a campaign.[63] However, the short reference comes much later in the narrative structure and timeline, with no further details or discussion, and with no links to the hagiographical material used by the *SynChron*. The *Synopsis Lambros* also omits the list of the past bishops of the city of Byzantium,[64] the description of the First Ecumenical Council, which is mentioned only briefly,[65] again drawing from Zonaras, and the extensive section on the succession of Metrophanes,[66] which is only mentioned in a short reference,[67] part of a longer segment that was also taken from Zonaras.

The problem of the participation of Alexander in the Council of Nicaea as bishop of Constantinople, another link between the *SynChron* and hagiography, is particularly interesting. The short reference of the *Synopsis Lambros* to the Council does not mention its presidents, and hence it does

---

[59] *SynChron*, 44.27–45.4; *Synopsis Lambros*, 320.22–321.16.

[60] *SynChron*, 45.10–20; *Synopsis Lambros*, 321.26–323.3.

[61] *SynChron*, 42.7–15; *Synopsis Lambros*, 312.25–313.10.

[62] *SynChron*, 46.31–48.16.

[63] *Synopsis Lambros*, 332.15–333.2.

[64] *SynChron*, 48.20–49.27.

[65] *SynChron*, 49.28–50.15; *Synopsis Lambros*, 331.2–8.

[66] *SynChron*, 51.3–52.16. The section of the *SynChron* (50.23–53.17) missing from the *Synopsis Lambros* is actually more extensive, and also includes Constantine's order for free provision of bread for the population of the City, the finding of the Holy Cross by Helen, two edicts by Constantine about the function of the Church, and a passage detailing the senators and nobles of Rome that were moved to Constantinople – all elements linked to the legend of Constantine.

[67] *Synopsis Lambros*, 331.24–332.9.

not allow us to ascertain the bishop of Constantinople. However, this can be deduced from the position of the reference on Metrophanes' succession in the structure of the section in the *Synopsis Lambros*; the passage is placed in the aftermath of the Council, before the sections on the deaths of Helen and Constantine, and indicates that its author was not aware of the alternative tradition (that Alexander participated in the First Ecumenical Council as bishop of Constantinople, which – of the later sources – is found only in the *SynChron*). In this instance, as in the others that we have discussed earlier, the *SynChron* presents specific events from Constantine's reign following its hagiographical sources, whereas the *Synopsis Lambros* tends either to ignore them, or uses more conventional historiographical texts, usually Zonaras. In the end, the differences between the two texts emphasize the disparity of focus of the two authors, especially in religious and ecclesiastical matters.

It has become evident that the presentation of the reign of Constantine in the *SynChron* was systematically constructed with extensive use of hagiographical material. Juxtaposition of the *SynChron* with the respective sections of the *Synopsis Lambros* suggests that the practice was not accidental but, rather, the conscious practice of the author. This can also be confirmed by the other sources that were available to the author of the *SynChron*, which either omit such incidents or present them in a different manner, with no apparent references to or from hagiography. It is possible that the hagiographical influence on the *SynChron* is linked to specific interests of its author. His interest in theology and ecclesiastical matters would lead him to a more extensive use and presentation of such material, especially when his usual sources do not convey a corresponding attitude: John Malalas, for example, whose lack of interest in theology can be seen in his short presentation of the First Ecumenical Council,[68] in contrast to the extensive account of the event in the *SynChron*. Theophanes' account, on the other hand, is immersed in the Arian debate and its reflection on the dispute about iconoclasm[69] and, as a result, approaches the reign of Constantine mainly through this prism. At the time of the composition of the *SynChron*, though, the iconoclasm debate had long ceased, and Theophanes' account would not have been a suitable source, especially for the presentation of Constantine. It is, however, plausible that the strong presence of hagiography in the *SynChron* reflects a contemporary perspective. It has been noted that, after the decline of hagiography during the Comnenian period,[70] there is a revival of interest in saints in the late thirteenth century, and the writing of hagiography begins again to assume its former

---

[68]   Scott, 'The image of Constantine in Malalas and Theophanes', 60.

[69]   Scott, 'The image of Constantine in Malalas and Theophanes', 68–70.

[70]   See P. Magdalino, 'The Byzantine holy man in the twelfth century', in S. Hackel, ed., *The Byzantine Saint* (London, 1981), 52–4.

importance.[71] It is possible that the strong presence of hagiography in the *SynChron* manifests this change in attitude, especially if we are to accept that the unknown author was a member of a circle that would be part of this regeneration of interest in hagiography.[72] We do know that the author was a cleric, with access to a variety of different sources that were used for the composition of the chronicle. His strong interests in matters religious and ecclesiastical are also evident from the special attention shown to them throughout the text. In the case of Constantine and the presentation of his legend, the particular personal interests of the author, in conjunction with the contemporary revival of hagiography, have led to a distinctive approach, through rare hagiographical texts and material, and ultimately to a unique portrait of *the* emperor, as a μέγας καὶ ἅγιος καὶ ἰσαπόστολος, καὶ πρῶτος τῶν χριστιανῶν βασιλέων.

---

[71]   See R. Macrides, 'Saints and sainthood in the early Palaeologan period', in Hackel, ed., *The Byzantine Saint*, 82–3.

[72]   Cf. I. Ševčenko, 'Society and intellectual life in the fourteenth century', in *Actes du XIVe Congrès International des Études byzantines*, I (Bucharest, 1974), 69–76, esp. 76, which provides an overview of intellectual life in the following century, especially with regard to different intellectual clusters and their respective social groups.

SECTION VII
Structure and Themes

14. Procopius' *Persian War*: a thematic and literary analysis

Anthony Kaldellis

Contents, composition and conclusions

Procopius' *Persian War*, comprising the first two books of his narrative of the wars of Justinian, is our main source for the conflicts between Rome and Persia in 502–49 AD. Long in preparation, the work was finished in 551.[1] But in 554 Procopius published a continuation of all three *Wars* (*Persian*, *Vandal* and *Gothic*) in a supplementary Book (8), extending the *Persian War* by narrating the conflict in Lazike in 550–51. Unlike the *Vandal War*, which narrates a single expedition against the Vandals in 533–34 followed by inconclusive wars with the Moors, and the *Gothic War*, which recounts a single long war after 535, the *Persian War* is discontinuous, with each raid provoking a counter-raid, which leads to a truce and possibly a peace, lasting in some cases for years. Unlike in Africa and Italy, the aggressor here was usually the Persian king, who wanted plunder and not conquest. The Romans had the worst of it, as Procopius tells it, but the border remained stable despite being violated often. The *Persian War*, then, recounts the confrontation with King Cabades in 502–506 (1.7–10), and then with Cabades and his heir Chosroes between 527 and 532, when the so-called Eternal Peace was signed (1.12–22).[2] Hostilities resumed again in 540 and lasted until 545, when a five-year truce was agreed; they resumed again in 549 in Lazike (this is covered in Book 2). Therefore, 'the war' in these Books was both chronologically spread out and discontinuous, with more years of calm than active warfare (especially between 506–27, 532–40

---

[1] For dates, see G. Greatrex, 'The dates of Procopius' works', *BMGS* 19 (1994), 101–14. Translations are from H. B. Dewing's Loeb, with modifications. The most recent survey of late antique (or early Byzantine) historiography is by W. Treadgold, *The Early Byzantine Historians* (New York, 2007), esp. 176–226 on Procopius.

[2] For this phase, see G. Greatrex, *Rome and Persia at War, 502–532* (Leeds, 1998).

and 540–49), but all within Procopius' lifetime and in a part of the empire not far from his native Caesarea.

The *Persian Wars*, as mentioned, is our principle source for these events, and it has mostly been used *as* a source by scholars interested in understanding the military history of those years. The text has therefore been treated primarily as a repository of factual knowledge, its testimony compared to that of other sources (when available), its consistency and plausibility scrutinized, and its biases identified and corrected. The challenges posed to modern historians by Procopius' text stem from the conflicting testimony that he offers in the *Secret History* about the same events (this was the work in which Procopius disclosed the dirty secrets of Justinian's regime); from the classicizing format of the *Wars*, which invited comparison with the great works of ancient historiography and imported their rhetorical modes to describe the realities of the sixth century AD; and from what many scholars have assumed were Procopius' biases in favour of Belisarius (Justinian's leading general) and the Roman war effort more generally, the *Persian Wars* being disappointing from this angle because Procopius had no great victories to recount. These were the themes that shaped Averil Cameron's major 1985 study of the author.[3]

In a recent monograph on Procopius, I have argued that these challenges have been posed and addressed in ways that have actually had a limiting effect on how the text has been read.[4] Procopius' engagement with classical literature and thought was far more sophisticated than previously believed (I offer more examples in the present study). Also, when read closely, the *Wars* reveals traces of the hostile attitude of the *Secret History*. Procopius' admiration for Belisarius in the *Wars* has been exaggerated, while it is wrong to consider him a supporter of Justinian's repressive policies. Beyond these particulars, a broad shift has been taking place within the study of ancient and Byzantine historical texts, of which the present volume is indicative. Narrative texts, including histories, are being seen increasingly as creative works of literary representation. Moving beyond the limiting concept of the historian's 'bias', often crudely reduced to social class or political faction, scholars are examining how narratives are structured by literary techniques that subtly encode nuanced reflections on events and personalities as well as by overarching themes that reflect the historian's thoughts on important, large-scale developments.[5] No one has yet attempted to identify the *themes* that preoccupied Procopius when

---

[3]   A. Cameron, *Procopius and the Sixth Century* (London, 1985; repr. 1996), 152–70, focuses on the *Persian War*, offering a summary of its contents with brief commentary on the major episodes (and on some minor ones as well).

[4]   See esp. Kaldellis, *Procopius of Caesarea*.

[5]   The distinction between using historical texts as sources and reading them as literature formed the basis of a paper on 'Byzantine historiography: the literary

he was writing the *Wars* (whereas classicists have discussed the theme of imperial overreach in his model Thucydides). Yet it seems as though Procopius did manage to impose considerable unity of style, coverage and outlook on material that he was collecting and revising for many decades, a substantial achievement.

Yet if it were possible to detect the compositional seams of the work and corresponding changes in Procopius' outlook, especially as the victorious 530s gave way to the disastrous and desultory 540s (to which shift the vicious *Secret History* has often been attributed),[6] then the thematic unity of the work might be compromised. Geoffrey Greatrex has astutely noticed and convincingly argued that the transitional sentence at the beginning of the *Vandal War* refers back not to the end of the *Persian War* as we have it now but to the end of 1.22, the signing of the Eternal Peace. Evidently, Procopius was originally planning to move from the Eternal Peace (532) to Belisarius' conquest of Africa (533–34); later, however, he broke the sequence into two geographical theatres and extended the *Persian War* to 549. The material on John the Cappadocian in 1.25 was also added later. This, Greatrex argues, was originally destined for the *Secret History*, but the prefect's disgrace and the death of Theodora enabled Procopius to put it in the public *Wars*. Procopius may have hoped that a change of regime would allow him to incorporate the material of the *Secret History* into the *Wars*, but Justinian's longevity forced him to settle for two works.[7] I shall argue that this strategic redeployment of material was consistent with the themes that the historian intended to develop in the *Wars* and does not reveal any incoherence in the work.

Other historians have perceived a change in Procopius' attitude towards Belisarius in the *Wars*, from enthusiastic in the coverage of the 530s, to cool and even critical later.[8] This point seems less plausible to me, as a close reading of the earlier passages fails to find the alleged enthusiasm and even turns up considerable criticism, often undisguised. Besides, Procopius

---

dimension', presented at the Twenty-First International Byzantine Congress, London 2006, and is a topic to which I intend to return.

[6]   The change in mood is evoked by T. Honoré, *Tribonian* (Ithaca, NY, 1978), 18–21.

[7]   G. Greatrex, 'The composition of Procopius' *Persian Wars* and John the Cappadocian', *Prudentia* 27 (1995), 1–13. For uniting the works, see G. Greatrex, 'Procopius the outsider?', in D. C. Smythe, ed., *Strangers to Themselves: The Byzantine Outsider* (Burlington, VT, 2000), 215–28, here 216–20. The possibility that the attack on John in 1.24–5 is taken from the secret work is strengthened by its Aristophanic language (1.24.12 = *Knights* 189; 1.25.8 = *Clouds* 225–8), a feature of the *Secret History*: Kaldellis, *Procopius of Caesarea*, 58, 149.

[8]   E.g., Cameron, *Procopius and the Sixth Century*, 8, 15, 52–4, and *passim*. This is a common position.

would have revised his earlier narrative to reflect later views, smoothing it out into a near-seamless whole, which is what I believe we have.

Much depends on whether we regard Procopius as pro- or anti-war. In some publications he is presented as a partisan of the regime and its imperialism, as though the *Secret History* did not exist.[9] That work should give us caution, as should our experience of the Iraq War. Few of those who are now called 'anti-war' really merit the title. Some were opposed to the war even before it began, but most – certainly most Americans – oppose it now because it failed. Had the predicted military 'cakewalk' led to a quiet regime change, none of the illegality or the death and destruction would have disturbed the approving consensus. Procopius *may* have favoured the restoration of imperial rule to North Africa. Little could be said for the Vandals. About Italy it is less certain. But certainly by the early 540s (and possibly earlier) he deplored the corruption, incompetence, illegality and folly that Justinian was bringing to the imperial endeavour, and set out to describe its extent and effects. Contrary to many publications that state or imply that Procopius was a partisan of the regime's wars, the *Wars* is an anti-war document, perhaps sympathetic to Roman imperial ideals but opposed to what Justinian was doing with (and to) them.

Procopius' anti-war stance is worth exploring further because it affects all attempts to read the text from a literary/thematic standpoint. The fact that each of the *Wars* ends badly has not been noticed or given due weight. In his preface Procopius highlights the endings by saying that his work will benefit others by showing the *outcomes* of events (1.1.2); the beginning – a heavily ironic preface – points directly to the end.[10] The *Vandal War* ends with conspiracy, murder and Pyrrhic victory over the Moors: 'Thus it came to pass that those Libyans who survived, few as they were and poor, at last and after great toil found some peace' (4.28.52). These are the last words of the text. The *Gothic War* ends with the ascendancy of Totila and the plundering of the Balkans by Slavs (7.40). The same is true of the extensions of the *Wars* in the supplementary Book 8. The last sentence of the page devoted to the African war reads, 'by reason of the previous wars and insurrections the land remained largely destitute of habitation' (8.17.22). The continuation of the *Gothic War* ends with a Roman victory,

---

[9] E.g., Cameron, *Procopius and the Sixth Century, passim*; P. Amory, *People and Identity in Ostrogothic Italy, 489–554* (Cambridge, 1997). The idea that Procopius distorted history to provide a *favourable* view of Justinian's wars appears in many publications, e.g. F. R. Trombley and J. W. Watt, *The Chronicle of Pseudo-Joshua the Stylite* (Liverpool, 2000), xxxvi.

[10] For the preface, see Kaldellis, *Procopius of Caesarea*, 17–24; and *idem*, 'Classicism, barbarism, and warfare: Prokopios and the conservative reaction to later Roman military policy', *American Journal of Ancient History* n.s. 3–4 (2004–2005 [2007]), 189–218.

but the final chapter is devoted to the heroism of the Gothic king Teias (8.35). Even the imperial victory is marred: 'for this victory turned out to be for the Roman senate and people a cause of far greater destruction', as the barbarians in Narses' army slaughtered the city's inhabitants (8.34.2).

In the following discussions, I shall attempt to identify some of the main historical themes of the *Wars*, the literary techniques by which Procopius wove them into his factual narrative, and their relation to his overall anti-war stance.

The indictment of Justinian: an overriding and underlying theme

The *Persian War* is a litany of Roman defeats and disasters and basically indicts Justinian's failure to protect his subjects. Procopius even has Belisarius say of the 'Great King', i.e. Justinian, 'he is altogether ignorant of what is happening here and unable to adapt his moves to opportune moments' (2.16.9–10). The fighting ends with a Roman victory, but matters remained inconclusive. After bitter warfare in Lazike, 'the fourth year of the truce between the Romans and Persians came to an end' (2.30.48). Some truce! Procopius has already told us that it was to last five years (2.28.11). This deliberate juxtaposition of truce and battle was probably picked up from Thucydides, who set his only full account of a hoplite battle in Book 5 of his *History*, during the truce.[11]

Beyond the fighting and Procopius' irony about the so-called truce, the two Books of the *Persian Wars* have a parallel set of endings that focus on the career of the execrable prefect John the Cappadocian. Book 1.25 is a character-assassination of the official on whom Justinian most relied; it exposes the devious machinations at the court, implicating Theodora and Antonina, and exposing Justinian's indulgence of his favourite's crimes. The page-long sequel about the former prefect's dismal career, which is then added on to the end of 2.30, closes the circle, linking strategic failure to disarray and wickedness at home at the end of both Books. If these sections were ripped from the *Secret History*, the condemnation of John in the *Wars* was meant to implicate the emperor, because that is the function of such condemnations in the *Secret History*. So, beginning and end are again linked; whereas in the anecdotes that introduce the *Persian War* the Emperor Arcadius is said to have had access to divine inspiration and wise advisors (1.2.6),[12] by the end of Book 1 Justinian emerges as a ruler with wicked and corrupt advisors who are hated by God (1.25.36). This is the first and only reference in Book 1 to God as an agent that is not in a

---

[11] Cf. W. R. Connor, *Thucydides* (Princeton, NJ, 1984), 144.
[12] For the anecdotes, see Kaldellis, *Procopius of Caesarea*, ch. 2.

speech. Yet Justinian, we are told, continued to favour and protect this man (2.30.49), his partner in crime.

The episodes about John are set into the narrative with no regard for chronology or military relevance. But this does not mean that their placement was random or merely 'convenient'.[13] Their positions are deliberate and they perform important ideological work at key moments. This is strengthened by the parallel of Herodotus, who placed in the conclusion of his account of the Persian wars a sordid episode from the Persian court that prominently features a plotting queen and a king who reluctantly abandons his favourite (9.108–13). In Procopius' account, which is linked to that of Herodotus both thematically and by a literary allusion,[14] it is the Roman court that takes the place of the Persian one, in accordance with Procopius' persistent linking of Justinian to the oriental despots of Greek literature.[15] We have seen how he makes Belisarius refer to him as the 'great emperor', which can be rendered as Great King (μέγας βασιλεύς).[16]

By so framing the *Persian War*, we gain a better view of its disposition. It is hardly favourable to Justinian. We should not, however, demean this aspect of the text by calling it a 'bias', a term that can refer to unconscious influences, mere prejudice, or self-interested distortion. We are dealing here with the considered judgement of an intelligent witness, one of the best historians of antiquity and Byzantium. Turning this judgement into a history involved deploying thematic and literary techniques.

We must appreciate the uniqueness of Procopius' position. His is the only surviving history of a ruling emperor (other historians covered events up to the reigning dynasty or ruler, because one could be more objective about the dead);[17] he happened to hate the regime in question; and that regime was one of the most intolerant and deadly in history. Given all

---

[13]   Greatrex, 'The Composition', 3, 9; cf. Cameron, *Procopius and the Sixth Century*, 169: 'less than satisfactory'.

[14]   Cf. Herodotus 9.109.2: τῇ δὲ κακῶς γὰρ ἔδεε πανοικίῃ γενέσθαι, with Procopius 1.25.26: χρῆν γὰρ αὐτῷ γενέσθαι κακῶς. For the story in Herodotus, see D. Lateiner, *The Historical Method of Herodotus* (Toronto, 1989), 46.

[15]   See Kaldellis, *Procopius of Caesarea*, 54–5, 74, 119–28, 141–2. Cf. the aborted parallelism between the adoption of Theodosius II by Isdigerdes (1.2.1–10) and the non-adoption of Chosroes by Justin I (1.11); the execution of Seoses and disgrace of Hypatius after the negotiations (1.11.31–9); and the parallel plots against the kings (1.23–4).

[16]   Cf. Procopius, *Wars*, 4.5.12–17 and 8.30.2 (in the context of enslaving nations); also 5.3.19, 5.8.16, 6.25.22, 7.11.8.

[17]   Agathias, Procopius' continuator, is explicit in his preface. Otherwise, one could discuss recent emperors under the guise of discussing past ones: R. Syme, *Tacitus* (Oxford, 1958).

this, we can understand the paranoia of the *Secret History* and praise the courage required by the seemingly neutral but really critical *Wars*. In the preface, Procopius draws attention to the problem of blaming the living (1.1.4–5), who could only be men and women of power, given the nature of the events.

Procopius certainly does not *praise* Justinian in the *Wars*, as authors in all genres writing about living emperors were expected to do (we will examine a passage where he implies it *might* be possible to do so). The absence of praise by itself was an act of courage. The challenge was to criticize, which could not be done in the *Wars* as easily as in the *Secret History*. Circumstances and the story that Procopius had to tell led him to adopt certain techniques of indirection. Most commonly, and less interestingly from a literary standpoint, Procopius reports facts and consequences in a deadpan way, leaving the reader to infer what kind of ruler Justinian was. For example, what are we to make of the fact that the emperor would not give Candidus, the bishop of Sergioupolis, a small sum to ransom prisoners from the Persians (in 540–41), despite the fact that Candidus had sworn an oath to the king that he would pay and repeatedly begged (ἱκετεύσας) the emperor for the funds? Candidus was tortured by Chosroes later, when he failed to pay (2.5.29–33, 2.20.3–4).[18] Procopius may not comment on Justinian's inaction, but this does not mean that he had no opinion about it.

Similar impressions are conveyed repeatedly concerning the men whom Justinian appointed to govern sensitive regions, particularly Armenia and Lazike. He emerges as susceptible to slander when he allowed Acacius to murder Amazaspes, the governor of Armenia, and take his place. Procopius states that the murder had 'the emperor's consent'. Acacius was wicked, cruel and avaricious, and was killed by his subjects (2.3.1–7). He was replaced by Sittas, who angrily butchered the women and children of potential allies, turning their men into enemies (2.3.18–19). When he too was killed, Justinian sent Bouzes, who proved to be faithless and murderous, driving the Armenians into the hands of the Persians (2.3.28–31). Likewise in Lazike. The Persians were invited into that land by the Lazi, because the Roman governor Peter was insolent and avaricious. Justinian then sent John Tzibus, 'the most accomplished villain in the world and most successful in discovering unlawful sources of revenue. This man unsettled and threw into confusion all the relations of the Romans and the Lazi' (2.15.9). This pattern of maladministration and poor appointments continues throughout the *Wars* and in Book 8 (e.g., 8.9.10–12 for Abchazia). In that Book, Procopius can hold back no longer and states that 'the emperor Justinian was accustomed to condone, for the

---

18 For Candidus and his see, see E. K. Fowden, *The Barbarian Plain: Saint Sergius between Rome and Iran* (Berkeley, CA, 1999), 133–4.

most part, the mistakes of his commanders and consequently they were generally found guilty of offenses both in private life and against the state' (8.13.14). Justinian's appointments contributed to the prolongation of the wars, and hence of the *Wars* too.

How to criticize a ruling emperor: the use of speeches

One of the standard ways for a historian to criticize the powerful or dissent from conventional notions was to put words into the mouth of one of his characters. Sometimes these artful simulations establish complex patterns of textual and metatextual resonance, as the alternation of voice and audience destabilizes frames of references. Consider the lie by which a peasant of the territory of Amida persuaded Glones, the commander of the newly installed Persian garrison, to leave the city and fall into a Roman ambush (1.9.5–19). He claimed that he had been robbed by some Roman soldiers, to whose hideout he wanted to guide Glones. The peasant paints a very convincing picture of illegality, violence and exploitation on the part of the Roman soldiers, and his complaint rings true, considering other evidence of military–civilian relations in the later empire.[19] Moreover, it reflects the incompetence and corruption that Procopius generally ascribes to the Roman army in the *Persian War*. But the speech is a *lie*: the alleged robbery never happened. Procopius has insinuated a true impression of a deep-seated problem through an invented *and* mendacious speech attributed to an anonymous man who never appears again in the narrative. Who is deceiving whom?

The speeches against Justinian, delivered to the Persian king by envoys of the Goths (2.2.4–11), Armenians (2.3.32–53) and Lazi (2.15.14–30), are strongly worded and compelling, and resonate closely with the spirit and even the letter of the *Secret History*.[20] The Goths accuse Justinian of overturning ancient orders and imperialism; the Armenians of creating confusion in settled places, excessive taxation, oppression, imperialism and treachery; and the Lazi of enslavement, tyranny, injustice, usurpation, avarice and robbery. It is significant that there is no counter-speech to these indictments, which are, moreover, supported by Procopius' own narrative. Enemies of Justinian provide the commentary that the historian could not write in his own name. There is only one passage where he attempts to counter them: it is brief and occurs right after the Gothic speech, which

---

[19]   Cf. R. MacMullen, *Soldier and Civilian in the Later Roman Empire* (Cambridge, MA, 1963). For versions of this event, see Greatrex, *Rome and Persia at War*, 98–9. For soldiers oppressing the cities during the war, see also the *Chronicle of Pseudo-Joshua the Stylite* 86, 92–4 (Trombley and Watt, 103–5, 111–13).

[20]   Cf. Kaldellis, *Procopius of Caesarea*, 49–50.

focuses on Justinian's imperialism (by contrast, the Armenian and Lazic speeches, which come *after* the Gothic speech, are not countered in any way). This proffered defence of Justinian is so weak that it must be *pro forma*; Procopius evidently had to keep up appearances (this was a concern also when it came to religion, as we will see).

What Procopius says in the emperor's defence is that the Goths 'were bringing as charges against Justinian things that would naturally be praise (encomia) for a worthy monarch, namely that he was struggling to make his realm larger and more splendid. For these accusations one might make also against Cyrus, king of the Persians, and Alexander, the Macedonian' (2.2.12–15). So what Procopius offers is not a defence but only a rhetorical *redescription* of the charge, moreover a redescription that is twice made in a potential sense through the optative + ἄν (these things *might* constitute praise); he does not *actually* praise Justinian. If one were so inclined, he says, one might praise Justinian (i.e., 'but I will not'). The defence is not only conditional but is inappropriate as Justinian did not bravely lead his armies as had Cyrus and Alexander; he hardly ever left the palace.[21] It is, moreover, fatally weak, because what Procopius implies is that the Goths' accusations may be countered only if one switches to another genre, that of the *encomium*, which, as both he and other historians knew, did not make truth its chief concern.[22]

It is also interesting to consider the figures with whom Procopius compares Justinian (hypothetically). The first is a Persian, reinforcing a recurring theme of the text that we have touched upon already. As for Alexander, though he could be a proper model of panegyrical comparison, he was also an ambivalent moral figure. Interesting in this connection was his transformation into a Persian monarch, noted in all the ancient accounts. There was also precisely his lust for world conquest. 'He was always insatiate in winning possessions', wrote Arrian. The theme of conquering 'other' worlds is relevant here. When he heard that Democritus had postulated multiple worlds, he was upset because he had conquered only one. On another occasion, he cried when the court sophist Anaxarchus read out a long list of lands because he realized there were many he had not yet conquered. In sum, as Juvenal put it, one world was not enough for him.[23] This material is relevant not only because he is mentioned as a

---

[21] For the comparison of Justinian to Achilles in the *Buildings*, see K. Gantar, 'Kaiser Iustinian "jenem Herbststern gleich". Bemerkung zu Prokops Aed. I 2, 10', *Museum Helveticum* 19 (1962), 194–6.

[22] Procopius, *Wars* 1.1.4; cf. the introduction of the *Buildings*. I discuss the tension between rhetoric and historiography in other publications.

[23] Arrian, *Anabasis of Alexander* 7.19.6; Aelian, *Various History* 4.29; Plutarch, *On Tranquility of Mind* 4 (= *Moralia* 466d); Juvenal, *Satires* 10.168–173; cf. Plutarch, *Alexander* 71.2 for world conquest. The negative tradition regarding Alexander is

possible model by Procopius but because it resonates in the indictment of Justinian by the Armenians, which follows Procopius' 'defence' of the emperor: 'The whole earth is not enough for the man; it is too small a thing for him to conquer all the world together. But he is even looking about the heavens and is searching the retreats beyond the Ocean, wishing to gain for himself some other world' (2.3.42–3; cf. also Proverbs 17:24). τὸν αἰθέρα περισκοπεῖ links up with the *Secret History's* περισκοπῶν τὰ μετέωρα (18.29), which leads back to Aristophanes, *Clouds* 225–8, one of Procopius' favorites. He would later vary it for Chosroes: μετεωρισθεὶς τὴν διάνοιαν ἐπὶ μακροτέρας ἐλπίδος ὠχεῖτο (*Wars* 8.7.11).

Who violated the Eternal Peace?

There are themes in the *Persian War* that go beyond Justinian and his policies. But before we discuss them, let us consider another issue of concern to Procopius, the responsibility for violating the Eternal Peace in 540, because it too illustrates the rhetorical techniques that Procopius used to expound some of his basic themes, and the fashioning of subtle impressions certainly falls under the category of literary devices. We are dealing here with what in the study of esoteric writing has been called the 'first impressions' that are modified by 'second impressions'. The first mislead us into a (false) sense of security, while the second considerably complicate matters.[24]

Chosroes' invasion of 540 AD was one of the worst the empire ever experienced, for it led to the plundering of many cities and the destruction of Antioch. There is no question that the Persian king was primarily responsible for this violation of the Peace. The beginning of Book 2 makes this clear.[25] Chosroes was looking for pretexts to invade, because he knew that the eastern provinces would be defenceless due to the wars in the west. Procopius had no intention of portraying him favourably, so there is no question about his sincerity here. As we read, however, a question begins to form about whether Chosroes was *exclusively* responsible. Chosroes claimed to have evidence that Justinian had attempted, during the peace, to subvert Persian allies to the Roman cause and encouraged the Huns to

---

documented in K. Simopoulos, Ὁ μύθος τῶν «Μεγάλων» τῆς ἱστορίας (Athens, 1995), ch. 1.

[24] Cf. L. Strauss, *Persecution and the Art of Writing* (Chicago, IL, 1952), and *idem*, *Thoughts on Machiavelli* (Chicago, IL, 1958).

[25] For the Thucydidean opening of Book 2, see C. F. Pazdernik, 'A dangerous liberty and a servitude free from care: political 'Eleutheria' and 'Douleia' in Procopius of Caesarea and Thucydides of Athens' (dissertation, Princeton University, 1997), 22–3.

attack Persia. We would not have to make much of these allegations were it not for Procopius' admission, placed significantly at the end of his account as a conclusion, that he himself did not know whether these charges were true or not (2.1.12–15). When a Roman historian attached to a leading general at the court declares this in a public work, we must suspect that there was reason to think that the charges *were* true, that he is not telling us all. Moreover, his profession of ignorance serves the rhetorical purpose of establishing the charges as *meaningful* because *possible*, that is, it mattered whether they were true or not.

Having sown doubt, Procopius waters its seeds. The subversion of Persian allies and incitement of the Huns are mentioned as hard facts by the Armenian envoys to Chosroes (2.3.47). Granted, they are hostile, even if Procopius' own narrative demonstrates that they had legitimate grievances. And their testimony is not the end of it. In a delicious twist, Procopius has Justinian himself basically admit to Chosroes in a letter that he did write letters to the Persian allies and the Huns (2.4.20). He is represented as making feeble excuses, saying that his intentions have been misinterpreted (ἑρμηνεύειν ἐσπούδακας, οὐχ ἧπερ ἡμεῖς διανοηθέντες γεγράφαμεν). He does not, however, clarify those intentions. Procopius' initial disclaimer (that he did not know whether the charges were true) is now superseded by a serious if not quite altogether damning confession, which the historian, for reasons of both safety and irony, attributes to the emperor himself. The question of responsibility is now unclear. In later formulations, Procopius carefully claims that Chosroes was 'most responsible', not *solely* responsible (2.9.10–11; the syntax here repays close study). Chosroes continues to insist that Justinian was responsible, listing the charges 'some of which', Procopius notes in his own voice, 'were serious, while others idle and fabricated' (2.10.16). The 'first impression' of 2.1.1 has been set aside. Justinian too was guilty.

This small and subtle matter alone proves that Procopius was not a court historian and that the *Wars* was not a work of propaganda for Justinian; quite the contrary.[26] Procopius certainly did not want to insinuate that Justinian was the guiltiest party in the destruction of the east; such a position would diminish his credibility. What he is implying is that Justinian's careless meddling, plotting and faithlessness gave the enemy of Rome the opportunity to attack at a moment when the east was undefended because of the emperor's imprudent wars in the west. Both Justinian's behaviour and Chosroes' greed and aggression contributed to the erosion of the trust required for the fragile peace. The theme of trust in the *Wars*, and how it is undermined, also deserves further study.[27]

---

[26]   Cf. J. Haury, *Zur Beurteilung des Geschichtschreibers Procopius von Cäsarea* (Munich, 1896), 35–6.

[27]   See Kaldellis, *Procopius of Caesarea*, 66–7, and cf. *Wars* 1.5.10–11, 2.10.10.

Religious war in the sixth century

We have examined some of the literary aspects of Procopius' representation of Justinian in the *Wars*, techniques by which the historian constructs and maintains deeper themes. It was a feat of subtlety to write the *Wars* – a seemingly neutral narrative – so that it cohered with the bitter denunciations of the *Secret History*. But the emperor's policies (and their failures) constitute only one of the work's themes. Procopius has infused the *Persian War* with narrative themes that do not have to do primarily with Justinian, or that transcend the narrow objectives of the emperor's policies. Specifically, he has contrived to make the Persian war take on the character of a religious struggle, which makes him the first ancient historian to make religious war one of his themes. Herodotus touches on it, while in Josephus' *Jewish War* only the religion of one side is of importance.

The existence or not of Holy War in Byzantium has been debated often.[28] Without entering the broad theoretical (and comparative) questions here, we may note at least that in the sixth century a zealously Christian Roman empire fought against a zealously Zoroastrian Persian empire, both of which were ruled by strong-willed theocrats, that is, kings who ruled in the name of their respective Gods, perceived their faiths as antagonistic, and felt that they had the right and duty to impose true worship on others. The time was ripe, if not for a theory of Holy War then at least for a thematic-historical representation of it. Ammianus could have offered this in the fourth century, but he does not, partly because the religious question within the empire of his time was unsettled and partly because the campaign against Persia that he recounts in detail was led by a non-Christian emperor.

As for Procopius, it has until recently been asserted that, in his effort to write a classicizing history, he omitted religion as too unclassical, distorting the events and 'flavour' of his times. I have argued elsewhere against this position, regarding both the alleged omission and distortion.[29] Procopius *was* interested in religious questions, though we should be very cautious in drawing conclusions about his own belief from the way he introduces and handles them. I shall argue that he drew attention to the religious dimension of warfare in the sixth century, a theme that has been missed by historians who assert that 'the Persian wars under Justinian seem not

---

[28]   The latest discussion is P. Stephenson, 'Imperial Christianity and Sacred War in Byzantium', in J.K. Wellman, ed., *Belief and Bloodshed: Religion and Violence across Time and Tradition* (Lanham, MD, 2007), 83–95.

[29]   Kaldellis, *Procopius of Caesarea*, 38–45; for his readiness to scrutinize religion, see, e.g., 138–41.

to have acquired a dimension of religious warfare'.[30] Moreover, he was one of the first to draw attention to this theme from a critical, even non-partisan point of view. His synopsis of Persian religion, for instance, is entirely neutral (2.24.1–2), unlike that of Agathias (or of any Christian writer).[31] What is fascinating in that synopsis is that he relates Zoroastrian 'fire-worship' to the ancient Roman worship of Hestia. In their religion, then, modern Persians are related to ancient Romans, which partly casts the struggle between Christian Rome and Zoroastrian Persia as an implied struggle between Christian and pagan Rome.

The potential for religious war was always present in the confrontation between Christian Rome and Iran. In the letters exchanged between commanders before the battle of Daras (530 AD), each invokes divine aid, the Romans 'God' and the Persians 'our gods' (1.14.9–11). It is possibly an aspect of Procopius' classicism at this stage in his narrative that the Romans invoke God based on considerations of justice and not on sectarian divisions (God is with us because we are just, not because we are opposing infidels). According to Belisarius before the battle of Callinicus in 531 AD (1.18.21), God's favour is swayed by pragmatic factors (not justice *or* faith here). Justinian later invokes God and Chosroes 'the gods' (cf. 2.4.17–25 with 2.7.22). When Chosroes occasionally invokes God (2.9.1–3), that would not necessarily make him a monotheist for Procopius' readers, as in Greek the singular can refer to the plural (cf. 'man' in English).[32]

The theme of religious confrontation becomes stronger in the second part of the work, which deals with the great invasion of Chosroes in 540 AD and the years of warfare following it. It is possible that, continuing his history in the late 540s, Procopius perceived something new in the relations between the empires and elaborated what had been only potential so far. Cabades, for instance, had tried to convert the Lazi to Zoroastrianism (1.12), provoking a Roman response. But in Book 2 these confrontations become more direct and pointed. In the next section I shall discuss the recurring episode of Christian bishops submitting to Chosroes and begging for mercy. Here I want to look at incidents of religious violence that frame those pathetic encounters, and at their implications. Basically, in the thematic economy of Procopius' history they highlight aspects of

---

[30] A. Kolia-Dermitzaki, Ὁ βυζαντινός «ἱερός πόλεμος»: Ἡ ἔννοια καί ἡ προβολή τοῦ θρησκευτικοῦ πολέμου στό Βυζάντιο (Athens, 1991), 154, who admits *Wars* 2.12 and 2.26 as exceptional, and discovers traces of religious warfare between Rome and Persia before and after the sixth century; cf. J. Haldon, *Warfare, State, and Society in the Byzantine World, 565–1204* (London, 1999), 18–19.

[31] But cf. *Wars* 2.28.25–6, for a curious description of Persian customs. For Agathias, see A. Kaldellis, 'The historical and religious views of Agathias: a reinterpretation', *Byz* 69 (1999), 206–52, here 247.

[32] For this passage and the theme of *tyche*, see Kaldellis, *Procopius*, 209.

Persian strength and Roman weakness in a way that reaches beyond the military sphere.

When Chosroes captured Antioch,[33] he proceeded straight to the church, where he 'found stores of gold and silver so great that, though he took no other part of the booty, he departed with enormous wealth'. He then had the entire city burned. The Roman ambassadors begged him (ἐδέοντο) to spare the church, and he yielded (2.9.14–18). In the next chapter, which is devoted to the *absence* of God's providence for Antioch, Procopius wryly notes that 'the entire city was destroyed except for the church, on account of the labour and foresight (πρόνοια) of the Persians assigned to this task' (2.10.6). This is the first instance of *pronoia* in the *Wars*, and it concerns the foresight of infidels in preserving a church while destroying the rest of the great city. Procopius may be responding here to claims that God preserved that church, because in the very next sentence he emphasizes that it was due to *human* providence: ἐκ προνοίας ἀνθρώπων τινός (2.10.7).

Chosroes moved on to Seleucia, where he swam in the sea, sacrificed to the sun, and called upon his gods (2.11.1). He then went to Daphne, the suburb of Antioch, where he sacrificed to the Nymphs (2.11.6). He also burned down the local church of the archangel Michael, in retaliation for the murder of one of his nobles, who was killed at a nearby church of the archangel by a local young man. The story is curious (2.11.6–13). This noble, mounted and armed, tried to ride down the young man, who was named Aeimachos ('He who Fights Always'). Aeimachos hit him on the head with a rock, then took his sword (presumably the Persian's: ἀκινάκης) and killed him; he stripped him of gold and arms, and escaped on the horse either by good luck or because he knew the terrain. This episode clearly alludes to David and Goliath (David also killed Goliath with Goliath's sword: 1 Samuel 17:51). I suspect that it was, if not largely invented, considerably embellished by Procopius; the lad's name is certainly invented (like Thucydides' speakers Sthenelaïdas, Diodotos and Euphemos). It is a minor symbolic Roman victory set in the midst of massive defeat. At Daphne, an Always-Fighting lad who reminds us of an Old Testament hero prevails while a Christian church burns. Antioch was left defenceless by the Roman army and destroyed except for a church, which the Always-Begging Romans begged for. There is a lesson here for victory and the relative worth of religious/ethical values. The tension is as much between Persia and Rome as it is within Rome. Viewed this way, the episode reinforces Procopius' admiration for common people who

---

[33]   For the city's destruction, see G. Downey, *A History of Antioch in Syria from Seleucus to the Arab Conquest* (Princeton, NJ, 1961), 533–46; H. Kennedy and J. H. W. G. Liebeschuetz, 'Antioch and the villages of Northern Syria in the fifth and sixth centuries A.D.: trends and problems', *Nottingham Medieval Studies* 32 (1988), 65–90, here 65–6.

defended themselves valiantly, when the institutions of Justinian's state failed them, rather than beg capricious tyrants for mercy (cf. the Edessenes in 2.26–7, who are the account's heroes despite the presence of some soldiers). The episode acquires additional symbolic significance when we remember that Justinian required magistrates to swear by God, the Virgin, the Gospels, and the archangels Michael and Gabriel upon taking office; the emperor himself was so devoted to the angels that in 563 AD he travelled to their shrine in Galatia. Thus the burning of a church, made possible by the complete failure of military policy, strikes symbolically at the heart of the regime's ideology.[34]

The theme of religious war peaks with Chosroes' two attempts to capture Edessa with the intention of striking a blow less against Justinian as against the Christian God himself (2.12.6–7, 2.26.2–4). He was incited by an alleged prophecy by Jesus that the city would never be taken (see below). As we saw, Persians and Romans, Christians and Zoroastrians, are groups that can also stand for broader ideological formations and polarities such as the pagan past and Christian present of Rome itself and the comparative strength and weakness that they display in responding to the Persian offensive.[35]

The conflict between Rome and Persia was not, for Procopius, essentially a religious war but acquired a religious dimension in 540. Religious differences were highlighted and soon became matters of policy, ideology and propaganda. Chosroes waived the tribute brought by the people of Harran 'because they adhered to the ancient religion' (2.13.7), another link between Roman paganism and Zoroastrianism.[36] Conversely, Belisarius freed the Christians of the Persian city of Sisauranon when he captured it (2.19.24–5). But the balance in the mid-sixth century, as any reader of the *Persian War* sees, tilted in favour of the 'ancient religion'. Procopius, then, was not averse to religion as a topic. But he enmeshed it in a set of polarities that expand the strange linkage in the *Persian War* between Rome and Persia.

Bishops and despots

When it came to matters of defence, Procopius firmly believed in the efficacy of arms. He rejected, for instance, the policy of paying barbarians

---

[34]   Oath: *Novel* 8 (this was pointed out to me at the Birmingham Symposium by Brian Croke); Pilgrimage: John Malalas, *Chronicle*, 18.148. Cf. Michael's churches built by Justinian: Procopius, *Buildings* 1.3.14–18, 1.8.2–19 (two), 1.9.14, 5.3.20.

[35]   We shall touch on this below from a different angle.

[36]   For Harran, see J.B. Segal, 'Mesopotamian communities from Julian to the rise of Islam', *Proceedings of the British Academy* 41 (1955), 109–39, here 124–6.

to refrain from invading Roman territory, which Justinian preferred, because it did not deter aggression and only whetted their appetite. 'With all the barbarians there is no means of compelling them to keep faith with the Romans except through the fear of soldiers to hold them in check' (1.19.33).[37] This indicts Justinian's policy in the east, which left prosperous provinces open to a warlike, treacherous, cruel and avaricious king – all so that the emperor could pursue dreams of conquest elsewhere.

The most striking image of Roman defencelessness in the east is that of bishops begging for mercy from Chosroes.[38] It is an image we confront too often in the *Persian War*, and it is not cast in neutral language. The bishops and the religious values encoded in the vocabulary that Procopius uses contrast with the valour of Aeimachos and the Edessenes (in the siege of 544), those self-helpers and 'always-fighters'. Let us, then, return to the invasion of 540. The first town that Chosroes took was Sura. After losing their commander to a chance arrow, its people became 'suppliants (ἱκέται)' of Chosroes (2.5.12). They sent their bishop, who brought fowl, wine and 'pure (καθαροὶ)' loaves of bread as offerings to the king (these symbolized perhaps the three parts of the Greek meal,[39] but also the Christian sacraments; cf. the Athenian and Spartan response in Herodotus to the king's demand for earth and water). The bishop fell to the ground and 'tearfully supplicated (ἱκέτευε) the king to spare such pitiable (οἰκτροὶ) people', who would give him ransom (λύτρα). Chosroes dissembled his anger and pretended to accept the 'entreaty (δέησις)', but was planning to make himself 'terrible (φοβερός)' to the Romans by the 'punishment (κόλασις)' of Sura. He sent the bishop back with some Persian nobles, who were 'to encourage him and cheer him with fair hopes (παρηγοροῦντας καί τισιν ἀγαθαῖς ἐπαίροντας ἐλπίσιν)'. When they reached the gates, they were to block the doors 'with a stone or piece of wood (ξύλον)'. This is mentioned again later when the deed was done (2.5.12–27). Note that ξύλον was a technical word for the Cross upon which Jesus suffered his 'punishment (κόλασις)', as Procopius relates only a few chapters later (2.11.14).

That the terms used to describe this encounter are central to the Christian liturgy and devotion requires no proof. Procopius has transposed this language to a different context, but he thereby makes the two contexts seem less different by suggesting affinities between them. After all, bishops

---

[37]   Cf. *Wars* 7.13–14, 7.33–4, 8.5.16–17, and *passim*.

[38]   For bishops pleading for their cities in general, see N. G. Garsoïan, 'Le rôle de l'hiérarchie chrétienne dans les rapports diplomatiques entre Byzance et les Sassanides', *Revue des études arméniennes* 10 (1973–74), 119–38, here 121–2.

[39]   Wine, bread and *opson*: J. Davidson, *Courtesans and Fishcakes: The Consuming Passions of Classical Athens* (New York, 1998), ch. 1.

were involved in both. Procopius makes unflattering comparisons with religious implications.

Learning the fate of Sura, the leading citizens of Antioch decided to bribe the king to spare their city. They sent Megas, the bishop of Beroia, to 'entreat (δεησόμενος)' him. Megas 'beseeched (ἐλιπάρει)' Chosroes to 'pity (οἰκτεῖραι)' those who had not 'sinned (ἥμαρτον)' against him. He later 'begged (ἱκετεύων)' Chosroes to quit Roman territory (2.6.17–25). When the king attacked Megas' city instead, desiring to impose 'punishment (κόλασις)'on it for resisting, Megas echoed the words of Sura's bishop by reminding him that he was attacking 'pitiful' folk 'lacking in honour'. Beroia should not be punished for defending itself, but rather 'pitied (ἐλεεῖσθαι)' (2.7.22–9). When Megas discovered that the defenders had no water, he returned 'in tears' and, 'lying prone on the ground', denied that the city had any money; he 'begged' Chosroes to spare its inhabitants. Chosroes was moved and granted the bishop's 'entreaty (δέησις)' (2.7.34–5).

We need not consider here every instance where Procopius reinscribes liturgical and devotional Christian language in the humiliating context of the bishops' submission to an oriental despot. A retrospective episode added into the account of the warfare and negotiations of late 540 (2.13.8–15) indicates that this theme occurred to Procopius in the 540s, after witnessing the wars of those years. This flashback concerns Cabades' plundering of the region around Amida in 503, and specifically his extortion of money from Constantina. The bishop was Baradotus, a man so pious that anything he asked of God came to pass. He approached Cabades bearing wine, figs, honey and 'pure' loaves, and 'entreated (ἐδεῖτο)' him not to harm the town, which was pitiful and had no army, only 'worthless (οἰκτροὶ)' inhabitants. This scene projects the recurring pattern of the 540s – demilitarized towns that could only beg for mercy in Christian terms – back on to the earlier war.[40] The result of Baradotus' entreaty was astonishing: Cabades spared the town (χαριεῖσθαι) and, moreover, supplied it with food from his own provisions, which modern historians have dismissed as an absurd statement. But I think Procopius is trying to make a point, namely to link Baradotus' ability to obtain whatever he wished from God to his ability to obtain favours from Cabades, a link with disturbing implications. Moreover, the bishop's *deesis* is not only about the state of Roman defences but about prevailing states of mind.[41] It is no accident that Procopius places his strongest statement on the cruel capriciousness of the 'God' who

---

[40]   For a different account, see Trombley and Watt, *The Chronicle of Pseudo-Joshua the Stylite*, 74, n. 352. Note, for instance, how differently the encounter in *Wars* 1.7.30–32 is presented.

[41]   Cf. Demetrios, *On Style*, 222; trans. D. C. Innes (based on W. Rhys Roberts), Loeb Classical Library 199 (Cambridge, MA, 1995), 480–81.

allowed Antioch to be destroyed by Chosroes (2.10) immediately after his most direct statement regarding Chosroes' (similar?) character (2.9).[42]

This inevitably brings us back to Justinian, for he, in addition to the God of the Christians and kings of the Persians, was the recipient of entreaties, whose humiliating ceremonial aspect is depicted negatively in the *Secret History*, as an aspect of tyranny. Again, the *Wars* and *Secret History* cohere thematically. For example, in the works of Procopius the most prominent recipients of *proskynesis* are Justinian and Theodora, the Persian kings, and the piece of the Cross in the church at Apameia.[43] Besides, 'liturgical petition shares elements common to the prescriptions for court ceremonial ... The language of petition is the language of prayer and the word *déêsis* (δέησις) is central to it'.[44] If other Byzantines could perceive or postulate a parallel between the heavenly and the imperial courts for the purposes of edification, then Procopius could also do so for other purposes.[45] It was easy to see the connection. It is in the *Persian War*, for example, that we meet the *referendarius* Theodore, who conveyed to the emperor his subjects' pleas: τῷ βασιλεῖ τὰς τῶν ἱκετῶν δεήσεις ἀγγέλων (2.23.6). That last participle yields a curious sense if read as a noun. *Deesis* in the *Persian War* is a troubling act, and the verbal linkage of its different planes is indicative of Procopius' view of the official religion.

---

[42]   Cf. Kaldellis, *Procopius of Caesarea*, 204–9.

[43]   For the latter, see *Wars* 2.11.15–16; for *proskynesis* and Justinianic tyranny, Kaldellis, *Procopius of Caesarea*, 128–42.

[44]   R. Macrides, 'The ritual of petition', in D. Yatromanolakis and P. Roilos, eds., *Greek Ritual Poetics* (Washington, DC, 2004), 356–70, here 357; also D. G. Letsios, Ἡ «Ἔκθεσις κεφαλαίων παραινετικῶν» του διακόνου Αγαπητού: Μια σύνοψη της ιδεολογίας της εποχής του Ιουστινιανού για το αυτοκρατορικό αξίωμα', *Δωδώνη* 14 (1985), 175–210, here 188 for the emperor's δεόμενοι; and M. McCormick, *Eternal Victory: triumphal rulership in Late Antiquity, Byzantium and the early medieval West* (Cambridge and Paris, 1986), 127–8 for ἱκέτης.

[45]   See, e.g., H. Maguire, 'The Heavenly Court', in *idem*, ed., *Byzantine Court Culture*, 247–58; H. Hunger, *Schreiben und Lesen in Byzanz: Die byzantinische Buchkultur* (Munich, 1989), 14–15; K. M. Ringrose, *The Prefect Servant: eunuchs and the social construction of gender in Byzantium* (Chicago, IL, and London, 2003), 143, 152; C. Kelly, *Ruling the Later Roman Empire* (Cambridge, MA, 2004), 232–45. For blurring imperial and divine attributes, see J. Moorhead, *The Roman Empire Divided, 400–700* (Harlow, 2001), 178 for the early seventh century; and S. Vryonis, 'Byzantine imperial authority: theory and practice in the eleventh century', in G. Makdisi *et al.*, *La notion d'autorité au Moyen Age: Islam, Byzance, Occident* (Paris, 1982), 141–61, for the eleventh.

Procopius and the Christian miracles at Apameia and Edessa

Let us turn, in conclusion, to two episodes in the *Persian War* that have occupied scholars' attention, especially those interested in Procopius' religion. Taken at face value, they should leave no doubt that he was a believing Christian. As the Persians marched on Apameia, the bishop Thomas showed the piece of the Cross to the people and all witnessed a miracle (θαῦμα) of light emanating from the relic. Chosroes plundered the town regardless, but Procopius notes that 'something divine (τι θεῖον)' or, indeed, 'God (θεὸς)' saved Apameia from total destruction (2.11.14–30).[46] As for Edessa, in explaining that its citizens believed their city to be invincible because of a promise made by Jesus to king Abgar, Procopius digresses to give an account of Jesus' ministry in language that only a believer would use (2.12.6–30).

And yet, despite these apparently strong declarations of belief, scholars have traditionally been reluctant to take Procopius at face value. Not only does he say other things in other places that call his sincerity into question, he lived in an age when all were required by law to profess Christianity in order to hold any official position or even function as legal persons. Towards the beginning of the *Persian War* he has one of his characters make a statement, redundant in its narrative context, about certain 'sophistries of speech that hide through a pretense of solemnity (σεμνότης) and for which the majority need an interpreter (ἑρμηνεύς)' (1.11.17). And Procopius included many passages in his works on how the clever can outwit the powerful, including how one could trick Justinian specifically about religion. So we need not take the passages about Apameia and Edessa at face value, which accords well with what we have seen of Procopius as a writer so far.[47]

Moreover, the events at Apameia and Edessa were already famous in Procopius' time, as evinced by the ecclesiastical history of Evagrius (who was present at Apameia), and Procopius could not omit them without undermining his credentials as a historian among Christian readers and

---

[46]   For the origins of the Cross at Apameia, see P. Athanassiadi, *La lutte pour l'orthodoxie dans le Platonisme tardif de Numénius à Damascius* (Paris, 2006), 64. For the sixth century, see J. C. Balty, 'Apamée au VIᵉ siècle: Témoignages archéologiques de la richesse d'une ville', in C. Abadie-Reynal *et al.*, eds., *Hommes et richesses dans l'empire byzantin* (Paris, 1989), 79–96.

[47]   For the religious question, see Kaldellis, *Procopius of Caesarea*, 56–60, and ch. 5. For a rejoinder, see M. Whitby, 'Religious views of Procopius and Agathias', in D. Brodka and M. Stachura, eds., *Continuity and Change: Studies in Late Antique Historiography* = *Electrum* 13 (2007) 73–93.

even his sincerity as a Christian.[48] We should note that Evagrius' versions are more Christianized than those of Procopius, both in language and even content; in the case of Edessa, he introduces the *mandylion*, a miraculous image of Christ.[49] Evagrius normally followed Procopius for this period, but here seems to have found him lacking in zeal.

More importantly, we must consider Procopius' representation of those events in light of the literary and thematic patterns of the *Persian War*. It is, for example, somewhat misleading to say that 'God saved Apameia' given that it was conquered and thoroughly plundered by Chosroes. The bishop's plea that he not take the box in which they kept the piece of the Cross (2.11.30) reminds us of the Antiochenes' plea that he spare their cathedral, highlighting the fact that both cities were at his mercy. And the 'divine something' that stopped Chosroes from destroying Apameia is too precisely localized in the king's arbitrary will. In his discussion of the fall of Antioch, Procopius had conjoined the arbitrariness of God's will with that of the king's whims; here, the two are brought even closer, the one depending on the other. Besides, while the people of Apameia naturally thanked God that Chosroes did not destroy them, a military historian must have had higher standards for success. It should never have come to that in the first place. There is historical irony in the declaration that God saved Apameia.[50]

That irony is perhaps rarefied, and requires that we consider the Apameia episode in the context of the *Persian War* as a whole. That is not so in the case of Edessa, where the irony is thick; in this case, it is extremely difficult to accept that Procopius believed his own theological acrobatics. He notes that Jesus' promise that Edessa would never be captured is not mentioned by those who wrote the history of that time, possibly referring to Eusebius' *Ecclesiastical History* 1.13. So right from the start he rejects the promise, the foundation of the Edessenes' hope that they (and other cities)

---

[48]   Evagrius, *Ecclesiastical History* 4.26–7 (the miracle at Apameia was commemorated in art). For the fame of Jesus' promise to Agbar, see the *Chronicle of Pseudo-Joshua the Stylite, passim*.

[49]   M. Whitby, 'Greek historical writing after Procopius: variety and vitality', in A. Cameron and L. I. Conrad, eds., *The Byzantine and Early Islamic Near East*, 1: *Problems in the Literary Source Material* (Princeton, NJ, 1992), 25–80, here 56–7. For the *mandylion*, see A. Cameron, 'The history of the Image of Edessa: the telling of a story', *Harvard Ukrainian Studies* 7 (1983), 80–94. For its later history, see Kolia-Dermitzaki, Ὁ βυζαντινός «ἱερός πόλεμος», 281–2.

[50]   K. Adshead, 'Procopius and the Samaritans', in P. Allen and E. Jeffreys, eds., *The Sixth Century: End or Beginning?* (Brisbane, 1996), 35–41, here 37 argues for irony on different grounds.

had inscribed over their gates, as inauthentic.[51] In fact, he adds, the city did subsequently come under Persian power, when one of Abgar's sons surrendered it to them. At this point there is a lacuna in Procopius' text, which is suspicious given the good state of preservation of the remainder. It is possible that what he argued there offended a Byzantine copyist (in this way, passages in the works of Julian and Zosimus were also lost). When the argument resumes, Procopius admits that 'the thought occurred to me that, if Christ did not write this very thing just as I have cited it, still, since men have come to believe in it, He wishes to preserve the city uncaptured for this reason, so that He may never give them any pretext for error' (i.e., scepticism).

This position is so absurd that it must be a joke, or at best an ironic cover of a sceptical exposé. It makes God the captive of human errors, requiring him to back up any fantastic notions that people believe for the sole purpose of not giving cause for scepticism.[52] The absurdity is compounded by the fact that Procopius three times depicts Chosroes as desiring to capture Edessa precisely to disprove God's promise (2.12.6–7, 2.12.31 and 2.26.2). So both God and Chosroes are motivated by an inauthentic text, the first to protect and the second to attack; both are the victims of a human error, from which apparently only the historian is free. In the detailed account of the siege of Edessa in 544 with which the *Persian War* closes (2.26–7), Abgar and Jesus' promise are not mentioned; the true heroes are the townsfolk of Edessa, which accords, as we have seen, with the broader themes of Procopius' history.

---

[51] See the studies cited by Trombley and Watt, *The Chronicle of Pseudo-Joshua the Stylite*, 6, n. 22, and L. M. White, 'Urban development and social change in imperial Ephesos', in H. Koester, ed., *Ephesos, Metropolis of Asia: An Interdisciplinary Approach to its Archaeology, Religion, and Culture* (Cambridge, MA, 2004), 27–79, here 38–40. The bibliography on late antique Edessa is extensive. See now A. Palmer, 'Procopius and Edessa', *Antiquité tardive* 8 (2000), 127–36.

[52] Cf. Bede, *Life of Cuthbert*, 23; trans. J.F. Webb, *The Age of Bede* (Penguin, 1983).

15. La chronique de Malalas entre littérature et philosophie

Paolo Odorico

La *Chronique* de Jean Malalas a connu un succès grandissant ces dernières décennies: considérée pendant longtemps comme le prototype d'une prétendue historiographie monastique, et donc a priori peu fiable, elle avait été méprisée par des générations de chercheurs. La langue très éloignée des modèles classiques, les références fantaisistes, l'anonymat substantiel de l'auteur, le modèle de composition qui échappe aux règles établies, autant d'éléments qui ont contribué à faire mépriser l'ouvrage. Les chercheurs étaient même parvenus à fabriquer une catégorie spéciale où confiner les chroniques universelles, dont Malalas était l'initiateur, celle de 'Mönchschronik': ces chroniques étaient le produit des gens incultes et substantiellement dépourvus de tout sens critique, et leur contenu ne pouvait servir, les cas échéant, qu'à fournir des renseignements historiques; elles ne pouvaient donc être prises en considération que pour des détails qui portaient sur l'histoire contemporaine de l'auteur, mais demeuraient en général peu fiables, étant le fruit de la superstition et du fanatisme. Sauf pour le respect qu'on portait aux chroniques plus récentes, comme celle de Théophane, ces compositions historiques étaient dans leur globalité mal comprises et non étudiées dans leur complexité.

Si la situation a changé, cela est dû aux efforts de plusieurs savants, en premier lieu de H.-G. Beck,[1] lequel, à raison, a refusé l'identification de ces produits littéraires avec les récits dont raffolaient les circuits monastiques, qui auraient été à la fois leurs auteurs et leurs destinataires. Il fallait bien pourtant expliquer la différence entre les constructions savantes de Procope et Agathias et celles des chroniqueurs universels: c'est pourquoi le très classicisant H. Hunger a eu recours aux ressources de la critique moderne en appliquant aux chroniques la définition (et les contenus) de la *Trivialliteratur*.[2] Dès lors, il était évident qu'il fallait reprendre la recherche

---

[1] Beck, '"Mönchschronik"', 88–97.

[2] Hunger, *Literatur*, 1, 257–78 ('Chroniken als Trivialliteratur'). La partie consacrée aux chroniques se trouve pp. 33–60 de la traduction grecque, vol. II

sur des bases nouvelles et sans les a priori dictés par la tradition classique: c'est à cette tâche que s'est attelée une équipe australienne, dans le but de reconsidérer l'œuvre de Malalas, et les efforts de ces chercheurs, qui ont réalisé un travail collectif sur cet auteur,[3] ont donné un nouvel élan aux recherches. Par la suite, une édition critique de la *Chronique* a vu le jour, tandis qu'en France deux colloques sur cet ouvrage ont été organisés par un groupe de chercheurs qui ont essayé de revenir sur le sujet.[4] Pour ma part, j'avais écrit un article[5] sur la conception du monde et de l'histoire de Malalas, article qui fut publié (avec retard) en 1995. Si je reviens aujourd'hui sur ce sujet, c'est parce que je crois qu'il me faut expliquer mieux mes propos de l'époque, et essayer d'insister sur la dimension philosophique de la *Chronique*.

Je ferai d'abord une considération générale, sans pourtant essayer de la justifier. Je crois fermement que la véritable historiographie byzantine se trouve justement dans les chroniques, car ce sont elles qui expriment une conception globale de l'histoire, en l'insérant dans un système philosophique qui prend en compte l'homme et son insertion dans l'espace et le temps, tandis que des historiens savants comme Psellos ou Anne Comnène devraient être plutôt rangés dans une catégorie différente, plus proche de celle des journalistes de grande envergure d'aujourd'hui. Cette question, comme aussi le rapport entre historiographie et littérature, a fait l'objet d'un colloque organisé par moi-même et par P. Agapitos et M. Hinterberger en 2004, dont les Actes viennent d'être publiés, colloque qui est étroitement en rapport avec le thème choisi cette année dans le Symposium anglais.

Pour revenir à Malalas, il faudrait bien expliquer la structure de son ouvrage et comprendre si sa signification va ou non au-delà d'un simple recueil de notices mal digérées, si l'enregistrement des événements ne suit qu'une logique héritée de la tradition *annalistique*, et de toute manière il faudrait comprendre cette sorte de frénésie d'exposition qui mélange avec la plus grande désinvolture noms de dieux et histoire biblique. Pour ce faire, je commencerai en faisant référence à une certaine forme de poésie

---

(Athènes, 1992), plus complète en ce qui concerne la bibliographie.

[3]   *Studies in John Malalas*, éd. E. Jeffreys, *et al.*; voir aussi *The Chronicle of John Malalas*, traduit par E. Jeffreys, *et al.*

[4]   *Recherches sur la Chronique de Jean Malalas*, vol. I, Actes du colloque organisé à Aix-en-Provence en mars 2003, éd. J. Beaucamp et al. (Paris 2004) (Centre de recherche d'histoire et civilisation de Byzance, Monographies 15); vol. II, éd. S. Agusta-Boularot, J. Beaucamp, A.-M. Bernardi, E. Caire (Paris, 2006) (Centre de recherche d'histoire et civilisation de Byzance, Monographies 24).

[5]   P. Odorico, 'L'uomo nuovo di Cosma Indicopleuste e di Giovanni Malalas', *BSl* 56 (1995), 305–15 (= *Stephanos, Studia byzantina ac Slavica Vladimiro Vavrinek dedicata*).

contemporaine, liée aux chanteurs qui ont tant de succès dans notre société. Le public très raffiné composé de gens instruits, formés à la tradition littéraire de par leurs études savantes, tombera probablement d'accord sur le fait que, parmi les poètes d'aujourd'hui, pourraient éventuellement être rangés Simon and Garfunkel, capables de provoquer en nous des frissons de jouissance lorsqu'ils exécutent 'Like a bridge over troubled water'; mais ces mêmes gens instruits jugeront la plupart des compositions d'autres auteurs assez banales, voire dépourvues de toute qualité artistique. Je voudrais présenter maintenant un chanteur italien peut-être moins connu à l'étranger, qui pourtant est extrêmement cultivé et fort intéressant du point de vue musical, Franco Battiato. Une de ses compositions présente le texte suivant:

> l'ira funesta dei profughi afgani
> che dai confini si spostarono nell'Iran
> Cantami o diva, dei pellirossa americani,
> le gesta erotiche di squaw Pelle-di-Luna
> le penne stilografiche con l'inchiostro blu,
> la barba col rasoio elettrico non la faccio più.

Ces lecteurs cultivés, auxquels je faisais référence, trouveront probablement que ces vers sont le résultat du délire contemporain, tout comme les lecteurs de Procope de Césarée auraient pu peut-être porter le même jugement sur l'étrange exposition historiographique de Malalas. Mais si nous essayons de comprendre ce petit texte, nous nous apercevons très vite que la réalité est plus complexe que celle qui peut apparaître à première vue. Battitato, je crois, fait référence à ce qui est au fondement du langage, de la culture et de la communication contemporaines, à savoir la télévision, avec ses journaux télévisés, ses histoires alléchantes à quatre sous (ce que Hunger définissait comme *Trivialliteratur*), et sa publicité. Il aborde les nouvelles politiques (la chanson date des années de l'invasion russe de l'Afghanistan), en demandant à la Muse de l'inspirer: les mots sont choisis de façon à rappeler au public une traduction de l'Iliade homérique très connue en Italie. Il passe ensuite de l'Orient, où vivent les Hindous (Indiens, en italien), aux Indiens d'Amérique, pour parler de sexe, à savoir des histoires qui intéressent le grand public, et les gestes dont il veut parler sont non héroïques, mais érotiques. S'ensuit l'espace de la publicité: en Italie les stylos à bille de la marque Bic étaient connus par une réclame qui montrait un chef indien avec une coiffe de plumes, où les plumes avaient été remplacées par des stylos rouges et bleus. Mais la même marque de stylos à bille était aussi celle des rasoirs jetables en plastique, d'où l'affirmation finale, qu'il n'utilisera plus le rasoir électrique. En d'autres mots, chaque idée présentée, loin d'être détachée des autres, lui est liée par un lien qui obéit à une structure différente de la logique d'enchaînement fondée sur la cause-effet, ou de la logique fondée sur des similitudes thématiques, mais sur une logique qui est plutôt associative, où des idées sont juxtaposées par effet d'évocations de concepts qui vont bien ensemble. Cet enchaînement se greffe sur un discours commun qui demeure le processus d'évocation possible, car ce discours est partagé et connu par tous: le cas échéant, il s'agit du discours télévisé, qui représente la référence et le point de communication partagés à notre époque entre auteur et destinataire.

La construction de ce texte est faite sur la base de la pensée associative ou, si on préfère, de l'analogie, mais cette analogie est supportée par un discours de référence, un langage sous-jacent sur lequel le raisonnement analogique se greffe et qui représente le véritable point de repère de la construction intellectuelle. Or, dans le cas de l'histoire, le discours analogique a reçu une définition par Claude Lévi-Strauss, en relation avec la pensée primitive, différente de la pensée traditionnelle qui puise dans la logique de la philosophie grecque son enchaînement. Voici la définition donnée par l'éminent anthropologue français:[6]

> It (traditional thought) remains different because its aim is to reach by the shortest possible means a general understanding of the universe – and not only a general but a *total* understanding. That is, it is a way of thinking which must imply that if you don't understand everything, you don't explain anything. This is entirely in contradiction to what scientific thinking does, which is to proceed step by step, trying to give explanations for very limited phenomena, and so on. As Descartes had already said, scientific thinking aimed to divide the difficulty into as many parts as were necessary in order to solve it. So this totalitarian ambition of the savage mind is quite different from the procedures of scientific thinking. Of course, the great difference is that this ambition does not succeed. We are able, through scientific thinking, to achieve mastery over nature … while, of course, myth is unsuccessful in giving man more material power over the environment. However, it gives man, very importantly, the illusion that he can understand the universe and that he *does* understand the universe. It is, of course, only an illusion.

On pourrait ajouter que la pensée analogique est étroitement liée à la pensée magique, et faire référence à la pensée de Carl Gustav Jung, mais de toute manière il s'agit d'un processus démonstratif qui est alternatif par rapport à la pensée grecque de la tradition aristotélicienne, et qui n'a pas besoin d'expliquer les phénomènes par rapport à leur cause directe, mais plutôt par rapport à une cause sous-jacente, à un langage autre, connu et

---

6   C. Lévi-Strauss, *Myth and Meaning* (Toronto, 1978), 17. Texte publié en anglais à la base des conférences données pour la radio canadienne.

partagé par les lecteurs. Mais même en laissant de côté Lévi-Strauss et la pensée primitive, ce que nous retiendrons est qu'une logique associative peut expliquer l'ensemble des phénomènes, sans obliger le discutant à entrer dans des détails ou des querelles philosophiques: cela est d'autant plus possible si cette logique associative est fondée sur un texte qui est le point de repère commun d'une communauté, connu par ceux qui discutent, et, plus important encore, reconnu en tant que texte sacré, ce qui est le cas pendant la période byzantine. Enfin, cette logique ne donne pas l'explication d'une action ponctuelle, mais, pour reprendre la formulation de Lévi-Strauss, donne l'illusion de pouvoir comprendre le tout dans son ensemble.

Revenons-en à Jean Malalas. Si nous observons sa façon de construire le discours historique, nous ne pouvons pas ne pas remarquer que les données sont disposées autrement que ce que nous avons l'habitude de rencontrer dans l'historiographie traditionnelle, même si apparemment une grande différence existe entre la partie consacrée à l'histoire ancienne et celle qui porte sur les événements contemporains à l'auteur. Autant dans la première et plus vaste partie Malalas essaie de fusionner les données pour construire un discours logique, fantaisiste certes, mais conséquent dans sa logique universelle, autant dans la partie qui porte sur les règnes des empereurs plus récents la méthode semble suivre entièrement la tradition des annales classiques, où les données sont rangées selon un critère strictement chronologique, sans lien apparent entre elles.

Mais cette confusion apparente, ce discours qui nous semble peu logique, ce mélange de renseignements hétéroclites et confus peuvent être expliqués: tout comme dans le texte de Battiato que je viens de citer, il y a un langage sous-jacent, qui représente la base commune entre auteur et lecteur, leur point de repère; ce langage est constitué à la fois par une base de données et par un questionnement complexe qui se greffe dessus, créant un lien très étroit, comme le journal télévisé et la publicité de Battiato. Nous devinons facilement que ce langage sous-jacent est constitué au premier chef par la Bible, sur lequel cependant se greffe une question qui a intéressé les philosophes, notamment à Alexandrie, de l'époque de Malalas, le VI siècle, et cette chronique universelle est en rapport immédiat avec ce débat. Au VI siècle, le christianisme, imprégné toujours davantage d'éléments de la pensée néoplatonicienne, continuait d'affronter la question du rôle du Démiurge dans la création du monde, et son intervention dans l'histoire de l'humanité, qu'Il avait voulue et de la volonté duquel découlait la réalité vécue, ce que rejetaient les païens. Des ouvrages du VI siècle portent sur cette question, comme le *De opificio mundi* de Jean Philopon. Fallait-il accepter la doctrine païenne, même transformée et adaptée aux besoins des chrétiens? Ou bien fallait-il se tenir exclusivement à un enseignement de base, sans étudier les discours des philosophes de l'Antiquité? Le débat était certainement ancien, et Basile de Césarée y avait déjà apporté sa contribution. Mais l'idée du refus de toute compromission avec la sagesse païenne était encore forte, surtout dans les provinces orientales, où était plus puissant le mouvement monastique souvent animé par des paysans dépourvus de culture de tradition païenne. Or, l'histoire de l'humanité depuis ses origines constitue exactement le sujet abordé par Jean Malalas,[7] qui essaie de raconter toutes les vicissitudes humaines en partant du récit biblique: c'est la Bible qui fournit non seulement les renseignements de base, mais aussi le cadre de la narration.

Il est intéressant de rappeler que maints ouvrages historiques de l'époque ont les mêmes préoccupations, comme l'histoire des Goths de Jordanès (*Getica* et *Romana*), ou encore la chronique de Victor de Tunnuna, écrits tous deux en latin,[8] dans la Constantinople du VI siècle, ouvrages où l'histoire universelle sert à expliquer le plan de la construction divine du monde, et à justifier les événements contemporains. Il suffit de citer un passage de Jordanès, où l'auteur déclare que le royaume des Romains, selon la prophétie de Daniel, est destiné à durer jusqu'à la fin du monde, et s'inscrit dans la succession des empires de l'Antiquité pour créer le nouveau monde voulu par Dieu.[9] Cosmas Indicopleustès suit le même principe, lorsqu'il soutient que l'Empire byzantin doit rester invincible et victorieux jusqu'à la fin du monde.[10] Il s'agit du même Cosmas qui, contre tout l'enseignement géographique bien installé dans les circuits savants, redessine la structure du monde, de façon à la faire ressembler à l'Arche de l'Alliance biblique. Mais la création toute entière est destinée à être détruite après la Deuxième Parousie, et le plan de la Divine Providence explique et justifie la structure même de l'univers. Ce n'est pas par hasard que Photios au IX siècle définit la *Topographie Chrétienne* comme un commentaire de la Bible.[11]

---

[7] Des renseignements très utiles en ce sens dans l'article de B. Croke, 'Byzantine Chronicle Writing. 1: The early development of Byzantine chronicles', *Studies in John Malalas*, éd. E. Jeffreys, *et al.*, 27–38.

[8] Sur Jordanès le livre de W. Goffart, *The Narrators of Barbarian History* (Princeton, NJ, 1988), 20–111 est toujours utile; voir aussi la traduction française: Jordanès, *Histoire des Goths*, introd., trad. et notes par O. Devillers (Paris, 1995). Sur Victor de Tunnuna on peut voir *Victoris Tonnennensis Episcopi Chronica*, éd. Th. Mommsen, in MGH, AA 11 (Berlin, 1894), et *Vittore da Tunnuna* Chronica. *Chiesa e impero nell'età di Giustiniano*, éd. A. Placanica (Florence, 1997).

[9] *Iordanis Romana et getica*, éd. Th. Mommsen, in MGH, AA 5.1 (Berlin, 1882), 84.27–8 (p.9.27–8).

[10] W. Wolska-Conus, *Cosmas Indicopleustès, Topographie Chrétienne*, 3 t. (Paris, 1968–73) (*Sources chrétiennes*, t. 141, 159 et 197), t. 159, 2.75.3–5: 391.3–4.

[11] Photios, *Bibliotheke*, cod. 36, I, 21.

Certes, comme il a été bien dit et démontré,[12] Malalas se préoccupe aussi de combiner sa construction chronologique avec les calculs millénaristes qui affolaient ses contemporains, mais à mon avis même ces calculs sont en lien étroit avec l'idée que le monde a été crée, comme la Bible le dit, et que l'intervention de Dieu dans la matière est immédiate. Cette considération a comme corollaire une autre conséquence, à savoir que la volonté de Dieu se manifeste tout au long de l'histoire humaine, qui de cette façon est une volonté uniforme, visant un but précis en ce qui concerne l'homme, son salut, qui était aussi le fondement de la construction de la géographie théologique de Cosmas Indicopleustès. En outre, d'un côté, l'histoire conçue de cette manière ne connaît pas (ou plus) de véritables mutations, pas de réelle évolution, et d'un autre côté, tout doit se rapporter d'une façon logique au seul texte qui nous parle de l'histoire ancienne, la Bible.

D'un côté donc, toute diversité dans le devenir du monde est niée, et l'histoire de l'humanité est l'histoire du projet divin, qui ne connaît ni alternatives ni mutations. De l'autre, par le biais d'un processus de rationalisation, tous les mythes anciens sont récupérés et insérés dans ce cadre. Prenons comme exemples les mythes d'Aphrodite et celui de Tirésias. Dans le premier,[13] Malalas réécrit le mythe d'Aphrodite, qui trompe avec Arès son époux Héphaïstos et est châtiée et exposée par lui à la risée des dieux de l'Olympe: dans la *Chronique*, elle devient une dame de la bonne société égyptienne qui commet l'adultère. Le pharaon Hélios, fils d'Héphïstos, apprend des faits et condamne à mort l'homme, en montrant à tous la femme adultère. Le deuxième exemple porte sur le mythe de Tirésias, le devin qui, ayant vu Athéna nue, avait été aveuglé, ou qui avait été transformé en femme, en punition du fait que, ayant vu deux serpents accouplés, il avait tué la femelle; enfin il avait reçu à Delphes le pardon des dieux. Pour Malalas,[14] Tirésias est un 'philosophe' homosexuel qui étudie la grossesse des femmes: c'est pourquoi on lui crève les yeux et on l'enferme, comme s'il s'agissait d'un condamné, dans un monastère.

La structure de la *Chronique* accepte la mythologie ancienne à la condition de l'insérer dans une optique symbolique et allégorique de normalisation, qui éloigne les phantasmes du paganisme, et insère la narration mythique dans un contexte d'allure chrétienne, pour démontrer que l'histoire sans ruptures de l'humanité suit un parcours qui est celui du salut, le parcours du plan divin de la Providence, qui intervient dans l'histoire humaine depuis la création et jusqu'à la fin déjà programmée. Cette opération est

---

[12]   Voir notamment les articles de B. Croke, 'Malalas, the man and his work', 1–25, et de E. Jeffreys, 'Chronological structures in Malalas' Chronicle', 111–66, dans *Studies in John Malalas*, éd. E. Jeffreys, *et al.*

[13]   *Chronographia*, 2.1: 17.9–18.22. Sur le mythe de Tirésias voir l'ouvrage de Luc Brisson, *Le mythe de Tirésias: essai d'analyse structurale* (Leiden, 1976).

[14]   *Chronographia*, 2.14: 29.37–51.

conduite par un rhéteur originaire de la très savante Antioche, qui sait utiliser une langue simple pour créer un imaginaire simple, fondé sur le fond de la cosmologie biblique, qui en constitue la langue sous-jacente, dans laquelle s'insèrent les données de la mythologie grecque rationalisée. En ce sens, toute l'histoire ancienne de l'homme est reconduite à l'espace prévu par la Bible. Les personnages mythiques ont des origines qui, d'une façon ou d'une autre, appartiennent à la géographie du Proche Orient, la même qui figure dans les Ecritures, et tous les personnages se déplacent pour donner naissance aux civilisations occidentales, tel Zeus Picus, assurant ainsi la liaison entre les différentes étapes de l'humanité, dont il rend compacte l'histoire selon le cadre prévu et voulu par la Divine Providence. Une fois construite l'histoire de l'humanité sur la base d'une pensée arrêtée, la pensée judéo-chrétienne, fondée sur la vérité exprimée par la Bible, Malalas peut participer au débat philosophique de son époque avec la démonstration imposée d'une non-évolution de l'histoire, établissant quelles sont les valeurs du peuple chrétien et quelle est sa philosophie de l'histoire. Tout est expliqué sur la base des connaissances globales, qui peuvent tout élucider à travers un jeu de renvoi du particulier au général, et ces connaissances sont fondées sur la Bible, comme la chanson de Battiato est fondée sur le langage télévisé.

Si dans le traitement de l'histoire ancienne cette façon de procéder de Malalas n'est pas sans rappeler les principes de l'analogie, ces mêmes procédés de la pensée associative sont aussi présents dans son exposition de l'histoire contemporaine. Evidemment, si dans le traitement de l'histoire ancienne le discours est assez explicite, dans l'histoire contemporaine le mécanisme est plus délicat, étant donnée la proximité des événements traités et la nécessité pour l'auteur de présenter leur enchaînement par le biais d'un procédé plus subtil, qui met en œuvre la démonstration assumée, celle d'un plan divin qui régit l'histoire de l'homme, à travers des associations entre les événements effectuées sur la base d'un langage subjacent, celui de la Bible. Voyons comment fonctionne cette pensée, en prenant en considération le XVIII livre, qui traite des événements du règne de Justinien. Je porterai d'abord l'analyse sur le traitement des nombreux tremblements de terre,[15] dont nous ne pouvons pas toujours avérer l'historicité.

Malalas cite onze séismes qui ont eu lieu sous Justinien (527–565) dans toute l'aire orientale: les sept premiers se placent pendant la première partie de son règne, caractérisée par la lutte acharnée contre l'Empire persan. Or, dans le texte, qui est constitué par une série de notices juxtaposées l'une à l'autre, sans lien apparent, la notice d'un tremblement de terre est souvent précédée ou suivie immédiatement par un renseignement concernant un accord passé entre le basileus et le roi des Perses, l'ennemi de l'Empire

---

[15]   Voir G. Dagron, 'Quand la terre tremble …', *TM* 8 (1981), 87–103.

chrétien, Byzance, le nouvel Israël. Ainsi, juste avant un séisme qui touche Antioche et Laodicée, il y a la notice d'une trêve dans la guerre entre Romains et Perses.[16] Après l'envoi d'une ambassade conduite par Hermogène auprès de l'Empire perse,[17] une catastrophe touche Amasée[18] et, la même année, Myra de Lycie.[19] Après plusieurs séismes qui frappent plusieurs localités orientales, on relate l'envoi d'un autre ambassadeur en Perse.[20] Une nouvelle ambassade est suivie par un incendie qui frappe Antioche.[21] La paix signée entre les deux puissances est précédée par des signes célestes et suivie par un tremblement de terre qui touche Constantinople,[22] et un autre, qui ne provoque pas de dommages importants, frappe Antioche après la promulgation de l'édit de Justinien sur la foi orthodoxe.[23] Le premier tremblement de terre, en revanche, suit la notice de l'exécution de certains évêques accusés d'homosexualité, auxquels le pénis est coupé à moitié: le séisme enregistré tout de suite après frappe Pompéopolis, où la terre s'ouvre au milieu.[24] Ce dernier tremblement de terre, à mon avis, nous donne aussi la clé de lecture des autres: il s'agit d'un acte contre nature qui détermine le déchaînement de la création contre l'homme, et la référence biblique sous-jacente est évidemment celle de l'épisode de Sodome et Gomorrhe. Mais une référence à la Bible peut-elle expliquer aussi les autres séismes? Le discours de Malalas suit-il un développement associatif?

Certes, nous pourrions imaginer que la narration suit un ordre d'exposition qui passe de la 'politique étrangère' aux faits majeurs de l'Empire, comme les catastrophes naturelles, et dans ce cas l'enregistrement de ces cataclysmes trouverait tout naturellement sa place à cet endroit précis de la narration, en admettant que par hasard la nature se soit déchaînée régulièrement après chaque trêve entre Byzance et la Perse, ou pour signaler une action mauvaise, comme lorsqu'un autre tremblement de terre secoue Cyzique: juste avant on dit que dans cette ville avait été exilé Jean de Cappadoce, le puissant et détesté préfet de Constantinople, qui à Cyzique avait participé au meurtre de l'évêque.[25] Mais nous pourrons aussi expliquer les autres tremblements, en imaginant que le discours de Malalas fait référence au récit biblique, qui demeure son texte de référence,

---

[16] Respectivement, *Chronographia*,18.27–8: 369.78–371.95 et 18.26: 369.69–77.
[17] *Chronographia*, 18.36: 375.87–90.
[18] *Chronographia*, 18.37: 376.91–3.
[19] *Chronographia*, 18.40: 376.10–12.
[20] *Chronographia*, 18.55–6: 384.79–83.
[21] *Chronographia*, 18.61–2: 390.3–391.11.
[22] *Chronographia*, 18.75–7: 401.16–36.
[23] *Chronographia*, 18.78–9: 402.37–403.42.
[24] *Chronographia*, 18.18–19: 364.42–365.59.
[25] Respectivement, *Chronographia*, 18.93: 408.20–21 et 18.89: 406.79–86.

son langage sous-jacent: en ce cas, les cataclysmes seraient considérés et présentés par l'auteur comme des actes 'contre nature', pour dire qu'à chaque fois que l'Empire des chrétiens accède à un pacte ou à un traité de paix avec les Perses, ennemis du peuple élu, la nature entière punit les comportements immoraux des Byzantins en les frappant d'un cataclysme. Si cela est le cas, la construction du récit historiographique serait déterminée par une autre manière d'exposer les événements par rapport à celle à laquelle nous, les héritiers de l'historiographie classique, sommes accoutumés: en ce cas, il s'agirait d'un discours qui se construit par analogie, pour tout expliquer sans entrer dans des longues analyses, mais pour tout comprendre sur la base du texte sacré. En d'autres mots, Malalas semble abandonner la pensée logique fondée sur le binôme explicité cause-effet, car son binôme à lui ne fonctionne que si on fait référence au texte biblique, qui devient de cette manière la clef pour tout interpréter: l'exposition ne serait donc pas dépourvue d'une logique, mais elle est 'autre' par rapport à la traditionnelle. Pour paraphraser la définition de Lévi-Strauss, Malalas, 'n'a pas une maîtrise sur la nature, mais l'illusion de pouvoir comprendre l'univers, et de le comprendre naturellement, effectivement', et cela sur la base de la référence continuelle aux Ecritures.

Si nous continuons dans notre analyse, nous pouvons constater que chaque tremblement de terre est suivi par une série de dispositions émanant de l'empereur qui, de quelque façon, servent à rétablir l'ordre divin perturbé. Certes, là encore on peut imaginer que la réponse impériale est tout à fait normale dans des conditions d'urgence, ou que la suite des événements narrés suit une logique d'exposition chronologique; cependant, ces renseignements nous font soupçonner une autre manière de lier les épisodes. Ainsi après le tremblement de terre d'Amasée, Justinien décide l'*anadikeusis ... ton palaion nomon*;[26] après celui de Myra et les troubles d'Antioche, Justinien prend des mesures contre les païens,[27] et peu après empêche l'enseignement de la philosophie et de l'astronomie à Athènes;[28] à noter que seul Malalas nous donne ce renseignement, tandis que nous savons par Agathias que les philosophes avaient simplement trouvé refuge auprès du roi de Perse, Chosroès, qui apparaissait comme protecteur de la philosophie et philosophe lui-même.[29] Nulle part chez Agathias se trouve une liaison entre des catastrophes naturelles et la décision des néoplatoniciens de quitter Athènes. Après des tremblements de terre multiples, Justinien envoie une délégation auprès des Axoumites,'accomplissant la volonté divine' (*poiesas theias keleuseis*).[30] Après le tremblement de terre qui frappe

---

26   *Chronographia*, 18.38: 376.94–5.
27   *Chronographia*, 18.42: 377.17–20.
28   *Chronographia*, 18.47: 379.67–9.
29   Agathias, *Histoires*, 2.30: 80; trans. M. Maraval (Paris, 2007), 120.
30   *Chronographia*, 18.56: 384.85.

Constantinople, Justinien 'dans les mêmes jours' envoie un édit sur la foi orthodoxe et contre les hérétiques.[31]

Voyons maintenant si ce type de comportement narratif, fondé sur un processus associatif, est fréquent dans son analyse historique des événements contemporains. Bien entendu, il serait inutile de rechercher à tout prix des automatismes constants dans l'exposition des faits : ce qui importe est de vérifier s'il existe un recours à la juxtaposition d'éléments sur la base d'une référence à une conception partagée par l'auteur et le récepteur. Pour ce faire, je prendrai en considération sa façon de traiter les statues dans les villes : l'analyse est rendue plus facile par un récent essai sur ce sujet.[32] Dans le XVIII livre de la *Chronique*, notre auteur parle de cinq statues : la première est celle de Julien l'Apostat, qui se trouvait dans le port de Julien ; la statue tombe et est remplacée par une croix. Juste avant cette notice, Malalas nous dit que Bélisaire a amené le roi d'Afrique prisonnier à Constantinople, avec son épouse et un riche butin.[33] La troisième est une statue qui s'élevait sur le Forum : à la suite d'un tremblement de terre, la lance que la statue tenait dans ses mains, tombe et s'enfonce dans la terre. Juste avant cette entrée, Malalas précise que Narsès avait battu le roi des Goths Totila à Rome, et qu'il avait envoyé à Constantinople (la Nouvelle Rome) ses vêtements tâchés de sang.[34] La quatrième statue est celle qui se trouvait sur une colonne à *Secoundianae*, tombée lors d'un séisme ; la notice est suivie d'un autre : l'étrange peuple des Huns, qui s'appellent les Avares, arrive à Constantinople.[35] Quant à la deuxième statue, son histoire diffère légèrement : dans un climat de catastrophes, de pandémies et de famine, envoyées par Dieu pour punir les hommes de leurs impiétés, l'empereur décide de faire transporter près de l'*Augoustaion* la statue d'Arcadius qui se trouvait *en to tauro* : la statue sera dorénavant celle de Justinien. Peu après, Malalas nous dit que le pape Vigile est arrivé à Constantinople, et que Rome a été prise par les Goths.[36]

Certes, comme dans le cas des séismes, nous pouvons penser que tous ces notices suivent un ordre purement chronologique, et que Malalas rapporte fidèlement les événements tels qu'ils se sont passés et quand il se sont passés, sans qu'il y ait aucun lien de nature associative entre les renseignements. Toutefois le rapport entre les statues et les peuples étrangers reste quand même intriguant, surtout si l'on songe à la dimension

---

[31]   *Chronographia*, 18.78 : 402.37–40.

[32]   C. Saliou, 'Statues d'Antioche de Syrie dans la *Chronographie* de Malalas', in S. Agusta-Boularot, J. Beaucamp, *et al.*, *Recherches sur la Chronique de Jean Malalas* (Monographies 24), II, 69–96.

[33]   Respectivement *Chronographia*, 18.82 : 404, 49–51 et 18.81 : 403.46–8.

[34]   Respectivement *Chronographia*, 18.118 : 416, 18–20 et 18.116 : 415.7–11.

[35]   Respectivement, *Chronographia*, 18.124 : 419.59 et 18.125 : 420, 67–8.

[36]   Respectivement, *Chronographia*, 18.94 : 408.22–5 et 18.97 : 409.32–4.

que les statues ont dans la pensée chrétienne: elles sont 'habitées' par une puissance surnaturelle, comme le démontrent les *Patria Constantinoupoleos*, et maints textes, qui en attribuent la fabrication à des mages. Pour donner un exemple, nous pouvons rappeler un épisode raconté quelques siècles plus tard par un autre chroniqueur, Syméon Magistros:

> Le 27 mai, l'astronome Jean dit à l'empereur Romain Lécapène que la statue qui s'élevait sur les arcades du Xèrolophos, et qui tournait son regard vers l'Occident, était celle de Syméon (le Tzar des Bulgares). 'Si tu coupe la tête de la statue, Syméon mourra au même moment'. Le basileus envoya donc des hommes pendant la nuit et fit couper la tête *de la statue, et à moment précis, Syméon mourut en Bulgarie.*[37]

Voici un autre témoignage de la même teneur, dû à un autre chroniqueur, Jean Skylitzès: au IX siècle, lorsque sur le trône siège Théophile et que le patriarche est Jean le Grammairien, connu comme sorcier, trois chefs barbares attaquent Constantinople: l'empereur ne sait plus quelles mesures prendre. C'est pourquoi il s'adresse à Jean, pour lui demander conseil. Le patriarche trouve la solution:

> parmi les statues de bronze érigées à l'hippodrome sur l'Euripe, il y en avait une représentée avec trois têtes. Jannès (le surnom de Jean), donc, donna ses instructions pour qu'on forgeât autant de marteaux qu'il y avait de têtes et pour que trois hommes au bras vigoureux, munis de ces marteaux, vinssent avec lui à une heure convenue de la nuit auprès de la statue. Lorsqu'il en donnerait l'ordre, ils cogneraient vigoureusement sur les têtes avec leurs marteaux jusqu'à ce qu'elles tombassent à terre. Une fois les statues décapitées et renversées, les rois barbares sont anéantis.[38]

Si nous observons de près le texte de Jean Malalas, nous constatons que dans sa *Chronique* la mention d'une statue érigée ou détruite s'accompagne toujours de la notice relative à un exploit des barbares ou des Byzantins sur les barbares. Or, les barbares sont les ennemis de l'Etat qui est fondé sur l'ordre divin et sur la loi. Dans la Bible, c'est en détruisant l'idole du faux dieu que Moïse rétabli la loi divine. En outre, le lien entre les peuples ennemis et leurs statues est souvent repris dans la Bible, comme chez Isaïe. S'agit-il encore une fois d'une coïncidence, ou bien le lien entre l'un passage de Malalas et l'autre existe, non comme dépendance directe, bien

---

[37]　Theophanes Continuatus, ch. 33: 740.4–8.

[38]　Skylitzes, 85.13–20, 86; traduction française: *Jean Skylitzès. Empereurs de Constantinople*, texte traduit par B. Flusin et annoté par J.-C. Cheynet (Paris, 2003) (Réalités Byzantines, 8), 76–7.

sûr, mais comme langage sous-jacent qui est connu par ses lecteurs, qui comprennent bien a quoi notre auteur fait référence? A mon sens, c'est là que Malalas construit son discours comme le fait Battiato dans la chanson que j'ai citée au début. Certes, il ne s'agit pas d'automatismes, et il ne faut pas chercher toujours des liens immédiats, mais il me semble qu'une lecture 'associative' de certains passages est bien possible, et cela d'autant plus si nous nous rappelons du contexte dans lequel s'insère la production de la *Chronique*.

Que ces liens soient moins apparents à nos yeux qu'à ceux des Byzantins, l'on voit bien en considérant ces mêmes références aux statues. Après chaque épisode où il est question d'une statue qui tombe, Malalas rapporte un fait qui se lie à différentes figures de hauts prélats ou de hauts fonctionnaires, qui auraient été déposés ou tués. Ainsi après la chute de la statue d'Arcadius, Malalas relate la déposition du patriarche Anthémios;[39] après le déplacement de la statue d'Arcadius et la prise de Rome par les Goths, le patriarche Ménas est déposé;[40] après le tremblement de terre et la chute de la lance que tenait une statue, le gouverneur est tué pendant une révolte en Palestine;[41] après la chute de la statue à Secundianae et l'arrivée des Avares à Constantinople, on relate la mort de l'évêque de Césarée, intervenue 'dans les mêmes jours', comme le dit Malalas.[42] La relation entre ces circonstances pourrait être encore une fois occasionnelle; et cependant les événements pourraient être liés par une logique associative, et en ce sens la lecture d'un passage des Continuateurs de la *Chronographie* de Théophane nous fait réfléchir. Dans ce récit du X siècle, il est question d'une série d'incursions des Russes et des Arabes, et de tremblements de terre qui auraient fait tomber plusieurs statues et églises. Ayant constaté qu'une statue située dans le Deutéron était tombée, Léon le Mathématicien émet une prophétie, en relevant que cet événement était le signe évident de la chute de l'empereur.[43]

Venons-en aux conclusions. Après avoir éliminé l'idée que la *Chronique* est un ouvrage de basse littérature, liée au monde monacal, on fait rentrer subrepticement le même jugement fondé sur des valeurs classicisants, mais en actualisant l'approche en parlant de '*Trivialliteratur*'. A mon avis la situation est fort différente, et je ne crois pas à la volonté de l'auteur de faire des 'clins d'œil' aux basses émotions d'un public hétéroclite. Au contraire, Jean est un personnage cultivé qui connaît bien son métier. Son choix d'utiliser une langue proche de la langue parlée n'est pas dû à un manque de capacité, étant donné qu'il pratique des lectures savantes, dont

---

[39]   *Chronographia*, 18.83: 404.52–6.
[40]   *Chronographia*, 18.98: 409.35–6.
[41]   *Chronographia*, 18.119: 417.29–32.
[42]   *Chronographia*, 18.126: 420.69–70.
[43]   Theophanes Continuatus, ch. 34: 196.6–197.5.

il relate le contenu en le transformant à ses fins. Son choix est délibéré: face à la tradition classiciste qui a ses repères dans la littérature de l'Antiquité, à la narration historique qui fait de Thucydide son modèle et à la philosophie qui suit la lignée classique, face à tous ces chrétiens qui adhèrent volontiers à ce monde qui sent le paganisme, Malalas propose une autre conception du monde et une autre langue pour la présenter.

A la philosophie classique, et à ses adeptes qui, comme Jean Philopon, essaient de trouver des compromis entre néoplatonisme et christianisme, s'oppose maintenant une nouvelle sensibilité plus 'orientale', celle-là même que Cosmas Indicopleustès expose dans le domaine de la géographie. Une idée du monde qui a comme point de repère la Bible, qui seule peut expliquer tout, parce qu'elle fournit un cadre total pour l'humanité. La *Chronique* a été imaginée pour donner une clef d'interprétation qui puisse justifier et expliquer l'histoire de l'homme en tant que développement homogène et compact de la volonté divine, une histoire sans mutation et sans changement au vu de la réalisation du plan de la Providence, un cadre où tout événement peut être expliqué en prenant les Ecritures comme motif de fond.

Malalas participe de cette manière au débat très vif qui accompagne la naissance d'une nouvelle civilisation, et propose une manière inédite de voir l'homme. De cette manière, reprenant la tradition des études sur l'histoire universelle, et en la développant à travers un exposé qui entre dans les détails au lieu de s'arrêter au schéma chronologique, Malalas propose une façon nouvelle et différente de juger l'action humaine par rapport à ce que font les historiens chrétiens de son époque. Il ne s'agit pas de relater les exploits des généraux, comme le fait Procope, ni de raconter l'histoire contemporaine pour fournir une explication dictée par l'engagement immédiat: cela, je l'ai dit au début, c'est ce que font les autres, qui parlent davantage de la contemporanéité pour soutenir une idée 'politique' du moment. Malalas propose une manière d'interpréter globale, qui, comme il le dit dans la préface,[44] doit être continuée par les générations futures, sans se soucier de changer le schéma: l'histoire est toujours pareille à elle-même, parce qu'elle n'est que répétition d'un modèle unique et invariable, dont la Bible, en tant que parole de Dieu, contient la clef. Et la chanson peut continuer avec d'autres mots qui ne seront que d'autres exemplifications de ce qui a déjà été présenté.

---

[44]   *Chronographia*, Prooimion, 3.12.

16. Rhetoric and history: the case of Niketas Choniates

Athanasios Angelou

If we are going to talk about the relationship of rhetoric and history in the work of Niketas Choniates, we should raise the question of where the authorial presence is traceable in the *Chronike Diegesis*. There are many ways of ascertaining this presence that could show that the rhetoric in Choniates the historian is not the work of a mere declaimer, however skilful, but that of a discriminating master involved in the narrative task of shaping the material to his historiographical purpose. The two most obvious approaches forcing themselves to our attention are to focus upon, and bring to the forefront, the author's manner of presenting the historical material available to him and, secondly, to study his vocabulary, both word choice and acoustical aspects. To investigate the lexical aspect properly, the words of Choniates would have to be studied beyond their literal surface meaning and measured, so to speak, by their ability to evoke an atmosphere through their qualities of sound, their classical associations or the capacious range of their meanings.[1] Here I would like to take into consideration the approach to authorial presence that has more to do with structural aspects, understood as both the sequence of themes and the construction of episodes, although the lexical and structural aspects may in due course have to be brought together.

Today we see a diversification of perspectives in historiographical research, and in many aspects of the genre of historiography a rethinking of our approach is under way. To be more open-minded, we should be ready to explore the possibility of viewing the *Diegesis* from different

---

[1]   See the comments by R. Browning in his article 'The language of Byzantine literature', in *History, Language and Literacy in the Byzantine World* (Northampton, 1989), study XV, 121: 'In his exploitation of the resources of "Atticism", as understood by the Byzantines, for the purposes of variety and novelty, he [Niketas Choniates] pushes the resources of the classicising language about as far as they will go. … Unlike those writers who try to produce a pastiche of Late Roman or Early Byzantine prose, he uses the redundancy, the suggestiveness, the flexibility of the learned language in an original way'.

angles. It may be restrictive to concentrate only upon assessing how accurate and comprehensive Niketas Choniates is in his historical writing. Adopting a multiplicity of approaches, we should explore other aspects of the *Diegesis* that include structure and sound. By following this line of approach we may end by seeing him as a rhetorician of history, a historian in the full Byzantine sense.[2]

If, then, we are going to investigate the *Chronike Diegesis*, or any other such text, from a rhetorician's point of view, what must be at the root of such an enquiry is the question of the creation or production of discourse. Now, there is a difficulty inherent in historiography. In other properly oratorical works, whether panegyric, homily, address or forensic rhetoric, the crafting of the structure is more easily detectable, especially the shift from subject to subject, the changes in argument, theme or topic, the passage from one subject to another whether in an expected or unexpected fashion. And in many cases, what at first sight looks like an unexpected change of topic further enquiry may show to be dictated by the theory of discourse respecting the specific genre. Even in discourses of mixed genres, such as sermons, with their apparent confusion of hortatory, epideictic and, on occasion, forensic rhetoric, once we identify the genre, embedded, so to speak, in the discourse, then what seems to be an unexpected topic that has suddenly arisen reveals itself as a requirement of that genre, only its position being left to the discretion of the individual rhetorician. With historiography, on the other hand, however rhetorical in practice or literary in intention the work may appear to be, we find something at first sight drastically unrhetorical: that is, the ordered succession of subjects is dictated by the course of events themselves. We could say that history has a starting-point that is essentially unrhetorical.

This tension between history and rhetoric is part of the problem posed to rhetoric itself by what lies outside its operations, ostensibly within its scope yet beyond the bounds of inventiveness, for example, legal documents or testimony by witnesses. Being external to rhetoric, these cannot be easily rearranged. You may interpret the law or question the witness, but there is a body of thoughts and expositions laid down in texts or statements that is external to rhetoric, outside its framework. Just as rhetoric faces a problem when it has recourse to documents that are legally binding and thus not malleable through authorial intervention, so by extension rhetoric may have a potential conflict with history as a whole, since the latter draws upon a body of evidence external to the operations of rhetoric, accessible initially only by enquiry or investigation with a logic of its own unlike that of rhetoric.

---

[2]   For a broadening of our perspective upon the presence of rhetoric in Byzantine life see M. Mullett, 'Rhetoric, theory and the imperative of performance: Byzantium and now', in Jeffreys, ed., *Rhetoric*, 151–70.

Greek rhetorical theory does discuss manners of handling a case when reference to law is required, and this occurs, among other places, in the so-called *nomikai staseis*. It has not, though, discussed similar issues concerning historical evidence, or certainly not to the same extent. For forensic discourse, and for whatever narrative it may include, there is no lack of rules. But the problem is, how do you handle a narrative when you must have recourse to historical evidence? Historical narrative as a genre, unlike forensic discourse, has received very little attention by the rhetoricians and to this question the handbooks give no consistent answer, if any answer at all.[3] Unless we develop a theory about Byzantine historiography, though, we cannot fully appreciate what our author, Choniates, or any other practising rhetorician of history, is doing. Without such a framework we run the risk of treating him only as an imaginative writer who may do violence to his facts, or as a mediocre enquirer falling short of the canons of objective historiography; whereas, if we are going to do justice to the rhetorical qualities of his work, we should be seeing him more along the lines of a speaker on history.

Having presented the problems involved in an enquiry into the rhetorical nature of the *Chronike Diegesis* and the prospects for solving them, we should now look in detail at a series of extracts from Choniates and see how an analysis can point to future research. So I choose extracts from the book on the boy Emperor Alexios II.[4] This book opens with an extensive description of the times, that is, the period immediately after the death of Manuel Komnenos. The characterization of the period is general and, apart from describing the character and habits of the young boy Emperor Alexios, what Choniates does is mainly to typify the various kinds of people prominent on the scene and in positions of power after the death of Manuel. He sorts them into categories, three in number, though without naming any specific people. They are all cases of self-interested behaviour: those who ingratiate themselves with the dowager Empress Maria of Antioch, those who appropriate public money and spend it lavishly, and those who seek power for themselves. The state of affairs is further characterized by a succession of images: it is compared to a building when its pillars are taken away, and to a classroom situation when the teacher is missing and the pupils go wild.

---

[3]   In Rufus' *Art of Rhetoric* there is an unusual tetrapartite division of the forms of rhetoric; see *Rhetores Graeci*, ed. L. Spengel, 1 (Leipzig, 1853), 463.13–14. Apart from the customary division into deliberative, epideictic and judiciary, a fourth is added: 'historical'. This was never really taken up and adopted into rhetorical theory in any consistent or systematic fashion. For an anti-rhetorical treatment of historiography see Lucian on *How to Write History*, ed. with German trans. H. Homeyer, *Lukian, Wie man Geschichte schreiben soll* (Munich, 1965).

[4]   Choniates, *Historia*, 223–74.

This depiction with its clear-cut scheme of reference to general characteristics of the times and a final comparison would not be out of place in the framework of the theory of *ekphrasis*. Whatever interpretation the Late Antique and Byzantine commentators placed upon the term, there are two dominant features that permeate all kinds of *ekphrasis*: whether the subject is a physical object of nature or a season, an art object in architectural space or a painting in two-dimensional space, an activity like a battle, a feast or hunting, all these objects and activities should be strongly visualized, with immediacy, as though one is present and seeing them. Secondly, each component should be enumerated and included, so to speak, in a tour of the subject, with everything divided into its dominant or striking characteristics.[5]

Ekphrasis has received considerable attention, particularly from art historians; but what is important for us here is another of its subjects. The rhetoricians tell us that we can have an *ekphrasis*, among other things, of *chronos* or *kairos*, time, and that there is such a thing as an *ekphrasis* of war-time; so, by extension, we could have an *ekphrasis* of *eirene*, peace-time, and other kinds of time.[6] In the opening stages of the book on Alexios, rather than telling of actions and agents, Choniates is describing a state of affairs in a particular period, by bringing out the component elements that determine this period, without naming any specific people, but conveying the activity of each in visual imagery: it may, for instance, be the courtiers dressing up to impress the empress so as to win her over, or the shrunken purse full now that its owner is rich. That is why we should be entitled to call it an *ekphrasis* of *kairos* and could gain in understanding if we characterized this particular period as an *ekphrasis* of anarchy-time.

From a structural point of view it is worth bearing in mind that what Choniates is doing here is to take advantage of an era coming to an end in historical time, with the changes brought about after the death of Manuel, and construct at this particular point in the narrative what we would like to call an *ekphrasis* of anarchy-time, amplifying it to considerable proportions, dressing it up in archaizing language and on occasion arranging the words

---

[5]   See the phrases applied to *ekphrasis*: ὑπ' ὄψιν ἄγων τὸ προκείμενον / τὸ δηλούμενον and λόγος περιηγηματικός, *Aphthonii Progymnasmata*, ed. H. Rabe (Leipzig, 1926), 36 and *Hermogenis opera*, ed. H. Rabe (Leipzig, 1913), 22. For a collection of *progymnasmata* in translation see G. Kennedy, *Progymnasmata: Greek Textbooks in Prose Composition and Rhetoric* (Leiden, 2003).

[6]   It is interesting to note that in Hermogenes historical time (periods of war and peace) is categorized as *kairos*, seasonal and festal time as *chronos* (spring/a feast), while specific activities in historical time, such as land or sea battles, are categorized as *pragma*. See *Hermogenis opera*, 22. For the subject of *chronos/kairos* in *ekphrasis* see R. Webb, *Ekphrasis, Imagination and Persuasion in Ancient Rhetorical Theory and Practice* (Farnham, 2009), 61–4.

according to their acoustic value.[7] We can fully appreciate this archaism and this sudden explosion of sound play only if we consider them part of an *ekphrasis* enhancing the visual imagery at this point, a kind of brief climactic performative act. After all it is only fitting that Choniates should begin with an *ekphrasis* of anarchy-time, providing an overall temporal framework for the subsequent episodes that in themselves rarely have any other temporal specification apart from their relative position in the narrative sequence. It is within this period of anarchy that the sacrilegious episodes concerning the church of Hagia Sophia take place, and also those duplicitous, vengeful and brutal activities of the coming usurper, both salient narrative examples of this anarchy-time. If we are to claim that, at least in some parts of the *Chronike Diegesis*, Choniates is a speaker on history, this combination of an account and a succession of visual images with acoustic enhancement provides some evidence.

The second topic in the series of themes is the current attitude of the Comnenian dynastic family, especially those members who had been prominent during the former emperor Manuel's reign. What is said about them concerns their reasons for disliking the new state of affairs whereby the *protosevastos* Alexios, the lover of Maria of Antioch, holds the real power in the empire.[8] There is a rather extended analysis of their feelings of insecurity and their indifferent attitude towards the boy emperor, and we are presented with what in the end will prove to be the motives underlying their future actions, though the actions rooted in the present *aitia* come much later in the story. From a narrative point of view, it is important to note that again no name is given: only a psychological state is analyzed, the mind of a group. This is in keeping with the variety of psychological motivation found in this book and across the whole of the *Chronike Diegesis*. Elsewhere also motivation is de-personalized, as here, but very often it is personalized as the driving-force of one individual.[9]

The next theme in the series returns to the first one, the state of affairs after the death of the Emperor Manuel, and continues the *ekphrasis* of *kairos*. Now the theme of anarchy-time comes back as a motif enhanced with more images, the first drawn from classical mythology, the giant Typhoeus with a hundred serpent-like heads, and the other from contemporary lore, the

---

[7]   See the passage in Choniates' *Historia*, 224.17 from ἤρων καὶ ἐπείρων to λιθοκόλλοις καὶ ὅλοις (l. 20).

[8]   *Historia*, 224.33–46.

[9]   Kazhdan observed Niketas Choniates' 'penchant for psychological portraiture', in A. Kazhdan and S. Franklin, *Studies in Byzantine Literature of the Eleventh and Twelfth Centuries* (Cambridge, 1984), 284. It remains to be seen exactly how much this psychological portraiture functions as a structural principle in Niketas Choniates' narrative across the entire length of his history.

portentous monstrous birth of a boy with a huge head and tiny body.[10] From a structural point of view these supplementary images, though related in content to the original nucleus of *ekphrasis*, are separated from it within the narrative space. Their function is to depict anarchy-time visually. This theme of anarchy is to be re-enhanced periodically across the whole narrative, underpinning it throughout.

The first person to be named in the narrative, and whose appearance marks the next subject in the series of topics, is a member of the dynasty who had been confined by the previous Emperor Manuel Komnenos to retirement at a secure distance from the capital; this is Andronikos Komnenos, the future usurper, the man lying in wait for his bid for power.[11] He is introduced directly as the subject of the sentence, in the nominative, as befits the protagonist of an objective historical narrative, to set the tone and mark him out rhetorically. The name of the person is followed appropriately by his relationship to the rest of the dynasty in the form of an apposition.[12]

Immediately after this naming of a protagonist, we are introduced to what will prove to be the dominant psychological motive for his action, and for all his further actions in this section of the narrative: this is an obsession for power that is accompanied, as will be disclosed later, by duplicity as a means of attainment. The technical term in rhetoric for the root cause or motivating force of *praxis* in a narrative is *aitia*, and it is important to bear in mind that an *aitia* comes, even in a condensed form, right after the naming of Andronikos, as if his outstanding characteristic opens a case against him. This is in general a recognizable pattern in the *Chronike Diegesis*, and it will reappear in the introduction of the next historical protagonist, Maria Komnene. What follows further along and till the end of the book can be construed as a chain of actions, interrupted or not by parallel actions of other protagonists or antagonists, that illustrate this ambition and this duplicity. As with the *aitia* of the members of the dynasty, so with the *aitia* of Andronikos, the narration diverts at this point, later resuming the theme to connect the motivation with actions further on and throughout.

After the motivation of Andronikos has been put in place, in that he is said to whet his appetite for power, there is a break in the narrative to bring in a flashback from Andronikos' earlier life.[13] Within the narrative space assigned to the flashback, where his flight to the Seljuks and his

---

[10]   *Historia*, 225.47–55.

[11]   *Historia*, 225.56–226.63.

[12]   For the use of the nominative for an agent, especially in *historiai*, see *Hermogenis opera*, 5.

[13]   *Historia*, 226.64–227.19. Upsetting the chronological order in a narrative is called *anastrophe* by Theon and is discussed in connection with *diegema*: *Progymnasmata*, ed. with French trans. M. Patillon (Paris, 1997), 86.

private life are dealt with in summary form, the historian suddenly focuses in, and allows the narrative to expand into an amplified visual scene, at the particular moment when Andronikos presents himself at court in the presence of Emperor Manuel asking for mercy. This is the first truly descriptive scene of the book.

There is a major shift here from a generalized summary account to an isolated and specific narrative; from hovering above, we could say, the narrative is now grounded in a specific scene of immediate reality. This is in marked contrast to what went before and in equally marked contrast to what will happen afterwards. The theme of Andronikos' submission is developed in its own separate self-contained narrative space, a unit devoted to a single theme following its own line, stylistically discontinuous from what went before and is to come. The details here are surprising in their visual eloquence, when the supplicant, as he lies on the floor, takes from inside his garment a chain attached to his body and stretches it out in front of the assembly of courtiers around the emperor, asking to be drawn forwards across the floor, and offering thus a vivid and palpable symbol of mock submission.[14]

The details of the scene are disproportionate both to the surrounding narrative and to their historical importance, especially if one bears in mind that nobody else, in power or demise, has been given such specialized narrative attention so far. However, the scene is proportionate to the *aitia*, illustrating it and introducing further the element of duplicity in the man. He would do anything he could and he would stop at nothing, however hypocritical or extreme or base or theatrical it is, if it steadies and furthers his course towards the seizure of power. The scene is also important as an instance of plot structure devised to connect a future event, the eventual lynching of Andronikos, with the participation in this scene of Isaac Angelos, the courtier who dragged him along by the chain across the floor, and who would also figure in his downfall. This connection is provided by the author himself, but the significance of the coincidence is hinted at in an enigmatic way when the author wonders whether it can be dismissed as devoid of meaning, implying that it may be a premonition of future events.[15]

Following the flashback from Andronikos' early life Choniates returns to a description of the times.[16] The original motif of the overture is now woven into the texture, as the theme of the current state of affairs recurs and the people prominent at this time are again characterized, but from

---

[14]   *Historia*, 226.86–227.7. A further extensive scene exhibiting duplicity occurs later (256.45–257.71) when the same agent, Andronikos, makes a public display of mock grief over the tomb of the Emperor Manuel.

[15]   *Historia*, 227.6–7.

[16]   *Historia*, 227.20–228.30.

a different point of view. The first incidence of the motif was, as we said, ekphrastic, the second drew upon classical legend and contemporary lore, but the third, while describing the same people in analogous terms, again without naming them, presents them now as part of a diagnosis by a protagonist, Andronikos, who is planning for his future and assessing how the current situation can be manipulated for his own purposes. With this change of perspective we now see roughly three types of people: the swine who are after money to enrich themselves, the goats who are after the tender shoot Alexios to ease him out, and the bees ranging far and wide in the provinces in lucrative government posts. The authorial voice is heard in true literary fashion, variegating the repetition of crucial themes and hiding behind the voice of the protagonist. The theme of the times (*kairos*), having received its ekphrastic amplification by the author himself at first hand, is now made into an *ethopoiia*: 'What Andronikos must have thought about the situation at the time'.[17]

This marked shift, in the case of Andronikos, from scenic narrative to political assessment leads on to a scene of its own, not public like the previous one, but private to fit the personal scheming. From a scene of action we pass to a scene of the mind where what is now presented is Andronikos struggling to find a pretext for his actions, while the narrative follows him as he is paging through a document, the narrative becoming very detailed as the protagonist searches for the passage expedient to him in the power struggle lying ahead.[18] In forensic rhetoric for a scene constructed in this way one would talk about *diaskeue*, a kind of narrative elaboration rendering all the stages of a composite activity, or about another kind of operation called 'from beginning to end', where the speaker moves away from the basic facts of a case and expands to all the attendant circumstances, mental or factual, in the interests of his own cause.[19] From

---

[17] An interesting *ethopoiia* appears further on in the narrative (256.64–257.71), where Andronikos is made to murmur to himself over the tomb of the Emperor Manuel that he now has Manuel in his hands and that he is going to destroy his family. This is a construction on the part of the author showing Andronikos' vengefulness: 'What Andronikos must have been saying to himself on the spot when he visited Manuel's tomb.'

[18] Choniates, *Historia*, 228.31–229.58. The document according to Choniates was an oath committed to paper that Andronikos swore to the Emperor Manuel and his son Alexios, and the crucial passage obliged Andronikos to inform them of potential threats to their position and guard against the danger.

[19] For *diaskeue* see *Hermogenis opera*, 166.20ff. and the commentators, e.g. *Rhetores Graeci*, ed. Chr. Walz, V, 417; VII, 791. A classic example for the commentators is *Iliad* 1.459 ff., where the sacrifice of an animal with a feast afterwards is set out in precise detail. For the technique of ἀπ' ἀρχῆς ἄχρι τέλους see *Hermogenis opera*, 47.7 ff. See translations by M. Heath, *Hermogenes on Issues* (Oxford, 1995), and M. Patillon, *Hermogène, La Rhétorique* (Paris, 1997), and also G. Kennedy, *Greek Rhetoric*

now on Andronikos appears in the persona of a guardian to the legitimate authority, purportedly in favour of the boy emperor.

When the narrative swings back to Constantinople and to Alexios, the *protosevastos*, the next person to be introduced by name, in much the same way as Andronikos, is Maria Komnene, daughter of Manuel and half-sister of the boy emperor.[20] She is introduced in the nominative, according to the 'ceremonious' grammatical protocol stipulated for such appearances in a historical *diegema*; her relationship to the dynasty is then set out, and immediately afterwards, as in the case of Andronikos, comes the psychological motivation for the actions that will follow. She is presented, straightaway, as not being able to stand the very image of her father's bed (where presumably her stepmother, the empress, still sleeps) being violated by the presence and lovemaking of the *protosevastos*, the wielder of power in this interim period; and we cannot have a deeper psychological motive than this. The analysis does not stop here. The second thing mentioned takes the *aitia* to another level, not now to a psychological state of mind but to her psychological make-up: Maria's hot-headed recklessness (*thermourgia*) and masculinity of temperament (*andrikon phronema*). Then, as though this is not enough, a third item is further introduced, referring to the typical situation she is in, that of a stepdaughter faced with a stepmother. She resents being pushed aside. The analysis of Maria's *aitia* is thus not only detailed, but categorized by a complex of three elements, so far: revulsion, rashness and alienation. What follows is an account of her decisions and actions, apparently stemming from such a psychology and such a character, regarding her attempted coup to seize power and oust the *protosevastos*; and here begins one of the longest episodes in the book, making up a more-or-less self-contained narrative with all the essential components of a *diegema*.[21]

It is helpful at this point, and indeed throughout the *Chronike Diegesis*, to remind ourselves of the kind of discourse that forms the parts that narrate action, as distinct from the ekphrastic passages. In Greek rhetorical theory '*diegesis*' is used in two senses. It can be a connected series of *diegemata*, and the analogy given is the narrative units of a Homeric epic making up the *diegesis* of the Iliad or the Odyssey.[22] Alternatively it can be a part

---

under Christian Emperors (Princeton, NJ, 1983), 85. Kennedy explains the use of this technique in laying out an account from the point of view of a prosecutor or defendant. The commentators make heavy use of it because it is closely related to the case itself: τὰ δὲ ἀπ' ἀρχῆς ἐστι τὰ πράγματα (*Rhetores Graeci*, ed. Walz, V, 56).

[20] *Historia*, 230.93–231.10.

[21] For a classic enumeration of the components of a *diegema* see *Aphthonii Progymnasmata*, 2–3.

[22] See *Aphthonii Progymnasmata*, 2; *Hermogenis opera*, 4.

of forensic discourse, coming after the prologue, and before the *agon* and the epilogue. Here the *diegesis* constitutes an account of the case under consideration, centring largely upon narrative and its implications.[23] The *diegema*, on the other hand, is what we could call a narrative unit around a central episode or a single action, with a series of connected elements: agent, time, place, deed, manner of action and cause or motive (*aitia*). An exemplary *diegema* would be the slaying of the suitors in the Odyssey.[24] The story of Maria has all the characteristics of a *diegema*: a connected series of actions all stemming from an initial motive or series of motives, interwoven into a spatial and temporal setting, and culminating in specific scenes where words are spoken. That is why it is of significance for the structural aspect of the book to observe whose motivation is analyzed and whose is not, which motivation leads to action *in extenso* or lies behind a specific scene, and which events are merely chronicled or narrated summarily, if we are to consider whether it is a series of *diegemata*, with a narrative logic of their own.[25]

The course of this narrative is complex, but it all forms one unit that is nothing other than the unfolding of a plot to oust Alexios, lover of the empress. The first plan is thwarted, so the narrative has to begin anew, and as its course develops so the narrative specificity of time, place and manner of action is increased, culminating in the famous battle-scene within the precincts of the church of Hagia Sophia, the main place (*topos*) of this *diegema*. The motives of the princess are not further characterized but are now worked into the narrative; nor are those of anybody else involved in the coup presented: there is hardly any more analysis of motives, only mention of strategic thoughts of the protagonists involved. The dominant agent here is the princess, and the dominant motive behind the scenes is that mentioned at the beginning of this narrative section, the princess's personal psychology; this is different from the psychology of Andronikos revealed earlier in the narrative, yet similar at its core in that it is personal rather than political.

---

[23]   See e.g. *Nicolai Progymnasmata*, ed. J. Felten (Leipzig, 1913), 4, 11.

[24]   See e.g. *Aphthonii Progymnasmata*, 3.

[25]   We recall what G. Kennedy wrote in *Greek Rhetoric under Christian Emperors*, 53: 'Much of later Greek literature can be analyzed in terms of structural units, such as the narrative … the *ekphrasis*, which are used as building blocks for larger works.' In John of Sardis' commentary on the *Progymnasmata* of Aphthonius, ed. H. Rabe (Leipzig, 1928) we read among the scholia on the *diegema* a remark that concerns historiography: '*Historia* is an exposition of consecutive *diegemata*' (30.23). The same Byzantine commentator makes a distinction between a narrative in itself and a narrative πρός τι (30.14–24), that is, between a narrative told for its own sake and a narrative making a point.

She is the only one of the protagonists in the coup against Alexios whose motives are analyzed, while all the rest simply perform their duties. Her husband speaks to the crowds, the conspirators meet, the patriarch offers her asylum. Narratively speaking, she is clearly the notable exception, whose frame of mind gives unity to the section. The only other agent, if it is an agent at all, that is described and analyzed *in extenso,* is not a person but a multitude: the crowd of Constantinople, which plays a big role in supporting the coup of Maria in the streets.[26] As Choniates analyzes the actions of a person behind the course of events, so he analyzes the people's mind as though the group is now the protagonist. Here again, in this depiction of the people we have a premonition: swayed to pity, the crowd by supporting Maria in the streets affect her decision to go ahead with her plan, so becoming an agent in the coup. Quickly turning from acceptance to rejection and disparagement, the crowd will eventually be responsible for the lynching of Andronikos. The crowd is introduced in the first stages of the action, as Maria is, and, in modern terms, this is one of the finest literary examples of mass psychology in Byzantium, centring on the shift from subservience to rebellion all within a mental framework of political ignorance.

After the specialized and localized narrative of the civil war, which receives a kind of epilogue with a moral judgement on the sacrilege involved, the action retreats to something less dense in detail with the quandary over the patriarch's future.[27] As to the princess, we are given no specific information about what happened: her story comes abruptly to an end as the amnesty is granted and she goes into the palace. Nothing is said about her subsequent position, though we might speculate that Choniates must surely not have lacked further information, even if only gossip or hearsay. Her attempt to oust the *protosevastos* is one of the most extended and detailed accounts in the whole book, and then she vanishes from the narrative, as far as her subsequent fate is concerned. She reappears only to die, allegedly from poisoning arranged by Andronikos. Her relationship with Andronikos, with whom she had been in correspondence at an earlier stage, is not mentioned even when he takes charge as master of the situation. It is important to reflect upon the effacement of this particular agent because she has been the centre of one of the longest and best constructed units. We can perhaps understand this only if we take into account that the narrative unit about Maria, her *diegema* based upon her *aitia* and its consequent actions, is now completed. It culminated in the sacrilegious use of the church of Hagia Sophia for motives that were really in the end very personal. The case against her, so to speak, has been put forward and, whatever her historical significance may subsequently have

---

[26]   *Historia*, 233.70–234.90.
[27]   *Historia*, 241.70–242.19.

been, her narrative significance has faded. What consequently happened to Maria is not of prime interest. Only her death is mentioned, and that in the context of Andronikos' persecutions.

The next scene that can claim to be closely focused and in marked contrast to the rest is a miniature scene concerning the return of the patriarch Theodosios to Constantinople, after his temporary exile on the charge of having colluded with Maria.[28] The detail of the scene is again disproportionate to its historical import, especially if one thinks of other events that have not been fully depicted. His banishment is not amplified, only referred to in general terms, but his return is. It is made into a scene: the route is given, the time taken for him to travel from one place to another, and even the scents for the occasion are mentioned, not just any aromatic fragrances but Indian sandalwood in particular. This is clearly a vignette again and the patriarch is accordingly a protagonist, though a minor one.

The narrative then, following its pendulum course, switches to the front, in Paphlagonia.[29] No specific visual account is given of Andronikos' march from the region. But the same elements concerning the narrative significance of Andronikos himself reappear. His love of power is reiterated; it is described as what bears him up (*kouphizomenos*). Letters from Constantinople make him buoyant (*pteroumenos*) and when his daughter comes to him from the capital, bringing news, all this marks an important step in his strategy towards seizure of power. It is the moment when he decides to march out to Constantinople; only the march itself is not crystallized in any amplified scene, though his duplicitous character in dealing with people in places he passes is reiterated.

When the narrator's pendulum swings back again to the capital the only detailed narrative we have is once more a scene illustrating a person's psychology,[30] this time that of Alexios the *protosevastos*. What is actually described in some detail is his private room, and we are told about the purple colour of the curtains and his manner of protecting himself from the sunlight, all characteristics of an effeminate man. It is clearly a vignette again and the *protosevastos* a sort of protagonist: not in the strong sense of an agent but as a rather passive object of circumstances.

The only places on Andronikos' march to Constantinople that receive some narrative attention are Nicaea and Nicomedia; otherwise the events impeding or speeding Andronikos' advance are sparsely indicated.[31] But when we move back to Constantinople we return to Alexios the *protosevastos* and for the first time a strategy of his for confronting Andronikos is now given with some idea of what he thinks he should and should not do,

---

[28]   *Historia*, 243.20–31.
[29]   *Historia*, 243.32–244.47.
[30]   *Historia*, 244.48–57.
[31]   *Historia*, 244.70–245.19.

or what he is forced to do in the circumstances.[32] He has decided to use the fleet to prevent Andronikos from moving further into the City. In no way does the description of the preparations for the naval engagement compare in detail and narrative qualities with that of the civil war started by the princess Maria. It is not a full narrative and it is partly exhausted in outlining the troops involved and the commanders appointed. It is an abortive narrative, and it was after all also an abortive undertaking.

It would be beyond the bounds of this provisional study to speak of every episode in the book on Alexios II similar in form and purpose to those we have been outlining up till now. There are various topics that are developed further on and built into narrative units. Some concern the preparations for the murder of the empress and her son towards the end of the book, but there are two other topics upon which I should like to concentrate.

After the reported naval preparations, no dramatic piece of narrative is developed concerning the outcome. In the end the downfall of the *protosevastos* was triggered by one of his admirals switching to the side of Andronikos.[33] This is one of the most crucial pivotal events of the story, yet it is not accounted for, just referred to, not narrated in detail, not explained in strategic or other terms: it is, in fact, one of the most shrunken pieces of narrative. What is accounted for and amply expounded is, on the contrary, the movement of the Constantinopolitan elite feeling free now to abandon the *protosevastos* in order to go over openly to Andronikos.[34] There is a description of the charms he casts on those who meet him, as though this is another of his actions. His charisma is described ironically, in terms of people tasting the honeycomb of his tongue, drinking him as the grass drinks dew, feasting on him as in myth or as at the table of the sun (an allusion to Herodotus), as though what Choniates is doing here is presenting a miniature *ekphrasis* of Andronikos' charisma. The firing of people's imagination concerning Andronikos is ekphrastically amplified and given more narrative space than the defection of Kontostephanos to him, which is merely mentioned. Nor is the fall of the *protosevastos* isolated into a unified dramatic piece of narrative. Rather, there is a more-or-less perfunctory account of the typical sequence of events expected when a potentate falls: he is arrested, placed under guard, bundled out of the palace, transferred to a secure place... It is a 'lean' type of narrative (*psile aphegesis*), a mere recital of the recognizable stages in the procedure. Instead of expanding this into a scene, Choniates expands, at this point, into authorial reflections upon the *protosevastos*: the inadequacies of his character, what he might have done and had been constitutionally unable to achieve, the instability of human affairs (of the type 'he who was

---

[32]   *Historia*, 246.20–248.58.

[33]   *Historia*, 248.59–61.

[34]   *Historia*, 248.63–75.

powerful ... is now powerless'), and the ironic reversal of fortune by which a man too fond of sleep is doomed to suffer the torture of sleeplessness in prison, the last being the only detail that is very specific to the man in his situation. In their pathos and irony these reflections function as another of Choniates' epilogues, this time bringing to a close the appearance of the *protosevastos* in the narrative, and clearly establishing a link with an 'audience', which is invited to consider the human situation in general, to feel the irony of Alexios' situation in particular, to judge him according to his lack of achievement, but finally to feel pity. Narratively speaking, the *protosevastos* is really in the end very few things: the effeminate man sequestered in his claustrophobic room and the ridiculous man of the final minuscule scene: brought by a pony to his victor and to his own doom, holding a flag on a reed. He may not be a πράττων any more, if ever he was, but he is definitely now a conspicuous πάσχων.[35]

The last person to go over and meet the victor is the patriarch. The meeting is made into a separate extended scene, one of the largest in the whole of the *Chronike Diegesis*.[36] What the patriarch is in narrative terms Choniates renders through selected images. After the heightened imagery of his return from banishment, in another scene of intense detail the patriarch is portrayed together with Andronikos. The preparatory dressing-up of Andronikos for the meeting is described in elaborate detail, a true amplification. The scene of the actual meeting is made into an opportunity for the author to show us the mind of the patriarch at work and is similar to the observation of Andronikos' mind at work when he was searching his documents for a pretext. The patriarch's reactions to Andronikos are described in ekphrastic amplification: what his eyes meant when they were looking, what his stance meant when he was posing, the significance of the repartee, the veiled insults and barbed comments exchanged. This may not be the patriarch of ecclesiastical history: the meeting is not evaluated from the point of view of ecclesiastical statesmanship, of any historical understanding or misunderstanding the two men reached, of a deal struck or not struck by two historical protagonists. But a man comes alive through this scene, presented as the dramatic encounter of a deep, experienced physiognomist with an arrogant hypocritical man of power, a usurper who is not himself a statesman but a hardened old adventurer.

Let us stand back now and see how we can comment on what is really a difficult undertaking – and I have offered only a sample. What Choniates is doing from a rhetorical point of view is assigning a protagonist and, in particular, specific actions of his, their own narrative space, where what is at play is really either the amplification or the shrinking of that space, enclosing the narrative in a self-contained unit round an *aitia* or in a self-

---

[35] *Historia*, 248.79–250.20.

[36] *Historia*, 252.70–253.3.

contained scene with the *aitia* in the background, personalizing its figures in dense detail or de-personalizing them in ekphrastic amplification, specifying or passing over events, setting and localizing scenes in time and space or broadly alluding to them. These are some of the main operations of his historiographical approach and what we should mean by rhetoric in Choniates, and these are some of the patterns, selected by our discriminating author, that we should be investigating in order to appreciate the significance of the text as it is built word by word. His techniques are so varied and subtle that though his material, as we said earlier, has an unrhetorical starting-point, he pushes the rhetoric as far as it will go.

There is in Choniates a structural design equivalent to an emplotment when he centres the episodes around a motivation.[37] The narrative may be deceptively linear, though it is in fact broken up, not only by various digressions but in another more radical way. Many episodes, especially those constructed around a nucleus of motivation, are just so many illustrations of one point concerning either personal or group psychology. So his lines of narrative come full circle: in their meaning they do not depend so much, or only, on what went before but rather home in upon a constant centre of motivation. The circle begins when the actor appears on the stage, and it is consummated with his removal from the theatre of action. So in a sense the history of Choniates is a coming together of these circles, overlapping or one inside the other.

There is another structural aspect of this emplotment that we have only touched upon, and this is when the narrative prefigures the kind of destiny that lies ahead for the characters. We have already alluded to this, but I should like to add one more example. When the princess Maria welcomes Andronikos and his scheme for disposing of the empress's lover, she is in fact foreshadowing her own death. This reference to the protagonist's final destiny – the end of the plot, as it were – is not expressed overtly but as a prophetic symbolic act, a figurative foreshadowing: the princess Maria in embracing Andronikos' cause is embracing her own doom.[38]

Some of the rhetorical operations effected by Choniates seem, in their general features, to have their counterparts in certain specific techniques developed by the theoreticians of rhetoric, especially those that deal with narrating cases based upon an issue. This is not to say that he is strictly adhering to specific rules of forensic or other rhetoric. Niketas, like his

---

[37]   For remarks on the significance of the character and actions of emperors in Choniates' narrative see the article by J. Harris, 'Distortion, divine providence and genre in Niketas Choniates's account of the collapse of Byzantium 1180–1204', *Journal of Medieval History* 26 (2000), 19–31.

[38]   *Historia*, 231.6–7: ἐὸν κακὸν ἀμφαγαπῶσα.

brother Michael, was a speaker experienced in performing publicly,[39] and we assume that he was familiar with the fundamentals of rhetorical theory, a large part of which offered a grounding in forensic rhetoric.[40] Historiography, though, is not forensic or panegyric rhetoric per se; but it can be rhetorical in its manner of handling narrative, description and thought, and in its reference to an 'audience' that 'hears' a *politikos logos* on a subject, public or private, that matters to the polity.[41] The classic tripartite division of rhetoric into deliberative, epideictic and judiciary is based upon the kind of audience we assume it is directed towards, which could be sitting in judgement, participating in a feast or waiting to be counselled. Many more kinds of audience exist, whether real or imaginary, at various periods, that fit into this scheme only by analogy. A greater sophistication is required on our part, and a corresponding degree of analysis, to appreciate the link the *Chronike Diegesis* is making with its 'audience', and to recognize how this affects the structure and production of a discourse in which the protagonists are delivered up for arraignment on the basis of their motivation, and their action intended or unintended, within the context of the decline of the Byzantine polity. As in the case of Procopius, whose *Secret History* was described by him, curiously for us,

---

[39]   His orations have been edited by J.-L. van Dieten: *Orationes et epistulae* (Berlin and New York, 1972).

[40]   If we judge on the basis of the information we have on the activities of Byzantine commentators, compilers and copyists, forensic rhetoric was studied in Byzantium. See Kennedy, *Greek Rhetoric under Christian Emperors*, 294: 'Stasis theory remained the core of formal rhetorical studies'. It is another matter whether it was practised for strictly forensic purposes, becoming real judiciary oratory delivered in front of a real court of justice. See P. Magdalino, 'The *Bagoas* of Nikephoros Basilakes: a normal reaction?', in L. Mayali and M. M. Mart, eds., *Of Strangers and Foreigners (Late Antiquity–Middle Ages)* (Berkeley, CA, 1993), 47–63 for a discussion on surviving evidence indicating circumstances under which forensic rhetoric was practised in Byzantium. See also R. Macrides, 'The Law outside the Lawbooks: Law and Literature', in *Fontes Minores* 11 (Frankfurt, 2005), 133–45; and *eadem*, 'Poetic Justice in the Patriarchate: murder and cannibalism in the provinces', in L. Burgmann, M. Th. Fögen and A. Schminck, eds., *Cupido Legum* (Frankfurt, 1985), 137–68 [= *Kinship and Justice in Byzantium, 11th–15th Centuries* [Aldershot, 1999], study XI], where potential evidence in a variety of surviving texts is studied as a possible reflection of actual practice.

[41]   Hermogenes in his treatise *On Ideas* (*Hermogenis opera*, 384.15) refers to *politikos logos* in much the same way as he refers to rhetoric in general: political discourse can be deliberative, judiciary or panegyric. In John of Sardis' Commentary to Aphthonius, 17, something political, as in the case of a narrative, is what happens within a polity, and what we use when we deliberate, sit in judgement or participate in a feast.

as an *agonisis*,[42] a word akin to *agon*, and inescapably alluding to a contest in discourse centred upon an issue, so in the *Chronike Diegesis* we may be inclined to see that behind the choice of material and the operations of rhetoric lies another *agon*, where people playing a major or minor role in Byzantine history are judged in a constructed historiographer's court of justice. And perhaps the *Chronike Diegesis* is a piece of writing intended for such a court.

---

[42]   *Secret History*, 1.4.

Index of Proper Names, Places, Terms

Index of Modern Authors